REVISION WORKBOOK

Law of The European Union

Third Edition

EDITOR: JOANNE COLES
LLB (Hons), LLM

OLD BAILEY PRESS

OLD BAILEY PRESS
at Holborn College, Woolwich Road,
Charlton, London, SE7 8LN

First published 1997
Third edition 2002
Reprinted 2004
Reprinted 2005

ISBN 1 85836 466 3

British Library Cataloguing-in-Publication.

A CIP Catalogue record for this book is available from the British Library.

Printed and bound in Great Britain.

Contents

Contents

Acknowledgement

Some questions used are taken or adapted from past University of London LLB (External) Degree examination papers and our thanks are extended to the University of London for their kind permission to use and publish the questions.

Caveat

The answers given are not approved or sanctioned by the University of London and are entirely our responsibility.

They are not intended as 'Model Answers', but rather as Suggested Solutions.

The answers have two fundamental purposes, namely:

a) to provide a detailed example of a suggested solution to an examination question; and

b) to assist students with their research into the subject and to further their understanding and appreciation of the subject.

Introduction

This Revision WorkBook has been designed specifically for those studying the Law of the European Union to undergraduate level. Its coverage is not confined to any one syllabus, but embraces all the major european law topics to be found in university examinations.

Each chapter contains a brief introduction explaining the scope and overall content of the topic covered in that chapter. There follows, in each case, a list of key points which will assist the student in studying and memorising essential material with which the student should be familiar in order to fully understand the topic.

Additionally in each chapter there is a key cases and materials section which lists the most relevant cases and legislative provisions applicable to the topic in question. These are intended as an aid to revision, providing the student with a concise list of materials from which to begin revision.

Each chapter ends with several typical examination questions, together with general comments, skeleton solutions and suggested solutions. Wherever possible, the questions are drawn from University of London external Law of the European Union papers, with recent questions being included where possible. However, it is inevitable that, in compiling a list of questions by topic order rather than chronologically, not only do the same questions crop up over and over again in different guises, but there are gaps where questions have never been set at all.

Undoubtedly, the main feature of this Revision WorkBook is the inclusion of as many past examination questions as possible. While the use of past questions as a revision aid is certainly not new, it is hoped that the combination of actual past questions from the University of London LLB external course and specially written questions, where there are gaps in examination coverage, will be of assistance to students in achieving a thorough and systematic revision of the subject.

Careful use of the Revision WorkBook should enhance the student's understanding of the Law of the European Union and, hopefully, enable you to deal with as wide a range of subject matter as anyone might find in a european law examination, while at the same time allowing you to practise examination techniques while working through the book.

Studying European Union Law

The recent recognition of the importance of European Union/Community law in many respects reflects the dramatic transformation which the European Community has undergone throughout the course of the last decade. The institutional changes in the structure of the Community, introduced by the Treaty on European Union (the Maastricht Treaty), transformed the Community from an essentially economic organisation into a European Union. Further, the growing volume of legislation emanating from the Community is itself evidence of the increasingly important role of the European Community as a source of legal principles.

European Community law is a sui generis species of law. It has been created by drawing upon the reservoir of legal principles contained in the legal systems of the Member States. For various reasons, the English legal system has not played a significant role in this evolution. Community law has been fashioned under the influence of the civilian legal systems of continental Europe. For that reason, students with common law backgrounds may not readily identify with some of the concepts and institutions of Community law. Students must therefore exercise patience when studying Community law in order to appreciate the unique nature of Community law.

To understand Community law, a basic comprehension of the fundamental elements of this system must be achieved. This requires intensive consideration of subjects such as the relationship between the Community legal order and the legal systems of the Member States, the different forms of Community legislation and the hierarchy which exists between them, the judicial techniques of the European Court and the fundamental principles of Community law which have been developed in order to allow the Community to function on the basis of the rule of law. These matters form the essential core of the Community legal system, and the edifice of Community law has been erected upon them.

Further, it is also important to acquire a comprehensive and overall perception of the subject and to understand how particular topics interrelate. European Community law is characterised by an extensive overlapping of topics. Points which are brought up in one particular section of the syllabus continuously recur in other areas of the subject. An overall general knowledge of each individual topic will ultimately facilitate the acquisition of an extensive and detailed knowledge of the complete subject.

Students should also adopt an appropriate methodology towards answering questions of Community law. Legal authority in Community law is derived primarily through the Community Treaties and secondarily through Community legislation, particularly Regulations and Directives, and the decisions of the European Court. The European Court has been responsible for a considerable number of the fundamental principles of the Community, and cases of important legal significance have been cited throughout the text. Familiarity with these precedents is absolutely essential to the study of Community law.

Once the basic skills and methodology have been acquired in approaching problems involving questions of Community law, the task of identifying and applying the relevant legal principles to the issue becomes increasingly simplified. These skills may best be acquired through a study and appreciation of the techniques involved in answering examination questions. The objective of this text is therefore not primarily to provide students with pro forma answers to questions, but to teach them the skills involved in approaching questions which have European legal implications.

Please note that references to EC secondary legislation contained in this book include reference to the institution from which the measure came: you would not be expected to supply this information in an examination, however.

Revision and Examination Technique

Revision Technique

Planning a revision timetable

In planning your revision timetable make sure you do not finish the syllabus too early. You should avoid leaving revision so late that you have to 'cram' – but constant revision of the same topic leads to stagnation.

Plan ahead, however, and try to make your plans increasingly detailed as you approach the examination date.

Allocate enough time for each topic to be studied. But note that it is better to devise a realistic timetable, to which you have a reasonable chance of keeping, rather than a wildly optimistic schedule which you will probably abandon at the first opportunity!

The syllabus and its topics

One of your first tasks when you began your course was to ensure that you thoroughly understood your syllabus. Check now to see if you can write down the topics it comprises from memory. You will see that the chapters of this WorkBook are each devoted to a syllabus topic. This will help you decide which are the key chapters relative to your revision programme, though you should allow some time for glancing through the other chapters.

The topic and its key points

Again working from memory, analyse what you consider to be the key points of any topic that you have selected for particular revision. Seeing what you can recall, unaided, will help you to understand and firmly memorise the concepts involved.

Using the WorkBook

Relevant questions are provided for each topic in this book. Naturally, as typical examples of examination questions, they do not normally relate to one topic only. But the questions in each chapter will relate to the subject matter of the chapter to a degree. You can choose your method of consulting the questions and solutions, but here are some suggestions (strategies 1–3). Each of them pre-supposes that you have read through the author's notes on key points and key cases and statutes, and any other preliminary matter, at the beginning of the chapter. Once again, you now need to practise working from memory, for that is the challenge you are preparing yourself for. As a rule of procedure constantly test yourself once revision starts, both orally and in writing.

Strategy 1

Strategy 1 is planned for the purpose of quick revision. First read your chosen question carefully and then jot down in abbreviated notes what you consider to be the main points at issue. Similarly, note the cases and statutes that occur to you as being relevant for citation purposes. Allow yourself sufficient time to cover what you feel to be relevant. Then study the author's skeleton solution and skim-read the suggested solution to see how they compare with your notes. When comparing consider carefully what the author has included (and concluded) and see whether that agrees with what you have written. Consider the points of variation also. Have you recognised the key issues? How relevant have you been? It is possible, of course, that you have referred to a recent case that is relevant, but which had not been reported when the WorkBook was prepared.

Strategy 2

Strategy 2 requires a nucleus of three hours in which to practise writing a set of examination answers in a limited time-span.

Select a number of questions (as many as are normally set in your subject in the examination you are studying for), each from a different chapter in the WorkBook, without consulting the solutions. Find a place to write where you will not be disturbed and try to arrange not to be interrupted for three hours. Write your solutions in the time allowed, noting any time needed to make up if you are interrupted.

After a rest, compare your answers with the suggested solutions in the WorkBook. There will be considerable variation in style, of course, but the bare facts should not be too dissimilar. Evaluate your answer critically. Be 'searching', but develop a positive approach to deciding how you would tackle each question on another occasion.

Strategy 3

You are unlikely to be able to do more than one three hour examination, but occasionally set yourself a single question. Vary the 'time allowed' by imagining it to be one of the questions that you must answer in three hours and allow yourself a limited preparation and writing time. Try one question that you feel to be difficult and an easier question on another occasion, for example.

Misuse of suggested solutions

Don't try to learn by rote. In particular, don't try to reproduce the suggested solutions by heart. Learn to express the basic concepts in your own words.

Keeping up-to-date

Keep up-to-date. While examiners do not require familiarity with changes in the law during the three months prior to the examination, it obviously creates a good impression if you can show you are acquainted with any recent changes. Make a habit of looking through one of the leading journals – *Modern Law Review, Law Quarterly Review* or the *New Law Journal,* for example – and cumulative indices to law reports, such as the *All England Law Reports* or *Weekly Law Reports,* or indeed the daily law reports in *The Times.* The *Law Society's Gazette* and the *Legal Executive Journal* are helpful sources, plus any specialist journal(s) for the subject you are studying.

Examination Skills

Examiners are human too!

The process of answering an examination question involves a communication between you and the person who set it. If you were speaking face to face with the person, you would choose your verbal points and arguments carefully in your reply. When writing, it is all too easy to forget the human being who is awaiting the reply and simply write out what one knows in the area of the subject! Bear in mind it is a person whose question you are responding to, throughout your essay. This will help you to avoid being irrelevant or long-winded.

The essay question

Candidates are sometimes tempted to choose to answer essay questions because they 'seem' easier. But the examiner is looking for thoughtful work and will not give good marks for superficial answers.

The essay-type of question may be either purely factual, in asking you to explain the meaning of a certain doctrine or principle, or it may ask you to discuss a certain proposition, usually derived from a quotation. In either case, the approach to the answer is the same. A clear programme must be devised to give the examiner the meaning or significance of the doctrine, principle or proposition and its origin in common law, equity or statute, and cases which illustrate its application to the branch of law concerned. Essay questions offer a good way to obtain marks if you have thought carefully about a topic, since it is up to you to impose the structure (unlike the problem questions where the problem imposes its own structure). You are then free to speculate and show imagination.

The problem question

The problem-type question requires a different approach. You may well be asked to advise a client or merely discuss the problems raised in the question. In either case, the most important factor is to take great care in reading the question. By its nature, the question will be longer than the essay-type question and you will have a number of facts to digest. Time spent in analysing the question may well save time later, when you are endeavouring to impress on the examiner the considerable extent of your basic legal knowledge. The quantity of knowledge is itself a trap and you must always keep within the boundaries of the question in hand. It is very tempting to show the examiner the extent of your knowledge of your subject, but if this is outside the question, it is time lost and no marks earned. It is inevitable that some areas which you have studied and revised will not be the subject of questions, but under no circumstances attempt to adapt a question to a stronger area of knowledge at the expense of relevance.

When you are satisfied that you have grasped the full significance of the problem-type question, set out the fundamental principles involved.

You will then go on to identify the fundamental problem (or problems) posed by the question. This should be followed by a consideration of the law which is relevant to the problem. The source of the law, together with the cases which will be of assistance in solving the problem, must then be considered in detail.

Very good problem questions are quite likely to have alternative answers, and in advising a party you should be aware that alternative arguments may be available. Each stage of your answer, in this case, will be based on the argument or arguments considered in the previous stage, forming a conditional sequence.

If, however, you only identify one fundamental problem, do not waste time worrying that you cannot think of an alternative – there may very well be only that one answer.

The examiner will then wish to see how you use your legal knowledge to formulate a case and how you apply that formula to the problem which is the subject of the question. It is this positive approach which can make answering a problem question a high mark earner for the student who has fully understood the question and clearly argued their case on the established law.

Examination checklist

a) Read the instructions at the head of the examination carefully. While last-minute changes are unlikely – such as the introduction of a compulsory question or an increase in the number of questions asked – it has been known to happen.

b) Read the questions carefully. Analyse problem questions – work out what the examiner wants.

c) Plan your answer before you start to write.

d) Check that you understand the rubric before you start to write. Do not 'discuss', for example, if you are specifically asked to 'compare and contrast'.

e) Answer the correct number of questions. If you fail to answer one out of four questions set you lose 25 per cent of your marks!

Style and structure

Try to be clear and concise. Fundamentally this amounts to using paragraphs to denote the sections of your essay, and writing simple, straightforward sentences as much as possible. The sentence you have just read has 22 words – when a sentence reaches 50 words it becomes difficult for a reader to follow.

Do not be inhibited by the word 'structure' (traditionally defined as giving an essay a beginning, a middle and an end). A good structure will be the natural consequence of setting out your arguments and the supporting evidence in a logical order. Set the scene briefly in your opening paragraph. Provide a clear conclusion in your final paragraph.

Table of Cases

Table of Community Legislation

Table of United Kingdom Legislation

Chapter I

The Origins and Nature of the European Union

1.1	**Introduction**
1.2	**Key points**
1.3	**Key cases**
1.4	**Questions and suggested solutions**

1.1 Introduction

The 'European Community' originally consisted of three separate, yet closely related, economic organisations each established by independent international agreements. The first Community was the European Coal and Steel Community (ECSC) formed under the Treaty of Paris signed in 1951. This was followed by two more Treaties, signed in Rome in 1957, namely the European Economic Community (EEC) Treaty and the European Atomic Energy (Euratom) Treaty. Of these, the most important is the EEC Treaty (now known as the European Community Treaty) which covers most economic activities other than those regulated under the two other agreements.

The six original Members of the Community – Belgium, France, Germany, Italy, Luxembourg and the Netherlands – have been joined by an additional nine Member States. In 1973, membership of the Community was increased by the admission of the United Kingdom, Ireland and Denmark. These three states were followed by Greece in 1981 and Spain and Portugal in 1986. Since 1 January 1995, membership of the Community has been increased to 15 Member States following the accession of Austria, Finland and Sweden. The European Community entered formal negotiations on membership in April 1998 with six other countries: Cyprus, the Czech Republic, Estonia, Hungary, Poland and Slovenia. It has also initiated accession discussions with five other countries that have applied to join, namely Bulgaria, Latvia, Lithuania, Romania and Slovakia.

The European Community has also significantly evolved from the embryonic organisation established under the EC Treaty. First, in 1986, the Single European Act 1986 was agreed which changed many of the internal institutional features and processes of the Community. A far more radical restructuring occurred when the European Union was inaugurated by the Treaty on European Union (TEU) 1992. Further alterations were introduced by the Treaty of Amsterdam 1997.

The European Community has not in fact ceased to exist but has now been subsumed within the broader umbrella of the European Union. The TEU has a constitutional structure based on three pillars: Pillar 1, which is the EC Treaty as (substantially) amended; Pillar 2, which comprises provisions relating to Common Foreign Policy and Security Policy; and Pillar 3, which contains provisions for Co-operation in the Fields of Justice and Home Affairs.

Although the European Union now incorporates the European Community, both the EC Treaty itself and the laws established thereunder remain important in the operation of the European Union for two reasons. First, the EC Treaty is one of the three cornerstones of the European Union. Second, the law of the European Community has developed over a period of more than 40 years, in contrast to the new legal principles being developed under the two other branches of EU competence.

The Treaty of Amsterdam 1997 made a number of further changes to the EC Treaty but these are relatively minor compared to the transformation brought about by the TEU. One important change which was made, however, was the re-numbering of almost all of the Articles of the EC Treaty. This re-numbering has been followed in this edition of the WorkBook, without cross-reference to the former Articles, in order to avoid confusion.

1.2 Key points

The treaties founding the European Community

The European Coal and Steel Community (ECSC) Treaty

The ECSC Treaty was signed in Paris on 18 April 1951 and consists of 100 Articles, three annexes and three protocols, together with a convention relating to transitory provisions. This Treaty established the world's first genuine supranational organisation. The purpose of the ECSC Treaty was to establish a common market for coal and steel products.

The ECSC Treaty required the Member States to abolish import and export duties and charges having equivalent effect, as well as quantitative restrictions, on the movement of coal and steel products. In addition, measures or practices which discriminated between producers, purchasers or consumers on the basis of nationality were prohibited. Restrictions were also placed on the rights of Member States to grant subsidies or aid in order to promote domestic production.

The Treaty rationalised coal and steel production throughout the six participating states and reduced levels of protectionism in these industrial sectors. The result was a more efficient industry and a significant increase in the gross national products (GNP) of the participating states.

The European Economic Community (EC) Treaty

The EC Treaty was signed in Rome on 25 March 1957. Article 2 of the Treaty originally identified four objectives for the common market: the promotion of harmonious economic development throughout the Community; continuous and balanced economic expansion among the Member States; the raising of standards of living among the population of the Community; and the development of closer relations among the Member States.

In order to construct the common market, art 3 of the Treaty originally instructed the Member States to pursue the following policy goals:

a) the elimination, as between Member States, of customs duties and of quantitative restrictions on the import and export of goods, and of all other measures having equivalent effect;

b) the establishment of a common customs tariff and a common commercial policy towards third countries;

c) the abolition, as between Member States, of obstacles to the free movement of persons, services and capital;

d) the adoption of a common agricultural policy;

e) the adoption of a common transport policy;

f) the creation of a Community competition policy;

g) the approximation of the laws of the Member States to the extent required for the proper functioning of the common market;

h) the creation of a European Social Fund to improve employment opportunity for workers;

i) the establishment of a European Investment Bank to facilitate the economic expansion of the Community; and

j) the association of overseas countries and territories in order to increase trade and promote economic development.

The states participating in the Treaty agreed to consolidate their individual economies into one single, enlarged internal market and to simultaneously form one single entity for the purpose of conducting economic relationships with non-participating states. Authority to administer the economic development of the organisation has been delegated to a centralised body with an institutional structure which functions independently from the influence of one or more Member States. The formation of the European Community involved the transfer of a considerable degree of national sovereignty to create a supranational body capable of regulating its economic affairs.

As we shall see later, the TEU, and subsequently the Treaty of Amsterdam, significantly amend many of these objectives with a view to establishing a European Union based on the EC Treaty, but supplemented by additional obligations contained in new Treaties and Protocols.

The European Atomic Energy (Euratom) Treaty

The Euratom Treaty was also signed in Rome on 25 March 1957, and contains 225 Articles. The purpose of this agreement is to create a specialist market for atomic energy. Euratom is designed to develop nuclear energy, distribute it within the Community and sell the surplus to non-Community states.

Since the objectives of Euratom differ from those of the ECSC Treaty and the EC Treaty, it is no surprise that the goals of Euratom are also different. Among the main goals of Euratom are the following:

a) to promote research and to ensure the dissemination of technical information throughout the Community;

b) to establish uniform safety standards to protect workers and the general public from atomic hazards;

c) to promote investment in the nuclear energy industry;

d) to maintain regular and reliable supplies of ores and nuclear fuels; and

e) to make certain that nuclear materials are not diverted for aims other than peaceful purposes.

The structure of the European Community

The EC Treaty seeks to achieve the creation of the common market by pursuing four fundamental principles.

a) The free movement of the factors of production – goods, labour, services and capital – within the territory of the Community.

b) The progressive approximation of economic policies among Member States, including the creation of common Community policies in key economic sectors such as agriculture, competition and transport.

c) The creation of a Common Customs Tariff (CCT) for the regulation and administration of trade between Community and non-Community countries.

d) The establishment of a Common Commercial Policy (CCP) for the conduct of economic relations between the Community and the rest of the world.

The first two of these principles are matters which fall within the internal competence of the Community, while the second two concern the external competence of the Community.

Again it should be noted that these fundamental principles have been supplemented by others, in particular by virtue of the TEU and the Treaty of Amsterdam.

The nature of European Community law

European Community law is a supranational species of law which prevails over the laws of all Member States, including the law of England. As the European Court has explicitly observed, the Community treaties have created a new legal order which now interacts to form part of the legal systems of all Member States and constitutes a body of principles which their courts and tribunals are bound to apply: *Costa v ENEL* Case 6/64 [1964] ECR 585.

This new legal order has a number of characteristic features.

a) Community law is a sui generis form of law which evades the traditional classifications made within English law. It transcends the distinction often drawn between public law and private law and also the distinction between civil and criminal law.

b) Community law not only provides a defence to legal proceedings, but may also furnish grounds for legal action or for interim injunction.

c) Community law – whether in the form of treaty provisions, Community regulations or unimplemented Community directives – prevails over prior and subsequent inconsistent provisions of national law.

The Treaty on European Union 1992 and the evolution of the Community into a European Union

The European Community has now undergone transformation from a primarily economic organisation into a true European Union. This was brought about the Treaty on European Union (TEU) 1992 signed in February 1992 at Maastricht. The Treaty entered into force in October 1993. Austria, Finland and Sweden acceded to the European Union, not only the European Community, and are therefore full members of both.

The Treaty itself consists of a number of titles dealing with different matters.

Title I: Common Provisions – this deals with the general principles behind the new European Union;

Title II: Provisions amending the EC Treaty (Pillar 1);

Title III: Provisions amending the ECSC Treaty;

Title IV: Provisions amending the Euratom Treaty;

Title V: Provisions on a Common Foreign Policy and Security Policy (Pillar 2);

Title VI: Provisions on Co-operation in the Fields of Justice and Home Affairs (Pillar 3); and

Title VII: Final Provisions.

The Treaty also contains a number of supplementary protocols defining or clarifying certain subjects and authorising derogations, including the Protocol on the derogation of the United Kingdom from the obligations established to further monetary union.

Titles II, V and VI define the organic and most significant competencies of the European Union and the remaining titles contain provisions designed to ensure that the powers conferred on the European Union under the three main pillars are exercised in an integrated fashion within a unified institutional framework. However, in essence, these three Titles together form the heart of the constitution of the European Union.

Pillar 1: The European Community Treaty

The TEU significantly amended the EC Treaty but, at the same time, the EC Treaty remains the most important pillar of the European Union at the present time. The main amendments made may be summarised as follows:

a) redefinition of the institutional and organisational structure of the decision-making processes within the organisation;

b) the addition of new areas of competence to the spheres of activity previously occupied by the European Community;

c) the creation of new principles to regulate the functioning of the European Union including the principle of subsidiarity;

d) the introduction of new provisions to regulate economic policy co-operation;

e) the incorporation of new competencies in the field of monetary policy co-operation;

f) the creation of the concept of the citizenship of the European Union.

Pillar 2: Common Foreign Policy and Security Policy

Title V TEU creates this competence, but in fact co-operation in this area has been taking place among the Member States for at least the last decade.

Three separate kinds of joint actions are contemplated in the field of the common foreign and security policy, namely: the definition of principles and general guidelines for the common foreign policy; the adoption of joint actions; and the adoption of common positions.

a) Defining principles and general guidelines

The European Council is authorised under art 13 TEU to define the principles and general guidelines for the common foreign policy. In addition, the European Council can also decide on common strategies to be implemented by the European Union in areas of foreign policy where the Member States have important interests in common. The Council of Ministers will implement common strategies by means of the adoption of both joint actions and common positions.

b) The adoption of joint actions

Joint actions address specific situations where operational action at a European Union level is necessary. Each of these measures must define their objectives, their scope and the means given to the European Union for their implementation, as well as the conditions required for giving effect to them.

Examples of joint actions taken by the Council of Ministers include: Council Decision 97/817/CFSP on the eradication of anti-personnel landmines; Council Decision 98/301/CFSP on action in support of the government of Montenegro; Council Decision 98/375/CFSP on the appointment of a special EU envoy to Yugoslavia; and Council Decision 97/288/CFSP on the promotion of transparency in nuclear-related export controls.

c) The adoption of common positions

Common positions differ from joint actions in that common positions require the Member States to adopt a united front to the international community, whereas joint actions involve a proactive element. Member States are obliged to ensure that their individual national policies are consistent with these instruments. Hence, common positions are more akin to statements of international policy.

Examples of common positions include: Council Decision 97/356/CFSP concerning conflict prevention and resolution in Africa; Council Decision 98/606/CFSP concerning the promotion of non-proliferation and confidence building in the South Asian region; and Council Decision 98/633/CFSP on stability and good-neighbourliness in south-east Europe.

In the area of security, the TEU envisages a strengthened role for the Western European Union (WEU), an organisation created in 1954 but which has largely remained dormant since its conception. This organisation is specifically identified as the 'defence component' of the European Union.

Pillar 3: Justice and Home Affairs

Co-operation on justice and home affairs is an inter-governmental matter which originally fell within the competence of the European Union under Pillar 3. The fields which were expressly included within the ambit of this policy included: asylum policy; control of external frontiers; immigration policy; drug enforcement policy; international fraud; co-operation between civil and criminal courts among Member States; customs co-operation; and co-operation among the police forces of the Member States.

The Treaty of Amsterdam brought a number of these competencies out of the scope of Pillar 3 and into Pillar 1 by amending the EC Treaty. Articles 61–69 EC contain provisions relating to free movement of persons, visas, asylum policy, immigration and judicial co-operation in civil matters. These subjects therefore no longer form part of Pillar 3 which, after the Treaty of Amsterdam, now concerns simply police and judicial co-operation in criminal matters.

The amended EC Treaty and the competencies established in relation to political, economic, monetary and fiscal affairs

Over and above its original objectives and purposes, the TEU inserted new competencies in the EC Treaty. The most important of these concern the political dimension, economic and monetary policy co-ordination and a series of new objectives to be pursued through the EC Treaty.

The political dimension – citizenship of the Union

Article 17 EC, as amended by the TEU, establishes the concept of European citizenship. Every person holding the nationality of a Member State is to be considered henceforth to be a citizen of the European Union. Citizens of the Union are to enjoy the rights conferred by the EC Treaty and are subject to the duties imposed by that agreement.

A slight modification was made to the original terms of art 17 by an amendment made by the Treaty of Amsterdam which clarifies the principle that citizenship of the Union is complementary to national citizenship and does not replace individual national citizenships.

Article 18 confers every citizen of the Union with the right to move and reside freely within the territory of the Member States, subject to the limitations and conditions laid down in the EC Treaty and by the measures adopted to give effect to this right.

Each citizen of the Union will have the right to vote and to stand as a candidate in the Member States where he or she resides, regardless of the nationality of that person under art 19(1). Council Directive 93/109/EC (1993) lays down the arrangements for allowing citizens of the European Union the right to vote and stand as candidates in elections for the European Parliament in the Member State in which they are resident. Similarly, Council Directive 94/80/EC (1994) creates rights to participate in municipal elections for citizens residing in Member States other than their own.

Economic policy coordination

The development of economic policy within the Community is based on the principle of an open market economy, with free competition, and a favouring of an efficient allocation of resources: art 98 EC.

The Commission is instructed to submit recommendations for the conduct of the economic policies of the Member States to the Council and the Council in turn is required, acting by a qualified majority vote, to draft broad guidelines on the basis of these recommendations.

The Council, acting on the basis of reports submitted by the Commission, is responsible for monitoring economic developments in each Member States as well as ensuring the consistency of the economic policies of Member States with the broad guidelines referred to above: art 99(3) EC, as amended.

The amendments made by the TEU to the EC Treaty are less than comprehensive in relation to the principles to be pursued for the purposes of economic policy coordination. The following are the few express principles stated in the amended Treaty:

a) Member States shall avoid excessive government deficits;

b) Member States are required to maintain budgetary disciplines and the Commission is empowered to monitor the development of the budgetary situation and of the stock of government debt in the Member States; and

c) overdraft facilities or any other type of credit facilities with the European Central Bank (ECB) or with the central banks of the Member States in favour of government bodies are generally prohibited.

Monetary policy coordination

The Treaty on European Union introduced a three stage programme towards monetary and fiscal union.

Stage 1

The first stage, outlined in the Single European Act 1986, was increased co-operation among the Member States within the framework of the European Monetary System. This required all Member States to:

a) eliminate all restrictions on the movement of capital both among themselves and between individual Member States and third countries; and

b) adopt programmes intended to ensure the lasting convergence necessary for the achievement of economic and monetary union.

Stage 2

For the second stage of the programme, the European Monetary Institute (EMI) was established in January 1994 on the basis of a statute laid down in a protocol annexed to the EC Treaty by amendments made after the approval of the TEU.

The EMI was the precursor to the European Central Bank (ECB). Its main tasks were to specify the regulatory, organisational and logistical framework necessary for the European Central Bank to perform its functions and tasks from the start of Stage 3. Throughout Stage 2, the EMI strengthened co-ordination of national monetary policy and made recommendations to national central banks relating to the conduct of their monetary policies.

In January 1997, the EMI published its main Report on the specification of the operation framework to achieve Stage 3 of monetary union. This Report set down the conditions and criteria for a strategy to create a single European currency by 1 January 1999.

Stage 3

The third stage of the project was the creation of the ECB and the introduction of the single European currency. Both of these objectives were achieved on 1 January 1999.

Eleven Member States fulfilled the criteria required for inclusion, and agreed to participate, in the single European currency programme which commenced on 1 January 1999. These countries were Austria, Belgium, Finland, Germany, Ireland, Italy, Luxembourg, The Netherlands, Spain and Portugal who collectively constitute the 'Eurozone'. Three Member States declined to participate, namely the United Kingdom, Sweden and Denmark, while Greece failed to meet the necessary requirements set down in art 121 EC. As a result, these currencies remain outside the Eurozone.

Council Regulation 974/98 confirms that the single European currency is called the 'Euro'. Under the Regulation, with effect from 1 January 1999, the Euro has been substituted for the currency of each of the participating Member States at fixed conversion rates. The actual conversion rates were not in fact definitively fixed until Council Regulation 2866/98 was adopted by the Council on 31 December 1998.

The Regulation also sets out measures which each participating Member State may take during the transitional period, notably to redenominate in the Euro unit any outstanding debt issued by the Member State's central government in its national currency unit, and to enable the change of the unit of account of their operating procedures from the national currency unit to the Euro.

Council Regulation 974/98 stipulated that on 1 January 2002 the ECB and the central banks of the participating Member States would put into circulation bank notes denominated in Euro, and from this date the Euro notes and coins have been legal tender. As from the same date participating Member States have issued coins denominated in Euro or in cents. Bank notes and coins in the national currency will remain legal tender within their territorial limits up until six months after the end of the transitional period at the latest, which is nearly due to pass at the time of writing.

The addition of new policy objectives to the EC Treaty

The TEU amends art 3 EC by adding a significant number of new policy objectives to that provision. Broadly speaking these may be grouped into three categories.

a) The development of new common Community policies

This requires the formulation of common policies in the following fields:

i)   encouragement for the establishment and development of trans-European transportation networks;

ii) the environment;

iii) consumer protection;

iv) the attainment of a high level of health protection.

b) The formulation of an industrial policy

This policy is intended to achieve three goals:

i) the strengthening of the competitiveness of Community industry;

ii) the promotion of research and technological development;

iii) the introduction of measures in the sphere of energy, civil protection and tourism.

c) The pursuit of a social and cultural policy

This is a miscellaneous classification involving the following objectives:

i) the strengthening of economic and social cohesion;

ii) formulation of a policy in the sphere of development co-operation;

iii) a contribution to education and training of quality and to the flowering of the cultures of the Member States.

In addition, the Treaty of Amsterdam inserted a further primary policy objective into art 3 EC, namely the promotion of co-ordination between employment policies among the Member States and the development of a co-ordinated strategy for employment issues.

The changes made by the Treaty of Amsterdam 1997

The Treaty of Amsterdam was signed on 2 October 1997 by the 15 Member States of the European Union and came into effect on 1 May 1999 after ratification by all the Member States. Its aims and objectives are, however, far more limited than its predecessor, the TEU. Indeed, most of the provisions of the Treaty of Amsterdam concern adjustments to the original EC Treaty and the TEU rather than any radical transformation of the institutional structure and competencies of the European Union.

In general terms, the four main aims of the Treaty of Amsterdam are to:

a) define with greater precision the scope of the common foreign and security policy and bring co-operation in justice and home affairs within the scope of the EC Treaty itself;

b) adjust earlier provisions of both the EC Treaty and the TEU to improve their efficiency and operation;

c) expand the participation of the European Parliament in the institutional decision-making process;

d) introduce a limited number of new policy areas and to strengthen certain existing ones.

Article 11 EC, which was inserted by the Treaty of Amsterdam, authorises groups of Member States to establish closer co-operation between themselves using the institutions, procedures and mechanisms contained in the EC Treaty. This type of co-operation is permitted as long as proposed measures or actions:

a) do not concern areas which fall within the exclusive competence of the Community;

b) do not affect Community policies, actions or programmes;

c) do not concern the citizenship of the Union or discriminate between nationals of Member States;

d) remain within the limits of the powers conferred upon the Community by the EC Treaty;

e) do not constitute a discrimination or a restriction of trade between Member States and do not distort the conditions of competition between these states.

This mechanism will allow the more progressive EU Member States to pursue closer economic, social and political integration without the need to continue to persuade less progressive countries to participate in such programmes. The ability of such groups to do so is, however, circumscribed by the above-mentioned conditions.

It should be noted, however, that the Treaty of Amsterdam amends both the TEU and the EC Treaty but continues to maintain a separation between competencies and powers established under Pillars 2 and 3 of the TEU, as adjusted, on the one hand, and those enshrined in the EC Treaty itself (Pillar 1) on the other.

The Treaty of Nice

The Treaty of Amsterdam (ToA) failed to provide the institutional changes required to expand membership of the European Union. All the ToA included on this important matter was a protocol that provided for a comprehensive review of the institutional infrastructure of the EU at least one year before membership exceeded 20 Member States. It was obvious, though, that this number was to be reached, and considerably exceeded, relatively quickly.

The TEU had charged the European Council with the obligation of ensuring that the necessary impetus was provided for further development, to define the political guidelines and to identify necessary amendments. The principal focus of the Inter-governmental Conferences (IGCs) following the ToA was to secure the necessary institutional changes required to cope with the proposed enlargement of the EU to 27 Member States by 2004. The main institutional reforms contained within the Treaty of Nice are:

a) altering voting weights in the Council of Ministers for qualified majority voting (QMV) and amendment of the formula required for minimum qualified majority voting success;

b) increased use of QMV;

c) changes to the allocation of seats in the Parliament;

d) reform of the judicial system by the creation of specialist chambers via the insertion of a new art 220(2) EC.

However, at the time of writing the Treaty of Nice is not in force. The Irish referendum on accepting the Treaty in June 2001 produced a no result and there may be some delay in the ratification process. This may, in turn, slow down the proposed expansion of membership.

1.3 Key cases

* *Accession of the Community to the ECHR, Re the* Opinion 2/94 [1996] ECR I–1759
  A decision confirming that the Community does not have the authority to accede to the European Convention on Human Rights, thereby circumscribing its competence in that field

* *Commission* v *Council (Re ERTA)* Case 22/70 [1971] ECR 263
  The Member States no longer have the right, acting individually or even collectively, to enter into international obligations with third states if the subject matter of such agreements falls within the scope of the Community treaties

* *Costa* v *ENEL* Case 6/64 [1964] ECR 585
  The Community treaties have established a new legal order stemming from the limitation of sovereignty or a transfer of powers from the Member States to the European Community and have thus created a body of law which binds both their nationals and themselves

* *Donkerwolke* v *Procureur de la République* Case 41/76 [1976] ECR 1921
  Member States are prohibited from enacting measures of national legislation on matters which fall within the competence of the Community by virtue of the Community treaties unless express authority to do so has been delegated

* *R* v *Secretary of State for Foreign and Commonwealth Affairs, ex parte Rees-Mogg* [1994] 1 All ER 457
  Decision from the Queen's Bench confirming the consistency of the statute ratifying the TEU with the constitution of the United Kingdom

1.4 Questions and suggested solutions

QUESTION ONE

'The Community constitutes a new legal order in international law, for whose benefit the States have limited their sovereign rights, albeit within limited fields, and the subjects of which comprise not only the Member States but also their nationals.' (Case 26/62 *Van Gend en Loos* v *Netherlands*.) Discuss.

University of London LLB Examination
(for External Students) European Community Law June 1989 Q1

General Comment

A basic question requiring the student to discuss the unique nature of the European Community.

Skeleton Solution

Nature of sovereignty: power to legislate – limits on state sovereignty – scope of Community law – rights of individuals under Community law.

Suggested Solution

The European Community is a supranational organisation. It is neither an international organisation nor a federal state. By merging certain aspects of their sovereignty, the Member States have created a unique legal structure. Further, the law which emanates from this structure also has a supranational character. By creating a Community of unlimited duration which has its own institutions, its own personality, its own legal capacity, a capacity to conduct international relations and real legislative powers stemming from the transfer of sovereignty from the Member States to the Community, the Member States have established a sui generis form of law – European Community law.

Membership of the European Community entails a significant transfer of sovereignty from the Member States to the Community. For example, Member States no longer possess sufficient sovereignty to enact legislation on matters which fall within the competence of the Community: *Donkerwolke* v *Procureur de la République* Case 41/76 [1976] ECR 1921. Equally, Member States can no longer enter international agreements with non-Community states if the subject matter of such agreements relates to issues within the domain of the Community: *Commission* v *Council (Re ERTA)* Case 22/70 [1971] ECR 263. However, perhaps the greatest limitation on the sovereignty of Member States is that Community law prevails over inconsistent prior or subsequent national legislation: *R* v *Secretary of State for Transport, ex parte Factortame Ltd and Others* Case C–221/89 [1991] ECR I–3905.

The European Community legal system is unlike the international legal system. While the jurisdiction of the International Court of Justice is confined to disputes among sovereign states, the EC Treaty expressly recognises the rights of individuals to challenge acts of the Community institutions in the European Court, and national courts are able to refer disputes involving individuals for consideration by the European Court under the preliminary reference procedure established by art 234 EC. The European Court has also expanded the application of Community law to individuals by recognising the right of individuals to rely upon Community treaty provisions, regulations and directives. National courts have greatly assisted in this process by acknowledging that the jurisprudence of the European Court requires that Community rights can be vindicated in national courts and tribunals by individuals.

While the force of Community law resides in the transfer of sovereignty by Member States, at the same time the European Court has recognised that the legal systems of the individual Member States form an integral part of the Community legal system: *Costa* v *ENEL* Case 6/64 [1964] ECR 585. Both the European Court and the House of Lords have recognised that rights of individuals under the Community treaties must be protected by national courts: per Lord Bridge of Harwich in *R* v *Secretary of State for Transport, ex parte Factortame and Others* [1990] 3 CMLR 59. Directly enforceable Community rights are part of the legal heritage of every citizen of the Member States of the Community. Such rights are automatically available and must be given unrestricted retroactive effect. The persons entitled to the enjoyment of such rights are also entitled to direct and immediate protection against possible infringement of them. The duty to provide such protection rests with the national courts.

Recognition by national courts of the rights of individuals under Community law allows individuals to rely on such rights in national courts and tribunals. Therefore, Community law can be used as a defence to a civil action or as a ground for initiating a civil action. Thus, in *Brown* v *Secretary of State for Scotland* Case 197/86 [1988] ECR 3205, the plaintiff founded upon Community law to establish rights in a civil action concerning the right of foreign nationals to seek state support for further education. Conversely, in *Société Technique Minière* v *Maschinenbau Ulm GmbH* Case 56/65 [1966] ECR 235, the defendants relied on art 81(2) EC as a defence to an action for breach of a contract dealing with exclusive sales rights. Equally, Community law can constitute a ground for a criminal prosecution or may be a defence to such an action. For example, in *Anklagemyndigheden* v *Hansen and Son* Case C–326/88 [1990] ECR 2911, the defendant was charged with violations of Community regulations concerning maximum permitted daily driving periods and compulsory rest periods and fined accordingly. Similarly, in *Pubblico Ministero* v *Ratti* Case 148/78 [1979] ECR 1629, an accused charged with failure to comply with minimum manufacturing standards relied on an unimplemented Council directive to avoid liability.

A number of corollaries stem from the principle that Community law confers rights on individuals which national courts and tribunals must recognise. First, the European Court will not permit the efficacy of Community rights to vary from one Member State to another. Community rights must be consistent throughout the Community. Second, Member States cannot maintain national measures which would deny access to such rights. Third, Member States cannot remove the power to enforce Community rights from national courts. Finally, where the legislation of a Member State is declared incompatible with Community law, the legislative bodies of the state are under an obligation to amend or repeal the offending legislation.

QUESTION TWO

'The structure of the EC Treaty suggests that the architects of the Community believed that economic integration was the road to political harmony.'

Discuss.

Written by the Editor

General Comment

A question requiring a simple narrative answer based on the functions of the European Community.

Skeleton Solution

The four fundamental principles of the economic integration within the EC – the four freedoms: coordination of economic policy; the CCT and the CCP – the failure of the Community to achieve these objectives – the amendments made by the Treaty on European Union and the Treaty of Amsterdam.

Suggested Solution

As expressed in the EC Treaty, economic integration between the Member States is to be achieved through adherence to four fundamental principles: the free movement of the factors of production – goods, labour, services and capital – within the territory of the common market; the progressive approximation of economic polices among Member States, including the creation of common Community policies in key economic sectors such as agriculture, fisheries and transport; the creation of a common customs tariff (CCT) for the regulation and administration of trade between the Community and non-Community countries; and the establishment of a common commercial policy (CCP) for the conduct of economic relations between the Community and the rest of the world.

The free movement of factors of production is pursued through the elimination and progressive reduction of four forms of discrimination: between domestic products and products originating from other Member countries as regards commercial transactions; between nationals and other Community citizens in the field of employment; between domestic suppliers of services and Community suppliers of similar services; and between domestic capital and similar forms of investment from Member countries. In particular, the elimination of discrimination requires the abolition of customs duties and quantitative restrictions on intra-Community trade. As a consequence of Community membership, Member States may no longer unilaterally impose tariffs or quotas on goods originating within the Community. Equally, laws and administrative practices which discriminate against workers from Community countries seeking employment in other Member States are contrary to Community law, as are national laws and practices which limit the supply of services or investment from Community countries.

Coordination of economic policy in fields such as agriculture, fishing, transport, competition, regional development and social policy is essential to ensure that these freedoms are promoted, and not gradually eroded or undermined by inconsistent national economic policies. The most successful, and also the most controversial, Community economic policy is the Common Agricultural Policy (CAP) which is designed to increase agricultural productivity, to ensure a fair standard of living among the agricultural community and to stabilise agricultural markets within the Community. Although most of the Community policies were originally specified under the Community treaties, a number of other policies, including the environment protection policy, the regional assistance policy and the energy policy, have been derived as a consequence of the functions of the Community.

The flow of commodities and products into the Community from foreign states is regulated by the common customs tariff which creates a single customs union from the individual customs territories of the Member States. In essence, the common customs tariff is a comprehensive tariff schedule which applies to goods entering the Community from destinations outside the Community. This system ensures that products entering the Community are liable to the same uniform rates of customs duties regardless of the port of entry in the Community. In addition to specifying applicable rates of duty on non-Community goods, the common customs tariff also regulates reliefs from duty, customs valuation and customs classification.

Functioning in conjunction with the common customs tariff, the common commercial policy serves to regulate the external economic policy of the Community towards non-Community states. In discharging its responsibilities under the common commercial policy, the Community enters into international economic agreements to regulate trading relationships between the Community and third states. The Community, through the European Commission, undertakes multilateral negotiations within the World Trade Organisation (WTO) and pursues bilateral economic negotiations with individual states. An extensive network of agreements now exists between the Community and third states regulating economic matters. These agreements may be classified according to form and content into four groups: multilateral trade agreements negotiated within the context of the WTO; bilateral free-trade agreements; association agreements, which are usually concluded with states about to become members of the Community; and development and assistance agreements with developing states.

The original draftsmen of the Community treaties clearly believed that the pursuit of these four fundamental objectives would ultimately achieve the creation of a comprehensive common market among the Member States of the Community. In reality, progress towards this goal was painfully slow. This lack of progress was generally attributed to the cumbersome decision-making processes within the Community which obstructed the adoption of measures to eradicate barriers and impediments to the free movement of goods, labour, services and capital. These failures led to a re-evaluation of the organisational structure and general goals of the Community, culminating in the adoption of the Single European Act 1986.

With the negotiation of the Treaty on European Union (TEU), it is clear that the EC Treaty, as amended, acted as a catalyst to closer integration among the peoples of Europe. This integration is no longer merely economic, but also political, social and cultural. The Treaty on European Union reflects this development and marked a significant step towards political harmony among the populations of the 15 Member States.

The Treaty itself recognises that it is a 'new stage in the process of European integration' initially started with the EC Treaty. In order to advance this process of integration, a concept of citizenship of the Union has been introduced as have mechanisms to increase economic, monetary and fiscal co-operation among the Member States.

In fact, the TEU has dramatically increased political, economic, monetary and social integration among the Member States participating in the organisation. A European citizenship has been established granting specific political rights, including the right to vote for non-nationals, to EC citizens in Member States other than their native countries. Economic and monetary union is being pursued vigorously with the creation of the single European currency. Furthermore, social integration is being achieved through a spectrum of policies and programmes. Each of these objectives have been continued, to differing degrees, by the amendments made to the EC Treaty and the TEU by the Treaty of Amsterdam.

None of these policy objectives could have been obtained without the foundations laid by the process of economic integration started by the EC Treaty and developed over the last 40 years. Hence, it is true to say that the architects of the EC Treaty were correct in identifying economic integration as the appropriate vehicle for achieving political harmony among the states of Europe.

QUESTION THREE

'The TEU and its three "pillars" have changed the balance of power between the Community institutions.'

Discuss, giving specific examples.

University of London LLB Examination
(for External Students) European Community Law June 1995 Q7

General Comment

This question relates to the new areas of competence added by the Treaty on European Union (TEU) and the changes in the power structure within the organisation. It is difficult to give many of the specific examples asked in the question since relatively few measures have been adopted in the new areas of competence. However, the main focus of the question lies in examining the role of the Community institutions outside the EC Treaty.

Skeleton Solution

The three pillars of the European Union: EC Treaty; Common Foreign Policy and Security Policy; Co-operation in the Fields of Justice and Home Affairs – limitations imposed on the ability of the Commission to participate in the processes outside the scope of the EC Treaty – examples of decisions of the Council in its new areas of competence – limitation of the ECJ's jurisdiction to conduct judicial review in these areas – some proposals being suggested for constitutional reform at the Intergovernmental Conference.

Suggested Solution

The Treaty on European Union (TEU) has transformed the European Community into a European Union by adding a number of new competencies to the constitutional structure of the organisation. This was achieved by creating an institution based on three pillars of broad competence. The TEU amended the EC Treaty to extend the Community's authority in several areas. The EC Treaty now stands as one pillar of competence of the organisation. The other two pillars are constituted by the provisions of the TEU dealing with the establishment of a Common Foreign Policy and Security Policy, on the one hand, and those relating to Co-operation in the Fields of Justice and Home Affairs on the other.

The first pillar – the European Community – is based on the amended EC Treaty. However, a number of substantial changes were brought by these amendments including the creation of the concept of European citizenship, the adoption of the principle of subsidiarity and a redefinition of the institutional and organisational structure of the decision-making processes within the organisation. In addition, new responsibilities were added in the field of economic and monetary policy with a view to creating a single European currency.

The second pillar – Common Foreign Policy and Security Policy – is contained in a separate title of the TEU. The European Union pursues a common foreign policy through procedures for systematic co-operation among the Member States in the formulation of policy. Gradually, Member States will implement a greater and greater volume of decisions on joint action in those areas where they have shared interests. Naturally, these areas will grow in size once the necessary momentum has gathered pace from the first decisions. The TEU also envisages the eventual framing of a common defence policy based on the Western European Union, a separate organisation but one in which joint decisions can be formulated on defence issues.

The third pillar – Co-operation in the Fields of Justice and Home Affairs – is composed of a number of areas of mutual interest among the Member States which involve elements of regulatory control. Thus, for example, the fields expressly included within the ambit of this policy are formulation of asylum policy, control of external frontiers, immigration policy, drug enforcement and co-operation among the police forces of the Member States.

Creating these three pillars has required reconfiguration of the organisational basis on which the organisation functions. In turn, this has changed the balance of power among the Community institutions, these being the Council, the Commission, the European Parliament and the European Court.

In the original EC Treaty, authority to enact Community measures was shared. The Commission proposed legislation and the Council adopted these proposals by the necessary vote. As a result, the Council could not legislate without a proposal from the Commission and, conversely, the Commission could not enact legislation without the stamp of the Council. Neither institution held an absolute balance of power; the need for co-operation ensured that both organs remained interdependent.

The TEU has altered this balance. In the two new areas of competence, the Council can act without a proposal from the Commission. Decisions concerning Common Foreign Policy and Security Policy can be enacted at the sole discretion of the Council. Member States consult among each other within the Council on future foreign policy to ensure that their combined influence is exerted as effectively as possible by means of concerted and convergent action. Similarly, common policies on issues are defined within the Council.

This is important because the new competencies granted under the provisions of the Common Foreign Policy are extensive. For example, since this procedure began operating in November 1993, decisions have been made by the Council on EU support for the transition of South Africa to a multiracial state, for the supply of humanitarian aid to Bosnia-Herzegovina and for the dispatch of observers for the parliamentary elections in Russia. Similarly, Council measures have been taken to approve joint action in preparation for the 1995 Conference on the Treaty on Non-Proliferation of Nuclear Weapons and in support of the Middle East peace process.

Action in the area of Police and Judicial Co-operation in Criminal Matters has not had as high an international profile but, behind the scenes, much activity has in fact occurred. Measures have been adopted, again by the Council acting alone, on co-operation among police forces. Joint action has been taken to create a Europol Drugs Unit and the negotiation of the Convention on the Simplification of Extradition Procedures. In these fields, Member States again consult with each other with a view to co-ordinating action.

The exclusion of the Commission from these activities is a significant shift in the balance of power inside the organisation in favour of the Council. The ability to formulate policy in these two important areas is a remarkable extension of authority on the part of the Council. Hence, it is significant that only the Council has changed its name after the TEU (to the Council of the European Union) while the European Commission has retained its former name.

As a further mark of the enhancement of the Council's position inside the organisation, it is to be noted that the European Court was not given power to conduct judicial review of the acts of the Council in the areas of Foreign Policy and Security Policy and

Police and Judicial Co-operation in Criminal Matters: art 46 TEU. In effect, this meant that the European Commission had very restricted power to bring the Council to the European Court to account for ultra vires actions in the same manner that it is able to do under art 226 EC. This limitation of jurisdiction effectively meant that the Council's actions were not subject to judicial review.

Parliamentary scrutiny of decisions taken in the two pillars outside the EC Treaty is also disturbingly weak. The European Parliament has limited rights to be consulted in the taking of certain decisions and can debate the ramifications of specific decisions. It cannot, however, veto the adoption of decisions in these fields or compel the Council to adopt amendments.

Inside the European Community itself, the TEU also brought about fundamental shifts in the balance of power by amending the EC Treaty. Parliament has greater rights to participate in the legislative procedure under the co-operation and co-decision procedures. It also has the power the approve the appointment of the President of the Commission, to ratify the accession of new Member States and to approve certain bilateral trade agreements, for example the EC-Turkey Customs Agreement 1995.

The shift in the balance of power towards the Council has therefore been tempered by the conferring of limited additional powers on the European Parliament, albeit in areas falling inside the EC Treaty and not in those new areas of competence under the other two pillars. At the same time, the TEU did not embrace the more radical changes in the constitutional structure of the organisation such as granting the Parliament equal powers relative to the Council to make laws, adopt the budget or participate in the formulation of general policy guidelines for the European Union.

While there was initial speculation that the Treaty of Amsterdam would entail significant changes in the balance of powers between the Community institutions, ultimately such a radical constitutional re-allocation of authority did not occur. True, the European Parliament acquired significantly greater influence in a number of areas by the extension of the co-decision procedure into fields previously excluded from its remit under this procedure. The EC pillar was also strengthened by simplification of the decision-making process. In addition, the range of competencies was extended so, for example, the provisions on the admission of third-country nationals was moved from the Justice and Home Affairs pillar to the European Community one and the Schengen Agreement and associated decisions were incorporated into the EC Treaty to replace provisions on social policy (new Pt Three, Title IV, EC Treaty). The ECJ's jurisdiction, subject to some limitations, was extended to this new Title and to those JHA provisions that remain in the TEU. The Treaty of Amsterdam also introduced the concept of 'closer co-operation'. This permits Member States to cooperate on matters should they so wish, if they are within the competence of the treaties but not currently subject to specific Community legislation. Under a new art 11 EC such action requires the involvement of a majority of the Member States, the extension of European Union objectives, and that the rights and obligations of non-participating Member States remain unaffected. However, even now, the European Parliament is far from being the initiator of legislative proposals or even an equal partner in the legislative decision-making process. These competencies continue to lie with the Commission and the Council respectively.

QUESTION FOUR

'The European Community has developed from a Community based on purely economic objectives to one with far wider aspirations.'

Discuss.

University of London LLB Examination
(for External Students) European Community Law June 1998 Q3

General Comment

This question is a very general one, requiring focus on the increasingly non-economic aspects of the European Union. The better response would have been one that could provide specific examples of the move away from more economic objectives.

Skeleton Solution

Original economic objectives – common market – workers' rights – extension of rights including to those not economically active – citizenship – human rights – Treaty of Amsterdam.

Suggested Solution

At its inception the European Community was named the European Economic Community. The name was changed by the Treaty on European Union (TEU) – a symbolic act recognising that in a number of areas the Community had become more than purely economic in its objectives.

In 1957 the then EEC's task was to establish a common market: art 2 EEC Treaty. The common market was to be a customs union that also permitted the free movement of factors of production, such as goods, services, persons and capital. One of the Community's objectives was to be the removal of barriers to such factors: art 3 EEC Treaty. However, even at this early stage of development there were references within the Treaty of Rome that suggested that the peoples of Europe were to be seen as more than merely units of production. For example, the preamble to the Treaty refers to the Member States' determination to 'lay the foundations of an ever-closer union among the peoples of Europe' and to improving 'the living and working conditions of their peoples'. Similarly, in relation to art 39 EC, which provides for the free movement of workers, the Advocate-General in the relatively early decision of *F (Mr and Mrs)* v *Belgium* Case 7/75 [1975] ECR 679 stated that workers must be considered as human beings and not merely as sources of labour. Since these early days the Community has seen an increasing shift from focus on economic objectives to those that are more politically orientated, emphasising that the citizens of Europe are entitled to fundamental rights and principles. This essay will concentrate on three examples of where this may be witnessed: the interpretation, application and extension of those rights available to workers; the introduction of European citizenship; and the development of human rights protection within EC law.

Article 39 EC provides for the free movement of workers (similar rights are available for the self-employed). The approach of the Community, witnessed in the decisions of the ECJ and the secondary legislation passed, has been to recognise that measures which assist in the integration of persons into the host state encourage the exercise of free movement rights. To acquire such rights the Community national must be a worker. The ECJ has stated that the term must have a Community definition so that the objective of free movement is not undermined: *Hoekstra v Bestuur der Bedrijfsvereniging voor Detailhandel en Ambachten* Case 75/63 [1964] ECR 177. In *Levin v Staatssecretaris van Justitie* Case 53/81 [1982] ECR 1035 the Court declared that a worker would be a person pursuing a genuine and effective economic activity that was not marginal or ancillary. It was further stated in *Kempf v Staatssecretaris van Justitie* Case 139/85 [1986] ECR 1741 that part-time work was capable of coming within this definition, even if the wages drawn were so low as to require the individual to apply for social assistance. Since the influential decision in the case of *R v Immigration Appeal Tribunal, ex parte Antonissen* Case C–292/89 [1991] ECR I–745, it is now possible under a teleological interpretation of art 39 EC to enter a Member State to search for work.

Workers have a range of rights under primary and secondary legislation. A worker has the right to residence under art 39(3) EC, the right to equality of treatment in employment under art 39(2) EC and the right to stay after employment has been terminated. Secondary legislation has augmented and clarified the rights available. Workers have the right to bring their families to live with them (as defined under art 10(1), Council Regulation 1612/68) regardless of their nationality. The worker and their family are entitled to the same social and tax advantages as nationals according to art 7(2) of the same Regulation. This has been interpreted generously by the ECJ to include all social advantages irrespective of whether they derive from the contract of employment: *Ministère Public v Even and ONPTS* Case 207/78 [1979] ECR 2019. In addition, the worker has the right to equality of access to housing (under art 9 of the Regulation) and their family has the right to access education (art 12 of the Regulation). Indeed, in this final example the rights extend to all opportunities designed to facilitate education, such as grants and loans: *Casagrande v Landeshauptstadt München* Case 9/74 [1974] ECR 773.

The extent of the rights referred to above and the wide range of their recipients may suggest that free movement has moved beyond the economic sphere. However, although it is true that the ECJ has interpreted these rights in a generous manner, the above provisions remain inextricably linked with the objective of establishing the common market. In recent years, though, there has been a move towards recognising the rights of those that are not economically active; in other words, a recognition of rights of free movement for European citizens rather than merely for workers (or the self-employed). A number of directives have been passed that extend rights of residence to categories of persons that are not economically active. This includes Council Directive 93/96, which extends the rights to students; Council Directive 90/364, which extends the rights to persons of independent means; and Council Directive 90/365, which relates to the retired. All such persons are entitled to movement and residence rights, although they must be medically insured and have sufficient means to avoid reliance on social assistance from the state. Consequently, whilst such developments are welcome in that they expand the focus of the Community towards less economic objectives, such rights are still dependent on those wishing to invoke these rights having some degree of financial independence.

Another example of the move towards less economic factors can be witnessed in the creation of the concept of European citizenship. This offers a clear recognition of the peoples of the European Union as individuals rather than as members of any labour force. The concept was introduced under the Treaty on European Union but is contained within arts 18–22 EC. Article 18 EC provides a right to free movement for every citizen of the Union and the right to reside in a Member State. In addition, citizenship entails the right to stand and vote in municipal and European Parliamentary elections; to petition the Parliamentary ombudsman and Parliament itself; to claim diplomatic protection outside of the EU from any of the Member States if their own national state has no consular or diplomatic protection available; and the right to access Community institutional documentation.

Unfortunately, the Treaty of Amsterdam introduced an amendment to art 17 EC, which states that citizenship of the EU can only complement and not replace national citizenship and, in addition, it is subject to certain limitations. In determining national citizenship the state retains complete control under principles of public international law: *Micheletti* v *Delegación del Gobierno en Cantabria* Case C–369/90 [1992] ECR I–4239.

A recent example of the institutions focus on less economic matters can be seen in the development of the law associated with protecting human rights. The original EC Treaty contained no such provisions, reflective perhaps of its emphasis on economics, and the EC was rather slow in recognising such rights as witnessed in *Stauder* v *City of Ulm* Case 29/69 [1969] ECR 419. In both *Internationale Handelsgesellschaft GmbH* v *EVGF* Case 11/70 [1970] ECR 1125 and *Nold* v *Commission* Case 4/73 [1974] ECR 491 the European Court pointed to the need to respect human rights since they were a part of the constitutional traditions of the Member States and because there were various international treaties protecting them. In *Nold* v *Commission* Case 4/73 [1974] ECR 491 the Court concluded that treaties could offer guidance of the rights to be protected and referred specifically to the European Convention for the Protection of Human Rights and Fundamental Freedoms (ECHR). However, in *Re the Accession of the Community to the ECHR*, Opinion 2/94 [1996] ECR I–1759 the Court concluded that the Community was incapable of actually acceding in its own right to the Convention. Since this decision the Community has expanded its own means of protecting human rights with the creation of a Charter, first published in July 2000.

The Charter extends protection to six fundamental values: dignity; freedom; equality; solidarity; citizenship and justice. The rights are available to the majority of people, although there are in addition some categories of people, such as children, that are offered additional protection. The Commission has extended its support for the Charter stating that it offers codified protection that collates both economic and social rights that for too long have been traditionally separate. It remains to be seen if future developments will include the transformation of this Charter from something that is merely declaratory to something that is legally binding and/or part of the EC Treaty.

Recent changes introduced by the Treaty of Amsterdam emphasise the continued move towards political rather than economic objectives. Article 12 EC, which prohibits discrimination on the basis of nationality, was extended by the introduction of a new art 13 EC permitting the Council to 'appropriate action to combat discrimination based on sex, racial or ethnic origin, religion or belief, disability, age or sexual orientation'. The increasing importance of protecting fundamental rights can also be witnessed in the amendment by the Treaty of Amsterdam of art 7 EC. Hence, if a Member State commits a serious and persistent breach of the principles of liberty, democracy, respect for human rights and fundamental freedoms or the rule of law it may be suspended from voting in the Council.

This increasingly important dimension to the development of the European Union, witnessed too in treaty developments that have extended competencies into areas such as Justice and Home Affairs, is expected to only continue in the future as the drive to 'ever-closer union' is maintained.

Chapter 2

The Institutions of the European Union

2.1   Introduction

2.2   Key points

2.3   Key cases

2.4   Questions and suggested solutions

2.1 Introduction

As originally conceived, each of the three separate European Communities possessed a separate Commission and Council but shared the same parliamentary assembly and Court of Justice. The Merger Treaty 1965 consolidated these institutions into one set for all the Communities.

The Single European Act 1986 recognised the status of the European Council within the Community framework but did not amend the EC Treaty to give this organ formal institutional status. At the same time, the Act gave the Council of Ministers formal authority to create a second division within the European Court to be known as the Court of First Instance.

The pre-existing institutional structure contained in the amended EC Treaty was not significantly altered by the Treaty on European Union although the Court of Auditors was given formal recognition as an institution of the European Community by an amendment to the EC Treaty to that effect. Hence, the institutional structure of the European Union is composed of these five organs although the Council of Ministers has changed its name to the Council of the European Union. The European Commission, the European Court of Justice (and the Court of First Instance) and the Court of Auditors remain, at least in name, institutions of the European Community. This is because the majority of the functions of these four organs are performed on the basis of the powers conferred under the EC Treaty, while the Council of Ministers exercises authority under all three pillars of the Treaty on European Union.

The Treaty of Amsterdam did not significantly disturb this constitutional structure. It merely added additional functions and powers and distributed these among the organs of the organisation in a way that enhanced the position of the European Parliament, particularly in the legislative process. The three pillars of the constitution therefore remain.

2.2 Key points

The European Council

Composition and structure

The European Council consists of all the Heads of Government of the Member States and their respective Foreign Ministers, together with the President of the European Commission who is assisted by another Commissioner. The Treaty on European Union specifies that the European Council shall convene twice each year: art 4 TEU.

Competence and powers

The European Council is designed to facilitate the coordination of European Foreign policy. Responsibility for the agenda lies with the Member State which has the Presidency of a separate Community institution – the Council of Ministers.

The Council possesses no formal powers. Rather, it is a forum for discussions, on an informal basis, relating to issues of common Community concern. However, the Treaty on European Union declares that the European Council shall 'provide the Union with the necessary impetus for its development and shall define the general political guidelines thereof'. Through consultations at this level, Member States agree to maximise their combined influence on global affairs through coordination, convergence, joint action, and the development of common principles and objectives.

The Council of Ministers

Composition and structure

The Council of Ministers consists of one national representative from each Member State, the exact composition varying according to the subject of discussions. A distinction is drawn between two types of Council meetings.

a) General Council meetings: these are attended by the Foreign Ministers of the Member States.

b) Specialised Council meetings: these meetings are attended by the various national Ministers with responsibility for the subjects on the agenda for discussion.

The office of the President of the Council rotates in alphabetical sequence among the Member States in six month periods. The Presidency of the Council of Ministers has been synchronised with the Presidency of the European Council. This ensures that a single Member State is responsible for the general progress of the Community as a whole during its period of tenure.

Since the government Ministers who participate in the Council of Ministers also have national responsibilities and therefore cannot be permanently present in Brussels, a subsidiary organ has been established in order to maintain consistency and continuity in the work of the Council. This organ, called the Committee of Permanent

Representatives (known by the French acronym COREPER), has been formed to perform two main functions:

a) to provide liaison between national governments and Community institutions for the exchange of informations; and

b) to prepare draft Community legislation with the Commission for final submission to the Council itself.

COREPER is composed of the ambassadors of the Member States accredited to the Community, often assisted by national officials from the civil services of their respective Member States. The individual members of COREPER represent the interests of their respective countries and not those of the Community.

Competence and powers under the EC Treaty

The Council of Ministers is the principal decision-making organ of the Community and has competence to deal with the following matters:

a) the adoption of Community legislation;

b) the formulation of Community policies;

c) the finalisation of international agreements with foreign states on matters which fall within the competence of the Community;

d) drafting the Community budget in conjunction with the European Parliament;

e) taking those decisions required to ensure that the objectives specified in the EC Treaty are achieved.

Article 202 EC allows the Council to delegate authority to the European Commission for the implementation of policies and rules established by the Council.

The most important power of the Council of Ministers is the capacity to enact Community legislation. The Community legislative process is exceedingly complex, particularly after the amendments made by the Single European Act 1986 and subsequently the Treaty on European Union. As a result of the amendments made by the Single European Act 1986, two legislative procedures existed:

a) the original legislative procedure (consultation); and

b) the 'co-operation procedure'.

The European Parliament is more closely involved in the law-making process when the co-operation procedure is required. Co-operation procedure extends to Community legislation regulating the following subjects:

a) the elimination of discrimination on the ground of nationality;

b) the freedom of movement of workers and the freedoms of providing services and establishment; and

c) harmonisation measures relating to the establishment and functioning of the internal market.

The co-operation procedure was retained in the post-Maastricht legislative structure under art 252 EC.

The Treaty on European Union added a third legislative procedure to this already confusing picture by introducing the 'co-decision procedure'. The co-decision procedure is regulated by art 251 EC and follows, in broad terms, the co-operation procedure although it is a more comprehensive legislative process.

Under the co-decision procedure, the Commission retains discretion to submit legislative proposals which are sent to both the Council and the Parliament. The Council, acting by qualified majority, and after obtaining the opinion from the Parliament, is required to adopt a common position on the proposal. This common position is communicated to the Parliament.

After examining the common position of the Council, the Parliament has four options:

a) to approve the common position in which case the measure returns to the Council for formal approval;

b) to take no action in which case, after a period of three months, the Council may adopt the proposal;

c) to suggest amendments to the common position which must be by an absolute majority and these suggested amendments are returned to the Commission and amended before being resubmitted to the Council; or

d) to reject the common position, again by an absolute majority, in which case a Conciliation Committee may be established to resolve the impasse.

The most significant amendment made by the Treaty of Amsterdam to the existing legislative process is that the co-decision procedure has been extended to a further 23 subject matters. The co-decision procedure itself is also refined. Specifically, the third reading in Parliament has been abolished. If the Council and the European Parliament do not reach a compromise in the Conciliation Committee, there is simply no agreement and the proposed measure falls. As a result of this change the two institutions are now obliged to produce some result or allow proposals to fall: art 251 EC.

Voting

Article 205 EC stipulates that 'save as otherwise provided, the Council shall act by a majority of its Members'. A common requirement is for the use of a qualified majority. A system of weighted voting has been created for the purpose of determining a qualified majority under art 205 EC. According to this scheme, votes are allocated on the following basis.

10 votes	–	Germany, France, Italy and the United Kingdom
8 votes	–	Spain
5 votes	–	Belgium, Greece, the Netherlands and Portugal
4 votes	–	Austria and Sweden
3 votes	–	Denmark, Ireland and Finland
2 votes	–	Luxembourg

The total number of votes stands at 87 votes. For the adoption of measures by a qualified majority, there must be at least 62 votes in favour where the EC Treaty requires such acts to be adopted on a proposal from the Commission, and 62 votes in favour, cast by at least ten members, in all other cases. Since the accession of the new Member States in January 1995, a blocking minority has become 26 votes. This number of votes allows a coalition of Member States to prevent the adoption of measures which require a qualified majority.

The use of majority voting in the Council has been more common since the passing of the Single European Act 1986 which extended majority voting to a more substantial range of matters than had previously been the case. Similarly, the Treaty on European Union continued this process and enlarged the number of areas subject to majority voting.

The legal basis for enacting measures and legislation

Since the Council of Ministers is the principal decision-making body of the Community, it is responsible for ensuring that the measures which it approves are adopted on the proper legal basis. The legal basis for the adoption of a measure depends on its subject matter and not the type of measure. Depending on the subject matter involved, different procedural and voting requirements must be respected.

Failure to comply with these requirements may render a measure open to challenge by the European Commission, the European Parliament, the Member States and, in certain circumstances, private individuals.

For example, in *United Kingdom* v *Council (Re Hormones)* Case 68/86 [1988] ECR 855, the UK challenged the legal basis on which the Council adopted a directive prohibiting the use of certain types of hormones. The measure was adopted under art 37 EC – which required a qualified majority – but the United Kingdom claimed that the proper legal authority was art 94 EC which required unanimity. The Court held that the proper legal basis was art 37 EC although the measure was declared void on technical grounds.

The Court has also interpreted the effect of the UK opt-out clause incorporated into the Social Charter and how this provision affects the legal basis for the adoption of measures under the EC Treaty. In *United Kingdom* v *Council (Re Working Hours Directive)* Case C–84/94 [1996] ECR I–5755, the Court considered the legal basis of a directive imposing a maximum 48 hour working week adopted by qualified majority by the Council on the basis of art 138 EC which relates to health and safety. The UK challenged the directive on the grounds that it had been adopted on the incorrect legal basis and that the UK could not be bound by such provisions because of its opt-out clause.

The Court held that the Council had not adopted the directive on an incorrect legal basis as far as the measures were designed to limit the maximum permissible hours that employees were required to work and the various other work-related measures. These were issues which fell inside the scope of the health and safety of workers and the Council was free to regulate such matters under art 138 EC. This also allowed the Council to act by a majority vote. The UK could not therefore validly exercise its reservation made to the Treaty on European Union.

It is also open to private parties to challenge the legal basis for the adoption of measures either under art 230 EC or the preliminary reference procedure of art 234 EC. An example of the latter procedure being used occurred in *Eurotunnel SA and Others* v *SeaFrance* Case C–408/95 [1997] ECR I–6315.

The European Commission

Composition and structure

The European Commission is composed of 20 Commissioners – two from each of the five largest Member States together with one from each of the smaller Member States. Commissioners are appointed by agreement between the various Member States and hold office for renewable periods of five years.

By virtue of art 214 EC, the members of the Commission are appointed for a period of five years. Their term of office is renewable. The governments of the Member States nominate by common accord the person whom they intend to appoint as President of the Commission. The nomination of the President has to be approved by the European Parliament. The governments of the Member States, by common accord with the nominee for President, nominate the other persons whom they intend to appoint as members of the Commission.

The Commission functions as a collegiate body and recognises the principle of collective responsibility. Voting within the Commission is by simple majority and deliberations are private and confidential. In order to ensure efficiency within the Commission, special responsibilities are distributed to each individual Commissioner.

The Commissioners are also assisted by a considerable body of Community civil servants. This Secretariat is organised into 23 departments known as Directorates-General. Each department is presided over by a Director-General who is responsible to the Commissioners whose portfolio includes that particular department.

Competence and powers

The Commission performs four separate functions which are set out in art 211 EC:

a) to ensure respect for the rights and obligations imposed on Member States and Community institutions by both the Community treaties and measures made under the authority of these agreements;

b) to formulate, participate and initiate policy decisions authorised under the Community treaties;

c) to promote the interests of the Community both internally and externally; and

d) to exercise the powers delegated to it by the Council for the implementation and administration of Community policy.

The Commission has ultimate responsibility to ensure that the interests of the Community are protected.

The most important power of the Commission is the ability to institute proceedings before the European Court against:

a) any Member State suspected of violating its Community obligations (art 226 EC); and

b) any Community institution considered to have acted outside its power (art 230 EC).

The Commission has also been delegated a considerable range of executive and legislative powers by the Council of Ministers. For example, art 83(1) EC authorises the Council to delegate responsibility for the administration of competition policy to the Commission. In the discharge of this function, the Commission has authority, in certain circumstances, to investigate complaints, to impose fines, and to require Member States to take appropriate action to prevent or terminate infringements of competition policy. Often delegated authority also vests power to legislate in the Commission.

The European Parliament

Composition and structure

Members of the European Parliament were originally appointed by their respective national parliaments according to internal parliamentary procedures. In 1976 the Member States agreed the Act Concerning the Election by Direct Universal Suffrage of Members to the European Parliament which facilitated direct elections to the European Parliament.

A total of 626 members of the European Parliament (MEPs) are elected for terms of five years. Seats are allocated to Member States in approximate proportion to their populations. The distribution of seats is as follows.

99 representatives – Germany

87 representatives – France, Italy and the United Kingdom

64 representatives – Spain

31 representatives – Netherlands

25 representatives – Belgium, Greece and Portugal

22 representatives – Sweden

21 representatives – Austria

16 representatives – Denmark and Finland

15 representatives – Ireland

6 representatives – Luxembourg

The distribution of seats within the United Kingdom is regulated by the European Parliamentary Elections Act 1978, as amended by the European Parliamentary Elections Act 1993. Constituencies are drawn up by the Boundary Commissioners and 72 seats are allocated to England, eight to Scotland, four to Wales and three to Northern Ireland.

Members of the European Parliament are seated according to their political affiliations and views and not their nationalities. The majority of parties in the European Parliament are coalitions between national parties. In July 1999, the European Peoples' Party was the largest single party, followed by the European Socialist Party, and then the European Democratic Party.

Competence and powers

The European Parliament represents the interests of the peoples of Europe. As originally conceived, the European Parliament lacked any real powers other than an essentially advisory competence. The Parliament has, however, gradually acquired a significantly more important role in the functioning of the Community.

Now the Treaty on European Union has been approved, the Parliament's legislative competence has passed through three distinct stages.

Stage 1: Original legislative role

Stage 2: The Co-operation procedure

Stage 3: The Co-decision procedure

In addition to its legislative functions, the Parliament also possesses a considerable number of powers, mainly over the European Commission as opposed to the Council of Ministers. In particular, the Parliament may exercise the following powers.

a) The consent of the Parliament is required for the admission of new Members into the Community and for the conclusion of association agreements between the Community and third countries.

b) The European Commission is obliged to answer questions submitted by Members of the European Parliament. Both written and oral questions may be submitted.

c) The Commission is required to submit an annual general report to the Parliament on the affairs of the Community which is the subject of an annual parliamentary debate.

d) The Community budget is prepared by the Commission and submitted to the Council of Ministers, but the Parliament may approve or modify the budget depending on the expenditure involved.

e) The opinion of the Parliament must be sought during the decision-making processes before the adoption of certain measures.

f) The Treaty on European Union introduced a petition procedure which entitles any citizen of the Community to petition the Parliament on matters which fall within the scope of the Parliament's competence.

While the European Parliament exercises considerable supervisory control over the Commission, the same cannot be said of its relationship with the Council of Ministers.

Power of censure over the European Commission

The European Parliament has the power to collectively dismiss the European Commission under art 201 EC, if a motion of censure is passed by a two-thirds majority.

In January 1999 the European Socialist Party in the European Parliament tabled a motion to compel the Commission, under the Presidency of Jacques Santer, to resign. This motion was defeated since the necessary two-thirds majority was not obtained. However, a commission of inquiry was established into allegations of maladministration by the Commission which resulted in an adverse report criticising a number of individual Commissioners. As a result, all the Commissioners resigned their positions since liability for maladministration involved collective responsibility of all members.

Power of the Parliament to compel judicial review of the acts of other institutions

The power of the European Parliament to challenge the validity of acts of other Community institutions and Member States was not originally included in the EC Treaty in the same way as the powers of both the Council of Ministers and the European Commission in this respect: see arts 230 and 232 EC.

Its right to bring actions for failure to act under art 232 EC was eventually recognised in *European Parliament* v *Council (Re Common Transport Policy)* Case 13/83 [1985] ECR 1513, where the Court held that the term 'institutions of the Community' included the European Parliament. Similarly, its right to initiate proceedings to protect its interests under art 230 EC was recognised in *European Parliament* v *Council (Re Chernobyl)* Case C–70/88 [1990] ECR I–2041 and *European Parliament* v *Council (Re Student Rights)* Case C–295/90 [1992] ECR I–4193.

Both these rights have now been recognised through amendments made to arts 230 and 232 EC by the Treaty on European Union.

The European Court of Justice

Composition and structure

The Court of Justice, which sits in Luxembourg, has 15 judges who are assisted by eight Advocates-General, although an additional Advocate-General has been appointed due to a political compromise reached during the accession of Austria, Finland and Sweden. Each Member State is entitled to appoint a judge of its own nationality.

Every three years there is a partial replacement of the judges (eight and seven after each three-year period) as well as Advocates-General (four on each occasion). Judges are eligible for re-election for another term. The President of the Court is elected by the judges from among their number for a term of three years, although again he or she may be re-elected.

In each case before the Court, an Advocate-General is appointed to deliver an impartial and legally reasoned opinion after the close of the pleadings by the parties, but before the judges sitting on the case render their decision. This opinion is a preliminary to a decision by the Court and the Advocate-General is not given a vote in the actual voting among the judges.

The structure and organisation of the Court is regulated by a separate Protocol to the EC Treaty – Protocol on the Statute of the Court of Justice. Matters of procedure are regulated by this Protocol, including the content of oral and written pleadings, rights of production, citation of witnesses, costs and expenses, and periods of limitation. These rules are supplemented by others contained in the Rules of Procedure of the European Court of Justice.

Jurisdiction

The jurisdiction of the European Court of Justice may be classified into three distinct categories.

a) Contentious jurisdiction: this refers to the right of the Court to hear direct actions between Member States and Community institutions, as well as actions by individuals against the acts of Community institutions.

b) Plenary jurisdiction: this refers to the right of the Court to award damages for unlawful acts committed by Community institutions.

c) Preliminary ruling jurisdiction: the European Court has jurisdiction to hear cases referred by the national courts of Member States on matters relating to the interpretation and application of Community law (art 234 EC).

The nature of the jurisdiction of the European Court forms the next two chapters of this book.

Advisory opinions

Both the Council of Ministers and the European Commission are authorised to submit legal questions to the European Court for advisory opinions. This power has been used most often by the European Commission to limit the competence of the Council to act, or alternatively to reinforce its own constitutional position: see *Commission* v *Council (Re ERTA)* Case 22/70 [1971] ECR 263.

Another important opinion concerned the possibility of the European Community acceding to the European Convention on Human Rights. In its opinion in *Re the Accession of the Community to the ECHR* Opinion 2/94 [1996] ECR I–1759, the Court ruled that there was no legal basis to allow accession of the European Community as a whole to the Convention. Such a putative act would amount to a usurpation of the constitutional system maintained in the Community.

Attempts have also been made to erect a legal structure to protect human rights and fundamental freedoms, although these attempts are far short of the wholesale incorporation of the European Convention of Human Rights into the structure of the organisation.

The Court of First Instance

Composition and structure

The Single European Act 1986 authorised the Council of Ministers to create a Court of First Instance (CFI) to alleviate the volume of work before the European Court of Justice. The Court of First Instance was established by Council Decision 88/591 and consists of 15 judges. Members of the Court are appointed by agreement between the Member States for periods of six years. The members of the Court of First Instance elect a President from among their own number.

No provision has been made in the Council Decision for the appointment of Advocates-General to the Court of First Instance. However, judges of the Court may be called upon to perform the task of an Advocate-General. The actual organisation of the Court is specified in the Rules of Procedure for the Court of First Instance.

The constitutional authority for the functioning and operation of the Court of First Instance has now been incorporated into the EC Treaty by amendments made by the Treaty on European Union. Article 225 EC regulates the composition of the Court as well as the extent of its jurisdiction.

Jurisdiction

The jurisdiction and powers of the Court of First Instance have been carved from those of the European Court of Justice itself. The Court of First Instance does not extend the jurisdiction of the European Court, but rather, it exercises certain aspects of the Court's functions. In particular, the creation of the new Court does not alter the jurisdictional relationships between the European Court system and the individual national courts and tribunals of the Member States.

This jurisdiction extends to the following classes of actions.

a) Actions or proceedings by the staff of Community institutions.

b) Actions for annulment and actions for failure to act brought against the Commission by natural or legal persons and concerning the application of arts 50 and 57–66 ECSC. Such actions relate to Commission decisions concerning levies, production controls, pricing practices, agreements and concentrations.

c) Actions for annulment or actions for failure to act brought by natural or legal persons against an institution of the Community under arts 230 and 232 EC.

Where these actions are accompanied by claims for damages, the Court of First Instance has jurisdiction to decide the related claim.

The Court of First Instance cannot hear cases brought by either Member States or Community institutions. Nor may the Court answer questions submitted by national courts through the preliminary ruling procedure which is reserved to the European Court of Justice.

Appeal from the Court of First Instance to the European Court is competent but only on point of law and subject to the appellant demonstrating the existence of one of the grounds of appeal specified in art 51 of the amended European Court of Justice Statute. Three grounds of appeal have been established.

a) Lack of competence on the part of the Court of First Instance, such as an excess of its jurisdiction.

b) A breach of procedure before the Court which has had an adverse effect on the interests of the appellant.

c) An infringement of Community law by the Court of First Instance, such as an error in the interpretation or application of Community legal principles.

A substantial number of appeals have now been heard by the European Court of Justice under the appeal procedure, the majority of which concern decisions of the CFI on competition matters: see, for example, *Publishers Association* v *Commission* Case C–360/92 [1995] ECR I–23. The Court, in particular, has assiduously stood by the principle that it will refuse to consider appeals alleging errors of fact as opposed to errors of law: see *Hilti AG* v *Commission (No 2)* Case C–53/92P [1994] ECR I–667.

The Treaty of Nice

The proposed expansion of membership to 27 Member States by 2004 led to demands for institutional reform and this forms the basis of the changes proposed by the Treaty of Nice. This Treaty is not to date in force and may face some delay because of ratification difficulties. The main institutional reforms are as follows.

a) Votes in the Council will be re-balanced for qualified majority voting (QMV) as from 1 January 2005. Votes have been allocated to the yet to join Member States even though they will join at different times. Voting weights have been determined by reference to population.

Existing Member States	QMV Weight Old	New	States yet to join	QMV Weight Old	New
Germany	10	29	Poland	0	27
United Kingdom	10	29	Romania	0	14
France	10	29	Czech Republic	0	12
Italy	10	29	Hungary	0	12
Spain	8	27	Bulgaria	0	10
The Netherlands	5	13	Slovakia	0	7
Greece	5	12	Lithuania	0	7
Belgium	5	12	Latvia	0	4
Portugal	5	12	Slovenia	0	4
Sweden	4	10	Estonia	0	4
Austria	4	10	Cyprus	0	4
Demark	3	7	Malta	0	3
Finland	3	7			
Ireland	3	7			
Luxembourg	2	4			
Total votes	87				345
	(62 qualified majority, 26 blocking minority)				(258 qualified majority, 88 blocking minority)

An affirmative majority vote will be when 75.1 per cent of the total votes cast are positive. In addition the use of QMV will be further extended, although the need for unanimity will probably be retained in specific areas that raise concern in Member States, such as harmonisation of internal taxation, for example.

b) In the Commission, Germany, the UK, France, Italy and Spain will have only one rather than two Commissioners from 2005. It is proposed that a rotation system will be put into operation to ensure that the Commission will have less than 27 members at any one time.

c) The number of seats in the Parliament will be reduced for all States except Germany. The allocation of seats for new States will be as follows.

Poland	50
Romania	33
Czech Republic	20
Hungary	20
Bulgaria	17
Slovakia	13
Lithuania	12
Latvia	8
Slovenia	7
Estonia	6
Cyprus	6
Malta	5

d) The judicial system will be reformed by the insertion of a new art 220(2) EC, which will provide for the creation of chambers attached to the CFI. This does, however, require unanimity in the Council and for the ECJ to pass comment, and as a result there may be alternative changes made in the future.

2.3 Key cases

- *European Parliament* v *Council (Re Chernobyl)* Case C–70/88 [1990] ECR I–2041
  First successful action by the European Parliament against the Council challenging the legal basis of a measure

- *European Parliament* v *Council (Re Student Rights)* Case C–295/90 [1992] ECR I–4193
  Confirmation of the right of the European Parliament to challenge measures under the authority of the EC Treaty

- *Hilti AG* v *Commission (No 2)* Case C–53/92P [1994] ECR I–667
  Appeal from the CFI to the European Court restricted to points of law

- *Re the Draft Treaty on a European Economic Area (No 1)* Opinion 1/91 [1991] ECR I–6079
  Reference by the European Commission of the constitutionality of the European Economic Area Agreement

2.4 Questions and suggested solutions

QUESTION ONE

To what extent is it true to say that the Council is the European Community's legislator?

University of London LLB Examination
(for External Students) European Community Law June 1991 Q6

General Comment

A question requiring a narrative, descriptive answer. In order to score well, it is not only necessary to identify the Council's role in the legislative process, but also the influence of the other bodies in the procedure.

Skeleton Solution

The strength of the Council's position in the legislative procedure – the influence of the Commission on the content of measures – the increasing influence of the European Parliament – the co-operation and co-decision procedures.

Suggested Solution

There is little doubt that the Council of Ministers is the principal decision-making organ of the Community. As a body composed of national representatives, it embodies the interests of the Member States of the Community and ensures that each state retains a voice in the formulation of Community policy and legislation. Its position in the hierarchy of institutions is such that virtually all the decisions and legislation passed at the Community level must be approved by the Member States through the medium of the Council.

The only limited exception to this general rule is that occasionally the Commission is authorised to enact regulations in particular sectors by the Council delegating authority to act or by the provisions of the Community treaties. For example, in the administration of competition policy, the Commission retains considerable discretion as to the application of the relevant rules of competition law.

While the Council exercises virtually unrestrained authority to enact legislative measures, this is not to deny that certain constraints are placed on the ability of the Council to influence the content of these rules. The final say in the enactment of Community legislation certainly resides with the Council, but in the formulation of these rules, both the European Parliament and the European Commission exercise some influence.

The European Commission has responsibility for proposing Community legislation and initiating policy. It is the Commission, in conjunction with the various consultative bodies, that constructs draft legislation. Naturally, in the discharge of this duty, the Commission retains considerable discretion as to the contents of a draft measure. At the same time, the Commission is often acutely aware that proposed measures that are too ambitious will be vetoed in the Council of Ministers. In practice, therefore, draft measures are often continuously passed between the Council and the Commission for revision and modification, a process that dilutes the Commission's influence in the drafting of legislation.

At the same time, the European Parliament has been given a greater role in the legislative process than originally envisaged under the EC Treaty. Before the Single European Act 1986, the function of the Parliament was essentially advisory. Although some provisions of the Treaty required the consent of the Parliament for the adoption of certain measures, on the whole Parliament could only provide advisory opinions and often the Commission was not even obliged to seek such an opinion, although in practice it often did so.

The Single European Act 1986 introduced the so-called co-operation legislative procedure. This procedure extends to the adoption of Community legislation in the following matters: the elimination of discrimination on the grounds of nationality; the free movement of workers and the freedom to provide services; and harmonisation of measures designed to implement the single internal market programme.

Under this procedure, the Commission continues to exercise responsibility for the initiation of proposals which are sent to the Parliament for an opinion before being sent to the Council of Ministers. The Council is then required to reach a 'common position' on the proposed measure, acting by qualified majority. A common position is simply a consensus on the basic elements of the proposal.

The Treaty on European Union (TEU) introduced a third type of procedure, namely the 'co-decision' procedure under what is now art 251 EC. Whenever the co-decision procedure applies, the Commission submits its proposals to both the Council and the European Parliament. After the proposal has been submitted, both organs consider the draft measure and the Council adopts a common position after having obtained the first opinion of the Parliament. The common position is then communicated to the European Parliament along with a statement of the reasons which led the Council to adopt the common position. The Parliament then has three months to react to the common position and this stage has become known as the second reading.

Under the co-decision procedure, the Parliament has three options that can be exercised during the three-month second reading. First, it can reject the common position by an absolute majority of its members, in which case the Council must reconsider the whole proposal. Second, it can propose amendments which are then notified to the Council for its consideration. Third, it can decline to act, which allows the Council to adopt the proposal. Where there is disagreement between the institutions, a conciliation committee may be established to adjudicate on the issue.

The Treaty of Amsterdam modified the co-decision procedure by shortening the options open to the conciliation committee to arbitrate in the event of failure to agree between the institutions. It also extended the scope of the co-decision procedure to subject matters which were previously excluded. These adjustments are widely seen as enhancing the position of the European Parliament in the legislative process.

It is therefore inaccurate to say that the Council of Ministers is the Community legislator. The power and influence of the European Parliament is now by no means negligible in this process. Ultimately, of course, the Council can veto all legislative measures if it so desires. In reality, however, this ultimate sanction is rarely applied. Instead, both organs have shown themselves increasingly willing to share in the legislative partnership which has developed, especially since the introduction of the co-decision procedure by the TEU.

QUESTION TWO

What role does the Commission play in the European Community's legal and institutional structure? What are the principal factors which have influenced the development of its role since 1958?

University of London LLB Examination
(for External Students) European Community Law June 1992 Q4

General Comment

This is a straightforward question in which students are required to provide a detailed description of the European Commission's role in the constitutional structure of the Community. Relatively high marks may be scored in the event that the student has a grasp of the basic elements of this part of the syllabus because of the general nature of the question.

Skeleton Solution

The constitutional position of the Commission in the instructional structure of the Community – powers: supervisory functions; initiation of policy; protection of the interests of the Community; exercise of powers conferred by both treaties and legislation – factors influencing the role of the Commission since 1958 – additional powers and functions exercised by the Commission today.

Suggested Solution

The European Commission plays an orchestrating role within the Community in the formulation of Community legislation and policy. While it performs its functions in conjunction with other Community institutions, particularly the Council of Ministers and the European Parliament, the Commission is ultimately responsible for the initiation of policy and legislative proposals.

Without the Commission, no Community legislation would be enacted, no international negotiations entered into with other countries, and there would be considerably fewer instances of Member States being brought before the European

Court for infringements of Community law. While the Council of Ministers represents the interests of the Member States and the European Parliament the interests of the peoples of Europe in the running of the Community, the Commission is the embodiment of the Community interests in the process. Ultimately, it is the European Commission that has responsibility to ensure that the interests of the Community are fully protected, particularly as against the Member States.

Originally the Commission was given four functions under art 211 EC.

First, the Commission is required to ensure respect for the rights and obligations imposed on both Member States and Community institutions by the Community treaties and Community legislation. Acting under this authority, the Commission regularly institutes proceedings against Member States alleged to have violated Community obligations (art 226 EC) and against Community institutions considered to have acted outside the scope of their powers (art 230 EC).

Second, the Commission has been given charge of formulating, initiating and participating in the policy-making process within the Community. It is this function that gives the Commission much of its power within the legislative process. While the Council of Ministers is the organ which eventually approves legislative proposals, the Commission has considerable discretion as regards the shaping and content of those proposals. It is true that both the Council of Ministers and the European Parliament are able to suggest amendments to proposals but, ultimately, without the drafting of proposed measures no policies would ever be formulated and no legislative measures ever enacted.

Third, it is required to promote the interests of the Community inside and outside the Community with regard to relations with other countries. Thus, the Commission is permitted to conduct negotiations with third parties on matters that fall within the scope of the Community's competence as defined in the constitutional treaties.

Finally, the Commission is instructed to exercise the powers delegated to it by the Council for the implementation and administration of Community policy. For example, the Commission has extensive powers as regards the enforcement of Community competition policy. It can enact decisions requiring private companies and firms to desist from certain anti-competitive practices and can impose fines subject to review by the European Court.

The functions and powers of the Commission were not substantially altered by the Merger Treaty in 1967. This agreement merely consolidated the functions and powers of the Commission in one single source.

The same cannot be said of the Single European Act (SEA) 1986 which significantly amended the EC Treaty. This agreement in fact had three separate effects on the powers of the Commission. Firstly, the Treaty altered the relationship between the Commission and the European Parliament in the legislative process as far as legislation on certain subjects was concerned. Secondly, the Act gave greater competencies to the Community in certain areas of policy. Since the Commission is in charge of the formulation of policy, any growth in the responsibilities of the Community necessarily entails a greater amount of power in the hands of the Commission. Thirdly, the role of the Commission in the external affairs of the Community was greatly enhanced through recognition of the institutional status of the European Council.

Obviously, any requirements imposed on the Commission to cooperate, consult or discuss proposed measures with another Community organ tend to dilute its power over the shape and contents of the proposed measure. The more influence Parliament acquired in the legislative process, the less dominance the Commission will be able to exercise. This development has required the Commission to change its role in the Community legislative framework in light of its changing function.

At the same time, the Single European Act 1986 considerably extended the areas of competence of the Community. Matters which were previously considered outside the remit of the Community were expressly included within its competence after the 1986 amendments. For example, the Community now has new responsibilities in the fields of consumer protection policy, environmental protection policy, economic co-operation, social policy and research and technological development.

The organic growth in responsibilities within the Community directly affects the powers and duties of the Commission. Essentially, the Commission can assert its competence over all matters falling within the scope of the Community treaties as amended. As the competence of the Community grows so too does the power and influence of the Commission. In the new areas of responsibility added by the SEA 1986, it is the Commission that has the power to influence the shape and content of these policies simply because it drafts proposals in these areas for consideration in conjunction with the other Community institutions.

The prospects for continued growth in the influence of the Commission have, to some extent, been marginalised by the Treaty on European Union (TEU) which created two additional 'pillars' of competence for the European Union. These two competencies concern Justice and Home Affairs, on the one hand, and Police and Judicial Co-operation on the other. In both these fields, the role of the Commission is relatively circumscribed. In contrast to its functions and powers under the EC Treaty, the Commission's powers to propose measures in these areas are relatively limited. Instead, it is the Member States themselves which decide the shape and content of initiatives in these sectors.

QUESTION THREE

'The choice of legal basis is a highly controversial, political matter.' What are the guiding principles governing the choice of legal basis? Illustrate your answer with reference to case law.

Adapted from University of London LLB Examination
(for External Students) European Community Law June 1993 Q1

General Comment

The question requires an examination of the principles behind the selection of the most appropriate basis for adopting Community measures. There is ample case law from the court in this connection which candidates are invited to use to illustrate the relevant principles. The subject of the question is relatively unusual.

Skeleton Solution

The proper choice of legal basis: voting requirements; consultations and procedure – the case law regulating legal principles applicable to the selection of the legal basis – the sanctions for exceeding the legitimate basis for adopting measures – the growing influence of the European Parliament.

Suggested Solution

All regulations, directives and decisions of the Council, and the Commission for that matter, must state the legal basis on which they were enacted, the reasons why the measures were required and also reference must be made to any proposals or opinions which were required prior to their adoption: art 253 EC. But, in any event, all acts of Community institutions must have a legal basis in the EC Treaty and, in the absence of a proper basis, such acts would be ultra vires.

The most important aspect of selecting the proper legal basis for a measure is that this choice determines the necessary procedural requirements including the necessary vote required in the Council of Ministers for the adoption of the measure, the degree of consultations required between the Council and the European Parliament and the decision-making processes which must be followed for the measure to be approved.

Voting requirements vary not according to the nature of the measure – a regulation, a directive or a decision – but rather according to the subject matter which the measure is intended to regulate. Article 205(1) EC specifies the general rule that, save as otherwise provided, the Council shall act by a majority of its members. But, in fact, the original EC Treaty required a unanimous vote for the adoption of most measures which resulted in a mere trickle of legislation being approved.

The voting criteria required for the adoption of a measure will, of course, significantly affect the nature and content of the final measure. Where unanimity is required, a single Member State may delay the adoption of a measure indefinitely. This has the effect of frustrating negotiations even when the other Member States are in unison. So, the legal basis and the voting requirements fundamentally shape the final form of the measure adopted quite simply because the minority of Member States have more ability and influence in the content of the final measure when unanimity is required than when a qualified majority is sufficient.

A substantial number of cases have come to the attention of the European Court for judicial review of the legal basis for the adoption of Community acts. While the selection of the appropriate legal basis is partly a political matter, the choice must be based on proper legal grounds. It is therefore inaccurate to claim that this selection is solely a political, and not a legal, matter. In fact, the European Court has built up a considerable reservoir of legal principles to allow the review of this selection.

First, the Council of Ministers cannot change the legal basis of a measure proposed by the Commission without proper justification. Thus, in *Commission* v *Council (Re Generalised Tariff Preferences)* Case 45/86 [1987] ECR 1493, the Commission proposed that the adoption of two measures should be based on art 133 EC which requires a qualified majority. The Council did not state the legal basis on which it finally adopted the measure – opening itself to an additional challenge under art 253 EC – but resorted to a unanimous vote which implied that the measure had been adopted under art 308 EC.

The Commission raised proceedings in the European Court which held that the Council had sufficient authority to adopt the measures under art 133 EC. Since unanimous voting had been used and not a qualified majority, the defect was not purely formal and therefore the Court declared the measures void.

Second, the choice of the legal basis for the adoption of a measure does not simply depend on the convictions of a Community institution as to the objective being pursued by the measure. The decision to adopt on the basis of a particular provision must be based on 'objective factors' which are amenable to judicial review: *Commission* v *Council (Re Generalised Tariff Preferences)* Case 45/86 [1987] ECR 1493.

Third, the previous practice of a Community organ in the adoption of similar measures has no bearing on the future voting practices of that organ. For example, a mere prior practice on the part of the Council cannot justify derogation from the strict requirements of the Treaty as regards legal basis: *United Kingdom* v *Council (Re Hormones)* Case 68/86 [1988] ECR 855.

Fourth, where authority to adopt a measure is split among two or more provisions, the institution exercising the power is required to adopt the measure in order to satisfy all the relevant provisions. Hence, for example, where a measure is being adopted on the basis of two provisions, one requiring unanimity and the other a qualified majority, the measure must be adopted unanimously.

But, the Court will not slavishly nullify a measure simply because a formal defect exists as regards the legal basis. So, for example, the Court will not declare a measure null and void where, although adopted on the incorrect legal basis, the proper legal basis imposes approximately the same procedural requirements.

The second important consequence of the selection of the proper legal basis is that many of the provisions conferring power to adopt measures can only be properly exercised after some form of consultation with the European Parliament. In this respect the Parliament's powers have grown considerably. Initially, Parliament's right to be consulted in the Community legislative and decision-making processes was extremely limited. However, failure to engage in consultations, in those few areas which required consultations, rendered a putative measure void: *SA Roquette Frères* v *Council* Case 138/79 [1980] ECR 3333.

The Parliament has actively challenged the legal basis for measures adopted by the Council. First in *European Parliament* v *Council (Re Chernobyl)* Case C–70/88 [1990] ECR I–2041, and then in *European Parliament* v *Council (Re Student Rights)* Case C–295/90 [1992] ECR I–4193, the Parliament sought judicial review of measures adopted by the Council alleging that the measures in question were enacted by the Council on inappropriate legal grounds.

Finally, the choice of legal basis will also determine the proper internal Community procedure to be followed for the adoption of a particular measure. For example, where a harmonising measure is adopted under art 94 EC, the co-decision procedure is not applicable and only informal consultations are required with the Council. But, if a measure is adopted under art 95(1) EC the co-decision procedure must be employed. This involves a different series of rights and duties for the Council and the Parliament, but also for the European Commission which has responsibility for drafting the final measure after the Council and the Parliament have had their say.

QUESTION FOUR

What is the role of the European Parliament in the institutional balance of the European Community? How has it developed since the inception of the Community and how might it develop in the future?

University of London LLB Examination
(for External Students) European Community Law June 1993 Q2

General Comment

This question involves a commonly recurring theme in past examination papers. The examiner is seeking to test knowledge of the institutional balance within the Community with special reference to the role of the European Parliament. This requires a statement of the constitutional balance vis-à-vis the European Parliament and the Council on the one hand and the Parliament and the Commission on the other. Essentially the question itself is relatively straightforward and should pose no problems for the well versed candidate.

Skeleton Solution

Doctrine of the separation of interests and the role of the European Parliament in this process – the powers of the Parliament over the Commission – the budgetary powers of the Parliament: the main power exercisable over both organs – powers over the Council and the legislative role played by the Parliament.

Suggested Solution

The EC Treaty, as the constitution of the Community, is based on the doctrine of the separation of interests rather than the separation of powers. The Council of Ministers embodies the interests of the Member States while the European Commission represents the fundamental interests of the Community. The role of the European Parliament is to preserve and protect the interests of the peoples of the Community. At present the Parliament remains ill-equipped and exercises insufficient authority to carry out this function particularly as regards the Council's activities.

The European Parliament was not intended originally to be a Parliament in the traditional, constitutional sense. The European Coal and Steel Community provided for an assembly comprised of delegates chosen by the six national Parliaments. Its purpose was predominately supervisory. When the EEC was established in 1957, the ECSC institution was shared between them. It had only a small range of powers, and even these were dependent upon the Commission. When, in 1966, the Luxembourg Accords were agreed, the Council became the most powerful organ, automatically making the powers of the Parliament of even less value. In 1974 the Tindemans Report proposed that there should be direct elections to this institution and that its powers should be strengthened. Direct elections were introduced in 1979, making the Parliament the only directly, democratically elected institution in the Community. As such there were criticisms that its lack of involvement only strengthened the claims that the EC suffered from a 'democratic deficit'. This essay will examine the powers of the Parliament and its increased role in the legislative process with reference to various treaty developments.

The powers of the Parliament over the Commission

The powers of the European Parliament in the institutional balance of the Community are, paradoxically, aimed at countering the exercise of authority by the European Commission rather than the Council of Ministers. This should not, strictly speaking, be surprising since the EC Treaty was drafted by representatives of the Member States. But, in fact the most constitutional authority within the Community institutional framework is vested in the Council of Ministers. Any further augmentation of powers for the Parliament should therefore be directed against checking the powers of the Council and not the Commission.

The original, primary power of the Parliament was to collectively dismiss the Commission: art 201 EC. Parliament's dissatisfaction with the conduct of the Commission was in part responsible for the resignation of the Commission in 1999. In practice, though, this power is considerably less powerful than it may appear. The entire Commission must resign, regardless of whether some Commissioners have not actually committed any indiscretion. The Parliament also had no influence in the selection of new Commissioners selected by the governments of the Member States. This has since changed and under art 214(2) EC the Parliament must be consulted on the nomination of the President and approve the appointment of Commissioners. The appointment of the Commission in its entirety must also be approved by the Parliament.

Parliament members are also permitted to put questions to Commission officials which the Commission staff are obliged to answer: art 197 EC. Questions may be submitted both orally and in writing. Commission officials may be subject to scrutiny in both the plenary session and committees of the Parliament. This power is part of the watchdog function carried out by the Parliament. Questions may also be asked of the Council, but these have neither the formal authority nor the same degree of compunction as those submitted to the Commission.

In a similar vein, the Commission is also required to submit an annual general report to the Parliament on the subject of the affairs of the Community: art 200 EC. This report forms the basis for the annual Parliamentary debate on the affairs of the Community.

Budgetary powers

One power, which is exercised over the Council as much as the Commission, is the Parliament's role in the budgetary procedure. The Community's budget is, at present, prepared by the Commission and submitted to the Council, but the Parliament may approve or modify the budget depending on the type of expenditure involved.

The Parliament has power to approve all non-compulsory expenditure – administrative and operational expenditure – which accounts for approximately 25–30 per cent of the total budget each year. In other words, the Parliament can modify this aspect of the budget to a considerable degree. But as regards the remainder of the budget – the compulsory expenditure – the power of the Parliament is confined to proposing modifications which are deemed accepted unless the Council rejects these proposals. The vote of the Council in such a matter is by qualified majority.

Ultimately, Parliament has authority to reject the budget as a whole if, acting by a majority of its members and two-thirds of the votes cast, it believes there are 'important reasons' to reject the draft budget: art 272(8) EC. In such an event, the Parliament may request that a new budget is submitted to it for approval. In fact, in 1979 the Parliament did reject the draft budget by a vote of 299 votes to 64, with one abstention.

The power to approve the budget is perhaps the main illustration of the Parliament's power to balance the institutional processes within the Community. It is a power that can be equally exercised over the Council and the Commission alike. However, again the power to veto the whole budget is one which the European Parliament must exercise carefully in order not to create havoc within the Community order.

In any event, the Council has constitutional authority to bring the European Parliament before the European Court if it is suspected that the Parliament has itself abused its powers over the budget: *Council* v *European Parliament (Re the Community Budget)* Case 34/86 [1986] ECR 2155.

As stated earlier, Parliament's influence over the Council is finite and takes two main forms: power to approve the admission of new members and limited participation in the legislative processes.

Under art 49 Treaty on European Union (TEU), the consent of the Parliament is required for the admission of new Members into the Community and for the conclusion of association agreements between the Community and third states. The negotiation of an association agreement is a preliminary step towards membership of the Community. The Parliament can technically veto the decision of the Council on admission and establishing association agreements which is a significant limitation on the Council's authority in this respect.

But, the historical impotence of the Parliament in restraining the actions of the Council is most evident in the legislative processes carried out within the Community. The legislative competence of the Parliament has progressed through three identifiable stages.

Parliament's legislative role

The original legislative role of Parliament was primarily consultative. The Parliament commented on proposals put forward by the Commission before the Council. It had a right to be consulted on certain matters, ie under arts 36, 44, 46 and 83 EC, but in practice the Commission frequently consulted the Parliament during the consultative phase of drafting legislation.

This consultative role was circumscribed in two respects. First, the vast majority of measures did not strictly require the views of the Parliament and so the Council could generally ignore its views. Second, unlike the Member States and the Commission, the Parliament was not permitted to bring proceedings in the European Court against the Council under art 230(2) EC. Hence, Parliament exercised little control over the activities of the Council.

The Single European Act 1986 altered the constitutional balance of authority in the Community slightly by introducing the co-operation procedure. The use of the co-operation procedure was required to enact legislation in specific subjects and especially the freedom of establishment, working conditions, and certain forms of harmonisation legislation. The co-operation extended the authority of the Parliament over the Council insofar as the Parliament was permitted two opportunities to discuss proposed measures but, as always, ultimate authority to adopt or reject measures resided in the Council of Ministers.

After the passing of the Single European Act 1986, the Parliament was also successful in persuading the European Court to recognise its standing to bring proceedings against the Council. After a series of unsuccessful cases (*European Parliament* v *Council (Re Common Transport Policy)* Case 13/83 [1985] ECR 1513 and *European Parliament* v *Council (Re Comitology)* Case 302/87 [1988] ECR 5615), the Court eventually recognised the standing of the Parliament to act to safeguard its powers under the Treaty as long as the action was raised solely with that objective: *European Parliament* v *Council (Re Chernobyl)* Case C–70/88 [1990] ECR I–2041.

The Treaty on European Union consolidates both these advances in the Parliament's authority over the Council. First, a new comprehensive legislative process modelled on the co-operation procedure will be introduced applying to all legislation, not just legislation on particular subjects. This process is to be known as the 'co-decision procedure' and is contained in art 251 EC. Second, Parliament's right to initiate proceedings against the Council of Ministers is formally recognised in an amended art 230(2) EC.

The Treaty of Amsterdam consolidated the gains made by the European Parliament, particularly in relation to the extension of the co-decision procedure to additional areas of competence. The co-decision procedure involves the Parliament in the legislative decision-making process far more extensively than was previously the case even under the co-operation procedure. The Parliament was also made the budgetary authority along with the Council. In addition, the Parliament was granted the right to be informed and consulted and to have its views taken into consideration in the field of Common Foreign and Security Policy. In this field, as with Justice and Home Affairs, the Parliament was also granted the right to ask questions and make recommendations.

In the final analysis, the European Parliament therefore exercises considerable supervisory control over the European Commission through the powers conferred under the EC Treaty. Its influence over the Council is more restrained although it is nevertheless significant, particularly when the co-decision procedure is invoked, when the European Parliament is almost a full partner in the legislative process. Since co-decision is becoming increasingly used, naturally the Parliament's position is gradually being enhanced. While it is a long way from being the exclusive legislative authority in the Community structure, it has certainly evolved an immense degree from its original role.

QUESTION FIVE

'The classic theory of separation of powers cannot be applied to the EC institutional structure. Subsequent treaties have not made any really significant changes in this respect.'

Discuss and illustrate your answer with examples concerning at least two of the institutions of the Community.

University of London LLB Examination
(for External Students) European Community Law June 1999 Q1

General Comment

A traditional question, often forming the basis of an examination question on the institutions of the European Union, which remains a popular choice. It should have been appreciated that merely describing the doctrine of the separation of powers and its application to the European Union was insufficient to adequately respond to the question. Candidates should have included discussion of the basic tasks, roles and powers of at least two of the institutions, and reference should have also been made to Treaty amendments, particularly in relation to the evolving legislative procedures.

Skeleton Solution

Introduce the institutions of the European Union – define the doctrine of the separation of powers – discuss the separation of interests between the European Union's institutions – describe the role and powers of at least two institutions – discuss the development of the legislative procedures from consultation, to co-operation and co-decision – include references to any relevant Treaty changes (eg Single European Act 1986, Treaty on European Union and Treaty of Amsterdam).

Suggested Solution

Whilst each of the European Communities originally possessed a separate Commission and Council and shared a Parliamentary Assembly and Court of Justice, the Merger Treaty 1965 consolidated these institutions so that one set exists for all the Communities. The tasks entrusted to the European Community under art 7(1) EC are carried out by the following institutions: a European Parliament, a Council, a Commission, a Court of Justice and a Court of Auditors (the latter being formally recognised under the Treaty on European Union). In addition, under the Single European Act 1986, the existence and functions of the European Council were formally recognised and the Court of First Instance, an institution attached to the Court of Justice, was established. Under art 7(2) EC two additional bodies with advisory roles in the decision-making process are named as the Economic and Social Committee and the Committee of the Regions.

The constitutional doctrine of the separation of powers, as developed by Locke and Montesquieu, is often described as one that is fundamental to the organisation of a State and to constitutionalism itself. The doctrine is based on the notion that there should be a clear demarcation of function between the various constitutional bodies, namely the legislature, the executive and the judiciary. Under the doctrine each institution is independent and has its powers and responsibilities clearly set out. This attempts to ensure that there is no excessive power within the hands of one of the bodies, and that they exist within a framework that provides for each to be a check and balance on the activities of the others. This demarcation is generally to be found within the constitution of a State, an often cited example being that of the United States of America, where the bodies exist in what has been called 'creative tension'.

The European Community, which as yet has no codified constitution, operates under a separation of interests, rather than powers. The Council embodies the interests of the Member States, whilst the Commission represents the interests of the Union. The role of the Parliament is to preserve and protect the interests of the peoples of the Union, although throughout its history it has often been argued that the Parliament has insufficient power or authority to carry out this function effectively. Consequently, the European Community institutions cannot be described, in traditional constitutional terms, as legislature, executive and judiciary. In addition, the various competencies of the institutions have fluctuated and various Treaty amendments have altered the original balance of power.

Articles 211–219 EC govern the Commission. Article 211 EC provides that the functions of the Commission include the following: to ensure that the provisions of the Treaty and the measures taken by the institutions are applied; to formulate recommendations or deliver opinions on matters under the Treaty; to participate in decision-making and the legislative processes of the Community along with the Council and the Parliament; and to exercise any powers conferred on it by the Council. Hence the Commission operates in part as the executive of the Community, drafts policy and ensures compliance with Community rules – a role often described as 'guardian of the Treaties' – but the Commission also has a role to play in the legislative processes.

The Council, renamed the Council of the European Union in 1993, is governed by arts 202–210 EC. It consists of the members of the governments of the Member States who are 'authorised to commit the government of that Member State' (art 203 EC). The function of the Council, as set out in art 202 EC, is to ensure that the objectives of the Treaty are attained by ensuring co-ordination of the general economic policies of the Member States and by making decisions. Indeed, in practical terms, decision-making is the most important role of the Council, and the vast majority of final decisions are still made by this institution.

The Parliament, consisting of 626 Members, is the only directly elected institution of the Community. It is not a Parliament in the traditional sense, since it lacks the power to initiate legislation or to impose taxes, but its role has developed from that originally envisaged. Under the EEC Treaty the Parliament was only an advisory body, but Treaty developments since then have increased the power of the Parliament in response to criticisms that there existed a democratic deficit within the institutional infrastructure of the Community. In brief, the principal powers of the Parliament are: to participate in the legislative processes; to act as a budgetary authority; and to supervise the Commission. It also produces reports and resolutions on a range of matters relevant to the Community.

In terms of the changes made to the power and functions of the institutions by the Treaties, the most significant are those in relation to the legislative processes. The Community has six distinct methods of creating legislation, a number of which were introduced and extended by later Treaty amendments. In recognition of the need for a greater democratic element in the creation of Community legislation, these processes have granted the Parliament a greater role.

The first process requires the Commission, acting alone, to create legislation, although this relates to only a few areas of policy. The second legislative process requires the Council to adopt a Commission proposal, without the need for the Parliament's consultation, although in practice consultation does often occur. This process, in which the interests of the Member States and Community and not its people are formally recognised, extends to some important areas of policy, such as the fixing of the Common Customs Tariff, Economic and Monetary Union and the free movement of capital. The commonest procedure early in the development of the Community, though, was that which required the Council and Commission to act after only having consultation with the Parliament. This indeed was the original role of the Parliament – to act only as a consultative body.

Under art 249 EC, the institutions have the ability to produce regulations, directives and decisions and to issue recommendations and opinions. According to this procedure the Commission proposes measures, the Parliament is consulted, and the Council makes the final decision. This final decision may be contrary to the Parliament's wishes, but it must be genuinely consulted and failure to do so is considered a breach of an essential procedural requirement that may render the measure void: *SA Roquette Frères* v *Council* Case 138/79 [1980] ECR 3333. This procedure still exists in a number of areas such as citizenship (arts 19 and 22 EC); State aid (art 89 EC); indirect tax harmonisation (art 93 EC); and employment (art 128 EC). Where this procedure remains it would be correct to state that the Parliament has little legislative power or involvement as would be expected under traditional constitutional arrangements.

However, in response to the demand for a greater democratic element, and the fact that the Parliament was the only directly elected body (elections being introduced in 1979), various Treaty amendments have extended the role of the Parliament from that originally envisaged.

Under the Single European Act (SEA) 1986 the co-operation procedure was introduced, the most striking feature of which is the ability of the Parliament to have a second reading of the measure and take action within a three-month time period. However, real legislative power under this process still rests with the Council, since it can override the wishes of the Parliament (and the Commission) as long as it acts unanimously. The areas in which this process is still used are rare, since a further Treaty amendment has introduced another legislative process providing a greater voice for the Parliament.

The co-decision procedure was introduced by the Treaty on European Union (TEU). This procedure was extended to more areas by the Treaty of Amsterdam (ToA). The ToA also simplified what had become a complex process by removing the third reading by Parliament (art 251 EC). The Commission is required under this procedure to submit legislative proposals to both the Parliament and the Council. The Council, acting by qualified majority after obtaining Parliament's opinion, adopts a common position. This is communicated to Parliament. The Parliament may then approve it, and the Council then adopts it. Similarly, if the Parliament makes no decision within three months, the Council may also adopt the measure. Alternatively, the Parliament may reject the common position and the act may not be adopted. However, if amendments are suggested, and the Commission and Council do not give positive opinions on them, the matter is referred to a Conciliation Committee. Under amendments introduced by the ToA if no agreement is reached the proposed measure falls (art 251 EC). If agreement is reached a joint text may be produced, which Parliament and the Council may approve by qualified majority or decline to approve within six to eight weeks, in which case the act is not adopted.

In short, this complex process exists because a range of competing interests, from the Member States' representatives to the peoples of the Community, have to be balanced. The introduction of this process shifts some power away from the Council to the Parliament since it can now veto a proposal from the Council. It should be noted though that the Parliament is not able to insist on its amendments being accepted. The Parliament has also rested some power from the hands of the Commission since, if a Conciliation Committee is required, the Parliament and Council can agree a joint text that may amend the Commission's initial proposal. This ultimately reduces to some extent the power of the Commission as initiator of policy and legislation. However, there remain limitations to this process in terms of placing the Parliament in the traditionally accepted role of legislator and in achieving any reduction in the so-called 'democratic deficit'. The Parliament has only an ultimate power of veto; in other words, it must reject everything or approve it. The Parliament must also negotiate with the Council to achieve any amendments it wishes, and the procedure does remain limited to certain areas only, albeit that the ToA expanded the range of areas in which this process is to be used.

The final legislative process is one in which we may more readily witness the Parliament exercising power in a manner similar to that of a traditional legislative body. The assent procedure, introduced by the Single European Act 1986, requires the Parliament to provide its assent before the measure may be passed. One important area in which this process is required is enlargement of the Communities beyond the current membership (art 49 TEU).

In conclusion, whilst Treaty amendments have extended the role and particularly legislative power of the Parliament, the institutions do not operate under the traditional constitutional doctrine of the separation of powers. Instead, the institutions compete within a complex system designed to balance competing interests within the Community.

Chapter 3

The Contentious Jurisdiction of the European Court of Justice

3.1   Introduction

3.2   Key points

3.3   Key cases and materials

3.4   Questions and suggested solutions

3.1 Introduction

The contentious jurisdiction of the European Court of Justice is the power of the Court to hear direct actions brought against Member States and Community institutions. Actions against Member States and institutions may be initiated by other Member States or institutions. Individuals and legal persons cannot bring a direct action against a Member State under the contentious jurisdiction of the European Court. However, they may institute an action under the contentious jurisdiction of the Court against an institution if they can successfully demonstrate that certain conditions have been satisfied.

3.2 Key points

Actions against Member States

An action relating to an infringement of Community law by a Member State may be raised by either another Member State or the European Commission acting on behalf of the Community.

Under art 227 EC, one Member State may bring a direct action against another if it considers that the Member State concerned has failed to fulfil its obligations under the Community treaties. The Court exercises exclusive jurisdiction over all disputes between Member States arising out of the subject matter of the Community treaties. Member States are expressly forbidden from resolving such disputes by any other means: art 292 EC.

A number of procedural preconditions must be satisfied before a Member State can initiate a direct action against another. These are explained below.

a) The Member State alleging the violation must bring the matter to the attention of the European Commission.

b) The Commission must deliver a reasoned opinion on the matter after allowing the parties in dispute to submit arguments.

c) Only after the Commission has delivered this opinion, or has failed to do so within the prescribed period of three months from notification of the matter, can the Member State continue its action.

d) If the Commission indicates that it has no intention of pursuing the action, the complaining State may bring the action itself.

e) The scope of any subsequent court proceedings under art 226 EC is circumscribed by the pre-litigation notification intimated by the Commission to the Member State: *Commission v Denmark (Re Taxation of Imported Motor Vehicles)* Case C–52/90 [1992] ECR I–2187.

Under art 226 EC, the European Commission is authorised to commence proceedings against any Member State suspected of violating its Community obligations. The same provision also specifies a formal pre-litigation procedure which must be exhausted before commencing actual proceedings in the Court.

a) While not strictly required under art 226 EC, the Commission informally notifies the Member State accused of violating its obligations of the allegations and invites comments on the behaviour under investigation. A failure by a Member State to justify its conduct will set the formal pre-litigation procedure in motion.

b) The Commission conducts an investigation into the matter and delivers a reasoned opinion on the subject after giving the Member State concerned an opportunity to submit its observations. Member States are under a separate obligation to cooperate with the Commission in its investigation and failure to do is a separate violation of Community law: *Commission v Greece* Case 272/86 [1988] ECR 4875.

c) If the Member State fails to comply with the terms of this opinion within the prescribed period, the Commission will bring the matter to the attention of the Court. However, the Commission must give the Member State a reasonable time to comply with the reasoned opinion: *Commission v Belgium (Re University Fees)* Case 293/85 [1988] ECR 305.

Violations of Community law may result from both acts and omissions by Member States. Article 10 EC requires Member States to take all appropriate measures to ensure respect for Community obligations and to 'abstain from any measure which could jeopardise the attainment of the objectives of this Treaty'. Common causes of action against Member States include the existence of incompatible legislation or the introduction of administrative practices which are inconsistent with Community law.

Member States cannot justify their failure to comply with their Community obligations by reference to their constitutional inability to control provincial or regional branches of government.

If the Court of Justice finds against a Member State, it does not pass a sentence but delivers a purely declaratory judgment which notes the fact that a Member State is in default. Originally, this judgment had no executory force and the European Commission or the Court were unable to impose sanctions to compel the offending state to redress its behaviour.

The Treaty on European Union introduced a new procedure by amending art 228 EC. Now the Commission is empowered to recommend that a Member State is fined if it fails to comply with an adverse judgment. Fines can be imposed by the Court on the basis of a second action brought at the instance of the Commission.

The Commission has adopted guidelines on how these fines will be calculated. Three principles will be applied to this determination: the seriousness of the violation, the duration of the infringement and the need to achieve a deterrent effect by preventing the repetition of the violation.

The starting point for calculating a fine is a basic amount of Euro 500 per day which applies for every day beyond the deadline for compliance. This sum is then multiplied by two co-efficients. The first relates to the seriousness of the violation which is evaluated on a scale of between one and 20. The Commission has drawn up rules to establish the seriousness of the violation. The second relates to the duration of the violation. In this context, the Commission will judge the degree of goodwill demonstrated by the recalcitrant States on a scale of between one and three.

As a final stage, this amount will be multiplied by a constant factor designed to express a Member State's ability to pay the fine. This factor is determined by reference to each Member State's gross domestic product and the number of votes which it can cast in the Council of Ministers. These constants vary from 1.0 for Luxembourg to 26.4 for Germany. The UK has been given a factor of 17.8 while France and Italy have been given the figures of 21.1 and 17.7 respectively.

Actions against Community institutions

A direct action may also be brought in the European Court to review the acts of Community institutions. The European Court has exclusive jurisdiction to review the legality of acts of Community institutions and has sole competence to declare an act of a Community institution invalid: *Firma Foto-Frost* v *Hauptzollamt Lübeck-Ost* Case 314/85 [1987] ECR 4199. The legal consequence of a successful challenge is that the Court will declare the measure null and void.

Community acts and measures which may be challenged include regulations, directives, decisions and all other acts capable of creating legal effects. Measures which have been held not to have such an effect include statements of objection, guidelines and internal procedural matters: *Partie Ecologiste Les Verts* v *European Parliament* Case 294/83 [1986] ECR 1339.

Member States, the European Commission and the Council of Ministers are privileged applicants for the purposes of initiating an action for judicial review of Community acts: *Italy* v *Council* Case 166/78 [1979] ECR 2575. The standing of these parties in such actions is presumed. The fact that a Member State challenges an act of an institution addressed to another Member State is not a bar to judicial review: *Italy* v *Commission* Case 41/83 [1985] ECR 873.

While art 230(2) EC explicitly recognises the standing of natural and legal persons to bring an action for judicial review directly to the European Court, such individuals must demonstrate that the act being challenged constitutes 'a decision which is of direct and individual concern' to the applicant. Decisions of the Council or the Commission addressed to a particular individual cause few problems in establishing direct and individual concern.

The fact that the act challenged by the individual is in the form of a Community regulation or a decision addressed to another person does not ipso facto exclude the possibility of establishing that the measure is a decision of direct and individual concern to an unrelated individual. In order to succeed, an individual must demonstrate that the regulation or decision addressed to another person is, despite its form or substance, a decision of direct and individual concern: *ARPOSOL* v *Council* Case 55/86 [1988] ECR 13; and *Sociedade Agro-Pecuaria Vincente Nobre Lda* v *Council* Case 253/86 [1990] 1 CMLR 105.

Private parties who can demonstrate direct and individual concern in a Community measure, and who decline to initiate direct proceedings against the Community institution on this basis, cannot later challenge the validity of the measure by bringing proceedings in a national court. In such circumstances, the European Court will decline to answer a preliminary reference from the national court: *TWD Textilwerke Deggendorf GmbH* v *Germany* Case C–188/92 [1994] ECR I–833.

Three separate grounds have been established by the Community treaties as a basis for judicial review of the acts of Community institutions. These are:

a) actions to annul an act of a Community institution;

b) actions against a Community institution for failure to act;

c) the plea of illegality.

Actions of annulment

Article 230 EC expressly confers on the European Court jurisdiction to review the legality of acts of both the Council of Ministers and the European Commission. Although the provision makes no reference to the acts of the European Parliament, the Court has reviewed such acts on a number of occasions. The Court is empowered to review all acts of the Community institutions other than recommendations and opinions: art 230(1) EC.

An act of a Community institution may be annulled on the basis of one of four separate causes.

a) Lack of competence on the part of an institution to adopt a particular measure.

b) Infringement of an essential procedural requirement.

c) Infringement of a provision of a Community treaty or a rule relating to the application of such provisions.

d) Misuse of power by a Community institution.

One illustration of a measure being annulled for breach of an essential procedural requirement occurred in *Germany* v *Commission (Re Constructive Products)* Case C–263/95 [1998] 2 CMLR 1235. Germany sought the annulment of an approval decision by the Commission granted on the basis of powers delegated to it. The German version of the draft measure had not been sent to its permanent representative nor the German member of the Commission within the time period specified in the delegating legislation. The Commission had acknowledged the delay in sending the German version but had circulated the English version of the draft decision in time to the German delegation. On this basis, it proceeded to adopt the approval decision, exercising its power to do so under delegated powers.

The Court held that the failure to send the German version to the German delegation, within the appropriate time limits, constituted an infringement of an essential procedural requirement justifying the annulment of the Commission's approval decision. The English version of the proposed measure could not be considered as an adequate substitute for the German language version. The Commission was bound to strictly adhere to the procedural requirements specified in the directive granting it delegated powers.

According to art 233 EC, where an act has been declared void by the Court, the institution which is responsible for the adoption of the putative measure is obliged to take the 'necessary measures' to comply with the judgment of the Court.

The limitation period for actions of annulment is two months from either the publication of the measure which is being challenged or from the date of the notification to the applicant: art 230(3) EC. This period applies regardless of whether the action is brought by a Member State, another Community institution or an individual. While these time limits are onerous, the Court has been prepared to extend the limitation period in cases where the measure being challenged lacks 'all legal basis in the Community legal system'.

Actions for failure to act

If a provision of the Community treaties imposes a duty to act on either the Council of Ministers or the European Commission, and one or other of these organs fails to take the appropriate course of conduct, proceedings may be instituted under art 232 EC (or the counterpart ECSC Treaty and Euratom Treaty provisions) for failure to act.

As a preliminary requirement to the initiation of an action for failure to act, the alleged omission must be brought to the attention of the institution concerned. Thereafter, the particular organ has two months to define its position. An organ may define its position without adopting a particular measure. For example, where the Commission has explained its position and justified its non-activity in terms which are consistent with its obligations under the Community treaties, the Court has held an action for failure to act inadmissible: *Lütticke (Alfons) GmbH* v *Commission* Case 4/69 [1971] ECR 325. This has created a distinction between a failure to act and a refusal to act. The former constitutes a prima facie ground for review while the latter amounts to a negative determination which must be challenged on grounds other than an action for failure to act.

Plea of illegality

Under art 241 EC, notwithstanding the expiry of the limitation period established for actions of annulment, any party may, in any proceedings which involve a Council or Commission regulation, invoke a plea of illegality in order to have the regulation declared inapplicable. This plea differs from the other grounds for judicial review in that it does not itself constitute a separate or independent cause of action, but allows a party to plead that a regulation is inapplicable in actions initiated on some other jurisdictional basis. The main purpose of this device is to allow challenges to be made to regulations outside the limitation period specified for actions of annulment: *Simmenthal* v *Commission* Case 92/78 [1979] ECR 777.

The fact that art 241 EC does not constitute a distinct ground for judicial review was made clear in *Worhrmann* v *Commission* Cases 31 and 33/62 [1962] ECR 501 where the Court stated:

> 'It is clear from the wording and the general scheme of this Article that a declaration of the inapplicability of a regulation is only contemplated in proceedings brought before the Court of Justice itself under some other provision of the Treaty, and then only incidentally and with limited effect.'

In order for a plea of illegality to be successful, the regulation upon which the plea is based must be applicable – directly or indirectly – to the principal issue with which the particular application to the Court is concerned: *Simmenthal* v *Commission*, above.

Plenary jurisdiction

The term 'plenary jurisdiction' is one more familiar to continental civilian lawyers than their common law counterparts. It refers to the ability of a Court to hear actions which require the Court to exercise its full powers. The plenary jurisdiction of the European Court extends to two principal forms of actions.

a) Actions for damages based on the non-contractual liability of the Community.

b) Actions to review penalties imposed by Community institutions.

A third ground of plenary jurisdiction related to cases involving disputes between the Community and its staff (staff cases) under art 236 EC. The jurisdiction to hear such cases was transferred to the Court of First Instance.

Actions based on the contractual liability of the Community do not fall within the plenary jurisdiction of the European Court because jurisdiction to interpret and enforce contractual obligations is governed by the choice of jurisdiction chosen by the parties to the contract: art 288(1) EC. Contractual disputes involving the European Community may therefore be brought before the appropriate national courts. The European Court only exercises jurisdiction over contracts involving the Community if a particular clause in the contract refers disputes to arbitration before the European Court.

Actions based on the non-contractual liability of the Community

The European Court has jurisdiction over non-contractual claims against the Community by virtue of art 235(1) EC. Non-contractual liability is a residual category which comprises all the liabilities of the Community other than contractual liability. The Court is instructed under art 288(2) EC to develop the Community law of non-contractual liability from 'the general principles common to the laws of the Member States' in order to 'make good any damage caused by its institutions or by its servants in the performance of their duties'.

One interesting case illustrates the elements required for a successful action based on the (non-contractual) liability of the Community. In *Sociedade Agro-Pecuaria Vincente Nobre Lda* v *Council* Case 253/86 [1990] 1 CMLR 105, the European Court observed that:

> '[T]he Court has held in previous decisions that by virtue of art 235(2) of the [EC] Treaty, the [non-contractual] liability of the Community presupposes the existence of a set of circumstances comprising the unlawfulness of the conduct alleged against the institution, actual damage and the existence of a causal link between the conduct and the alleged damage.'

Three elements are therefore necessary to establish the non-contractual liability of the Community: an unlawful act (or omission) which can be attributed to the Community; injury on the part of the applicant; and a causal connection between the act itself and the commission of the injury: *Embassy Limousines & Services* v *European Parliament* Case T–203/96 [1999] 1 CMLR 667.

In certain circumstances, non-contractual liability may be imputed to the Community even although the national authorities of a Member State were actually responsible for the commission of the act which is alleged to give rise to the liability. In *Krohn & Co Import-Export GmbH & Co KG* v *Commission* Case 175/84 [1986] ECR 753, the European Court established the principle that, where a national authority or body is obliged under Community law to comply with the instructions of the European Commission, any claim for compensation based on non-contractual liability should be directed against the Commission and not the national authorities.

Actions to review penalties

The European Court has jurisdiction to review penalties imposed by Community institutions. Article 229 EC authorises the Council of Ministers to enact regulations to regulate this aspect of jurisdiction. However, in the past, the Council of Ministers has tended to grant this authority in specific regulations dealing with particular subjects, rather than to adopt a comprehensive regulation to govern this aspect of the Court's jurisdiction.

A typical illustration of the Council granting such a power of review is contained in Council Regulation 17/62 which concerns the administration of Community competition policy. As regards competition policy, the jurisdiction of the Court is defined in the following terms:

> 'The Court shall have unlimited jurisdiction within the meaning of [art 229] of the [EC] Treaty to review decisions whereby the Commission has fixed a fine or periodic payment; it may cancel, reduce or increase the fine or periodic payment imposed.'

Unlimited jurisdiction permits the Court to cancel, reduce or increase a penalty imposed on a commercial enterprise by the Commission.

Jurisdiction of the Court under the Treaty on European Union

By art 46 TEU the jurisdiction of the European Court expressly covers the interpretation and application of the EC Treaty, the ECSC Treaty and the Euratom Treaty. As a consequence of the coming into force of the Treaty of Amsterdam, the Court also has jurisdiction to give rulings on the validity and interpretation of decisions, on the interpretation of conventions, and on the validity and interpretation of measures implementing conventions adopted in the area of Co-operation in Justice and Home Affairs.

3.3 Key cases and materials

- *Commission* v *Belgium (Re University Fees)* Case 293/85 [1988] ECR 305
  The Commission must give Member States a reasonable time period to comply with a reasoned opinion

- *Commission* v *Denmark (Re Taxation of Imported Motor Vehicles)* Case C–52/90 [1992] ECR I–2187
  The Commission is limited in any subsequent action under art 226 EC to the matters which were brought to the attention of the Member State in the pre-notification procedure

- *Firma Foto-Frost* v *Hauptzollamt Lübeck-Ost* Case 314/85 [1987] ECR 4199
  The European Court has exclusive competence to declare an act of a Community institution null and void and this power cannot be exercised by a national court

- *France* v *United Kingdom (Re Fishing Mesh)* Case 141/78 [1979] ECR 2923
  The sole illustration of a complaint by one Member State against another proceeding to judgment by the Court

- *Star Fruit Co SA* v *Commission* Case 247/87 [1989] ECR 291
  A private individual does not have the right to compel the Commission to institute proceedings against a Member State suspected of violating Community law

- EC Treaty

  - art 226 – European Commission authorised to bring proceedings against Member States suspected of violating Community obligations

  - art 227 – Member States may bring direct actions against other Member States for failure to comply with Community obligations

  - art 230 – the ECJ can review acts of the Council of Ministers and the European Commission

  - art 232 – jurisdiction to the ECJ to hear actions for failure to act

  - art 235 – actions based on the non-contractual liability of the Community

  - art 241 – for pleas of illegality to have a regulation declared inapplicable

3.4 Questions and suggested solutions

QUESTION ONE

'The right to challenge the legality of acts of Community institutions extends to institutions and Member States, but also individuals.'

Discuss and compare these different rights.

University of London LLB Examination
(for External Students) European Community Law June 1994 Q6

General Comment

This is a fairly common subject for examination and in this particular case the examiner is asking for a comparison of the different rights of Member States, Community institutions and private individuals to bring direct actions in the European Court.

Skeleton Solution

The requirements of art 230(1)–(5) EC as amended – standing of Member States – standing of Community institutions – differences between the Council, Commission and Parliament – the standing requirements of private individuals: a decision; direct and individual concern.

Suggested Solution

Community institutions must act within their scope of competencies as defined in the EC Treaty and failure to respect these limitations will render an institution liable to an action in the European Court of Justice for review of the legality of its actions. Exclusive jurisdiction to review the acts of Community institutions has been granted to the European Court. No such proceedings may be competently raised in a national court or tribunal: *Firma Foto-Frost* v *Hauptzollamt Lübeck-Ost* Case 314/85 [1987] ECR 4199.

Article 230(1) EC, as amended by the Treaty on European Union, authorises the judicial review of the legality of acts adopted jointly by the European Parliament and the Council as well as the acts of the Council, the Commission and the European Central Bank (when constituted), other than recommendations and opinions, together with those acts of the European Parliament intended to produce legal effects vis-à-vis third parties.

For the purposes of standing to bring such actions, a distinction is made between Member States and Community institutions, on the one hand, and private individuals on the other hand. This distinction is based on the separate locus standi requirements which must be satisfied before standing will be acknowledged by the European Court. Member States and Community institutions are considered privileged applicants for the purposes of initiating actions for judicial review of Community actions. In contrast, private individuals must establish that the measure being challenged is a decision of direct and individual concern to them.

Member States

Member States are entitled to initiate proceedings for the judicial review of the acts of the Council of Ministers, the European Commission and the European Parliament. The interest of a Member State in the actions of a Community institution is presumed and hence there is no need to establish standing in addition to a ground for review. In fact, even if a Member State challenges an act of a Community institution addressed to another Member State, interest and standing are still both presumed: *Italy* v *Commission* Case 41/83 [1985] ECR 873.

Member States frequently bring actions to protect their rights from the incursions of the European institutions. The European Commission is the most frequent target for such proceedings.

Proceedings are also brought against the Council of Ministers and the European Parliament by Member States but such cases are relatively rare. Actions against the Council of Ministers are infrequently initiated by states because that organ consists of national representatives. One rare instance of such proceedings occurred in *United Kingdom* v *Council (Re Hormones)* Case 68/86 [1988] ECR 855, when the United Kingdom challenged the competence of the Council to adopt Community legislation by simple majority instead of a qualified majority which was the voting requirement the United Kingdom believed applied. In this particular case, the European Court agreed with the United Kingdom and held that the measure was invalid.

Actions against the European Parliament are also not common, with one or two well-publicised exceptions: see, for example, *Luxembourg* v *European Parliament* Case 230/81 [1983] ECR 255.

Community institutions

In the original art 230(2) EC, only the standing of the Council of Ministers and the European Commission was recognised and their standing to bring actions against other Community institutions was also presumed. No express reference was made to the power of the European Parliament to commence this type of proceedings.

In a series of cases, the European Parliament tried to persuade the European Court that it also has a similar capacity but this right was initially refused by the Court: *European Parliament* v *Council (Re Comitology)* Case 302/87 [1988] ECR 5615. The Court subsequently reversed itself in *European Parliament* v *Council (Re Chernobyl)* Case C–70/88 [1990] ECR I–2041, and permitted the European Parliament to contest the legal basis on which a Council regulation had been adopted. Having regard to the institutional balance within the Community, the Court held that the Parliament was able to proceed if two conditions were satisfied. First, the Parliament must demonstrate 'a specific interest in the proceedings'. Second, the action must seek to safeguard the powers of the Parliament and must be based exclusively on the infringement of those powers: *European Parliament* v *Council (Re Student Rights)* Case C–295/90 [1992] ECR I–4193.

This formula, originally devised by the Court, has now been incorporated into the terms of art 230 EC by the amendments made by the Treaty on European Union. Article 230(3) EC now reads:

'The Court shall have jurisdiction under the same conditions [outlined in art 230(2) EC] in actions brought by the European Parliament and the ECB for the purpose of protecting their prerogatives.'

The standing of the European Parliament is not therefore unqualified, as it is for the Council of Ministers and the European Commission. The Parliament must, as a prerequisite for standing, establish a specific interest in the proceedings and that the action is necessary to safeguard its prerogatives.

Private individuals

The final category of persons entitled to challenge the legality of acts of the Community institutions are private legal persons and individuals. Article 230(4) EC provides:

'Any natural or legal person may ... institute proceedings against a decision addressed to that person or against a decision which, although in the form of a regulation or a decision addressed to another person, is of direct and individual concern to the former.'

Private individuals are not privileged applicants for the purpose of reviewing the legality of the acts of Community institutions. To obtain standing, they must demonstrate that two pre-conditions are satisfied. First, the measure being challenged must be a decision. Second, the decision must be of direct and individual concern to them.

If the measure is a decision, as defined in art 249 EC, the first condition will be satisfied. However, if the measure takes the form of a regulation, the applicant must show that, while the measure has the form of a regulation, it is in fact a series of individual decisions in the form of a regulation. The European Court has stated that even where a measure is generally applicable it may in fact amount to 'a conglomeration of individual decisions taken by the Commission' under the guise of a regulation: *International Fruit Company* v *Commission* Cases 41–44/70 [1971] ECR 411.

Once this requirement has been settled, if the decision is not addressed to the applicant, then he or she must show that the decision is of 'direct and individual concern'. In the event that the decision is addressed to the applicant alone or as one of a limited group of individuals, the condition will be satisfied. The difficulties arise when the decision is addressed to another person or is a regulation which apparently has general application. In both these cases, the need to establish direct and individual concern poses a considerable handicap to private individuals seeking to obtain standing.

Direct concern means that the applicant must demonstrate that the measure applies without the intervention of any state authorities. If national authorities exercise a discretion as to the means of implementing a measure, or are involved in the administration of the measure, direct concern will not be established.

The test for individual concern requires the applicant to prove that the decision affects its legal position 'because of some factual situation which differentiates it individually in the same way to the person to whom it is addressed': *Sociedade Agro-Pecuaria Vincente Nobre Lda* v *Council* Case 253/86 [1990] 1 CMLR 105. Individual concern is difficult to establish when the applicant has not been specifically identified in the decision. If a measure applies to objectively determined situations and entails legal effects for categories of persons generally and in the abstract, it has general application and is incapable of having individual effect.

Conversely, individual concern has been held to exist where a regulation of general application named specific companies and firms and applied specific measures to them, and where a regulation had as its subject matter the individual circumstances of the named importers. Similarly, individual concern has been established where a decision was issued by the Commission in response to the request of a particular group for relief even though the final decision itself was addressed to another person.

In practice, direct and individual concern is notoriously difficult to establish when general measures are involved, a situation which prevents private individuals obtaining access to the European Court to challenge the acts of Community institutions. This contrasts with the position of both Member States and Community institutions which do not have to cross this hurdle because both are considered privileged applicants.

QUESTION TWO

By what procedures can the European Court of Justice review actions of the Member States and the other institutions? Are there any areas where it has no such power?

University of London LLB Examination
(for External Students) European Community Law June 1996 Q3

General Comment

This is a wide-ranging question which deals with the jurisdiction of the ECJ over actions against Member States and Community institutions. The answer is long as a result of details provided about the procedures. Clearly, such detail would not be necessary in an exam. Only a passing reference need be made to art 234 EC.

It should be noted that when this question was written the ECJ did not have jurisdiction to hear cases on the interpretation or application of the two inter-governmental pillars, ie Common Foreign Policy and Security Policy and Co-operation on Justice and Home Affairs (art L TEU), except where by means of a convention the Council stipulated that the ECJ had jurisdiction (art K(e) TEU). This position has since changed.

Skeleton Solution

Review of Member States' actions: arts 226 and 227 EC – preliminary ruling procedure: art 234 EC – review of Community institutions – ECJ jurisdiction originally excluded from inter-governmental pillars.

Suggested Solution

The ECJ has widespread powers to review the actions of both Member States and Community institutions. However, those powers are circumscribed by the EC Treaty. The ECJ, in common with other Community institutions, can only exercise those powers of review insofar as permitted to do so under the Treaty.

Review of Member States

Under arts 226 and 227 EC, the ECJ is given jurisdiction to hear enforcement actions against Member States by the Commission (art 226 EC) and other Member States (art 227 EC) for alleged breaches of Treaty obligations.

The decision whether or not to bring an enforcement action against a Member State under art 226 EC is a matter for the Commission alone: *Star Fruit Co SA v Commission* Case 247/87 [1989] ECR 291.

When the Commission considers that a Member State has failed to fulfill its obligations under the Treaty, they will initially enter into informal discussions with the Member State concerned in an attempt to resolve the matter amicably. If this cannot be done, a formal letter of notice will sent to the Member State setting out the facts of the case alleged against the State. The State has an opportunity to make observations on the allegations. A reasoned opinion is then sent by the Commission to the State which will form the basis of the legal arguments against the Member State. The reasoned opinion will give a time-limit within which the State concerned must remedy their breach. Failure to comply with the opinion may lead to the case being brought before the ECJ.

If the ECJ consider that a State is in breach of its Treaty obligations, the Court will issue a declaratory judgment to that effect. Under art 228(1) EC, a Member State is obliged to take 'all necessary measures to comply with the judgement' as soon as possible. Failure to comply with a judgement under art 226 EC may lead to a further art 226 EC action for breach of art 228(1) EC.

The Treaty on European Union amended the EC Treaty to confer a power on the ECJ to impose a lump sum or penalty payment upon a Member State which fails to comply with its judgement. Under art 228(2) EC, the Commission must permit the Member State to make submissions concerning its alleged default. The Commission must then issue a reasoned opinion setting out particulars of the State's default and giving the State a time limit within which to remedy its default. If appropriate action is not taken within the time limit, the State may be referred to the ECJ by the Commission with a recommendation for the amount of penalty to be imposed. The ECJ is free to impose a penalty of its choice if it finds the default proved.

Article 227 EC provides a rarely used procedure for Member States to bring enforcement proceedings against other Member States for breach of a Treaty obligation. A complainant Member State must first inform the Commission of the breach. The Commission will receive observations from both parties and will deliver a reasoned opinion on the allegations. The Member State concerned may bring the matter before the ECJ within three months of notifying the Commission. There has only been one concluded art 227 EC action, that of *France v United Kingdom (Re Fishing Mesh)* Case 141/78 [1979] ECR 2923. Member States are understandably reluctant to take such action because of the adverse political implications and the costs involved.

Article 234 EC provides an indirect process of review of Member States' actions. It provides a procedure whereby national courts may and, in the case of courts of last resort, sometimes must refer a question of Community law to the ECJ for a preliminary ruling. This discretion and/or obligation mainly arises where national courts, when hearing an action, are faced with a question on the interpretation of the Treaty or the validity and interpretation of the acts of Community institutions. A reference by the national court to the ECJ is only appropriate where a ruling on the question is necessary to enable it to give judgement in the domestic proceedings: *Society for the Protection of Unborn Children (Ireland) v Grogan* Case C–159/90 [1991] ECR I–4685.

The art 234 EC procedure provides a neat illustration of the extent of and limit on the ECJ's powers. Only the ECJ have the power to declare acts of Community institutions invalid: *Firma Foto-Frost v Hauptzollamt Lübeck-Ost* Case 314/85 [1987] ECR 4199. Equally, however, the ECJ has no power under art 234 EC to rule on the validity of national laws or their compatibility with Community law: *Costa v ENEL* Case 6/64

[1964] ECR 585. The ECJ's role under art 234 EC is to provide rulings on the interpretation and validity of Community laws, not to adjudicate in the national proceedings. The Court does not therefore investigate the facts of an art 234 EC ruling nor apply their interpretative rulings to the facts of the national proceedings: *Van Gend en Loos* v *Netherlands* Case 26/62 [1963] ECR 1.

Review of Community institutions

Under art 230 EC, the ECJ has the power to review the legality of acts of the Council, the Commission, the European Central Bank (ECB), the European Parliament (EP) and the joint acts of the European Parliament and the Council. This power is subject to a number of limitations.

The only acts of the Council, the Commission, the ECB and the joint acts of the EP and the Council that are reviewable are those other than recommendations or opinions. The ECJ has interpreted this to mean that the reviewable acts are those that are intended to have legal effect: *Commission* v *Council (Re ERTA)* Case 22/70 [1971] ECR 263. In relation to the EP acting alone, the ECJ can only review those acts intended to produce legal effects vis-à-vis third parties: *Partie Ecologiste Les Verts* v *European Parliament* Case 294/83 [1986] ECR 1339.

In addition, art 230 EC distinguishes between privileged and non-privileged applicants. The category of privileged applicants consists of Member States, the Council and the Commission. All these parties have unlimited locus standi to bring judicial review proceedings before the Court. The EP has locus in such actions to protect its prerogative powers: *European Parliament* v *Council (Re Chernobyl)* Case C–70/88 [1990] ECR I–2041.

Non-privileged applicants, that is, private parties, have limited locus standi. Private parties are able to challenge a decision addressed to them or a decision (which may be in the form of a regulation) which, although addressed to a third party, is of direct and individual concern to them. These are very restrictive conditions which have had the effect of excluding many judicial review applications made by natural and legal persons.

The ECJ has insisted that a non-privileged applicant cannot challenge a true regulation: *Calpak* v *Commission* Cases 789 and 790/79 [1980] ECR 1949. In order to determine whether an act is a regulation or a decision, it is necessary to look behind the label attached to the act to its nature and content. A regulation is a normative act applicable to abstract categories of persons, whilst a decision is addressed to a limited number of people.

If the decision is not addressed to the applicant, it will be necessary for them to establish direct and individual concern. Direct concern is established by showing a causal link between the act of the institution and its effect on the applicant. Individual concern is established by demonstrating that applicants are affected by the decision as a result of characteristics peculiar to them or because of circumstances by which they were differentiated from others: *Plaumann and Co* v *Commission* Case 25/62 [1964] ECR 95.

The test may be fulfilled by the applicant showing that they belong to a closed group of persons, fixed and ascertainable at the time of the decision. The grounds upon which the acts can be challenged are set out in art 236 EC.

Under art 232 EC, the ECJ also has jurisdiction in actions where it is alleged that the EP, the Council or the Commission has failed to act when under a legal duty to do so. Again a distinction is made between privileged and non-privileged applicants. Member States and all Community institutions have unlimited locus standi to bring an art 232 EC action, whilst private parties are only able to challenge acts other than recommendations or opinions. The ECJ has interpreted this to mean that individuals are only able to challenge a failure to address to that individual a measure which they were legally entitled to claim: *Bethell* v *Commission* Case 246/81 [1982] ECR 2277.

The procedure under art 232 EC means that few applications are successful. The applicant must request the relevant institution to act. The institution then has two months to take action or to define its position. A definition of the institution's position brings art 232 EC proceedings to an end: *Lütticke (Alfons) Gmbh* v *Commission* Case 4/69 [1971] ECR 325. If the institution concerned fails to act or define its position within a period of two months, proceedings may be commenced.

The ECJ also has powers under arts 241, 235 and 288 EC. Article 241 EC is not an independent action in its own right but permits a party, in an action based upon another Article of the Treaty, to dispute the legality of a regulation which is in issue in the proceedings: *Milchwerke Heinz Wöhrmann & Sohn KG* v *Commission* Cases 31 and 33/62 [1962] ECR 501. Articles 235 and 288 EC give the ECJ jurisdiction in claims in tort for damage caused by Community institutions: *Adams* v *Commission (No 1)* Case 145/83 [1985] ECR 3539.

Before the Treaty of Amsterdam the ECJ did not have jurisdiction to rule on those matters under the Treaty on European Union (TEU). In particular, the ECJ did not have jurisdiction to hear cases on the interpretation or application of the two inter-governmental pillars, ie Common Foreign Policy and Security Policy and Co-operation on Justice and Home Affairs (art L TEU), except where by means of a convention the Council stipulated that the ECJ had jurisdiction (art K(e) TEU). However, the Treaty of Amsterdam introduced the ability of the Court to hear matters on the Justice and Home Affairs (JHA) pillar, although the agreement of the individual Member States must be gained first. In addition, the Court gained jurisdiction to hear certain JHA matters when some of them were transferred to the EC Treaty. In relation to this latter point, the Court unfortunately has limitations imposed on its jurisdiction. For example, only a court of final instance may make a reference on such matters (art 68 EC) and the Court is excluded from hearing cases on matters that involve national security (art 68(2) EC). The academic Steiner suggests that this is a 'worrying' development for two reasons: it undermines the extent and uniformity of the Court's jurisdiction (compared to the jurisdiction offered under art 234 EC in relation to all other EC Treaty matters) and limits the protection available to individuals.

QUESTION THREE

Liquidgold plc is one of only four manufacturers in the European Community of a new type of liquid sweetener manufactured from barley. Drinkitdown Ltd, a manufacturer of soft drinks, was so attracted by the economics of using this type of sweetener that it has installed new machinery in its factory suitable for use with the barley sweetener. In January it entered into a contract with Liquidgold to purchase 10,000 tonnes of the sweetener each year for the next five years, this quantity being the amount needed to meet its current production requirements.

Last month, fearing adverse effects on the Community sugar industry, the Council adopted a Regulation imposing production quotas on the barley sweetener. An annex to that Regulation, which expressly refers to the four manufacturers by name, fixed Liquidgold's annual quota at 7,500 tonnes.

Having discovered that the other three manufacturers are already bound by contracts covering the whole of their permitted production, Drinkitdown is faced with a choice between cutting back its production or converting its factory to use sugar at a cost of £500,000.

Advise Drinkitdown as to the remedies available to it with regard to the Council Regulation.

University of London LLB Examination
(for External Students) European Community Law June 1990 Q4

General Comment

A typical problem-type question which requires the application of the relevant law to the facts of the question.

Skeleton Solution

The applicable substantive principles of Community law – standing to challenge a regulation – problem of time bar; plea of illegality – possibility of an indirect challenge through the art 234 EC procedure.

Suggested Solution

In order to mount a successful challenge against the Council Regulation which imposes production quotas on the barley sweetener, Drinkitdown must establish the existence of one of four separate causes of action: lack of competence; infringement of an essential procedural requirement; infringement of a provision of a Community treaty or a rule relating to the application of such provisions; or the misuse of power by a Community institution. From the facts of the case, the only possible cause of action would be on the basis of an infringement of the terms of the Community treaties or the principles of Community law which have been derived from these treaties.

The Regulation was adopted as a measure to protect the Community sugar industry and would therefore be subject to the Common Agricultural Policy (CAP), the objectives of which are set out in art 33 EC. This Article recognises the general principle of proportionality. This principle requires that measures introduced to regulate a particular activity must be not be disproportionately onerous in relation to their derived benefit. In other words, if the harm caused by the introduction of a regulation outweighs any possible benefit, the measure may be challenged as being contrary to the principle of proportionality which is a recognised rule of Community law. If Drinkitdown could establish that the Council Regulation limiting the production of the sweetener caused more injury than assistance, the Regulation could be challenged on this basis.

Alternatively, Drinkitdown could attempt to demonstrate that the enactment of the Regulation contravenes the principle of legitimate expectation. For example, in *Mulder v Minister of Agriculture and Fisheries* Case 120/86 [1988] ECR 2321, the European Court held that a farmer who had suspended milk production pursuant to a Community scheme could not be subsequently excluded from the allocation of milk quotas after the scheme had been discontinued. The Court held that the farmer had a legitimate expectation that at the end of the programme he would be in a position no less favourable than that which he would have enjoyed had he not acceded to the scheme. Clearly, Drinkitdown could argue that it had a legitimate expectation that its expenditure on plant conversion would not be misspent as a result of a Community measure.

While Drinkitdown may have a legitimate cause of action to challenge the Council Regulation, in order to show standing art 230(2) EC requires individuals and legal persons to demonstrate that the act being challenged constitutes a decision which is of 'direct and individual concern' to the applicant. The fact that the act challenged by the individual is in the form of a regulation or a decision addressed to another person does not ipso facto exclude the possibility of establishing the measure is a decision of direct and individual concern. However, an action for judicial review of a regulation or a decision addressed to another person is considerably more onerous than review of a decision explicitly addressed to an individual.

The Council Regulation imposing the production quotas refers to four manufacturers by name, including Liquidgold, but does not refer to Drinkitdown. Drinkitdown must therefore establish that the Regulation is in fact a 'decision' under art 230(2) EC, in which it has a direct and individual concern. In order to show that the Regulation is a decision, Drinkitdown must prove that, while the measure takes the form of a regulation, it is in fact a series of individual decisions in the form of a regulation. An example of applicants successfully proving that a regulation made by the Commission constituted a decision is *International Fruit Company v Commission* Cases 41–44/70 [1971] ECR 411. In this case, the particular Community Regulation challenged established a system of import licences to limit the importation of dessert apples into the Community according to supply and demand in the market. Importers could only receive an import licence if the volume of their proposed imports did not exceed a certain level. The Court held that this Regulation was not a generally applicable measure, but a 'conglomeration of individual decisions taken by the Commission under the guise of a regulation'. This determination was made on the basis that applications over a certain quantity were automatically disqualified from the competition for import licences. In the present case, it would be relatively simple to establish that the Regulation is in fact a conglomeration of individual decisions since the Regulation itself is expressly confined to the activities of four businesses.

If Drinkitdown can establish that the Regulation is in fact a decision, it must then be shown that the decision is of direct and individual concern. In order to have direct concern, the effects of the decision must immediately affect the applicant without depending on the exercise of discretion by another body. Thus, in *ARPOSOL v Council* Case 55/86 [1988] ECR 13, the European Court held that the applicants could not establish direct concern because the implementation of the Community measure depended on the intervention of the national authorities of Member States. However, where the national authorities have no discretion in implementing a Community measure, direct concern may be established: *Sofrimport Sàrl v Commission* Case C–152/88 [1990] ECR I–2477. The criterion of direct concern may therefore be presumed.

In addition to having a direct concern in the decision being challenged, Drinkitdown must also establish an individual concern. When a decision is not expressly addressed to an individual, in order for the measure to be of individual concern, it must be demonstrated that it affects 'their legal position because of a factual situation which differentiates them individually in the same way as to the person to whom it is addressed'. The contested measure must affect the applicant by reason of certain peculiar attributes or factual circumstances which differentiate the applicant from all other persons: see *Sofrimport* case, above. The mere ability to ascertain more or less precisely, or even to establish the identity of the persons to whom a measure applies, does not immediately imply that the measure is of individual concern to them: *Cargill and Others v Commission* Case 229/88R [1988] ECR 5183.

Individual concern has been established where a regulation named specific undertakings and applied specific measures to them, where the regulation had as its subject matter the individual circumstances of three named importers, and where a decision was issued by the Commission in response to the requests of a particular group, even although the final decision was addressed to another person. Conversely, if an act applies to objectively determined situations and entails legal effects for categories of persons generally and in the abstract, it has general application and is incapable of having individual effect. Drinkitdown might therefore have difficulty establishing that the Regulation is of individual concern.

If Drinkitdown was successful in challenging the validity of the Regulation, it could also be successful in obtaining compensation from the Community for injury sustained as a result of the unlawful measure. Article 288(2) EC states that, in the case of non-contractual liability, the Community shall, in accordance with the general principles common to the laws of the Member States, make good any damage caused by the institution responsible for the unlawful measure. Article 235 EC confers jurisdiction on the European Court to decide disputes relating to damages on the basis of the non-contractual liability of the Community.

Alternatively, Drinkitdown may indirectly challenge the validity of the Regulation on any legal grounds by means of reference for a preliminary ruling by a national court to the European Court under art 234 EC. Such a reference may be made where it is relevant to the outcome of pending legislation. Indeed, in *Firma Foto-Frost* v *Hauptzollamt Lübeck-Ost* Case 314/85 [1987] ECR 4199, the European Court held that such a reference was necessary in a case involving a challenge to a Community measure because only the European Court had the power to render such an act invalid. An art 234 EC reference may be made regardless of the locus standi of the applicant and any time limits: *International Fruit Company* v *Commission* Cases 41–44/70 [1971] ECR 411.

If the European Court was prepared to declare the Regulation invalid, it would not be applicable to Liquidgold and therefore Drinkitdown could rely on the sales contract negotiated between itself and Liquidgold.

QUESTION FOUR

'Direct actions against Community institutions can be brought without great difficulty by privileged applicants. The procedure is much more difficult for non-privileged applicants.'

Explain and illustrate.

University of London LLB Examination
(for External Students) European Union Law June 1997 Q5

General Comment

This is a straightforward question concerning the locus standi of natural and legal persons under the judicial review provisions of the EC Treaty – an area that many students find difficult and complex. A thorough understanding of the ECJ's case law is required in order to answer such a question well.

Skeleton Solution

Definition of direct action – explanation of judicial review provisions of the EC Treaty – distinction between privileged and non-privileged applicants – explanation of locus standi for non-privileged applicants – only de facto decisions challengeable – individual concern – the *Plaumann* test – direct concern – art 241 EC.

Suggested Solution

In the context of EC law, a direct action is one that begins and ends in the European Court of Justice (ECJ) and is contrasted with an indirect action, which commences in a national court, is referred to the ECJ for a ruling on the point of law and then returned to the national court for a decision. Article 234 EC proceedings represent the only form of indirect action. Direct actions, however, cover arts 226 (enforcement actions), 230, 232 and 241 (judicial review) and 228(2) EC (non-contractual liability) proceedings. Since the distinction between privileged and non-privileged applicants is relevant only to judicial review proceedings, this essay will focus on arts 230, 232 and 241 EC.

Articles 230 and 232 EC permit the challenge of EC institutions for unlawful action and unlawful failure to act. The consequence of a successful art 230 EC action is that the unlawful act is declared void under art 231 EC. In relation to a successful art 232 EC action, an institution's failure to act is declared contrary to the EC Treaty. In both cases that institution concerned must take 'necessary measures to comply with the judgment of the Court of Justice'. The judicial review provisions of the Treaty are, therefore, a powerful means of challenging the way in which the Community institutions exercise their power. It is therefore unsurprising that rigorous limitations are imposed on the ability of certain parties to make such applications.

Both arts 230 and 232 EC make a similar distinction between what are known as privileged and non-privileged applicants. Privileged applicants are those parties that do not have to demonstrate any interest in the proceedings in order to commence with the judicial review. Under art 230 and 232 EC, privileged applicants are the Member States, the Council and the Commission.

Non-privileged applicants (that is natural and legal persons) have limited locus standi under arts 230 and 232 EC. Under art 230(4) EC, a natural and legal person (hereafter the applicant) may challenge certain acts. First, the applicant may challenge a decision addressed to them; second, they may challenge a decision addressed to another party but which is of direct and individual concern to the applicant; and finally, a decision in the form of a regulation that is of direct and individual concern to the applicant may also be challenged. In terms of trying to establish the necessary locus standi, the principal difficulties for the applicant are in identifying that the measure is a de facto decision (in the case of a regulation) and that it is of direct and individual concern to the applicant.

Formerly, the distinction between a true regulation and a decision (sources of secondary legislation stemming from art 249 EC) was found in the general application or otherwise of the measure. In other words, the substance, and not the form, of the measure was the important point. In *Calpak* v *Commission* Cases 789 and 790/79 [1980] ECR 1949 a regulation was said to apply to 'objectively determined situations and produces legal effects with regard to categories of persons described in a generalised and abstract manner'. Conversely, decisions are addressed to only a limited number of persons. However, more recently the issue of the nature of a measure has been subsumed into the inquiry concerning whether there is direct and individual concern. Hence, if a measure is shown to directly and individually affect/concern the applicant, it may be unnecessary to establish whether the measure is a regulation or decision: *Extramet Industrie SA* v *Council* Case C–358/89 [1991] ECR I–2501.

According to *Plaumann and Co* v *Commission* Case 25/62 [1964] ECR 95 individual concern is shown when the applicant establishes that they are affected by the decision 'by reason of certain attributes which are peculiar to them or by reason of circumstances in which they are differentiated from all other persons ... just as in the case of the person addressed'. The *Plaumann* test is most easily satisfied when it can be shown that the applicant belongs to a closed group of persons affected by the decision at the time it is adopted. A closed category of persons is one that is fixed and ascertainable and will generally only arise when a decision has retrospective effect.

It is noteworthy, however, that in some specific types of case the ECJ has been rather more generous in its interpretation of the concept of individual concern. In cases concerning challenges to anti-dumping regulations, competition decisions and State aids the ECJ has considered the issue of individual concern in the light of alternative criteria. Where applicants in such cases have been able to show involvement in the proceedings leading up to the challenged measure, individual concern has been established. For example, in *Metro-SB-Grossmärkte GmbH & Co KG* v *Commission* Case 26/76 [1977] ECR 1875, individual concern was established by the complainant whose actions initiated the Commission investigation. Similarly, in *Timex Corporation* v *Council* Case 264/82 [1985] ECR 849 the complainant in anti-dumping proceedings was individually concerned, as was the exporter of products affected by the anti-dumping duty in *Allied Corporation* v *Commission* Cases 239 and 275/82 [1984] ECR 1005.

The establishment of direct concern is essentially an issue of causation. The applicant must prove a causal link between the institution's act and its effect on the applicant: *Alcan Aluminium Raeren* v *Commission* Case 69/69 [1970] ECR 385. In cases where a Member State has discretion in the implementation of a Community measure, an applicant will be unable to establish direct concern and instead should challenge the national, not Community, decision.

Article 232 EC makes a similar distinction between privileged and non-privileged applicants. Whilst privileged applicants (Member States and Community institutions) may challenge the failure to adopt any act having legal effects, non-privileged applicants (natural and legal persons) are said to be able to challenge only the failure to address to them any act other than a recommendation or opinion: art 232(3) EC. However, it has been argued that similar principles should apply to art 232 EC as apply to art 230 EC, because they are opposite sides of the same legal remedy. This is generally referred to as the unity principle and it has been invoked to ensure that non-privileged applicants may challenge the failure to adopt any measure that would, if adopted, be challengeable under art 230 EC: *Nordgetreide GmbH & Co KG* v *Commission* Case 42/71 [1972] ECR 105.

Lastly, art 241 EC sets out the so-called 'plea of illegality'. Under art 241 EC the legality of a regulation may be challenged as a matter ancillary to another claim. Thus, in a challenge to the legality of a decision, the legality of the regulation upon which the decision is based may be contested: *Simmenthal* v *Commission* Case 92/78 [1979] ECR 777. Article 241 EC, therefore, permits non-privileged parties to contest the validity of measures that are regulations in both substance and form.

QUESTION FIVE

'The structure of art 230 of the EC Treaty shows that it was probably intended to be mainly used by the institutions.'

Discuss.

University of London LLB Examination
(for External Students) European Union Law June 2000 Q3

General Comment

This essay style question required discussion of the standing of the Community institutions before the European Court of Justice. Emphasis in this context should have been placed on the extension of standing to the Parliament by the ECJ and the recognition of this development by the Treaty on European Union (TEU). The essay particularly required analysis of whether individuals are capable of having standing, and the difficulties that may be encountered in gaining such standing, with reference to relevant cases.

Skeleton Solution

Direct action under art 230 EC judicial review – action for the review of the legality of acts of the Community institutions – role of art 230 EC – Community institutions with standing – the extension of such standing to the Parliament – TEU amendment to art 230 EC – the standing of individuals – need for the measure to be a decision of individual and direct concern to the applicant – problems in defining who has sufficient interest.

Suggested Solution

The EC Treaty creates an extensive and complex system of judicial review of the acts of Community institutions in order to protect the rights of both the Member States and private individuals. The system is designed to ensure that the Community institutions operate within their respective competencies as identified under the EC Treaty. The direct actions that may be taken to secure judicial review include: actions to review the legality of acts of the Community institutions under art 230 EC; actions for failure to act under art 232 EC; and actions for damages under art 288 EC. This essay will examine art 230 EC in the context of analysing and identifying those that may have standing (locus standi) to appear before the European Court of Justice to challenge an act of the Community institutions.

Article 230 EC provides the Court with the jurisdiction to review the legality of certain Community acts, and as such fulfils a dual function. First, it provides a means of controlling the legality of binding acts of the Community institutions. Second, it offers a form of legal protection to those that find themselves subject to the legislative and executive competencies of the Community.

Whether the act is reviewable by the Court depends to a certain extent on the identity of the entity making the application. Hence, if the applicant is a Member State or Community institution, the acts that may be reviewed include acts of the Council and the Commission, other than recommendations and opinions. To be reviewed, the act must be binding, and the Court places emphasis on examining a measure's content, subject matter and legal effect rather than its form or designation: *Commission v Council (Re ERTA)* Case 22/70 [1971] ECR 263. For example, in *Council v European Parliament* Case 34/86 [1986] ECR 2155 the Court concluded that a declaration made by the President of the Parliament at the conclusion of the budget debate had the character of a legal act and was therefore subject to proceedings under art 230 EC. However, for an act of the Council to be reviewable, it must be acting as the Council and not, for example, as merely government representatives. This was the case in the attempt to review the legality of the decision to grant aid to Bangladesh in *European Parliament v Council and Commission* Cases C–181 and 248/91 [1993] ECR I–3685.

If the applicant is a private party the measure will have to be a 'decision'. In the context of art 230 EC the definition of a decision is a wide one, in that the measure need not take the strict legal form of a decision under art 249 EC to still be capable of being reviewed. Hence, for example, the decision by the Commission to close a file on a complaint made alleging a breach of competition law was held to be a reviewable decision in *SFEI and Others v Commission* Case C–39/93P [1994] ECR I–2681. This issue is discussed in further detail below.

There have been suggestions that art 230 EC was to be primarily relied on by the Community institutions, and in its original form this would have only included the Council and Commission. However, in practice the bodies that may have the necessary standing to bring an action in the ECJ is wider and may be broadly classified into two main categories: first, Community institutions and Member States; and second, private parties.

Paragraph 2 of art 230 EC specifically refers to Member States, the Council and the Commission as having the necessary standing to bring an action for judicial review. They are consequently referred to as privileged applicants. Indeed, Member States are presumed to have an interest in the legality of all Community acts. This can be witnessed in the decision of the Court in *Italy v Council* Case 166/78 [1979] ECR 2575 where the Court concluded that every Member State has the ability to challenge a Council regulation regardless of its position at the time of adoption. This right presumably extends to all other acts too.

According to the original terms of art 230 EC the only Community institutions that had standing were the Council and the Commission. The Parliament was not referred to within art 230 EC as being capable of having the necessary standing. In a series of cases the Parliament was denied the ability to seek review under art 230 EC by the Court; for example, in *European Parliament* v *Council (Re Comitology)* Case 302/87 [1988] ECR 5615 the Court rejected the Parliament's argument that it should have the same unlimited standing as the other privileged applicants.

The issue of whether the Parliament was capable of having standing was re-examined in the case of *European Parliament* v *Council (Re Chernobyl)* Case C–70/88 [1990] ECR I–2041. This case rested on a Regulation adopted by the Council after the Chernobyl incident, which sought to establish a maximum level of radioactive contamination for food and feedstuffs. The Parliament desired the review of the legal basis for the measure, arguing that it should have been based on art 95 EC, which would have required the co-operation procedure to have been used and would consequently have given the Parliament greater involvement. The Court concluded that the lack of any express provision in the EC Treaty granting it the right to bring an action for annulment was a 'procedural gap', but that this oversight should not take priority over the fundamental need to maintain and observe the institutional balance. Thus the Court concluded that the Parliament did have the necessary standing to bring an action under art 230 EC. The Treaty of European Union amended art 230(3) EC to formally reflect and enshrine this decision.

The second category of those with standing are private parties, otherwise referred to as non-privileged applicants. However, they do not have unfettered access to seek judicial review under art 230 EC. Non-privileged applicants may seek judicial review in three situations. First, if they are the addressee of the decision; second, if the decision is addressed to another but is of direct and individual concern to them; and third, if the decision is in the form of a regulation and is of direct and individual concern to them. The Court has had some considerable problems in identifying whether there is the necessary direct and individual concern.

The test used to establish whether such concern exists was created in the case of *Plaumann and Co* v *Commission* Case 25/62 [1964] ECR 95. According to the Court in *Plaumann*, an individual that is not the addressee will be individually concerned if they are in some way differentiated from all other persons because of distinguishing features. These distinguishing features mean that they are affected in the same way as the addressee themselves. It appears that, even if an undertaking is adversely affected by a decision, if it is not of individual concern to them, they will not be considered as having sufficient interest to have standing. In *Plaumann and Co* v *Commission* Case 25/62 [1964] ECR 95 the applicant was concluded to be one of an open class and therefore was not individually concerned, even though they had been adversely affected.

To be of direct concern the decision must produce immediate, automatic and inevitable, not merely possible, disadvantageous effects. Hence, in *Piraiki-Patraiki* v *Commission*

Case 11/82 [1985] ECR 208 the contested decision related to the authorisation of quota systems by the French government on imports of Greek yarn. Those traders that had entered into contracts before the date of the decision, which were to be performed for larger quantities than permitted under the system during the period it was in force, were granted standing. Other yarn traders not in that position were refused standing, since they were not directly or immediately concerned.

Generally, it appears that an applicant will be directly concerned if the decision imposes a disadvantage, or denies an advantage, to a class of persons of which the applicant is a member. Alternatively, they may be directly concerned if the decision grants an advantage or terminates an advantage imposed on the applicant's competitors, but only if these results follow automatically from the decision. Where the results are 'likely' to follow but depend on the intervention of certain third parties or on the fulfilment of certain criteria, there will be no direct concern. This can be illustrated using the following example. Companies may apply for import licences to import certain goods into the EC. The Commission decides whether such licences should be granted. In such cases, according to *L'Etoile Commerciale* v *Commission* Cases 89 and 91/86 [1988] 3 CMLR 564 the companies that applied will be directly and individually concerned with the decision made. However, if the allocation of such licences is then placed at the discretion of the national authorities and the allocation is to be on the basis of future quotas to companies not traditionally known for importing such products, proving direct concern will be very difficult, as illustrated in the *Piraiki* decision.

The final situation in which a non-privileged applicant may have standing under art 230 EC is where there is a regulation that is, in reality, a decision, which is of direct and individual concern to them. Such claims have not traditionally been extremely successful, and the approach adopted by the Court in assessing such claims has been inconsistent. If the measure is indeed a true regulation, even if it affects only a small number of people, it will not be subject to review under art 230 EC proceedings. If the regulation is of a general nature, as was found in the case of *Calpak* v *Commission* Cases 789 and 790/79 [1980] ECR 1949, it too will not be open to review. However, if the regulation is intended to affect only a specific group of undertakings it may, as was held in the case of *International Fruit Company* v *Commission* Cases 41–44/70 [1971] ECR 411, be concluded to be a collection of decisions merely in the form of a regulation and hence subject to review under art 230 EC.

Indeed, the Court has generally construed the concept of direct and individual concern very narrowly. For example, the Court of First Instance denied employees' representatives standing to challenge Commission decisions in *Comité Central d'Enterprise de la Société Générale des Grandes Sources* v *Commission* Case T–96/92 [1995] ECR II–1213 even though decisions, which approved mergers, were to result in redundancies. This has been described as making it in practice very difficult for an applicant to secure the necessary locus standi – an almost impossible right to assert. The explanation generally offered for the Court's strict test for non-privileged applicants to secure standing under art 230 EC is that it wishes not to open the floodgates to claims from bodies supposedly affected by Community law.

Hence, it is not accurate to state that only Community institutions as privileged applicants have the right to seek judicial review under art 230 EC, since individuals may secure the necessary locus standi as non-privileged applicants. However, they may find this extremely difficult, and this position is not helped by the Court's somewhat inconsistent approach. It is a situation that the Court itself has declared to be one that is perhaps ineffective in securing adequate protection for Community individuals, but is one that has not been resolved by any Treaty amendment.

Chapter 4

The Preliminary Ruling Jurisdiction of the European Court of Justice

4.1   Introduction

4.2   Key points

4.3   Key cases and materials

4.4   Questions and suggested solutions

4.1 Introduction

To ensure the uniform, consistent and harmonious application of Community law throughout the national legal systems of the Member States, the Community treaties establish a procedure to allow national courts to refer questions of Community law to the European Court for consideration. These references from national courts (sometimes referred to as an indirect action) fall within the preliminary ruling jurisdiction of the Court. Article 234 EC establishes the essential principles and procedures which govern this aspect of the jurisdiction of the European Court.

4.2 Key points

Scope of the preliminary ruling jurisdiction

Article 234 EC confers jurisdiction on the European Court to render preliminary ruling decisions which relate to:

a) the interpretation of the Community treaties;

b) the validity and interpretation of acts of the Community institutions;

c) the interpretation of statutes of bodies established by the Council of Ministers where the relevant statutes so provide.

In addition, a number of Conventions among the Member States of the Community provide for preliminary references from national courts to the European Court for the interpretation of intra-Community agreements.

The discretion to request a preliminary ruling – lower courts

All national courts and tribunals, other than those against which there is no appeal, have discretion whether or not to refer a case involving a question of Community law to the European Court. If the issue arises before a court against whose decision there is no judicial remedy under national law, technically that court is obliged to refer the matter to the European Court: art 234(3) EC.

Courts and tribunals which exercise a discretion to refer a question should be satisfied that two preconditions exist before making a reference, namely:

a) the court or tribunal must believe that the case involves an issue of Community law; and

b) the court or tribunal must be satisfied that a decision on the question is necessary to decide the merits of the case.

A prima facie question of Community law will arise where a party relies on a provision of a Community treaty, or a measure of Community law such as a regulation, a directive or a decision, or a precedent of the European Court (and now also the Court of First Instance).

The obligation to request a preliminary ruling – courts of final instance

National courts and tribunals of final instance (or last resort) are subject to a different set of obligations as regards seeking preliminary references from the European Court. Article 234(3) EC declares that these courts are bound to refer a question of Community law to the European Court for a preliminary reference.

This absolute duty has been qualified by the European Court itself, particularly in *CILFIT* v *Ministry of Health* Case 283/81 [1982] ECR 3415. Where a question of Community law arises before a national court of final appeal, such a court need not refer the matter for a preliminary ruling if the question has already been settled by the European Court (acte clair). This discretion applies only 'where previous decisions of the [European] Court have already dealt with the point of law in question, irrespective of the nature of the proceedings which led to those decisions, even although the questions at issue are not strictly identical': *CILFIT*, above.

The European Court has also established a number of guidelines to ensure that this privilege is not abused. A court of final instance which decides not to refer a question to the European Court because of an earlier precedent must give special consideration to the 'characteristic features of Community law and the particular difficulties to which its interpretation gives rise'. Special consideration must be given to the following matters.

a) Community legislation is drafted in several different languages all of which are equally authentic and proper interpretation often involves comparisons with different language versions.

b) Community law has acquired its own terminology and legal concepts do not necessarily have the same meaning in Community law as in national law.

c) Every provision of Community law has to be placed in its proper context and interpreted in light of the system established by the Community treaties, having regard both to its objectives and to the state of the law at that particular point: *Lister* v *Forth Dry Dock and Engineering Co* [1989] 1 All ER 1134.

In many respects the decision of the European Court in *CILFIT* v *Ministry of Health* Case 283/81 [1982] ECR 3415 case reduces the discretion of courts of last instance to decide questions of Community law themselves because it establishes rigourous criteria for deciding whether or not to refer a question to the European Court.

The nature of the question submitted for a preliminary ruling

There are no formal requirements regulating the content of a question submitted for a preliminary reference, although obviously the greater the degree of precision, the more accurate the response of the European Court. A Practice Direction has, however, been published by the Lord Chief Justice for references made by the Court of Appeal and the High Court: [1999] 2 CMLR 799.

The European Court decides whether the requirements of the preliminary reference itself satisfy the terms of art 234 EC. In the past, the Court has had to decide:

a) whether a body in national law is a court or tribunal for the purposes of art 234 EC: *Pretore Di Salo* v *Persons Unknown* Case 14/86 [1987] ECR 2545;

b) whether a reference is premature or may have the effect of precluding a later reference from the same court in the same case;

c) if the question asked of the Court is too vague, or general, or involves questions of national law; and

d) if a preliminary ruling is competent in the event that a higher court had already ruled on the matter: *Society for the Protection of Unborn Children (Ireland)* v *Grogan* Case C–159/90 [1991] ECR I–4685.

The Court will not answer questions considered to be contrived or hypothetical. For example, in *Foglia* v *Novello (No 1)* Case 104/79 [1980] ECR 745, the Court declined to answer a reference which it considered contrived on the grounds that there was no real dispute between the parties.

Similarly, in *Meilicke* v *ADV/ORGA FA Meyer* Case C–83/91 [1992] ECR I–4871 the Court rejected a reference from a German court concerning a dispute that had not yet arisen between the parties but had been made to resolve a hypothetical and abstract point of law.

In fact, as a general principle, the Court has recently become more and more reluctant to accept loose references made by national courts if either the facts stated are too vague or the legal principles sought to be clarified inadequately specified: *Pretore Di Genoa* v *Banchero* Case C–157/92 [1993] ECR I–1085. This represents a reversal of its earlier policy of flexibility in these circumstances.

The authority of a preliminary reference

The term 'preliminary reference' is somewhat misleading. A preliminary ruling is not an advisory opinion but rather a decision which the referring national court is obliged to apply to the facts of the case: *Brown* v *Secretary of State for Scotland* Case 197/86 [1988] ECR 3205. A preliminary reference is binding upon the court which referred the question for consideration in the sense that it represents an authoritative determination of Community law.

Not only are decisions rendered through the preliminary reference procedure binding on the court which referred the question, but they may also be cited as precedents in those Member States which adhere to the principle of stare decisis. Decisions of the European Court are therefore binding as precedents on British courts when they relate to identical points of Community law.

The functions and responsibilities of the European Court

The primary responsibility of the European Court in a preliminary reference is to decide the legal merits of the case in terms of Community law. Therefore, the European Court cannot expressly declare that provisions of national law are inconsistent with Community law; this is a matter for the national court. As the Court has expressly observed:

'[T]he Court is not empowered under [art 234] of the [EC] Treaty to rule on the compatibility with the Treaty of provisions of national law. However, it has jurisdiction to provide the national court with all such matters relating to the interpretation of Community law as may enable it to decide the issue of compatibility in the case before it.' (*Schumacher* v *Hauptzollamt Frankfurt am Main-Ost* Case C–215/87 [1991] 2 CMLR 465.)

The European Court also cannot take notice of the facts of a particular case. Ascertaining the relevant facts is the concern of the referring court: *Simmenthal SpA* v *Amministrazione delle Finanze dello Stato* Case 35/76 [1976] ECR 1871.

Equally, the Court refrains from criticising the reasons behind a particular reference although on occasion the Court has rejected references which have been contrived between the litigating parties for the purpose of obtaining a particular ruling. Thus, in *Foglia* v *Novello (No 1)* Case 104/79 [1980] ECR 745, the Court held that it had no jurisprudence to pronounce on the merits of a case where the parties to the principal action had initiated the proceedings for the sole purpose of obtaining a ruling that a particular law of another Member State was inconsistent with Community law.

The relevance of precedents in the jurisprudence of the European Court

The European Court, in common with other systems of law based on the civilian model of law, does not adhere to the doctrine of precedent. The Court has, however, adopted a policy of referring to earlier decisions in the course of judgments and repeating, occasionally with slight modifications, parts of decisions from earlier relevant cases. This technique ensures consistency throughout the jurisprudence of the Court.

The Court has even recently declined to issue a fresh judgment in a particular case where the facts stated or questions raised are similar to earlier decisions. For example, in *Rochdale Borough Council* v *Anders* Case C–306/88 [1993] 1 All ER 520, the Court declined to issue a fresh judgement and cited its earlier judgment as authority for its refusal to issue a complete report.

But, in legal theory at least, the previous decisions of the Court do not constitute binding precedents and on occasion the Court has radically departed from its previous course of decisions. Compare *European Parliament* v *Council (Re Comitology)* Case 302/87 [1988] ECR 5615 with *European Parliament* v *Council (Re Chernobyl)* Case C–70/88 [1990] ECR I–2041.

4.3 Key cases and materials

- *Brown* v *Secretary of State for Scotland* Case 197/86 [1988] ECR 3205
  A preliminary ruling is a decision that the referring court is obliged to apply to the facts of the case

- *CILFIT* v *Ministry of Health* Case 283/81 [1982] ECR 3415
  Elaboration of the criteria required in order to allow a court of final instance to refuse a preliminary reference to the ECJ

- *Foglia* v *Novello (No 1)* Case 104/79 [1980] ECR 745
  The Court asserts that it has jurisdiction to determine whether to hear the reference or reject it, in this case because the sole purpose was to obtain a ruling that the law of another Member State was inconsistent with Community law. The Court will not hear hypothetical or contrived references on the basis that there is no real dispute between the parties

- *Pretore Di Genoa* v *Banchero* Case C–157/92 [1993] ECR I–1085
  The Court will not hear references that are too vague or lacking adequate clarification of the legal principles involved

- EC Treaty, art 234 EC – confers jurisdiction on the ECJ to render preliminary rulings

4.4 Questions and suggested solutions

QUESTION ONE

Should the European Court ever refuse a national court's request for a preliminary ruling?

University of London LLB Examination
(for External Students) European Community Law June 1990 Q3

General Comment

A difficult essay type question which, although requiring a narrative answer, refers to a particular topic on which there is little legal authority.

Skeleton Solution

The provisions of the EC Treaty – the policy of the European Court – case law – conclusions.

Suggested Solution

Initially, the European Court adopted an extremely liberal policy regarding the admission of references from national courts and tribunals. No formal examination was undertaken into the admissibility of such cases: *Simmenthal SpA* v *Ministero delle Finanze* Case 35/76 [1976] ECR 1871. This was due not only to the relatively light case load of the Court during the early years of the Community but also to a desire, on the part of the Court, to influence the evolution of the Community by forging fundamental principles of Community law.

In recent times there have been signs that this policy has changed due for the most part to the substantial increase in the workload of the Court. Thus, for example, in *Pretore Di Genoa* v *Banchero* Case C–157/92 [1993] ECR I–1085, the Court rejected a preliminary reference from an Italian court on the basis that the facts on which the reference was requested were inadequately stated. Similarly, in *Rochdale Borough Council* v *Anders* Case C–306/88 [1993] 1 All ER 520, the Court declined to issue a fresh judgment in this reference because the questions referred had already been addressed in an earlier reference. Nevertheless, in cases raising novel or controversial questions of law, the Court has been keen to address these issues to advance the frontiers of Community law.

In the pursuit of this policy, the European Court has been anxious to admit references in order to have an opportunity to fashion principles of Community law through interpretation. Equally, encouraging national courts to refer cases to the Court served the dual purpose of both ensuring uniform interpretation of Community law and acquainting the national courts with the existence of Community law.

The success or otherwise of this process has depended on the co-operation of the national courts. In order to assist national courts to accept the principle of the supremacy of Community law over national law, the European Court has emphasised the importance of co-operation rather than insisting on the development of a hierarchical structure which placed the European Court above national courts and tribunals. Instead the Court has evolved a careful delimitation of responsibilities between the Community system and the legal systems of the Member States, with the European Court interpreting Community law and the national courts applying this interpretation to the facts of the case before them.

A careful balance has been struck by the European Court between furthering the aims of the Community by ensuring the successful development of the Community legal order and consideration for the sentiments within the national legal systems of the Member States.

The practical utility of this policy, together with a growing awareness within the national courts about the existence of Community law, has meant that the European Court has become a victim of its own success. The sheer volume of references from the national courts has meant that a reference can take up to two years before a decision is rendered. Such a heavy workload also implies that the quality of individual judgments may decrease. Further, the quantity of judgments risks diluting their importance.

Yet in the leading case where the Court declined jurisdiction – *Foglia* v *Novello (No 1)* Case 104/79 [1980] ECR 745 – the European Court did not specifically address this issue. The case itself turned on its particular facts.

In *Foglia* v *Novello*, a reference was made by an Italian court in an action between two Italians who had entered into a sales contract requiring delivery of the goods in France. The contract provided that the buyer would not be responsible for the payment of any taxes imposed in contravention of Community law. The goods were duly delivered. The seller was required to pay a consumption tax in France and claimed reimbursement from the buyer who refused to pay on the ground that the tax was contrary to Community law. Thus, the Italian courts were required to decide whether the French tax was in accordance with Community law.

The Italian court referred the question to the European Court. The Court took exception to this question because it involved a challenge to the sovereign rights of one Member State in a legal forum where the state was not in a position to defend itself.

More importantly, there were a number of grounds for believing that the whole transaction had been contrived in order to present a test case to the European Court. For these reasons, the European Court refused to accept the reference on the basis that there was no genuine dispute between the parties. The Italian court declined to accept this decision and made a second reference to the Court: *Foglia* v *Novello (No 2)* Case 244/80 [1981] ECR 3045. However the European Court again rejected the reference on the same grounds.

This ruling was subject to a considerable amount of criticism, not least because it interfered with the delicate relationship between the national courts and the European Court. By substituting the criteria of 'a real dispute between the parties' for 'a question on matters of Community law' (as specified by the EC Treaty), the European Court created a ground for reviewing decisions of national courts to refer a case for a preliminary reference. The Court could therefore investigate the reasons for the reference and the relevance of the question referred.

This development broke down the cooperative framework which the European Court had patiently developed throughout the course of its jurisprudence and substituted a more hierarchical structure. In addition, the Court conferred upon itself power to investigate the facts of a case in order to ascertain the intention of the parties. This power trespassed on the role of the national court as the finder of facts.

Logic would suggest, however, that there are circumstances in which the Court should, and indeed has, declined a reference. The first ground relates to instances in which the Court determines that the matter at issue has no connection with Community law. The second ground is where the requirements of art 234 EC are not satisfied – the reference was not made by a court or tribunal or, alternatively, the question referred does not concern the interpretation of Community law or the validity of a Community measure. The third possibility is when the reference is an abuse of the procedure – an amorphous heading. In *Matthews* [1978] ECR 2203, the Court declined jurisdiction when it decided that the questions referred were purely hypothetical and that the parties had attempted to compel the national court to make a reference, thus depriving it of its discretion under art 234(2) EC. In *Foglia* v *Novello (No 1)* Case 104/79 [1980] ECR 745, it could be argued that jurisdiction had been declined because the art 234 EC procedure was being abused because it was being employed to indirectly challenged a French tax when proceedings under art 230 EC would have been more appropriate.

It could also be argued that fictitious litigation is an abuse of procedure, since mere academic consultation on a hypothetical issue is not the purpose of art 234 EC. It is, however, difficult to develop reliable criteria for determining the existence of fictitious litigation.

In between the two rulings in the *Foglia* affair, two other references were made to the European Court by courts in Italy: *Chemical Farmaceuticic* v *DAF SpA* Case 140/79 [1989] ECR 1; and *Vinal* v *Orbat SpA* Case 46/80 [1981] ECR 77. Both cases involved facts similar to those in *Foglia* except that the disputed tax was Italian and not French and the disputes were considered 'not to be manifestly bogus'. In both cases, the European Court accepted the reference. It seems likely that the European Court's real reason for its decision in the *Foglia* cases was comity – a desire not to offend France.

The hostile reception received by the decision of the Court in *Foglia* and the potentially devastating consequences of the ruling on the intra-judicial relationship previously built up by the Court may mean that the European Court will adopt a policy of only reluctantly interfering in matters which fall within the competence of national courts. The Court has, however, attempted to alleviate the workload before it by following another tactic – the development of the acte clair doctrine after *CILFIT* v *Ministry of Health* Case 283/81 [1982] ECR 3415. By establishing criteria which allow national courts of final instance to decide cases without reference to the European Court, the Court itself has developed a doctrine which builds on European-national judicial co-operation rather than encroaches on the role of national courts and tribunals in the preliminary reference procedure.

QUESTION TWO

Discuss the purposes of art [234] EC and evaluate the extent to which these purposes have been achieved. To what extent is art [10] EC a necessary complement to art [234] EC?

University of London LLB Examination
(for External Students) European Community Law June 1992 Q5

General Comment

A question requiring detailed knowledge of the purpose and function of the art 234 procedure as well as an insight into the relevance of art 10 EC in the structure of the Community.

Skeleton Solution

Purposes of art 234 EC: assistance in interpretation and uniform application of Community law – the pursuit of these objectives through art 234 EC – relevance of art 10 EC – limitations: direct actions; state liability.

Suggested Solution

Article 234 EC allows national courts to refer questions of Community law to the European Court for interpretation and for pronouncements on the validity and interpretation of acts of the Community organs. Several conventions negotiated among the Community's Member States, such as the Convention on the Jurisdiction and Enforcement of Judgments 1968, also provide that national courts can refer questions of interpretation to the Court for a ruling.

As the European Court itself pointed out in *CILFIT* v *Ministry of Health* Case 283/81 [1982] ECR 3415, the procedure under art 234 EC is designed to encourage 'the proper application and uniform interpretation of Community law in all the Member States'. The mechanism establishes a procedure whereby national courts and the European Court can cooperate to ensure that there is little possibility of decisions of national courts on questions of Community law differing from the judgments of the European Court on the same issues. Thus, the preliminary ruling procedure allows the Court to maintain an element of consistency on both a geographical level and at a jurisprudential level.

However, it should be noted that art 234 EC does not establish a hierarchy between the European Court and national courts. The preliminary ruling procedure does not mean that the ECJ is a court of final appeal on matters of Community law. Rather, art 234 EC creates a system whereby national courts and tribunals can seek guidance from the European Court rather than having a decision imposed on them.

An example of this relationship working in practice is the policy of the European Court to only answer questions of Community law. It will not respond to questions of fact or matters requiring an interpretation of national law. In the event that a national court refers a question dealing with points of national law, the European Court merely extracts the relevant points of Community law from the reference before conveying its responses to the national court.

As observed above, the purpose of art 234 EC is two-fold. First, to ensure the proper application and effectiveness of Community law and, second, to guarantee the uniform interpretation of Community law throughout the Community.

For present purposes, proper application is synonymous with effective enforcement. Article 234 EC itself assists to ensure this objective by requiring all national courts of final instance seized of a question of Community law to refer the issue to the European Court for interpretation. While not all lower courts are required to make such a reference, this avenue is, of course, open to them should they wish to do so.

The important point is that art 234 EC envisaged all questions of Community law, at least potentially, being interpreted by the European Court. This scheme would ensure proper and effective enforcement by creating an all-embracing scheme to coordinate the implementation of Community law through the European Court.

However, in certain respects, the European Court has contributed itself to the demise of this system. In *CILFIT* v *Ministry of Health* Case 283/81 [1982] ECR 3415, the Court, under considerable pressure from national courts, developed the doctrine of acte clair. Courts of final instance would no longer be required to make a mandatory reference if previous decisions of the European Court dealt adequately with the point at issue. In other words, if there was an earlier judgment of the court dealing with similar facts, national courts were released from the obligation to refer.

While it is true that the European Court set down rules for the application of the doctrine of acte clair, at the same time it is clear that it has undermined the effective application of Community law. National courts do not feel themselves under so much pressure to refer questions to the European Court. While this development was largely predictable once Community law had grown into a sizeable corpus of law with the assistance of the Court, nevertheless there are undoubtedly side-effects as regards effective enforcement of Community obligations.

On the other hand, the uniform interpretation of Community law has been achieved by the Court actively encouraging national courts to make preliminary references. For example, the Court will accept virtually all cases referred to it by national courts, no matter how trivial, if there is a genuine dispute.

However, this policy of the Court has also had unfortunate and unseen consequences. The present volume of cases was never anticipated and now the average period of delay between the initial reference and a decision on the matter stands at approximately two years. This delay is unacceptable once it is acknowledged that the matter may have been before a national court for some time prior to the reference.

The relationship of art 10 EC to art 234 EC is largely a separate issue. Article 234 EC is a procedure designed to ensure the effective enforcement and uniform application of Community law in national courts. Article 10 EC is intended to be a substantive obligation imposed on all governmental organs and agencies of Member States to ensure respect for Community law. Thus, while art 234 EC promotes compliance with Community law by national courts and tribunals, art 10 EC is a broader obligation imposed on all government organs.

Article 10 EC has been used extensively by the European Court to keep Member States in line with their Community obligations. For example, this provision forms the basis for the principle of the direct effect of unimplemented directives since the decision of the European Court in *Marleasing SA v La Comercial Internacional de Alimentacion SA* Case C–106/89 [1990] ECR I–4135. In that case, the European Court held that art 10 EC requires all Member States to take all appropriate measures to ensure the fulfilment of their Community obligations and it follows from this that their national laws must be interpreted to achieve this aim.

The same Article also forms the basis for most of the actions brought by the European Commission against Member States for non-implementation of Community regulations and directives. Equally, actions brought by the Commission for failure by a Member State to abide by the terms of an adverse ruling in the European Court are brought under this provision and not the article providing grounds for the first offence.

The scope of art 10 EC is considerable. It applies not only to acts attributable to Member States, but also to their omissions. This Treaty Article has also formed the basis of the creation of the principle of State liability. In *Francovich and Bonifaci v Italian Republic* Cases C–6 and 9/90 [1991] ECR I–5357 the European Court upheld the existence of a duty in European law to make reparation for injury caused by a Member State failing to comply with its obligations. The Court made specific reference to art 10 EC, stating the Member States were obliged to ensure the full effect of Community law and to guarantee the rights of private individuals under EC law. The effectiveness of these rights would be undermined if individuals were unable to secure compensation when they were breached through the illegal activities of the Member States. This principle of EC law has since been further clarified: *Brasserie du Pêcheur SA v Federal Republic of Germany; R v Secretary of State for Transport, ex parte Factortame Ltd* Joined Cases C–46 and 48/93 [1996] ECR I–1029.

While arts 234 and 10 EC can be seen in the broadest context as complementing each other, their relationship is not an essential one. Both serve to ensure compliance with Community law, one from a procedural perspective, the other from a substantive perspective. They are not, however, interdependent on each other.

QUESTION THREE

Distinguish situations in which a court may make a reference under art 234 of the EC Treaty from ones in which a reference must be made.

University of London LLB Examination
(for External Students) European Community Law June 2000 Q4

General Comment

This basic essay style question rests on knowledge on the preliminary reference procedure under art 234 EC. The emphasis should have been placed on distinguishing between paragraph one situations, in which Member States' courts may exercise discretion in referring to the European Court of Justice, and paragraph two situations, where a court is obliged to make a reference. The answer needed to address what a court of last resort is, but should also have considered situations where no reference need be made due to development of the law by the ECJ. This required analysis of cases such as *CILFIT* v *Ministry of Health* Case 283/81 [1982] ECR 3415 and *Foglia* v *Novello (No 1)* Case 104/79 [1980] ECR 745.

Skeleton Solution

Article 234 EC role and purpose – the distinction between courts that may make and reference and those that must – courts of last resort defined – situations where a reference is not required – acte clair and the *CILFIT* case – *Foglia* and the lack of a question.

Suggested Solution

Article 234 EC provides the European Court of Justice with jurisdiction to provide preliminary references or rulings on a request from the courts of the Member States. The Court has jurisdiction to provide such rulings in relation to the interpretation of the treaties and acts of the institutions; to determine the validity of acts of the institutions; and to interpret the statutes of bodies established by acts of the Council.

This jurisdiction of the European Court fulfils two important functions. First, it provides for legal integration; it offers a means of promoting and ensuring uniformity in the interpretation of Community law. The preliminary reference procedure puts in the hands of the ECJ alone the ability to provide this uniform interpretation, which in turn ensures that Community law maintains supremacy. Second, the preliminary reference procedure provides a means of legal protection for individuals; it complements and completes a system of remedies offering protection via direct actions. Hence, the preliminary reference procedure is referred to as an indirect action. An individual may therefore have recourse to the preliminary reference procedure where there is no other remedy available.

Article 234 EC refers to any court or tribunal of a Member State having the ability to seek a preliminary ruling. The interpretation of such bodies has been a wide one. The determination of the body under national law is, according to *Politi v Italian Ministry of Finance of the Italian Republic* Case 43/71 [1971] ECR 1039, irrelevant. The European Court has instead used a number of criteria to determine whether the body is able to make a reference, such as: whether it is established by law; whether it is permanent; whether it has compulsory jurisdiction; whether its procedure is inter pares; whether it applies rules of law; and whether it is independent. Hence, in *Nordsee Deutsche Hochseefischerei GmbH v Reederei Mond Hochseefischerei Nordstern AG* Case 102/81 [1982] ECR 1095 an arbitral tribunal was capable of making a reference to the ECJ.

According to the terms of art 234 EC, paragraph one, the power of a court or tribunal to request such a reference is within their discretion. They may make a request at any stage of the proceedings where they believe it is necessary, although the Court has stated that it generally prefers some inter pares proceeding to have taken place first if possible: *Eurico Italia Srl v Ente Nazionale Risi* Cases C–332, 333 and 335/92 [1994] ECR I–711. There are only two conditions before this discretion can be exercised. First, that there should be a question of interpretation or validity of Community law and, second, that the providing of a preliminary ruling is necessary to enable the body to give judgement.

Paragraph two of art 234 EC, however, places an obligation to refer on one particular type of court or tribunal. These bodies are those against which there is no judicial remedy under national law, in other words, the court of last resort in a Member State's judicial system is obligated to request a preliminary reference if there is a question on the interpretation or validity of Community law requiring an answer before judgement may be given. Determining what a court of last resort is has proved problematic, particularly in Member States where there is a system in operation that results in there being no right of appeal from a particular court or tribunal in the case at hand.

This was the situation in one of the earliest preliminary references to the European Court – *Costa v ENEL* Case 6/64 [1964] ECR 585. In this case there was no appeal available from the magistrate's decision because the amount being claimed was too small. Hence, the magistrate's decision was final in the case at hand. The Court concluded that this situation was one in which the national court was obligated to make a preliminary reference. This was confirmed in *Hoffman-La Roche v Commission* Case 85/76 [1979] ECR 461. In this case the question was whether a court of last resort was the highest appeal court in the national legal system, or one where there was no right of appeal in the case at hand. The Advocate-General argued that a reasonable interpretation of the obligation to refer would be one that rested on the highest court in the actual case – sometimes referred to as the concrete theory.

After some controversy, the UK adopted the concrete theory. The problem in relation to the UK's legal system is the position of the Court of Appeal. In order to access the jurisdiction of the House of Lords, the highest court of law in the land, the House must give its leave, which may be refused. This in turn places the Court of Appeal in the position of being the court of last resort, although it would not have such status of the

House did grant leave. If we apply the concrete theory, the Court of Appeal becomes a court obligated to make a reference under the terms of art 234 EC if leave to the House of Lords is refused. Obviously, if it is granted the House of Lords becomes the court of last resort and is obligated to refer. This indeed was the conclusion in *Chiron Corporation v Murex Diagnostics Ltd* [1995] All ER (EC) 88.

However, there are two situations where even a court of last resort need not make a preliminary reference. These limitations were created and developed by the ECJ, partly as a means of exercising control over the ever-increasing quantity of references made. The first of these limitations on the obligation to refer originates in the decision of the Court in *Da Costa en Schaake NV* v *Nederlandse Belastingadministratie* Cases 28–30/62 [1963] ECR 31. In this case the Court stated that a previous ruling of an identical nature could remove the need to refer. A court could still refer a question to the ECJ if, for example, there were new facts or argument, but if there were not the ECJ would merely refer the national court to the previous ruling.

This development was expanded upon in the case of *CILFIT* v *Ministry of Health* Case 283/81 [1982] ECR 3415 in which the Court declared that the obligation to refer would be removed if there were a previous decision of the Court on the matter, even if the facts were not strictly identical. In other words, previous decisions of the Court may result in an answer being so obvious to any national court that comes across the same point of Community law that there becomes no need to request the ruling. This is referred to as the acte clair doctrine.

To aid national courts in deciding whether the need to refer is unnecessary, the Court provided guidelines in *CILFIT*. The national court should take note of the fact that European Community legislation is drafted in several different languages and comparison should be made between them in order to come to the most accurate interpretation. The Court also pointed out that legal concepts in Community law may not necessarily mean the same as they do in national law. Finally, the Court warned that provisions of Community law have to be put in context and interpreted in the light of the objectives of the treaties. If, with these considerations in made, the national court feels able to rely on the previous rulings of the European Court it may decline to make a preliminary reference.

The acte clair doctrine therefore establishes an informal or de facto doctrine of precedent on which national courts may rely. They are provided with guidelines to help them exercise their discretion, but it should be noted that this discretion is possibly open to abuse. In such cases, there will have been a need to refer but the national court will have made the decision to deal with the Community legal point itself. In the UK such potential for abuse was not helped by the judgement of Lord Denning in *Bulmer (HP) Ltd* v *J Bollinger SA* [1974] Ch 401. In this case Lord Denning provided guidelines for when a preliminary reference was necessary, which included considering: whether the point was conclusive; previous rulings; acte clair; and that the facts should be decided first. At this point the court would have discretion in exercising whether a reference was required, and would do so by applying the following criteria. First, to consider the length of time it would take to receive a ruling from the ECJ. Second, to avoid overloading the European Court. Third, that any question should be clearly formulated and it should be assessed in terms of its difficulty and importance. Finally, the expense that could be incurred and the wishes of the parties were to be considered before any reference was made.

These subjective criteria attracted considerable criticism and resulted in a number of cases where there was a clear need for a reference not finding their way to the ECJ. Over the years though these criteria, whilst still referred to in some instances, have become less significant and courts in the UK are increasingly using the acte clair doctrine appropriately. In *R v International Stock Exchange, ex parte Else* [1993] QB 334, Bingham MR stated that a court should refer unless it had complete confidence in its ability to provide the answer; if it had any real doubt it should refer.

The second limitation on the need or obligation to make a reference stems from the Court's decision in *Foglia v Novello (No 1)* Case 104/79 [1980] ECR 745. Prior to this decision the Court had a very open approach to accepting references, in that it would not criticise why it had been made or would attempt to identify the nature of the question itself, seen, for example, in *Simmenthal SpA v Ministero delle Finanze* Case 35/76 [1976] ECR 1871. However, the Court has since adopted a more rigorous approach, as a means of both reducing its high workload and of asserting its superiority over national courts. In *Foglia* the Court declared that a reference was not necessary because the question being asked was artificial since there was no real dispute between the parties. This was further expanded on in *Foglia v Novello (No 2)* Case 244/80 [1981] ECR 3045. In this case the Court stated clearly that it would not be prepared to provide rulings on matters that were general or hypothetical and that it would check references before accepting them on this basis.

The application of this limitation can be seen in *Meilicke v ADV/ORGA FA Meyer* Case C–83/91 [1992] ECR I–4871 in which the Court declined a reference on the basis that the dispute had not in fact arisen and was therefore merely a hypothetical question on an abstract point of law. Further, in *Pretore Di Genoa v Banchero* Case C–157/92 [1993] ECR I–1085 the Court declined the reference because it was inadequately framed, preventing it from providing any useful interpretation of Community law.

Guidance Notes on References by National Courts for Preliminary References produced in 1996 offer the national courts with help on requesting proper references. The national court must provide: full reasons for its request; the essential facts; the relevant provisions of national law; and, if appropriate, a summary of the parties' arguments.

The preliminary reference procedure provided for under art 234 EC has contributed greatly to the development and uniformity of Community law, ensuring its supremacy over conflicting national law. It has provided the Court with a valuable means of expanding Community law and of 'plugging' gaps in the treaties and secondary legislation. Many important concepts of Community law have been both created and expanded on by the use of this procedure, such as the doctrine of direct effect and State liability. The wide interpretation of a body capable of making such a reference and those bodies obligated to make such a reference have only served to strengthen the reference procedure. The ECJ was never intended to be hierarchically superior to the national courts – they each had separate but equal functions to perform. However, the development of the acte clair doctrine and the ECJ's assertion of its right to check the validity of references has promoted the Court to the apex of the judicial system of the Community.

Chapter 5

The Supremacy of Community Law

5.1   Introduction

5.2   Key points

5.3   Key cases and statute

5.4   Questions and suggested solutions

5.1 Introduction

Community law does not function detached from the legal systems of the Member States, but forms an integral part of each of these individual systems. Principles of Community law may be enforced in the national courts and tribunals of each of the Member States of the Community, including the courts and tribunals of the United Kingdom. Further, within the United Kingdom, even accepted constitutional doctrines and precepts require modification in order to facilitate the reception of Community law.

5.2 Key points

The supremacy of European Community law

None of the treaties, including the EC Treaty, contain express provisions referring to the question of the supremacy of Community law over national law. Notwithstanding this omission, in *Costa* v *ENEL* Case 6/64 [1964] ECR 585, the European Court of Justice, using teleological interpretation, resolved the issue in the following terms:

> '[T]he law stemming from the Treaty, an independent source of law, [cannot], because of its special and original nature, be overridden by domestic legal provisions, however framed, without being deprived of its character as Community law and without the legal basis of the Community itself being called into question.'

Community law therefore prevails over inconsistent provisions of national law, whether passed before or after the Community treaties entered into force. Further, as formulated by the ECJ, the principle of supremacy of EC law must be given effect even within the national legal systems of the Member States. A number of subsequent decisions of the European Court have elaborated on the implications of this doctrine.

a) The principle applies irrespective of whether the inconsistent provision of national law has a civil or criminal character: *Procureur du Roi* v *Dassonville* Case 8/74 [1974] ECR 837.

b) Community law prevails even over inconsistent provisions of the constitutional law of the Member States: *Internationale Handelsgesellschaft GmbH* v *EVGF* Case 11/70 [1970] ECR 1125.

c) The formal source of national law is irrelevant to a determination of supremacy. Both inconsistent legislation and judicial precedents have been declared inapplicable. Even rules of professional bodies may, in certain circumstances, be held inconsistent and thereby inapplicable: *R* v *Royal Pharmaceutical Society of Great Britain, ex parte Association of Pharmaceutical Importers* Cases 266 and 267/87 [1989] ECR 1295.

d) The European Court has extended the principle of supremacy not only to provisions of Community treaties, but also to Community regulations and, in certain instances, to Community directives (see, for example, *Becker (Ursula)* v *Finanzamt Münster-Innenstadt* Case 8/81 [1982] ECR 53 and *Salumificio di Cornuda* Case 130/78 [1979] ECR 867). In addition, general principles of EC law will prevail over inconsistent national law, as in *Wachauf* v *Germany* Case 5/88 [1989] ECR 2609.

e) Member States are obliged to repeal national legislation found to be inconsistent with Community law: *Commission* v *United Kingdom (Re Origin Marking Requirements)* Case 207/83 [1985] ECR 1202.

While the ECJ has vigorously asserted the supremacy of Community law over national law within the Community legal system, a number of national courts initially expressed reservations in relation to this doctrine. These reservations are traditionally examined in relation to the United Kingdom.

Incorporation of Community law into the United Kingdom

Community law became part of the law of the United Kingdom by virtue of the European Communities Act 1972. Section 2(1) of this statute provides:

'All rights, powers, liabilities, obligations and restrictions from time to time created or arising by or under the Treaties, and all such remedies and procedures from time to time provided for by or under the Treaties, as in accordance with the Treaties are without further enactment to be given legal effect or used in the United Kingdom shall be recognised and available in law, and be enforced, allowed and followed accordingly.'

The European Communities Act 1972 was amended by the European Communities (Amendment) Act 1986 in order to give force to the changes to the Community treaties made by the Single European Act 1986.

Similarly the 1972 Act was again amended by the European Communities (Amendment) Act 1993 to give effect to the Treaty on European Union and by the European Communities (Amendment) Act 1998 for the Treaty of Amsterdam.

The effect of the European Communities Act 1972, as amended

The European Communities Act 1972 makes no distinction between Community law enacted before the entry into force of the statute and Community law established after this date. Consequently, in legal proceedings before national courts and tribunals in the United Kingdom, the jurisprudence of the European Court may be invoked regardless of whether the decision in question was rendered before or after 1972. Similarly, Community legislation has force within the United Kingdom regardless of the date of adoption by the Council or Commission.

Judicial notice of all decisions of the European Court has also been taken and matters concerning the interpretation and application of Community law are to be treated as questions of law and not questions of fact, as would be the case if Community law was to be considered 'foreign law' under English conflict of law principles: s3(2) 1972 Act.

Ministerial powers to implement subordinate legislation

Section 2(2) of the 1972 Act allows designated Ministers to make subordinate legislation for the purposes of implementing Community obligations. This provision allows Ministers to fulfil the obligations of the United Kingdom as a consequence of Community directives. In addition, Ministers may provide criminal sanctions in order to enact certain Community measures.

This prerogative is restricted by a number of limitations on the prerogatives of Ministers to enact subordinate legislation. Ministers are not allowed to enact measures which:

a) impose or increase taxation;

b) create new criminal offences punishable by more than two years of imprisonment;

c) sub-delegate legislative authority to other bodies or persons; or

d) introduce subordinate legislation having a retroactive effect.

Power to enact subordinate legislation may only be exercised by the Minister responsible for the administration of the particular Community subject matter.

Parliamentary control over Community secondary legislation

Primary control over Community legislation is exercised by Parliamentary Committees which examine and comment on draft proposals for Community legislation. Each House of Parliament has established select committees to evaluate the implications and ramifications of Community legislation on the political and legal constitution of the United Kingdom.

The House of Commons Select Committee on European Secondary Legislation

The House of Commons Select Committee on European Legislation is better known as the 'Scrutiny Committee'. This committee has been given the following mandate by resolution of the House of Commons:

'To consider draft proposals by the Commission of the European Communities for legislation and other documents published for submission to the Council of Ministers or to the European Council whether or not such documents originate from the Commission.'

The Scrutiny Committee reports on whether or not such proposals raise issues of significant legal or political importance and gives reasons for its opinion.

The House of Lords Select Committee on the European Communities

The House of Lords has established a parallel body known as the Select Committee on the European Communities. The mandate of this body has been given in the following terms:

'To consider Community proposals, whether in draft or otherwise, to obtain all necessary information about them, and to make reports on those which, in the opinion of the committee, raise important questions of policy or principle, and on other questions to which the committee consider that the special attention of the House should be drawn.'

The House of Lords Committee functions through a number of sub-committees which deal with individual subjects of relevance to the Community such as finance, law and external relations. On a number of occasions, the House of Lords Committee has produced reports of exceptional quality and detail concerning the functions of the Community.

Authority of the Select Committees

Neither the House of Commons nor the House of Lords Select Committees has direct influence over the Community decision-making processes. Control over the final content of Community legislation is maintained on the basis of the principle of ministerial responsibility.

The Council of Ministers of the Community is composed of one representative from each Member State. In the case of the United Kingdom representative, he or she will be the Minister of the Crown with responsibility for the particular subject matter upon which Community legislation is being passed. As a consequence of the Parliamentary convention of ministerial responsibility, the same Ministers participating in the Council are also answerable to the British Parliament. This dual responsibility ensures that the scrutiny of Parliament over Community secondary legislation continues.

The reception of Community law by the British courts

The principle difficulty faced by the British courts has been to resolve the doctrine of Parliamentary supremacy with that of Community law. According to Professor Dicey, Parliament may legislate on any matter and no other body may question the validity of a statute (the enrolled act rule). Each successive Parliament is supreme and therefore no one Parliament may be bound by its predecessors or bind a successor by entrenching legislation (implied repeal). Consequently, under the traditional concept of

Parliamentary sovereignty the European Communities Act 1972 (an ordinary statute) should be subject to implied repeal by any latter legislation.

The courts and tribunals of the United Kingdom have generally reacted positively towards the reception of Community law as part of the UK legal system. The following are the main instances of this attitude.

a) The courts have been willing to utilise the procedures established for preliminary references to the European Court.

b) The House of Lords itself has embraced the teleological approach to the interpretation of Community law as opposed to the literal approach used in the interpretation of English law: *Lister* v *Forth Dry Dock and Engineering Co* [1989] 1 All ER 1134.

c) UK court will apply Community law without prompting from the European Court: *Kirklees Metropolitan Borough Council* v *Wickes Building Supplies* [1992] 3 WLR 170.

d) The British courts have accepted the notion that Community law overrules pre-1972 statutes since the 1972 Act incorporated all existing Community law at that date into UK law: *Shields* v *E Coomes (Holdings) Ltd* [1979] 1 All ER 456.

e) In *R* v *Secretary of State Transport, ex parte Factortame and Others* [1990] 3 CMLR 59 the House of Lords accepted that EC law was supreme over national law, regardless of the fact that the statute (Merchant Shipping Act 1988) had been enacted after the European Communities Act 1972. Consequently, the constitutional principle of implied repeal had to be set aside to secure protection for the EC rights of Community individuals. Lord Bridge concluded:

> 'Under the terms of the 1972 Act it has always been clear that it was the duty of a United Kingdom court, when delivering final judgment, to override any rule of national law found to be in conflict with any directly enforceable rule of Community law.'

f) The British courts, though, have asserted that should Parliament expressly state that the provisions of a statute are to stand, regardless of whether they are inconsistent with the 1972 Act or Community law, they will simply apply the statute: *Macarthys* v *Smith* [1979] 3 All ER 325 and *Garland* v *British Rail Engineering* [1982] 2 All ER 402 (HL).

5.3 Key cases and statute

- *Bulmer (HP) Ltd* v *J Bollinger SA* [1974] Ch 401
  Lord Denning's much criticised attempt to formulate rules to regulate the discretion of British courts to refer questions of Community law to the European Court

- *Commission* v *United Kingdom (Re Origin Marking Requirements)* Case 207/83 [1985] ECR 1202
  Member States are obliged to repeal national legislation found to be inconsistent with Community law

- *Costa* v *ENEL* Case 6/64 [1964] ECR 585
  That EC law has supremacy over conflicting or inconsistent national law

- *Internationale Handelsgesellschaft GmbH* v *EVGF* Case 11/70 [1970] ECR 1125
  Community law prevails even over inconsistent provisions of the constitutional law of the Member States

- *Lister* v *Forth Dry Dock and Engineering Co* [1989] 1 All ER 1134
  Application by the House of Lords of the teleological approach to interpretation adopted by the European Court

- *Macarthys* v *Smith* [1979] 3 All ER 325; *Garland* v *British Rail Engineering* [1982] 2 All ER 402 (HL)
  Should Parliament expressly state that the provisions of a statute are to stand, regardless of whether they are inconsistent with the European Communities Act 1972 or Community law, the courts will simply apply the statute

- *R* v *Secretary of State for Transport, ex parte Factortame and Others* [1990] 3 CMLR 59
  EC law is supreme over national law, regardless of whether the legislation is enacted after the European Communities Act 1972. Consequently, the constitutional principle of implied repeal has to be set aside to secure protection of EC rights

- European Communities Act 1972 – incorporates Community law into the law of the United Kingdom

5.4 Questions and suggested solutions

QUESTION ONE

'Among all the Member States of the European Community, the United Kingdom has demonstrated the greatest reluctance to observe the obligations imposed by the Community treaties and the duties created thereunder.' Discuss.

Written by the Editor

General Comment

A narrative question requiring a descriptive answer.

Skeleton Solution

The nature of the obligation to respect Community law: art 10 EC – the record of the United Kingdom – examples of deviance from the principles of Community law – the record of the United Kingdom in contrast to other Member States.

Suggested Solution

Violations of Community obligations may arise from both positive acts and omissions on the part of Member States. Article 10 EC requires Member States to take all appropriate measures to ensure respect for Community obligations and to 'abstain from any measure which could jeopardise the attainment of the objectives of this Treaty'. Acts and omissions by Member States may also contravene the express provisions of the Community treaties or may infringe the contents of measures of secondary legislation lawfully enacted under the Community treaties.

A common ground of action against a Member State is the existence of national legislation which is incompatible with either the Community treaties or Community legislation. For example, in 1988, the United Kingdom enacted the Merchant Shipping Act 1988 which required that a number of conditions be satisfied before a fishing vessel could be registered as British. A fishing vessel was eligible for registration only if the vessel was British-owned, was managed or operated from the United Kingdom, or was owned by a British company. The European Commission took the view that this legislation constituted discrimination on the basis of nationality, contrary to arts 10 and 43 EC. After entering into unsuccessful discussions with the United Kingdom, the Commission initiated proceedings against the United Kingdom for enacting legislation which contravened the terms of the Community treaties: *Commission* v *United Kingdom* Case C–246/89R [1989] ECR I–3125.

Member States may also be held to have infringed Community law as a result of the enactment of secondary legislation. Thus, in *France* v *United Kingdom (Re Fishing Mesh)* Case 141/78 [1979] ECR 2923, the European Court held that the United Kingdom had violated its Community obligations by enacting an Order in Council which imposed a minimum mesh size for fishing. This requirement was held to contravene Community law on the ground that appropriate consultations had not been held prior to the enactment of the measure.

Administrative practices may also be held to contravene Community law. Customs measures and practices are most susceptible to action by the Commission for failure to observe Community law. For example, in *Conegate Limited* v *HM Customs and Excise* Case 121/85 [1986] ECR 1007, the United Kingdom customs authorities took the view that inflatable dolls manufactured in Germany could not be imported into the United Kingdom on the ground that they were indecent and therefore contrary to the rules established for the administration of imports. The European Court held that such practices contravened Community law because the United Kingdom did not prohibit the manufacture of such products within the United Kingdom and consequently such practices constituted a measure having an equivalent effect to a quantitative restrict.

Proceedings are also frequently initiated against Member States for failing to implement measures of Community law, and in particular directives. The United Kingdom has often been taken to the European Court for failing to implement directives, particularly in relation to gender discrimination; for example, *Marshall* v

Southampton and South-West Hampshire Area Health Authority (Teaching) (No 1) Case 152/84 [1986] ECR 723. However, in part this possibility has been mitigated by the doctrine of vertical direct effect adopted by the Court.

Neither the constitutional structure of a Member State nor pre-existing provisions of national law constitute a defence against a Member State for the enforcement of Community law. This is so even when a constituent part of a Member State – such as a region or a province – exercises exclusive authority over a particular subject matter, independently of the control of the central government. Consequently, the liability of a Member State arises whatever the agency of the state whose action or inaction is the cause of the failure to fulfil its obligations, even in the case of a constitutionally independent institution.

A Member State may even theoretically be liable for the acts of judicial bodies or tribunals for rendering decisions which are contrary to Community law. Thus a refusal of a national court of final instance to refer a question of Community law under the preliminary reference procedure could constitute a violation of Community law, unless the conduct of the court could be justified under the criteria established in *CILFIT* v *Ministry of Health* Case 283/81 [1982] ECR 3415. This applies despite the fact that the constitutions of a number of Member States rest on the doctrine of the separation of powers. During the five-year period between 1993 and 1998, the United Kingdom and Denmark had the least enforcement actions initiated against them. While Denmark had less than 15 actions brought against it in the European Court, the United Kingdom had less than 20. These statistics contrast extremely favourably against those of a number of the original Member States of the Community. Italy was the Member State which was the subject of most actions, with approximately 100 actions initiated against it. France and Belgium maintained equally unimpressive records during the same period. Consequently, it is completely inaccurate to suggest that the United Kingdom is the worst offender in respecting its Community obligations.

Further, the United Kingdom also maintains an impeccable record as regards implementing the adverse decisions of the European Court when cases are decided against its favour. Since the European Community is an organisation based on the rule of law, it is wholly appropriate that disputes between the United Kingdom and the Commission be settled through litigation. It is, however, indefensible that some states refuse to implement the decisions of the Court in full knowledge that they are contravening their Community obligations. The fact that the United Kingdom rarely, if ever, adopts such a policy is a reflection of the true commitment of the United Kingdom to the spirit and idea of the Community.

QUESTION TWO

'The principle of supremacy of Community law over national law has been accepted more readily by some Member States, more grudgingly by others.'

Discuss this development with reference to the United Kingdom and at least one other Member State.

University of London LLB Examination
(for External Students) European Community Law June 1995 Q1

General Comment

This question in fact has two separate parts. The first requires analysis of the case law of the English courts applying the principle of the supremacy of Community law. The second requires discussion of the attitude of the courts of another Member State relative to the application of the principle. While the first part of the question is relatively straightforward, the second part is not normally within the scope of the syllabus for this subject and therefore presents more difficulties.

Skeleton Solution

The creation of the principle of supremacy through the jurisprudence of the ECJ – the European Communities Act 1972 and the post-*Factortame* judgments of the English courts – the judgments of the House of Lords in the *Factortame* series of cases – the jurisprudence of the German constitutional courts: *Internationale Handelsgesellschaft* and *Brunner* v *The European Union Treaty*.

Suggested Solution

No provision of the EC Treaty contains an express term regulating the issue of the supremacy between Community and the various national laws of the Member States. The only implied reference to the issue of supremacy is art 10 EC which imposes a duty on all Member States to adopt appropriate measures to ensure that the obligations of the Treaty are observed, together with an additional duty to abstain from all acts which might jeopardise the achievement of the objectives of the Treaty.

Nevertheless, the principle of the supremacy of Community law over national law is a well-established principle, having first been recognised by the European Court of Justice in *Costa* v *ENEL* Case 6/64 [1964] ECR 585. In that case, the ECJ held that the objects and purpose of the Community would be frustrated if national law was allowed to deviate from Community law. Community law therefore prevailed over inconsistent provisions of national law, whether passed before or after the EC Treaty entered into force.

The ECJ has also extended the application of the principle of supremacy to different forms of Community law. Clearly the most obvious application of the principle is in cases of inconsistency between provisions of national law and the terms of the EC Treaty. However, the doctrine extends to conflicts between national laws and Community regulation. In addition, the Court has even upheld the supremacy of unimplemented directives, which are capable of direct effect, over inconsistent provisions of national law: *Marshall* v *Southampton and South-West Hampshire Area Health Authority (Teaching) (No 1)* Case 152/84 [1986] ECR 723.

While the ECJ has embraced and vigorously promoted this principle, the same cannot be said for the national courts of the Member States. Many of these have expressed reservations and reticence at accepting the doctrine. To a certain extent, this opposition has varied throughout the Community but, until recently, the courts of the United Kingdom were widely seen as the last bastion of defiance.

The English courts, including the Court of Appeal, were initially adverse to embrace the doctrine of the supremacy of Community law. This opposition was based on the belief that the principle of Parliamentary sovereignty was an unimpeachable basis of British constitutional law. Since not even a British Parliament could bind its successor, it was difficult to see how the legislative hands of Parliament could be tied by a foreign supranational organisation.

The European Communities Act 1972 made no reference to the principle of supremacy. It merely provided that all Community law provisions which are directly effective became part of United Kingdom law. Section 2(4) did state that 'any enactments passed or to be passed, other than one contained in this Part of the Act, shall be construed and have effect subject to the foregoing provisions of this section'. This was held by some commentators to mean that the United Kingdom courts must interpret Community law in accordance with the principles laid down by the ECJ, including the principle of supremacy. However, the English courts did not, in general, accept this interpretation willingly.

Initially, the English courts adopted a number of diverse tactics to reconcile the doctrine of supremacy with that of the principle of Parliamentary supremacy. There was little doubt that Community law prevailed over pre-1972 British legislation quite simply because of the force of that legislation itself and the general principle that earlier statutes must give way to later statutes. The courts were therefore perfectly willing to accept that Community law overruled pre-1972 statutes: *Shields* v *E Coomes (Holdings) Ltd* [1979] 1 All ER 456. There was, however, considerable difference of opinion as to how the principle of supremacy would apply to post-1972 statutes.

To avoid potential conflicts between Acts of Parliament and Community law, a series of principles of interpretation were derived by the English courts to assist in the application and construction of inconsistent provisions. Thus, statutes of Parliament were to be interpreted in such a manner as not to conflict with Community law: *Garland* v *British Rail Engineering* [1982] 2 All ER 402. In the event of an inconsistency, such a defect could be attributed to the oversight of the Parliamentary draftsmen. On this basis, even Lord Denning was prepared to give precedence to Community law and in *Shields* v *E Coomes (Holdings) Ltd* after referring to *Costa* v *ENEL* Case 6/64 [1964] ECR 585 and *Simmenthal* v *Commission* Case 92/78 [1979] ECR 777, he declared that '[i]f a tribunal should find any ambiguity in the statutes or any inconsistency with Community law, then it should resolve it by giving primacy of Community law'. However, in a rejoinder to this dictum, the qualification was made that this principle only applied in the event of accidental oversight and not when Parliament had expressed a deliberate intention to repudiate Community law. A clear intention on the part of Parliament to deviate from Community law would therefore be given effect by the English courts.

It was not until the issue was raised in *R v Secretary for State for Transport, ex parte Factortame Ltd and Others* [1990] 2 AC 85, that the House of Lords had to directly address the issue of application of a United Kingdom statute which was inconsistent with the terms of Community law. In this case, the House of Lords considered whether the terms of the Merchant Shipping Act 1988, which prevented non-British merchant ship-owners from registering their vessels as British, were consistent with the principle of non-discrimination on the grounds of nationality imposed by art 12 EC.

The House of Lords referred the issue of supremacy to the European Court for a ruling and the ECJ ruled ([1990] ECR I–2433) that Community law precludes the application of a rule of national law which would constitute an obstacle to the application of Community law. This was consistent with the views of Lord Bridge of Harwich who, when referring the issue to the European Court, observed that rules of United Kingdom law which render the exercise of directly enforceable Community rights excessively difficult or virtually impossible must be overridden.

Once the decision of the European Court was returned to the House of Lords, that court was required to apply the judgment of the ECJ to the facts of the case before it. In doing so, Lord Bridge felt compelled to address the public criticisms of the House of Lords and its readiness to accept the principle of the supremacy of Community law. In particular, he observed:

> 'Some public comments on the decision of the ECJ, affirming the jurisdiction of the courts of Member States to override national legislation if necessary ... have suggested that this was a novel and dangerous invasion by a Community institution of the sovereignty of Parliament. But such comments are based on a misconception. If the supremacy within the European Community of Community law over the national law of Member States was not always inherent in the EC Treaty it was certainly well established in the jurisprudence of the ECJ long before the United Kingdom joined the Community. Thus, whatever limitation of its sovereignty Parliament accepted when it enacted the European Communities Act 1972 was entirely voluntary.' (*R v Secretary of State for Transport, ex parte Factortame and Others* [1990] 3 CMLR 59.)

In fact, the English courts have accepted the fact that the sovereignty of Parliament, exercised in the form of statutes, is no longer absolute with considerable dignity. Acceptance of the doctrine by the House of Lords was a resounding endorsement of the principle that Community law prevails over English law, regardless of the academic constitutional obstacles to the adoption of the principle. Subsequently, the English supreme courts have applied the principle of supremacy without even requiring a preliminary reference to the European Court for guidance: *R v Secretary of State for Employment, ex parte Equal Opportunities Commission* [1995] 1 AC 1. Therefore, it can be said with some authority that, despite the grudging acceptance of the English courts to the principle, it has now become a fundamental principle of British constitutional law.

It is also true that other Member States of the Community have reluctantly endorsed the principle of the supremacy of Community law. Even the German courts were initially sceptical of endorsing it. Indeed, in *Internationale Handelsgesellschaft GmbH v EVGF* Case 11/70 [1970] ECR 1125, the German courts appeared ready to refuse to accept the doctrine. The facts behind this case are as follows. A number of Community regulations specified that companies would lose deposits lodged with Community authorities if full use was not made of certain export licences. These deposits were required in order for licences for exports to be granted. This scheme was challenged by a German company as being inconsistent with German constitutional law because it infringed the constitutional principle that the reasonable freedom of an individual to carry on business should not be unduly infringed.

The German supreme court referred this question to the ECJ for a preliminary reference, but in the terms of reference it was made clear that the German courts would refuse to accept that Community law prevailed over a fundamental freedom embodied in the German constitution. In fact, the ECJ reasserted the principle of the supremacy of Community law once again, but managed to avoid direct confrontation by stating that such fundamental human rights were also part of Community law and could also be enforced through the Community legal system. Hence, there was no inconsistency in applying the German constitutional principle.

Quite clearly, from the point of view of the German constitutional courts, this matter remained unresolved. However, over the course of time, the German courts have also softened their position. Indeed, in light of the German constitutional court's decision in *Brunner* v *The European Union Treaty* [1994] 1 CMLR 57, it is unlikely that the German courts would refuse to accept the principle of the supremacy of Community law. In that case, the constitutional court ruled that no provision of the European Union Treaty infringed the German constitution. Since the Treaty on European Union amended the EC Treaty, from which the principle of supremacy is derived, this was an indirect endorsement of the principle of supremacy. It is therefore highly unlikely that a German court would refuse to accept the force of this principle even in the event of a conflict with the terms of the German constitution.

QUESTION THREE

'The supremacy of EC law over national law has been accepted throughout the Community. However, some courts and countries have experienced particular difficulties in this respect.'

Discuss.

University of London LLB Examination
(for External Students) European Community Law June 2000 Q5

General Comment

This basic essay style question requires knowledge of the doctrine of supremacy of Community law. To offer a successful answer to this question, discussion of the ECJ's jurisprudence was essential. However, the question asks for more than a simple explanation of cases establishing the principle, in that it also requires analysis of the application of the principle in various Member States. Reference to the UK would have gone some way to achieving this, but the better answers would have referred to the problems encountered in other Member States such as, for example, France and Germany.

Skeleton Solution

The definition of supremacy and its development by the ECJ – relevant cases such as *Van Gend en Loos, Costa, Internationale Handelsgesellschaft, Simmenthal* etc – problems in selected Member States – France, Germany, Italy, Belgium and the United Kingdom.

Suggested Solution

None of the treaties expressly assert that Community law has precedence over national law. The creation and development of this most fundamental of Community law principles was achieved by the European Court of Justice.

In *Van Gend en Loos* v *Netherlands* Case 26/62 [1963] ECR 1 the Court concluded that the EEC Treaty was not a mere agreement binding only the Member States. This was supported by the fact that institutions had been established with sovereign rights; a new legal order had been created and the Member States had limited their sovereign rights on membership.

The principle was developed in the case of *Costa* v *ENEL* Case 6/64 [1964] ECR 585 in which the Italian government argued that the ECJ lacked the jurisdiction to hear a reference since the case involved national law that had been passed subsequent to the EEC Treaty. The European Court emphasised three aspects of the Community: it was of unlimited duration; it had autonomous power; and the Member States had limited their competence by transferring power to the Community institutions. Thus, Community law had been integrated into the Member States' legal systems and was binding on them. In justifying this conclusion, the ECJ pointed to the spirit of the EEC Treaty – Member States had accepted the new legal order, which was a permanent limitation on their sovereign rights, and were unable to subsequently establish a contrary body of national law – and the wording of art 249 EC. Under this provision, regulations could be passed that would have direct applicability in all Member States. Such a measure would be meaningless if Member States were then able to pass later inconsistent legislative measures.

The obligation placed on national courts to secure the primacy of Community law was explained in *Simmenthal* v *Commission* Case 92/78 [1979] ECR 777. Every national court is required to apply Community law in its entirety and set aside any conflicting national law, whether prior or subsequent to the relevant Community rule; only in this way could the rights of Community individuals be protected.

This obligation applies regardless of the nature of the conflicting national law, be it legislative, administrative, jurisdictional or indeed a constitutional principle. For example, in *Internationale Handelsgesellschaft GmbH v EVGF* Case 11/70 [1970] ECR 1125 the German court believed that a system imposed under EC regulations was unconstitutional, because it breached freedoms enshrined in the German constitution. The ECJ held that the validity of a Community measure may not be questioned by reference to national law, even if it was a fundamental constitutional right.

The principle of supremacy is an essential one to the success of the Community legal order, but it is one that has caused difficulties for the national courts in a number of Member States.

France

The French courts have had some difficulty in accepting the supremacy of Community law. To do so they have used a variety of rather contrived methods, for example, in *Administration des Douanes v Société 'Cafés Jacques Vabre' et SARL Weigel et Cie* [1975] 2 CMLR 336 the Cour de Cassation relied on Article 55 of the French constitution to achieve supremacy of EC law. However, in *Von Kempis v Geldof* [1976] 2 CMLR 152 the same court relied on the jurisprudence of the ECJ to achieve supremacy of EC law.

The Conseil d'Etat, the supreme French administrative court, had the most difficulties accepting the principle. This court refused to grant EC law supremacy in the case of *Syndicat Général de Fabricants de Semoules de France* [1970] CMLR 395 but this initial reluctance has since been overcome. In *Nicolo (Raoul Georges)* [1990] 1 CMLR 173 the Conseil d'Etat recognised that Treaty Articles would take precedence over all national law and in *Boisdet, Re* [1991] 1 CMLR 3 that regulations were supreme. However, the Conseil d'Etat has been less willing to accept another principle of Community law, namely the direct effect of directives. It has consistently refused to permit individuals to rely on the direct effect of a directive as the basis for an action to annul an individual administrative act: *Minister for the Interior v Cohn-Bendit* [1980] 1 CMLR 543.

Germany

The German judicial response to *Internationale Handelsgesellschaft*, described above, was not a promising start to acceptance of the supremacy of EC law. The German federal constitutional court refused to acknowledge the absolute supremacy of EC law and adhered to German constitutional rules, justified on the basis that their constitution offered greater protection of human rights. This position was finally reversed in *Application of Wünsche Handelsgesellschaft (Solange II)* [1987] 3 CMLR 225 where the court recognised that EC law offered human rights protection and that consequently a preliminary reference of the ECJ would not be subject to review. The principle of supremacy of EC law was specifically affirmed a year later in *Kloppenberg, Re* [1988] 3 CMLR 1. This decision though must be contrasted with the federal court's conclusions in *Brunner* v *The European Union Treaty* [1994] 1 CMLR 57. In this case, which involved a challenge to the German Parliament's ability to ratify the Treaty on European Union, the federal constitutional court indicated its respect for the principle of supremacy, but also made it clear that it this was the case because German law provided for it. If it wished, the German Parliament could pass a contrary act, which would revoke membership. In a delicate balancing act, therefore, the German court recognised the supremacy of Community law whilst retaining ultimate German State sovereignty – a position not unlike that of the UK.

Similar to the French courts, the German courts have had difficulties with the effect of directives, but in this case in relation to indirect effect. For example, in *A Rehabilitation Centre, Re* [1992] 2 CMLR 21 the Federal Supreme Court refused to accept the obligation to interpret national law in the light of Council Directive 76/207.

Italy

The German response was that initially also adopted by the Italian courts after the decision in *Costa* v *ENEL* Case 6/64 [1964] ECR 585, described above. The Italian Constitutional Court preferred to abide by national constitutional principles. The process of accepting the supremacy of EC law began in *Frontini* v *Ministero delle Finanze* [1974] 2 CMLR 372 where the court based its decision largely on ECJ jurisprudence. However, the court also claimed it had the ability to check EC secondary legislation to ensure its compatibility with Italian constitutional principles. Its right to do this was reaffirmed in *SpA Fragd* v *Amministrazione delle Finanze* [1989] 72 RDI. However, the court has generally accepted the supremacy of Community law and has shown willingness to use the ECJ's jurisprudence in coming to its judgments.

Belgium

Belgium is a dualist State, like the United Kingdom, but has had far fewer problems in accepting the supremacy of Community law. For a treaty in a dualist State to create rights and obligations enforceable in national courts, it must be incorporated into national law by the passing of legislation. This was achieved in Belgium by statute; however, the Belgian constitution did not expressly state that international law was supreme to national law. Consequently, the incorporating statute was vulnerable to the doctrine of lex posterior. The Belgian Cour de Cassation removed this potential threat to the supremacy of Community law in *Ministre des Affaires Economiques* v *SA Fromagerie Franco-Suisse 'Le Ski'* [1972] CMLR 330 by concluding that the lex posterior rule did not apply – a later statute would never be intended to conflict with the EC Treaty because a treaty was a superior form of law.

The United Kingdom

The UK's constitution is both dualist and based on the doctrine of parliamentary sovereignty. Parliament may legislate on any matter and that each successive Parliament is supreme, unable to bind either its predecessors or successors. This is achieved through the doctrine of implied repeal; if two statutes conflict, the later will prevail. In order for the rights and obligations under the Treaty to be enforceable in the UK, legislation was required. The UK passed the European Communities Act (ECA) 1972, which would have been subject to repeal by any inconsistent later legislation. It is this problem – reconciling the supremacy of Community law with parliamentary supremacy – that rests at the heart of the difficulties faced by the courts.

The most important provisions of the ECA 1972 are ss2(1) and 2(4). The former provides for the direct applicability of Community law in the UK. The latter requires that any enactment passed, or to be passed, shall be construed and have effect subject to Community law obligations.

Originally, the courts appeared to have considerable difficulty in accepting the doctrine of Community law supremacy. In *Bulmer (HP) Ltd* v *J Bollinger SA* [1974] Ch 401 Lord Denning stated that the Treaty had no more force than a statute. In *Felixstowe Dock and Railway Company* v *British Transport and Docks Board* [1976] 2 CMLR 655 Lord Denning also suggested that if an Act was passed that conflicted with Community law, it would be the duty of the courts to uphold the Act, regardless of the ECA 1972.

However, a change of attitude occurred when the courts used s2(4) ECA 1972 as a rule of construction. In other words, the courts concluded that were obligated under the ECA 1972 to interpret national law in accordance with Community obligations. This approach was adopted by the Court of Appeal in *Macarthys* v *Smith* [1979] 3 All ER 325 and the House of Lords in *Garland* v *British Rail Engineering* [1982] 2 All ER 402.

The doctrine of the supremacy of Community law requires more than simply interpreting national law to comply with Community law, especially since this may not always be possible particularly if the national law is in direct conflict. The courts appeared willing to accept the notion that pre-1972 national laws in conflict with Community law were invalid, as held in *Sheilds* v *E Coomes (Holdings) Ltd* [1979] 1 All ER 456. The problem was whether a UK statute post-1972 that directly breached Community law would be applied in accordance with the doctrine of implied repeal, or whether the courts would be prepared to accept the supremacy of Community law. This did not occur until the landmark case of *R* v *Secretary of State for Transport, ex parte Factortame Ltd and Others* [1990] 2 AC 85.

In this case the statute was the Merchant Shipping Act 1988. The Act directly contravened the EC Treaty in terms of both discriminating on the basis of nationality and depriving the claimants of the right to freedom of establishment. The issue was whether, according to the basic principle of implied repeal, it would be upheld by the courts. On a request for a preliminary reference by the House of Lords, the ECJ concluded that any provision of national law that impaired the effectiveness of Community law by preventing national courts from setting aside national law in contravention of Community law, thereby denying individuals their Community law rights, had to be set aside. Thus, even the constitutional principle of implied repeal had to be set aside to secure individuals their Community law rights.

The House of Lords, granting the applicants interim relief, concluded that under the terms of the ECA 1972 it was the duty of the UK courts to override any rule of national law found to be in conflict with any enforceable rule of Community law. This decision abides by the doctrine of the supremacy of Community law, but does so in a way similar to the German courts, in that it maintains the doctrine of supremacy of Parliament too. Thus, the House of Lords concluded that EC law was supreme because Parliament intended that to be the case when it voluntarily joined the Community. This conclusion is also witnessed in the judgements of Lord Denning and Lord Diplock in *Macarthys* v *Smith* [1979] 3 All ER 325 and *Garland* v *British Rail Engineering* [1982] 2 All ER 402. In both of these cases, their Lordships concluded that if Parliament produced a statute that expressly stated it was intended to breach Community law, the courts would uphold it. The ECA 1972 is semi-entrenched in that it cannot be subject to implied repeal; however, it could be expressly repealed. Of course, the chance of this occurring is small and in this light membership of the EC, whilst claimed by the UK courts to be as a result merely of a delegation of sovereignty, could perhaps be concluded to be a more permanent limitation on parliamentary supremacy.

The UK courts though have had similar problems to France and Germany in relation to the direct effect of directives. In particular, there have been problems in relation to indirect effect. In *Duke* v *GEC Reliance* [1988] 2 WLR 359 the House of Lords refused to accept the principle that national law had to be interpreted in the light of a non-directly effective directive. Since then there have been examples, such as *Lister* v *Forth Dry Dock and Engineering Co* [1989] 1 All ER 1134, of where the courts have been prepared to interpret national law in the light of directives. In contrast, the court in *R* v *British Coal Corporation and Secretary of State for Trade and Industry, ex parte Vardy* [1993] ICR 720 refused to interpret a statute in line with a directive because it was clearly intended to be contrary to the directive.

In conclusion, the doctrine of supremacy created via teleological interpretation of the EC Treaty by the European Court is one fundamental to Community law. It requires all national law, be it administrative, judicial, legislative or even fundamental to the constitution of the Member States, to be set aside. The principle has caused difficulties in some national courts and some of these problems remain in relation to the effect of directives, but generally the principle of supremacy of EC law is one accepted by the Member States.

Chapter 6

Fundamental Principles of European Community Law I: Direct Effect and State Liability

6.1   Introduction

6.2   Key points

6.3   Key cases and materials

6.4   Questions and suggested solutions

6.1 Introduction

The Community treaties create a new legal order, which interacts with the legal systems of all the Member States. This unique form of law required the development of fundamental principles to provide a basis for its proper functioning. Many of these essential principles were not originally stated in the treaties, but have been developed by the European Court of Justice using teleological (purposive) interpretation. Examples of this phenomenon include the principle of supremacy, considered in the previous chapter, and direct effect and state liability, discussed in this chapter. Other examples include human rights protection, non-discrimination on the basis of nationality and non-discrimination on the basis of gender. The latter two were elaborated on in the treaties, but all these principles have been substantially developed by the European Court. These principles will be considered in Chapter 7. Before proceeding to discuss the principles of direct effect and state liability, it is important to identify the primary and secondary sources of EC law.

Primary sources consist of the international agreements entered into by the Member States for the purpose of establishing the constitution of the Community. Secondary sources are measures enacted by Community institutions exercising the authority vested in them by the Community treaties. Naturally, primary sources of Community law prevail over secondary sources in the event of a conflict.

6.2 Key points

Primary sources of Community law

The three Community treaties, together with a number of international agreements formally amending these treaties, form the constitution of the Community and are the ultimate source of legal authority within the Community system. These treaties function as primary sources of law in two ways.

a) The Community treaties prescribe the powers of Community institutions to promulgate secondary legislation. Failure on the part of an institution to respect the limits of authority prescribed in the treaties will render a putative measure null and void: *Commission* v *Council (Re Generalised Tariff Preferences)* Case 45/86 [1987] ECR 1493.

b) The Community treaties, in certain circumstances, establish fundamental principles of Community law which have direct effect and may be relied upon by individuals before national courts and tribunals.

Community agreements with third states

Each of the three Community treaties confers authority on the Community to enter into international agreements with third states dealing with matters which fall within the competence of the Community. These agreements are also capable of providing a source of directly effective principles of Community law: *Demirel* v *Stadt Schwabisch GmbH* Case 12/86 [1987] ECR 3719. The Court has also held that such agreements prevail over inconsistent provisions of national law: *Hauptzollamt Mainz* v *Kupferberg* Case 104/81 [1982] ECR 3641.

In certain circumstances, the decisions of bodies established to administer such treaties may also be given such an effect. For example, in *SZ Sevince* v *Staatssecretaris van Justitie* Case 192/89 [1990] ECR I–3461 the Court held that a decision made by a body established by virtue of a Community agreement may be directly effective when, regard being had to its wording and the purpose and nature of the agreement itself, the provision contains a clear and precise obligation.

No decision has yet been rendered on the issue of whether the terms of such agreements would prevail over inconsistent secondary legislation. However, under no circumstances would the European Court support the principle that the terms of such agreements are capable of prevailing over conflicting provisions of the Community treaties.

Intra-Community agreements

Member States are authorised to negotiate intra-Community agreements to regulate particular subjects including the protection of persons and the protection of individual rights against discrimination, the abolition of double taxation within the Community, mutual recognition of corporations having their seat of incorporation in another Member State, and a system for the reciprocal recognition and enforcement of judgments among Member States.

A number of Conventions have been negotiated among the Member States to achieve certain of these objectives including the following.

a) The Convention on Jurisdiction and Enforcement of Judgments in Civil and Commercial Matters 1968.

b) The Convention on the Law Applicable to Contractual Obligations 1980.

c) The Convention on the Mutual Recognition of Companies and Bodies Corporate 1968.

In addition, the Lugano Convention on Jurisdiction and the Enforcement of Judgments in Civil and Commercial Matters 1988 extends the terms of the 1968 Jurisdiction and Judgments Convention to the European Free Trade Association (EFTA) countries on the basis of reciprocity with Community Member States.

In the past, these Conventions have been given effect through the traditional national procedures for the incorporation of international agreements. Within the United Kingdom, this procedure involves the enactment of enabling legalisation. For example, the 1968 Jurisdiction and Judgments Convention has force of law within the United Kingdom by virtue of the Civil Jurisdiction and Judgments Act 1982.

Secondary sources of Community law

Both the Council of Ministers and the European Commission have authority to enact secondary legislation although in order to do so they must have authority over the particular subject matter by virtue of the terms of the Community treaties. Article 249 EC specifies three separate forms of Community secondary legislation.

Regulations

A regulation is a general legislative instrument which is binding in its entirety throughout the Community and which is directly applicable within the legal orders of the Member States without the need of intervention on the part of national legislative bodies.

Directives

A directive also has binding effect, but only against the Member State to whom it is addressed and only in relation to the result to be achieved. Directives are not automatically applicable within Member States since Member States exercise a discretion to select the appropriate form of domestic law to incorporate the obligations arising from the directive into national law.

Decisions

A decision is binding in its entirety, but only upon those to whom it is addressed. Decisions may be addressed to both Member States and individuals.

Authority is also conferred upon the Council of Ministers and the Commission to make recommendations and to deliver opinions. Neither of these acts involves the creation of measures that have legal effect.

The distinction between the direct applicability and the direct effect of Community law

The concept of direct applicability only applies to Community regulations and is derived from art 249 EC which provides that regulations shall be 'directly applicable in all Member States'. The quality of direct applicability means that regulations are automatically incorporated into the domestic laws of the Member States immediately upon enactment by the appropriate Community institution. Individual and legal persons may therefore rely on rights and duties created by Community regulations before national courts and tribunals.

The quality of direct applicability was only expressly conferred upon Community regulations. Neither individual Treaty provisions nor Community directives were intended to be directly applicable. In fact the EC Treaty expressly provides that the national authorities of the Member States retain discretion in selecting the appropriate instrument of national law to implement Community directives. However, the European Court has significantly modified this provision by establishing the principle of direct effect which applies to Treaty provisions and also directives that have not been implemented by Member States within the prescribed period.

While the principles of direct applicability and direct effect perform the same function – to create enforceable rights on behalf of individuals – each principle applies to different forms of Community legislation in different ways.

The direct applicability of Community regulations

The essence of the principle of direct applicability is that a Community regulation which has entered force may be enforced by or against the subjects of the regulation and that the application of such a measure is independent of any measure of national law.

In the case of *Politi v Italian Ministry of Finance of the Italian Republic* Case 43/71 [1971] ECR 1039 the Court declared that 'by reason of their nature' regulations had direct effect. Regulations are capable of creating both vertical and horizontal directly effective rights.

However, whilst regulations have direct applicability, some require further legislative action to be taken and in such cases, will not necessarily be capable of having direct effect: *Leonesio v Italian Ministry of Agriculture and Forestry* Case 93/71 [1972] ECR 287. In addition, some regulations are addressed not to individuals but to Member States. In such cases, whether the regulation is capable of creating enforceable rights will depend on its subject matter and the nature of the group to which it is addressed: *Becker (Ursula) v Finanzamt Munster-Innenstadt* Case 8/81 [1982] ECR 53.

Direct effect and Community treaty provisions

No provision of any Community treaty expressly authorises the use of individual treaty provisions as a reservoir of legal principles, but from the very formation of the Community the European Court has sought to achieve this object. In *Van Gend en Loos v Netherlands* Case 26/62 [1963] ECR 1, the European Court held that where a Treaty Article imposes a clear and unconditional obligation upon a Member State, unqualified by any reservation reserving the right of legislative intervention, such a provision could be capable of direct effect and individual rights could be created which were enforceable in municipal courts.

Three specific conditions are therefore required for a provision of a Community treaty to have direct effect.

a) The provision being relied upon must be clear and precise: *Gimenez Zaera v Instituto Nacional de la Seguridad Social* Case 187/85 [1987] ECR 3697.

b) The term must be unqualified and not subject to a right of legislative intervention (unconditional): *Diamantarbeiders v Brachfeld & Chougol Diamond Co* Cases 2 and 3/69 [1969] ECR 211.

c) The obligation must not confer a discretion on either Member States or Community institutions to act (non-dependent): *Salgoil SpA v Italian Ministry for Foreign Trade* Case 33/68 [1968] ECR 453.

The Court will not necessarily give general retroactive validity to treaty provisions which have direct effect. Thus, in *Defrenne v Sabena (No 2)* Case 43/75 [1976] ECR 455, the Court held that the direct effect of art 141 EC applied only from the date on which the judgment was rendered, except as regards those litigants who had already instituted legal proceedings: *Barber v Guardian Royal Exchange Assurance Group* Case C–262/88 [1990] ECR I–1889.

In *Blaizot et al v University of Liège* Case 24/86 [1988] ECR 379, the European Court outlined its policy towards the non-retroactive application of treaty Articles given direct effect. It expressly observed:

' ... in determining whether or not to limit the temporal effects of a judgment it is necessary to bear in mind that although the practical consequences of any judicial decision must be weighed carefully, the Court cannot go so far as to diminish the objectivity of the law and compromise its future application on the grounds of the possible repercussions which might result, as regards the past, from a judicial decision.'

There are two types of direct effect. If a provision of EC law has vertical direct effect, it may be enforced against the 'State'. Horizontal direct effect results in the EC provisions being enforceable as against another natural or legal person.

Direct effect and Community directives

Since Community directives are given legal force through national measures, rights and duties are conferred on individuals only after incorporation into national law. Individuals and legal persons may, of course, rely on rights established by directives after the enabling legislation has been enacted. Frequently time limits are placed on implementation in order to ensure that Member States do not postpone incorporation indefinitely.

Where a Member State has failed to adopt a directive within the prescribed time period the European Court has, on certain occasions, been prepared to give direct effect to the contents of unimplemented directives notwithstanding the fact that the Member State has not incorporated the measure into internal law. The rationale for the development of this principle has been expressed by the Court in the following terms:

> 'It would be incompatible with the binding effect given by art 249 [EC] to directives to refuse in principle to allow persons concerned to invoke the obligation imposed by the directive ... Especially in cases where the Community authorities, by means of a directive, oblige Member States to take a specific course of action, the practical effectiveness of such a measure is weakened if individuals cannot take account of it as part of Community law.'
> (*Grad* v *Finanzamt Traunstein* Case 9/70 [1970] ECR 825.)

Strictly speaking, the provision of an unimplemented directive is not actually given direct effect in the same sense as the application of this concept to Community treaty provisions. Rather, a Member State is prevented from invoking its own omission or deficiency as a defence to an otherwise competent action.

A number of conditions must be satisfied before direct effect can be given to a term of a Community directive:

a) the term must be sufficiently precise;

b) the provision in question must specify an obligation which is not subject to any qualification, exception or condition;

c) the provision must not require intervention on the part of a Community institution or a Member State: *Van Duyn* v *Home Office* Case 41/74 [1974] ECR 1337.

The difference between this test and the analogous test for the direct effect of a treaty provision is that the condition requiring the non-discretionary implementation of the provision is easier to satisfy in the case of directives than for treaty provisions: Advocate-General Warner in *R* v *Secretary of State for the Home Department, ex parte Santillo* Case 131/79 [1980] FLR 1585.

Two important limitations are placed on the application of this principle.

a) The principle only applies to directives that are unimplemented after the date set for implementation. The application of directives which have been adopted, but which have not yet entered into force, cannot be anticipated or pre-empted: *Pubblico Ministero* v *Ratti* Case 148/78 [1979] ECR 1629.

b) The Court has only been prepared to apply this doctrine to the relationship between individuals and the state. In other words, directives are only capable of 'vertical direct effect'.

In the case *Marshall* v *Southampton and South-West Hampshire Area Health Authority*

(Teaching) (No 1) Case 152/84 [1986] ECR 723, the Court confirmed that while a directive might be upheld against defaulting Member States, it cannot be invoked directly against other individuals.

Hence, one main distinction between directives and regulations is that whilst the latter is capable of having both vertical and horizontal direct effect, directives may only create vertical direct effect. The 'State' has been defined broadly for such purposes. In *Marshall* v *Southampton and South-West Hampshire Area Health Authority (Teaching) (No 1)* Case 152/84 [1986] ECR 723 the Area Health Authority was concluded to be the State. In *Foster and Others* v *British Gas plc* Case C–188/89 [1990] ECR I–3313 the ECJ concluded that the provisions of a directive could be relied upon as against a body that provides a public service under the control of the State and which has powers in excess of those that result from the normal rules applicable in relations between individuals. The legal form of the body is irrelevant. For examples of the UK courts' response to this matter, see *Doughty* v *Rolls Royce* [1992] 1 CMLR 1045, in which Rolls Royce was not concluded to be an emanation of the State, and *Griffin* v *South West Water Services* [1995] IRLR 15, in which a privatised water authority was considered to be an emanation of the State/a public body.

While the Court of Justice has refused to recognise the concept of the 'horizontal direct effect' of directives (*Faccini Dori* v *Recreb Srl* Case C–91/92 [1994] ECR I–3325), it has sought to achieve the same effect through the process of interpretation – known as 'indirect effect' or 'sympathetic interpretation': *Von Colson and Kamann* v *Land Nordrhein-Westfalen* Case 14/83 [1984] ECR 1891. For example, where the Court is interpreting the terms of an unimplemented directive as it applies between private individuals, the Court observed:

> 'In applying national law, whether the provisions in question were adopted before or after the directive, a national court called upon to interpret it is required to do so, as far as possible, in light of the wording and purpose of the directive in order to achieve the result pursued by the latter…' (*Marleasing SA* v *La Comercial Internacional de Alimentacion SA* Case C–106/89 [1990] ECR I–4135.)

However, it is not clear what limitations are imposed on this means of indirectly applying unimplemented directives to the relationships between private individuals by way of interpretation. Certainly the UK courts have been reluctant to follow the European Court's lead on this point; for example, *Webb* v *EMO Air Cargo* [1993] 1 WLR 49.

The liability of Member States to private individuals for breaches of Community law

There is no provision in the EC Treaty that expressly permits private individuals to initiate proceedings against Member States for breaches by those States of Community law. A relatively ineffective Community enforcement process, and the apparent reluctance of national courts to grant relief to private individuals under national law for injury caused by acts of the Member States committed in violation of Community law, merely served to magnify the impact of the omission.

To plug this gap, the European Court developed a principle of Community law which provides that national courts are required to grant relief to private individuals who suffer injury as a result of a breach of Community law by a Member State. This principle is certainly destined to become a fundamental principle of EC law.

The case in which the principle was first established was *Francovich and Bonifaci* v *Italian Republic* Cases C–6 and 9/90 [1991] ECR I–5357. The Court held that a Member State was liable to private individuals for breaches of Community law if three conditions were satisfied:

a) the Community obligation had to be capable of conferring rights on private individuals;

b) the content of those rights had to be identifiable from the content of the measure; and

c) there had to be a causal link between the failure of the Member State to comply with Community law and the injury sustained by the private individual.

This right is to be vindicated in the national courts and private individuals remain unable to bring direct actions in the European Court.

Further clarification of this principle of EC law has been given in the joined cases of *Brasserie du Pêcheur SA* v *Federal Republic of Germany; R* v *Secretary of State for Transport, ex parte Factortame Ltd* Joined Cases C–46 and 48/93 [1996] ECR I–1029. State liability can attach to both acts and omissions by any organ of the State, including the legislature. The principle is also both alternative and additional to that of direct effect, although failure to use the route of direct effect, if available, may result in an inability to mitigate loss. In addition, non-directly effective Community law, if breached, may incur State liability.

The Court concluded that State liability should be analogous to that of the Community institutions themselves under art 288 EC and provided a three-part test to establish liability:

a) the rule of law infringed must be intended to confer rights on individuals;

b) the breach must be sufficiently serious; and

c) there must exist a direct causal link between the breach of Community law and the damage sustained.

To ascertain whether the breach is sufficiently serious the Court declared that the State must be shown to have 'manifestly and gravely disregarded the limits on its discretion'. This may be identified by considering factors such as: the clarity of the rule breached; the measure of discretion left by the rule; whether the breach was intentional or involuntary; whether there was an excusable error of law; whether a Community institution contributed to the breach; and whether there was any retention or adoption of national measures or practices contrary to Community law.

Cases since *Brasserie* have applied the test, but not necessarily in a consistent manner. In *R v Her Majesty's Treasury, ex parte British Telecommunications plc* Case C–392/93 [1996] ECR I–1631 the Court concentrated on whether the breach was sufficiently serious, and through application of the above principles concluded that the breach had been committed in good faith on the basis of a reasonable interpretation of an unclear directive: see also *Denkavit International BV v Bundesamt für Finanzen* Cases C–283, 291 and 292/94 [1996] ECR I–5063 and *Brinkman Tabakfabriken GmbH v Skatterministeriet* Case C–319/96 [1998] ECR I–5255. Applying the test in *Rechberger and Greindl v Austria* Case C–140/97 [2000] 2 CMLR 1, the Court concluded that Austria had incorrectly implemented a clear and precise directive and therefore the breach was manifestly serious.

In contrast, though, the Court in some preliminary references has considered the 'mere infringement' itself as a basis for State liability. In *R v Ministry of Agriculture, Fisheries and Food, ex parte Hedley Lomas (Ireland) Ltd* Case C–5/94 [1996] ECR I–2553, the Court declared that the UK's breach of art 29 EC was not justifiable under art 30 EC. In addition, the situation had been one in which the UK had had no, or very little, legislative discretion and consequently the mere infringement was sufficiently serious enough to incur liability. The same approach was adopted in *Dillenkofer and Others v Federal Republic of Germany* Cases C–178, 179, 188, 189 and 190/94 [1996] ECR I–4845, in which Germany had failed to implement a directive by its prescribed deadline. The Court declared this a per se serious breach of Community law: *Norbrook Laboratories Ltd v Minister of Agriculture, Fisheries and Food* Case C–127/95 [1998] ECR I–1531.

6.3 Key cases and materials

- *Brasserie du Pêcheur SA v Federal Republic of Germany; R v Secretary of State for Transport, ex parte Factortame Ltd* Joined Cases C–46 and 48/93 [1996] ECR I–1029
  State liability should be analogous to that of the Community institutions themselves under art 288 EC; the case redefines the test to be used to establish the existence of liability

- *Commission v United Kingdom (Re Tachographs)* Case 128/78 [1979] ECR 419
  If a Community regulation is re-enacted into national legislation in order to provide a greater degree of specification, the legislation must satisfy all the obligations incumbent on the Member State

- *Dillenkofer and Others v Federal Republic of Germany* Cases C–178, 179, 188, 189 and 190/94 [1996] ECR I–4845
  Germany had failed to implement a directive by its prescribed deadline; the Court declared this a per se serious breach of Community law

- *Foster and Others v British Gas plc* Case C–188/89 [1990] ECR I–3313
  Offers a definition of the State, for the purpose of applying directives, as a body that provides a public service under the control of the State and which has powers in

excess of those that result from the normal rules applicable in relations between individuals

- *Francovich and Bonifaci* v *Italian Republic* Cases C–6 and 9/90 [1991] ECR I–5357
  First case where a Member State was liable to private individuals for breaches of Community law

- *Hauptzollamt Mainz* v *Kupferberg* Case 104/81 [1982] ECR 3641
  The terms of Community agreements with third states may be given direct effect if the condition being relied upon is unconditional and precise, and also capable of conferring individual rights

- *Marleasing SA* v *La Comercial Internacional de Alimentacion SA* Case C–106/89 [1990] ECR I–4135
  National law should be interpreted in the light of EC directives, regardless of whether their implementation deadline has expired

- *Marshall* v *Southampton and South-West Hampshire Area Health Authority (Teaching) (No 1)* Case 152/84 [1986] ECR 723
  While vertical direct effect may be given to unimplemented directives, the European Court was unwilling to accept a similar application of the concept of horizontal direct effect

- *Pubblico Ministero* v *Ratti* Case 148/78 [1979] ECR 1629
  In order for a directive to be non-dependent (ie require no further legislative action to be taken) the date for implementation of the directive must have expired. Should the State fail to take the necessary action by such a date, it will be estopped from relying on its own failure

- *R* v *Her Majesty's Treasury, ex parte British Telecommunications plc* Case C–392/93 [1996] ECR I–1631
  The breach had been committed in good faith on the basis of a reasonable interpretation of an unclear directive and therefore did not attract State liability

- *SZ Sevince* v *Staatssecretaris van Justitie* Case 192/89 [1990] ECR I–3461
  Direct effect of decisions of bodies set up under the authority of Community treaties with third states

- *Van Duyn* v *Home Office* Case 41/74 [1974] ECR 1337
  Directives may be capable of creating directly effective rights that must be upheld in the national courts; to do so the directive must meet the *Van Gend en Loos* criteria

- *Van Gend en Loos* v *Netherlands* Case 26/62 [1963] ECR 1
  The EC Treaty creates a new legal order that is capable of generating rights for individuals that they may enforce in their national courts – direct effect. The conditions necessary for a provision of EC law to have direct effect are that it must be clear and precise, unconditional and non-dependent

- *Von Colson and Kamann* v *Land Nordrhein-Westfalen* Case 14/83 [1984] ECR 1891
  Application of unimplemented directives between private individuals through interpretative means

- EC Treaty

  - art 249 – provides authority to the Council of Ministers and European Commission to enact secondary legislation

  - art 288 – provides for the conditions to establish liability of the Community institutions

6.4 Questions and suggested solutions

QUESTION ONE

'Arguably the greatest achievement of the European Court of Justice is the development of the doctrine of direct effect.'

Discuss with reference to application to different types of EC primary and secondary legislation and to case law.

University of London LLB Examination
(for External Students) European Community Law June 1994 Q1

General Comment

This is a broad question requiring the application of a single principle to four separate sources of Community law. The answer is relatively long due to the sizeable volume of case law on this subject. However, in the final analysis, the question itself is relatively straightforward and involves one of the most basic concepts of Community law.

Skeleton Solution

Direct effect of EC primary legislation: EC Treaty provisions and international treaties – conditions required for application of the principle to primary legislation – direct effect of EC secondary legislation: regulations and directives – conditions required for application of the principle to secondary legislation.

Suggested Solution

When negotiating the EC Treaty the draftsmen envisaged Community law being created through the institutional framework created by the Treaty itself. The principal sources of law were to be regulations, directives and decisions according to art 249 EC. These laws were to be enacted by the Council of Ministers and the European Commission in accordance with the procedures laid down in the Treaty.

Had this remained the position, many of the fundamental principles of EC law would never have seen the light of day. For example, the principles of non-discrimination on the grounds of nationality or on the ground of gender were not enacted by Community institutions nor was the principle of the supremacy of Community law over national law. These concepts were created by the European Court through the direct application of the EC Treaty provisions.

In a deliberate act of judicial activism, the European Court created the doctrine of direct effect in order to expand the scope of the legal principles of Community law. Initially, this doctrine was applied to EC Treaty provisions to allow private individuals to rely on the terms of that agreement. Gradually, the doctrine was extended to encompass international agreements entered into by the Community with third states and to directives. So, while originally only Community regulations were intended to have the quality of direct effect, after the Court's interventions EC Treaty provisions, Community treaties with non-EC countries and directives are all capable of having direct effect if certain circumstances are satisfied.

The circumstances and conditions under which these measures have direct effect differ and therefore it is appropriate to consider each separately.

Direct effect of EC Treaty provisions

In *Van Gend en Loos* v *Netherlands* Case 26/62 [1963] ECR 1, the European Court held that where a provision of the EC Treaty imposes a clear and unconditional obligation on a Member State, unqualified by any reservation preserving the right of Member States to give effect to the provision in the form of a national law, such a provision may be capable of direct effect. The quality of direct effect creates private rights for individuals which can be enforced by bringing legal proceedings in national courts and tribunals.

Examining this decision in detail, three specific conditions are therefore required for a term of a Community treaty to have direct effect. First, the provision being relied on must be clear and precise: *Gimenez Zaera* v *Instituto Nacional de la Seguridad Social* Case 187/85 [1987] ECR 3697. Second, the term must be unqualified and not subject to the actions of national authorities for its operation: *Sociaal Fonds voor de Diamantarbeiders* v *Brachfeld and Chougol Diamond Co* Cases 2 and 3/69 [1969] ECR 211. Finally, the obligation established must not leave substantial discretion to Member States or the European Commission to effect its performance: *Salgoil SpA* v *Italian Ministry for Foreign Trade* Case 33/68 [1968] ECR 453.

Among the Articles which have been given direct effect by the European Court are art 12 EC (non-discrimination on the grounds of nationality), arts 23 and 25 EC (elimination of customs duties and charges having an equivalent effect), art 28 EC (elimination of quantitative restrictions and measures having an equivalent effect), arts 81 and 82 EC (European Community competition policy) and art 141 EC (non-discrimination on the grounds of gender).

Direct effect of Community treaties

The second source of primary legislation, in addition to the Community treaties, is international agreements entered into by the Community with non-Community States. These agreements are also capable of providing a reservoir of directly applicable principles of Community law: *Hauptzollamt Mainz* v *Kupferberg* Case 104/81 [1982] ECR 3641. Further, the European Court has also held that such agreements prevail over inconsistent provisions of national law.

The case of *Kupferberg* provides an interesting illustration of the application of the principle to agreements entered into by the Community. Kupferberg, a German importer, was charged duties on imports of Portuguese port. He believed these charges were contrary to the terms of the Association Agreement between the European Community and Portugal which prohibited, on a reciprocal basis, discriminatory internal taxation between imported and domestic products. The matter was referred by the German court to the European Court for a preliminary ruling.

The European Court held that, since international responsibility for breach of such treaties rested with the Community, the Court must recognise the need to ensure uniform application of these obligations within the Community. Hence, the terms of the agreement could be given direct effect if the provision being relied on was unconditional and precise and also capable of conferring individual rights which could be enforced in national courts or tribunals: *Bresciani* v *Amministrazione Italiana delle Finanze* Case 87/75 [1976] ECR 129.

It should be noted that the conditions required for the direct effect of international agreements entered into by the Community on the one hand, and those for direct effect of provisions of the EC Treaty on the other hand, differ in some respects.

Direct effect of regulations

Under art 249 EC, regulations are 'binding in their entirety and directly applicable in all Member States'. Community regulations which have entered into force may be enforced by or against the subjects of the regulation and the application of such measures is independent of any supplementing measure of national law: *Politi* v *Italian Ministry of Finance of the Italian Republic* Case 43/71 [1971] ECR 1039.

Direct effect of directives

'Vertical direct effect' may be given to directives which have remained unimplemented by Member States after the period provided for the adoption of the measure into national law: *Van Duyn* v *Home Office* Case 41/74 [1974] ECR 1337. In other words, the Court has been prepared to refuse to allow the failure of a State to adopt a directive as a justification for denying private individuals their legitimate rights.

The right to rely on the terms of an unimplemented directive is not absolute. Three conditions must be satisfied before reliance can be placed on the measure. First, the terms of the directive must be sufficiently precise to allow the creation of directly enforceable legal obligations. Second, the provision must specify an obligation which is not subject to any qualification, exception or condition. Third, the provision must not require intervention on the part of a Community institution or a Member State.

There are, however, two major limitations placed on the application of the principle of direct effect to Community directives.

First, the principle applies only to directives which remain unimplemented after the date has passed for adoption. The entry into force of directives which have been adopted, but which have not yet entered into force, cannot be anticipated or pre-empted: *Pubblico Ministero* v *Ratti* Case 148/78 [1979] ECR 1629.

Second, and more importantly, the Court has only been prepared to apply this principle to the relationships between individuals and the national authorities as opposed to the relationships among private individuals themselves. In other words, while an individual can invoke an unimplemented directive against national authorities, the rights conferred by the unimplemented directives cannot be enforced in private relationships: *Faccini Dori* v *Recreb Srl* Case C–91/92 [1994] ECR I–3325.

The application of the principle of direct effect to private relationships is known as 'horizontal direct effect' as opposed to 'vertical direct effect', which refers to the relationship between individuals and the State. In *Marshall* v *Southampton and South-West Hampshire Area Health Authority (Teaching) (No 1)* Case 152/84 [1986] ECR 723, the European Court denied that unimplemented directives were capable of horizontal direct effect.

That is not, however, the end of the matter. The situation has been made more complex by decisions of the Court which, while continuing the general policy of refusing to give horizontal direct effect to directives, have nevertheless opened an alternative channel to allow relief to private individuals denied their rights against other individuals because a Member State has failed to implement a directive in time.

In *Von Colson and Kamann* v *Land Nordrhein-Westfalen* Case 14/83 [1984] ECR 1891, and in *Marleasing SA* v *La Comercial Internacional de Alimentacion SA* Case C–106/89 [1990] ECR I–4135, the Court has given indirect effect to unimplemented directives via art 10 EC. This Article requires Member States to 'take all appropriate measures' to ensure the fulfilment of the obligations arising out of the Treaty.

While the Court rejected the notion of horizontal direct effect, it observed that art 10 EC placed Member States under an obligation to give effect to Community obligations. Spanish law had to be interpreted in light of this obligation. Hence, Spanish company law was to be interpreted and applied in terms compatible with the directive. Since the directive exhaustively listed all the grounds for annulling a company, the Spanish company could not be annulled for lack of consideration. Hence the directors were not personally liable for the debts of the company.

It is difficult to avoid the conclusion that this decision was simply a means of permitting horizontal direct effect through interpretative sleight of hand. In other words, the Court is prepared to apply the terms of unimplemented directives to the relationships between individuals where this can be achieved by means of interpretative implication.

In conclusion, the ECJ's judicial activism in creating the doctrine of direct effect has done much to ensure the effectiveness of Community law. Given the weaknesses of the original enforcement procedure envisaged in the EC Treaty, direct effect permitted individuals to enforce their rights throughout the Community, thereby compelling Member States to comply with their obligations. However, problems persist over the issue of the direct effect of directives, and this remains a controversial aspect of EC law.

QUESTION TWO

'To give what is called "horizontal effect" to directives would totally blur the distinction between regulations and directives which the Treaty establishes in Articles [249 and 254].' Advocate-General Slynn in Case 152/84 *Marshall* v *Southampton and South-West Hampshire Area Health Authority*.

Discuss.

University of London LLB Examination
(for External Students) European Community Law June 1989 Q3

General Comment

A problem concerning the application of the doctrine of direct effect of unimplemented directives which also requires consideration of the relationship between the various secondary sources of Community law.

Skeleton Solution

The legal effect of Community regulations – the legal effect of Community directives – the concept of horizontal effect and its consequences – contrast between the effects of regulations and unimplemented directives.

Suggested Solution

Article 249 EC provides that regulations 'shall be binding in their entirety and directly applicable in all Member States'. The quality of direct applicability means that regulations are immediately and automatically incorporated into the legal systems of the Member States without the need for intervention on the part of a legislative body such as the British Parliament. Individuals and legal persons may therefore vindicate rights and duties created by Community regulations before national courts and tribunals. An institution of the Community would pass a regulation when it was deemed undesirable that the national authorities of a Member State should be allowed to intervene in its promulgation.

Community directives do not possess the same quality. In fact, art 249 EC expressly provides that the national authorities of the Member States retain discretion in selecting the appropriate instrument of national law to implement Community directives. Directives are employed where an institution of the Community intends to create standards which need not be identical throughout the Community.

obligation of Member States under art 10 EC to interpret national law in a manner consistent with unimplemented directives.

Article 10 EC requires Member States to take 'all appropriate measures ... to ensure fulfilment of the obligations arising out of [the EC] Treaty'. In *Marleasing* (above), the Court was required to answer the question whether Council Directive 68/151 on company law harmonisation, which had not been implemented in Spain, could be relied upon to override a provision of Spanish law allowing the nullity of a company on the ground of lack of consideration. The directive exhaustively enumerated the grounds on which the incorporation of a company could be declared void. Spanish law therefore contradicted Community law, but the directive remained unadopted.

The Court held that national law must be interpreted in conformity with the directive and any attempt to dissolve a company on grounds other than those set out in the directive was incompatible with Community law. This decision was reached on the basis of a point of interpretation, namely that Spanish law must be interpreted in a manner consistent with Community law.

The impact of this decision has been to give horizontal direct effect to directives in an indirect manner. While the Court expressly rejected the possibility of directives having horizontal direct effect, its method of interpretation arrived at the same effect.

QUESTION THREE

Trace the development of the doctrine of direct effect from the inception of the Community to the present day. Does it retain its original importance or has its impact been lessened?

University of London LLB Examination
(for External Students) European Union Law June 1997 Q1

General Comment

This essay question requires the student to trace the development of the doctrine of direct effect and to assess its continuing importance in the Community legal order. In particular, this question requires an analysis of the relatively recent establishment of the principle of direct effect and its impact on direct effect. This question requires discussion of a considerable range of concepts and cases and the answer is therefore a relatively long one.

Skeleton Solution

Definition of direct effect – vertical and horizontal direct effect – treaty Articles, regulations and directives – role of direct effect in the legal order of the Community – inadequacy of direct effect to ensure protection of individual rights – indirect effect – State liability for damages – *Brasserie* case.

Suggested Solution

A provision of EC law that is directly effective is one that gives rise to rights and obligations enforceable by the individual in their national courts. Vertical direct effect results in the provisions of the Community law being enforceable against the State. Horizontal direct effect results in the provisions being enforceable against other natural or legal persons. The concept is one that has been created and developed by the European Court through teleological interpretation.

The concept was first established in *Van Gend en Loos* v *Netherlands* Case 26/62 [1963] ECR 1. In this seminal judgment the Court concluded that the Treaty was not only capable of creating obligations binding at an international level enforceable by the Commission under art 226 EC, but was also capable of conferring rights on individuals that became part of their legal heritage. The case also established the criteria that a provision must comply with in order to have direct effect. The criteria are: that the provision must be clear and precise; unconditional (in that the provision must not require the discretion of another body to be exercised); and non-dependent (in that it must not require further legislative action to be taken). Since the decision in this case, the ECJ has had to rule upon forms of Community law that may have the quality of direct effect.

Treaty Articles

In *Van Gend en Loos* v *Netherlands* Case 26/62 [1963] ECR 1 it was established that Treaty Articles may be capable of direct effects. In the case the issue was whether a Treaty Article was capable of having vertical direct effect; that is, enforceable by the individual against the State. Subsequently, in *Defrenne* v *Sabena (No 2)* Case 43/75 [1976] ECR 455, the Court concluded that Treaty Articles may also be enforceable against a private body or person, so-called horizontal direct effect.

Regulations

Article 249 EC states that regulations are directly applicable. This results in regulations being automatically incorporated into the corpus juris of each Member State. In *Politi* v *Italian Ministry of Finance of the Italian Republic* Case 43/71 [1971] ECR 1039 the Court declared that 'by reason of their nature' regulations had direct effect. Regulations are capable of creating both vertical and horizontal directly effective rights. However, some regulations require further legislative action to be taken, or are not addressed to individuals, and in such cases will not necessarily be capable of having direct effect: *Leonesio* v *Italian Ministry of Agriculture and Forestry* Case 93/71 [1972] ECR 287; *Becker (Ursula)* v *Finanzamt Münster-Innenstadt* Case 8/81 [1982] ECR 53.

Directives

Article 249 EC provides that directives are binding as to the result to be achieved, but leave the choice of form and method of achieving this result to the Member State. In other words, the Member State is required to implement the directive. Thus, directives are by their nature dependent and hence seem incapable of achieving the *Van Gend en*

Loos criteria. If the Member State takes the necessary measures and implements the directive fully and correctly, there are no difficulties, since individuals will rely on the national implementing measures. However, if the State fails to take the necessary measures, the question arises as to whether individuals are capable of relying on the directive itself. In other words, despite the fact that on face value directives fail the *Van Gend en Loos* test, are they still capable of creating directly effective rights?

In *Van Duyn* v *Home Office* Case 41/74 [1974] ECR 1337, the ECJ concluded that directives were capable of having direct effect. In order to have direct effect the directive must be clear and precise, unconditional and the deadline for implementation contained in the directive must have expired: *Pubblico Ministero* v *Ratti* Case 148/78 [1979] ECR 1629. Reasons in support of the direct effect of directives were identified as: the binding nature of such sources of Community law; the fact that the effect of directives would otherwise be diminished; and that Member States should not be permitted to rely upon their own failure to implement a directive against an individual attempting to assert rights contained in a directive.

Subsequently, in *Marshall* v *Southampton and South-West Hampshire Area Health Authority (Teaching) (No 1)* Case 152/84 [1986] ECR 723, directives were found to be capable of being invoked against the State only. In other words, directives may only be capable of vertical direct effect. This decision was reaffirmed in *Faccini Dori* v *Recreb Srl* Case C–91/92 [1994] ECR I–3325 despite powerful arguments to the contrary. The 'State' was interpreted broadly in *Foster and Others* v *British Gas plc* Case C–188/89 [1990] ECR I–3313 as a body that provides a public service under the control of the State and which has powers in excess of those that result from the normal rules applicable in relations between individuals.

The doctrine of direct effect is of enormous significance in Community law. The combined effects of supremacy and direct effect means that Community law should, in principle, apply uniformly throughout the EC independently of Member States' implementation. Moreover, individuals are able to enforce rights and claim remedies in their national courts even if their State has failed to grant them such rights. This has led to more widespread compliance with Community obligations by Member States, and goes some way to improving the often criticised public enforcement process under art 226 EC, since individuals can initiate proceedings to enforce their rights in the national legal system.

Despite the great significance of direct effect, the decision that they are not capable of horizontal direct effect has left a lacuna in the protection of individual rights in the Community legal order. The result of *Marshall* v *Southampton and South-West Hampshire Area Health Authority (Teaching) (No 1)* Case 152/84 [1986] ECR 723 is that there are two classes of Community individual: those who have a claim against the State who may rely on the terms of an unimplemented directive; and those that have a claim against a private party who are unable to rely on the unimplemented directive. This is clearly unjust. Moreover, the lack of horizontal direct effect for directives threatens the uniform application and integrity of EC law throughout the Community. In an effort to resolve these issues, and to further strengthen the supremacy of EC law in general, the ECJ has established two further principles, namely indirect effect and the principle of State liability.

In *Von Colson and Kamann* v *Land Nordrhein-Westfalen* Case 14/83 [1984] ECR 1891 the ECJ concluded that national courts were obligated under art 10 EC to interpret national law to comply with EC law, including the terms of a directive. This obligation applies regardless of whether the deadline for implementation of the directive has expired, and applies irrespective of whom the obligation in being imposed against, the State or a private party: *Marleasing SA* v *La Comercial Internacional de Alimentacion SA* Case C–106/89 [1990] ECR I–4135. Sometimes referred to as 'sympathetic interpretation', this obligation has permitted individuals to rely on the terms of directives against other individuals, and has been described as achieving horizontal direct effect through the 'backdoor'. However, the success of this concept is dependent on the willingness of national courts to carry out the interpretative exercise, especially in light of whether they are constrained by any national rules on interpretation.

Finally, the European Court has established the principle that Member States are liable in damages to individuals for breaches of Community law that cause damage: *Francovich and Bonifaci* v *Italian Republic* Cases C–6 and 9/90 [1991] ECR I–5357. This principle has been clarified in *Brasserie du Pêcheur SA* v *Federal Republic of Germany; R* v *Secretary of State for Transport, ex parte Factortame Ltd* Joined Cases C–46 and 48/93 [1996] ECR I–1029. State liability, can attach to both acts and omissions by any organ of the State, including the legislature. In addition, non-directly effective Community law, if breached, may incur State liability, thereby maximising the effectiveness of Community law.

The Court concluded that State liability should be analogous to that of the Community institutions themselves under art 288 EC and provided a three-part test to establish liability. First, the rule of law infringed must be intended to confer rights on individuals. Second, the breach must be sufficiently serious and, third, there must exist a direct causal link between the breach of Community law and the damage sustained. To ascertain whether the breach is sufficiently serious, the Court declared that the State must be shown to have 'manifestly and gravely disregarded the limits on its discretion'. This may be identified by considering factors such as: the clarity of the rule breached; the measure of discretion left by the rule; whether the breach was intentional or involuntary; whether there was an excusable error of law; whether a Community institution contributed to the breach; and whether there was any retention or adoption of national measures or practices contrary to Community law.

In *R* v *Her Majesty's Treasury, ex parte British Telecommunications plc* Case C–392/93 [1996] ECR I–1631 the Court concentrated on whether the incorrect implementation of a directive was sufficiently serious, and through application of the above principles concluded that the breach had been committed in good faith on the basis of a reasonable interpretation of an unclear directive: see also *Denkavit International BV* v *Bundesamt für Finanzen* Cases C–283, 291 and 292/94 [1996] ECR I–5063 and *Brinkman*

Tabakfabriken GmbH v *Skatterministeriet* Case C–319/96 [1998] ECR I–5255. Applying the test in *Rechberger and Greindl* v *Austria* Case C–140/97 [2000] 2 CMLR 1, the Court concluded that Austria had incorrectly implemented a clear and precise directive and, therefore, the breach was manifestly serious.

In contrast, though, the Court in some preliminary references has considered the 'mere infringement' itself as a basis for State liability. In *R* v *Ministry of Agriculture, Fisheries and Food, ex parte Hedley Lomas (Ireland) Ltd* Case C–5/94 [1996] ECR I–2553, the Court declared that the UK's breach of art 29 EC was not justifiable under art 30 EC. In addition, the situation had been one in which the UK had had no, or very little, legislative discretion, and consequently the mere infringement was sufficiently serious to incur liability. The same approach was adopted in *Dillenkofer and Others* v *Federal Republic of Germany* Cases C–178, 179, 188, 189 and 190/94 [1996] ECR I–4845, in which Germany had failed to implement a directive by its prescribed deadline. The Court declared this a per se serious breach of Community law: see also *Norbrook Laboratories Ltd* v *Minister of Agriculture, Fisheries and Food* Case C–127/95 [1998] ECR I–1531 and *Francovich and Bonifaci* v *Italian Republic* Cases C–6 and 9/90 [1991] ECR I–5357.

In terms of whether the creation and development of State liability has reduced the impact of direct effect, it is worth noting the comments of the European Court in *Brasserie* (above). The Court concluded that State liability, as a route of action, is also both alternative and additional to that of direct effect. However, failure to use the route of direct effect, if available, may result in an inability to mitigate loss. Hence, if an individual attempts to secure monetary compensation in a situation where they could in fact secure their rights through direct effect, any damages they are entitled to could be reduced. Thus, the doctrine of direct effect retains its significance in the Community legal order, but its inadequacies have led to the creation of additional concepts to ensure that Community law remains both effective and enforceable. Clearly, the creation of these concepts increases the pressure on Member States to ensure the full application and implementation of Community law, and assists the individual in enforcing and securing their individual rights.

QUESTION FOUR

'The doctrine of direct effect was developed gradually by the Court of Justice after its initial definition. It applies to different types of Community law in different ways.'

Discuss.

University of London LLB Examination
(for External Students) European Community Law June 1999 Q2

General Comment

This is an essay style question on the important concept of direct effect in Community law. The question is a standard one requiring a basic appraisal of the definition, development and application of direct effect to different types of Community law.

Candidates should have appreciated that this question required emphasis on direct effect in general, rather than discussion of indirect effect and/or State liability or emphasis solely on the difficult issue of the direct effect of directives. Whilst indirect effect and State liability could be included, they should have in no way constituted the main part of the answer.

Skeleton Solution

The definition and types of direct effect – the reasons for the creation of direct effect by the European Court of Justice – the conditions necessary for direct effect – relaxation of the conditions and the extension of direct effect to secondary sources of Community law, such as regulations, decisions and international agreements – direct effect and directives – the lack of horizontal direct effect for directives and extension of the definition of the State – the concepts of indirect effect and State liability.

Suggested Solution

Direct effect refers to a quality that a provision of Community law may have if it meets certain criteria. If a Community measure has direct effect, its obligations may be enforced by individuals in their national courts. Direct effect may be of a vertical nature in that it may be enforceable against the State, but in some cases the measure may also attract horizontal direct effect, in that individuals may rely on the measure as against other natural or legal persons.

Traditionally, under international law, treaties do not create rights for individuals and the draftsmen of the Treaty of Rome envisaged Community law being created through the institutional framework created by the Treaty itself. The principal sources of such secondary Community law are regulations, directives and decisions: art 249 EC and in many areas of Community law the institutions were required to produce legislation to achieve certain goals. However, had this remained the position many of the most important principles of Community law would have been of little value. For example, the principles of non-discrimination on the grounds of nationality or on the grounds of gender were not enacted by the Community institutions, nor was sufficient legislation produced on the harmonisation of qualifications in order to ensure freedom of establishment and services. In addition, many Member States failed to take appropriate action to secure Community law objectives (such as implementing directives), with the only recourse under the Treaty being the rather ineffective enforcement process in the hands of the Commission: art 226 EC.

In a deliberate act of 'judicial activism' the concept of direct effect was created and developed by the European Court of Justice (ECJ) via teleological interpretation. In other words, in the opinion of the Court the purpose and spirit of the EC Treaty would have been undermined if individuals were deprived of the right to enforce Community law by accessing their national legal systems. Direct effect therefore increases or maximises the scope and effectiveness of Community law.

Originally the ECJ applied direct effect to provisions of the Treaty, and laid down certain strict criteria that a provision had to meet to have direct effect. However, over time the ECJ relaxed the application of these criteria, making direct effect the norm rather than the exception. The ECJ has also extended the range of Community legislation that may have direct effect.

In *Van Gend en Loos* v *Netherlands* Case 26/62 [1963] ECR 1 the ECJ was asked to consider whether a company could rely on a provision of the EC Treaty. The ECJ concluded that the Community was a sui generis legal system capable of creating rights for individuals that could be enforced by bringing legal proceedings in national courts and tribunals. In order to acquire such direct effect, the Court declared that the Treaty provision would have to impose a clear and precise, unconditional obligation that was also non-dependent. It terms of being unconditional, the measure must not depend on the discretion or intervention of another body, be it the State or the Community institutions: *Sociaal Fonds voor de Diamantarbeiders* v *Brachfeld and Chougol Diamond Co* Cases 2 and 3/69 [1969] ECR 211. To be non-dependent the measure must require no further legislative action to be taken by the State or by the Community institutions: *Salgoil SpA* v *Italian Ministry for Foreign Trade* Case 33/68 [1968] ECR 453.

Treaty provisions are capable of vertical direct effect and thus may act as a means of establishing a defence to an action, or as grounds for an action in relation to the State: *Brown* v *Secretary of State for Scotland* Case 197/86 [1988] ECR 3205. The ECJ has in addition concluded that certain Treaty provisions may also be capable of creating horizontally effective rights, in that they may be invoked as against other individuals. This, for example, can be witnessed in relation to art 141 EC as concluded in the case of *Defrenne* v *Sabena (No 2)* Case 43/75 [1976] ECR 455. Should a Treaty provision require further legislative measures to be taken, it will fail the third criteria of the *Van Gend en Loos* v *Netherlands* Case 26/62 [1963] ECR 1 test. However, the Court has concluded that once the time period set down for those measures has expired, it may be granted direct effect, as long as the other criteria are met. For example, art 43 EC, providing for freedom of establishment, required the issuing of directives by the Community institutions, yet in *Reyners, (Jean)* v *Belgium* Case 2/74 [1974] ECR 631 the Court held that art 43 EC was still capable of creating directly effective rights.

Another source of primary Community law is international agreements concluded by the Community. Such agreements have also been granted direct effect: *Bresciani* v *Amministrazione Italiana delle Finanze* Case 87/75 [1976] ECR 129. In *Hauptzollamt Mainz* v *Kupferberg* Case 104/81 [1982] ECR 3641 the Court held that art 21 of the EC/Portugal Agreement was directly effective. This was because the Community was responsible for the breach of such treaties, and the Court recognised the need to ensure uniform application of these treaty obligations. Hence, if the terms of the agreement were precise, unconditional and capable of conferring rights on individuals, they would attract direct effect.

Secondary legislation produced by the Community under art 249 EC includes regulations, decisions and directives. A regulation is defined in art 249 EC as having 'general application', and to be 'binding in its entirety and directly applicable in all Member States'. Hence, a regulation will generally automatically become part of the legal system of the Member States. In *Politi v Italian Ministry of Finance of the Italian Republic* Case 43/71 [1971] ECR 1039 the Court recognised that, by their very nature, regulations are generally capable of direct effect in both a vertical and horizontal manner.

A decision is defined in art 249 EC as 'binding in its entirety upon those to whom it is addressed'. Whilst lacking direct applicability, the Court has concluded that decisions are capable of having direct effect, as long as they meet the necessary criteria: *Franz Grad v Finanzamt Traunstein* Case 9/70 [1970] ECR 825. The case of *Grad* also hinted at the extension of direct effect to other forms of secondary Community law, such as directives.

Directives are defined in art 249 EC as 'binding as to the result to be achieved' but which 'leave to the national authorities the choice of form and methods' of achieving the desired result. Directives are not directly applicable and it appears on face value that they are also not capable of creating directly effective rights. This is due to the need for further legislative action on the part of the Member State – a breach of the need for the measure to be non-dependent. However, in the case of *Van Duyn v Home Office* Case 41/74 [1974] ECR 1337 the ECJ concluded that art 3(1) of Council Directive 64/221 was capable of generating directly effective rights. The Court concluded that it would be incompatible with the binding effect attributed to directives by art 249 EC to exclude them from creating rights enforceable by individuals in their national courts.

However, in order for a directive to comply with the need to be non-dependent, the Court has stated that the time-limit imposed in the directive for the necessary national implementing measures to have been passed must have expired: *Pubblico Ministero v Ratti* Case 148/78 [1979] ECR 1629. Thus the Court has made it clear that direct effect only potentially exists once the Member State has failed to exercise its discretion to implement a directive within the prescribed period. It is only at this point that an individual may rely on the terms of a directive as against the defaulting State, and acquire rights that must be protected by the national court. In addition, a directive must also meet the remaining two criteria, in that it is clear and unconditional.

The application of direct effect to directives, in comparison with other sources of Community law, reveals one striking difference, however. The Court concluded in the case of *Marshall v Southampton and South-West Hampshire Area Health Authority (Teaching) (No 1)* Case 152/84 [1986] ECR 723 that directives, in this case Council Directive 76/207, were not capable of creating horizontally effective rights. This was confirmed in the case of *Faccini Dori v Recreb Srl* Case C–91/92 [1994] ECR I–3325.

The creation and extension of the doctrine of direct effect to various sources of Community law has achieved in part the desire of the ECJ to maximise the effectiveness of Community law. However, this effectiveness is limited by the Court's continued refusal to grant directives horizontal direct effect. This leaves those attempting to enforce unimplemented, or inadequately implemented, directives being capable of only doing so as against the State. On a positive note, the definition of the State has been extended to include all organs of the administration and decentralised bodies (*Fratelli Constanzo SpA* v *Commune di Milano* Case 103/88 [1989] ECR 1839). The State also includes, according to *Foster and Others* v *British Gas plc* Case C–188/89 [1990] ECR I–3313, all bodies providing public services under the control of the State and/or which have powers in excess of those resulting from normal rules applicable in relations between individuals.

Some relief to the lack of horizontal direct effect for directives can be found in the Court's creation of indirect effect in the cases of *Von Colson and Kamann* v *Land Nordrhein-Westfalen* Case 14/83 [1984] ECR 1891 and *Harz* v *Deutsche Tradax GmbH* Case 79/83 [1984] ECR 1921. In these cases the Court concentrated not on direct effect, but on the obligation found in art 10 EC that Member States ensure that all appropriate measures are taken to ensure that the objectives of the Treaty are fulfilled. This obligation extends to national courts, which are therefore under a duty to interpret national law in the light of Community law to ensure that Community law obligations are fulfilled. The case of *Marleasing SA* v *La Comercial Internacional de Alimentacion SA* Case C–106/89 [1990] ECR I–4135 extends this obligation to consideration of directives, regardless of whether their date of implementation has expired. This obligation, though, does rest on the willingness of national courts. There have been examples of where courts have been unprepared to interpret national law to the extent required to provide individuals with their Community law rights: for example *Duke* v *GEC Reliance* [1988] 2 WLR 359 and *Webb* v *EMO Air Cargo* [1993] 1 WLR 49.

An alternative route of redress is to seek damages for breaches of Community law under the principle of State liability: *Francovich and Bonifaci* v *Italian Republic* Cases C–6 and 9/90 [1991] ECR I–5357 and developed in *Brasserie du Pêcheur SA* v *Federal Republic of Germany; R* v *Secretary of State for Transport, ex parte Factortame Ltd* Joined Cases C–46 and 48/93 [1996] ECR I–1029. The threat of damages may impose a strong obligation on Member States to abide by their Community obligations. It also encourages Member States to implement directives by their expiry period since, according to the decision of the ECJ in *Dillenkofer and Others* v *Federal Republic of Germany* Cases 178, 179, 188, 189 and 190/94 [1996] ECR I–4845, failure to do so automatically incurs liability. However, the Court has also clearly stated that failure to use any available directly effective rights may result in an inability to mitigate any loss. Thus direct effect remains an important aspect of Community law, and one that individuals will continue to rely on in national courts to secure their Community rights.

QUESTION FIVE

The case of *Van Gend en Loos* established direct effect for Treaty Articles. Does this apply to all Treaty Articles? Can direct effect also apply to directives? If so, when does it apply and in what ways does it differ from direct effect for Treaty Articles?

University of London LLB Examination
(for External Students) European Community Law June 2000 Q1

General Comment

This is a rather basic essay style question on the important concept of direct effect. The question is a standard one that is actually comprised of four separate questions, which should all be tackled. Candidates should appreciate that this question requires emphasis on direct effect in general, and a definition of what direct effect is must be included. The distinction between vertical and horizontal direct effect is also essential in order to identify the differences between Treaty Articles and directives in terms of them having direct effects.

Skeleton Solution

The definition and types of direct effect – the conditions necessary for direct effect – the application of direct effect to Treaty Articles – the extension of direct effect to secondary sources of Community law, including directives – the lack of horizontal direct effect for directives and extension of the definition of the State – indirect effect and State liability.

Suggested Solution

Direct effect refers to a quality that a provision of Community law may have should it meet certain criteria. If a Community provision has direct effect individuals, in their national courts, may seek to rely on it. Direct effect may be vertical in nature, which means that the provision may be enforced against the State. However, in some cases the measure may also attract horizontal direct effect, which means that individuals may rely on the measure as against other individuals.

Traditionally, under international law, treaties do not create rights for individuals, but in a deliberate act of 'judicial activism' the concept of direct effect was created and developed by the European Court of Justice (ECJ) via teleological interpretation. In other words, in the opinion of the Court the purpose and spirit of the EC Treaty would have been undermined if individuals were deprived of the right to enforce Community law by accessing their national legal systems. Direct effect therefore increases or maximises the scope and effectiveness of Community law. One of the earliest and most important cases in EC law was that of *Van Gend en Loos* v *Netherlands* Case 26/62 [1963] ECR 1 in which the Court delivered a preliminary reference (art 234 EC) outlining the doctrine of direct effect.

The direct effect of Treaty Articles

In *Van Gend en Loos* the ECJ was asked to consider whether a company could rely on a provision of the EC Treaty. In this case, the Treaty Article in question was art 12 EC, which required that there be no increase in customs duties. When the company found itself subject to such an increase imposed by the Dutch government, it sought to enforce the prohibition in the Treaty Article in a vertical manner against the Dutch authorities.

The ECJ concluded that the Community was a sui generis legal system capable of creating rights for individuals that could be enforced by bringing legal proceedings in national courts and tribunals. In order to acquire such direct effect, the Court declared that the Treaty provision would have to impose a clear and precise, unconditional obligation that was also non-dependent. It terms of being unconditional, the measure must not depend on the discretion or intervention of another body, be it the State or the Community institutions: *Sociaal Fonds voor de Diamantarbeiders* v *Brachfeld and Chougol Diamond Co* Cases 2 and 3/69 [1969] ECR 211. To be non-dependent the measure must require no further legislative action to be taken by the State or by the Community institutions: *Salgoil SpA* v *Italian Ministry for Foreign Trade* Case 33/68 [1968] ECR 433.

Treaty provisions are therefore capable of vertical direct effect and thus may act as a means of establishing a defence to an action, or as grounds for an action in relation to the State: *Brown* v *Secretary of State for Scotland* Case 197/86 [1988] ECR 3205. The ECJ has in addition concluded that certain Treaty provisions may also be capable of creating horizontally effective rights, in that they may be invoked against other individuals. This, for example, can be witnessed in relation to art 141 EC, as concluded in the case of *Defrenne* v *Sabena (No 2)* Case 43/75 [1976] ECR 455 where the right to equal pay for equal work was enforced by an air stewardess against her employers.

Should a Treaty provision require further legislative measures to be taken, it will fail the third criteria of the *Van Gend en Loos* test. However, the Court has concluded that once the time period set down for those measures has expired, it may be granted direct effect, as long as the other criteria are met. For example, art 43 EC, providing for freedom of establishment, required the issuing of directives by the Community institutions, but proved to be extremely time-consuming. Fortunately, in *Reyners (Jean)* v *Belgium* Case 2/74 [1974] ECR 631 the Court held that art 43 EC was still capable of creating directly effective rights.

In some cases, however, it appears that a Treaty Article will be incapable of having direct effect. In some cases this is because they are concluded to be unclear, such as, for example, art 10 EC. Article 10 EC requires that Member States take all appropriate measures to fulfil the obligations stemming from the EC Treaty, but in *Schlüter (Carl)* v *Hauptzollamt Lörrach* Case 9/73 [1973] ECR 1135 it was concluded by the ECJ to be too vague to create directly enforceable rights. In other cases the Treaty Article may not be granted direct effect because, it appears, of the practical or political consequences that may result. This may be witnessed in the case of *R* v *Secretary of State for the Home Department, ex parte Flynn* [1997] 3 CMLR 888.

In *Flynn* the national court examined whether art 14 EC was capable of having direct effect. The Article requires Member States to create a single market, which is to be an area without internal frontiers in which the free movement of goods, persons, services and capital is ensured. Flynn had been subject to detainment for questioning at Dover, and sought to impose a directly enforceable right to free movement within a single market under art 14 EC. It was concluded that the provision did not impose an obligation on Member States, and certainly not one that was in any way clear or precise. It could, however, be argued that the decision was perhaps based on policy grounds because of the possible implications that would result from extending direct effect to such a provision.

Direct effect of directives

Secondary legislation produced by the Community under art 249 EC includes regulations, decisions and directives. Directives are defined in art 249 EC as 'binding as to the result to be achieved' but which 'leave to the national authorities the choice of form and methods' of achieving the desired result. Directives are not directly applicable, and it appears on face value that they are also not capable of creating directly effective rights. This is due to the need for further legislative action on the part of the Member State – a breach of the need for the measure to be non-dependent. However, in the landmark case of *Van Duyn* v *Home Office* Case 41/74 [1974] ECR 1337 the ECJ concluded that art 3(1) of Council Directive 64/221 was capable of generating directly effective rights. The Court concluded that it would be incompatible with the binding effect attributed to directives by art 249 EC to exclude them from being capable of having direct effect.

However, in order for a directive to comply with the need to be non-dependent, the Court stated in *Pubblico Ministero* v *Ratti* Case 148/78 [1979] ECR 1629 that the time limit imposed in the directive for the necessary national implementing measures must have expired. It is only at this point that an individual may rely on the terms of a directive and acquire rights that must be protected by the national court. In addition, a directive must also meet the remaining two criteria, in that it is clear and unconditional.

The application of direct effect to directives, in comparison with Treaty Articles, reveals one striking difference, however. The Court concluded in the case of *Marshall* v *Southampton and South-West Hampshire Area Health Authority (Teaching) (No 1)* Case 152/84 [1986] ECR 723 that directives, in this case Council Directive 76/207, were not capable of creating horizontally effective rights. The reasoning for this was, and remains, based on the fact that directives are only addressed to Member States and not to individuals. It was also argued that directives were not officially published, and therefore it was extremely difficult for individuals to be aware of the obligations stemming from them.

Since the decision in *Van Duyn* v *Home Office* Case 41/74 [1974] ECR 1337 the situation has changed, in that directives are now officially published under amendments (introduced by the Treaty on European Union) to art 254 EC. This, combined with the fact that Community citizens are now far more aware of Community law, prompted some to suggest that it was now appropriate to grant directives horizontal direct effect. This indeed was the suggestion put forward in a persuasive argument by the Advocate-General in *Faccini Dori* v *Recreb Srl* Case C–91/92 [1994] ECR I–3325. However, the ECJ declined to agree with the Advocate-General's opinion and confirmed the position in *Marshall* v *Southampton and South-West Hampshire Area Health Authority (Teaching) (No 1)* Case 152/84 [1986] ECR 723 that directives were not capable of granting horizontal direct effect.

The creation and extension of the doctrine of direct effect to various sources of Community law has achieved in part the desire of the ECJ to maximise the effectiveness of Community law. However, this effectiveness is limited by the Court's continued refusal to grant directives horizontal direct effect. This leaves those attempting to enforce unimplemented, or inadequately implemented, directives being capable of only doing so as against the State. On a positive note, the definition of the State has been extended to include all organs of the administration and decentralised bodies. The State also includes all bodies providing public services under the control of the State and/or which have powers in excess of those resulting from normal rules applicable in relations between individuals: *Foster and Others* v *British Gas plc* Case C–188/89 [1990] ECR I–3313.

Some relief to the lack of horizontal direct effect for directives can be found in the Court's creation of indirect effect in the case of *Von Colson and Kamann* v *Land Nordrhein-Westfalen* Case 14/83 [1984] ECR 1891. In this case the Court concentrated not on direct effect, but on the obligation found in art 10 EC. This obligation extends to national courts, which are therefore under a duty to interpret national law in the light of Community law. The case of *Marleasing SA* v *La Comercial Internacional de Alimentacion SA* Case C–106/89 [1990] ECR I–4135 extends this obligation to interpret national law in light of directives regardless of whether their date of implementation has expired and regardless of whom the obligation is being enforced. Thus, horizontal direct effect is achieved, but only via a 'backdoor', or indirect, route.

An alternative route of redress is to seek damages for breaches of Community law under the principle of State liability: *Francovich and Bonifaci* v *Italian Republic* Case C–6 and 9/90 [1991] ECR I–5357 and developed in *Brasserie du Pêcheur SA* v *Federal Republic of Germany; R* v *Secretary of State for Transport, ex parte Factortame Ltd* Joined Cases C–46 and 48/93 [1996] ECR I–1029. Failure to implement a directive by its deadline will, it appears, automatically incur liability: *Dillenkofer and Others* v *Federal Republic of Germany* Cases C–178, 179, 188, 189 and 190/94 [1996] ECR I–4845. For those that suffer damage and can prove a causal link between the failure to implement the directive and that damage, this provides the ultimate protection should they be unable to secure their directly effective rights because of the lack of any horizontal direct effect.

However, in *Brasserie du Pêcheur SA* v *Federal Republic of Germany; R* v *Secretary of State for Transport, ex parte Factortame Ltd* Joined Cases C–46 and 48/93 [1996] ECR I–1029 the European Court also clearly stated that failure to use any available directly effective rights could result in an inability to mitigate any loss. Thus, direct effect remains an important aspect of Community law, and one that individuals will continue to rely on in national courts in order to secure their Community rights. Finally, whether directives should be capable of horizontal direct effect remains an important and controversial issue in Community law; any decision to award them such effect would certainly go some considerable way to fully maximising the effectiveness of Community law.

Chapter 7

Fundamental Principles of European Community Law II: Non-discrimination, Protection of Human Rights and Proportionality

7.1   Introduction

7.2   Key points

7.3   Key cases and materials

7.4   Questions and suggested solutions

7.1 Introduction

This chapter will focus on other fundamental principles in the Community legal order. Some of these principles were contained within the treaties and have been expanded on by the European Court using teleological interpretation. They have also been expanded by the creation of secondary legislation widening their scope, and/or Treaty amendments. In contrast, the European Court has created some principles itself, for example the protection of human rights. In the case of this example, the Community itself has become involved only recently. One interesting feature of this area is that these examples of fundamental principles of Community law reveal the development of the Community beyond the original purely economic aims of the EEC Treaty to aims that are social in nature.

7.2 Key points

The interpretation of Community law

Since the European Court is engaged in the interpretation of Treaty law and legislation enacted thereunder, the Court has consistently prescribed the teleological or 'purposive' method for the interpretation or construction of Community law. This is the method used to ascertain the content of international obligations and contrasts with the 'literal meaning' approach preferred by the English courts.

The teleological approach is intended to allow flexibility in the interpretation process by emphasising the purpose of a measure and not its strict terminology. The first step in this process is to ascertain the purpose of the particular legislative measure. Article 253 EC requires that measures of secondary legislation 'shall state the reasons on which they are based'. The purpose of a Community measure, therefore, can be determined by reference to the preamble or recital which precedes the actual provisions of any Community measure. Once the purpose of the legislation has been identified, its provisions can be interpreted with this purpose in mind.

Section 3(1) European Communities Act 1972 specifically requires that any question relating to the meaning or effect of a provision of Community law before a court or tribunal in the United Kingdom is to be treated as a question of law and interpreted in accordance with the provisions laid down by the relevant decisions of the European Court.

The teleological approach to interpretation also means that measures of Community law incorporated into English law must be construed to give effect to the Community measure. For example, legislation implementing Community directives must be interpreted in light of the purpose of the original measure: *Lister* v *Forth Dry Dock and Engineering Co* [1989] 1 All ER 1134.

This chapter focuses on some of the fundamental principles developed by the European Court and includes discussion of: non-discrimination on the basis of nationality; non-discrimination on the basis of gender; and the protection of human rights.

Non-discrimination on the basis of nationality

Article 12 EC establishes the fundamental principle that 'any discrimination on the grounds of nationality shall be prohibited'. This obligation extends to all activities within the scope of the Treaty and, in particular, to the exercise of the rights of the free movement of goods, persons, services and capital. The same obligation is repeated in a number of subsequent provisions of the EC Treaty which stress the importance of this principle as a fundamental rule of Community law. Both direct and indirect discrimination are prohibited: see, for example, *Union des Associations Européennes de Football* v *Jean-Marc Bosman* Case C–415/93 [1995] ECR I–4921.

The obligation of non-discrimination on the basis of nationality has a number of important effects.

a) This obligation precludes Member States from levying tariffs or charges having an equivalent effect.

b) No Member State can impose, either directly or indirectly, any form of internal taxation on the products of other Member States in excess of that imposed on identical or similar domestic products.

c) Member States cannot discriminate between domestic and Community suppliers of services nor between domestic investors and Community investors.

d) The European Court has extended the principle of non-discrimination not only to the freedom to supply services, but also the freedom to receive services: *Cowan* v *Trésor Public* Case 186/87 [1990] 2 CMLR 613.

e) The obligation of non-discrimination applies to the protection of all economic rights falling within the scope of the EC Treaty and, in particular, intellectual and industrial property rights: *Collins (Phil)* v *Imtrat Handelsgesellschaft mbH* Cases C–92 and 362/92 [1993] ECR I–5145.

The principle of non-discrimination on the basis of nationality also applies to workers, whose free movement is secured under art 39 EC. Thus, Community nationals are entitled to the same kind of employment protection as nationals of the host Member State, as well as the same social and tax advantages under Council Regulation 1612/68, art 7(2). Such rights are considered in more detail in Chapter 8.

Article 13 EC, inserted by the Treaty of Amsterdam, gives the Council of Ministers power to adopt legislation to expand the prohibition against discrimination to include grounds other than nationality. Community measures may now be adopted to prohibit discrimination based on sex, racial or ethnic origin, religion or belief, disability, age or sexual orientation. As regards discrimination on the grounds of sex, there is an overlap with art 141 EC. However, the other grounds on which discrimination will be prohibited are innovations as far as Community law is concerned.

Non-discrimination on the basis of gender

Another fundamental objective of the EC Treaty, stated in art 141 EC, is recognition of the basic principle that men and women should be entitled to receive equal pay for equal work. The European Court has ruled on a number of occasions that art 141 EC is capable of having direct effect. In particular, in *Defrenne* v *Sabena (No 2)* Case 43/75 [1976] ECR 455, the Court held that art 141 EC prohibited direct and overt discrimination, a concept which was identified by reference to the twin criteria of equal work and equal pay which are specified in the Article itself. Unfortunately, the effect of the Court's decision in this case was limited because, according to the Court, the provision could only support claims relating to pay periods after the date of judgment.

Another illustration of de facto discrimination contrary to art 141 EC concerned the dismissal of a female employee on account of her pregnancy. In *Webb* v *EMO Air Cargo* Case C–32/93 [1994] ECR I–3567, the European Court held that art 141 EC and Council Directive 76/207 prohibited the dismissal of a female employee who was unable to fulfil the terms of her employment contract due to her absence for maternity leave. The Court found that the maternity leave for her condition could not be equated to a period of absence attributable to a comparable medical condition in a male employee which would justify dismissal.

As a result of the Court's decision in *Jenkins* v *Kingsgate (Clothing Productions) Ltd* Case 96/80 [1981] ECR 911, discrimination in relation to pay that is disguised or indirect may also come within the ambit of art 141 EC. Indirect discrimination exists when the discrimination is not based on sex per se but results in detrimentally affecting a considerably higher proportion of one sex. The applicant must therefore first establish that they are in a class of persons predominately of one sex: *Enderby v Frenchay Health Authority and the Secretary of State for Health* Case C–127/92 [1993] ECR I–5535. Under Council Directive 97/80 the employee only has to offer facts from which it may be presumed that there has been indirect discrimination.

In cases of direct discrimination there may never be a justification. However, in cases of indirect discrimination the employer has the opportunity to objectively justify the difference in treatment according to the ECJ in *Jenkins* v *Kingsgate (Clothing Productions) Ltd* Case 96/80 [1981] ECR 911. In *Bilka-Kaufhaus GmbH* v *Karin Weber von Hartz* Case 170/84 [1986] ECR 1607 the Court established a test that an employer is required to meet in order to objectively justify indirect discrimination. The test requires that the employer prove that their measures correspond to a real need; that they are proportionate to that need; and that they are necessary. Whether this is the case is a matter for the national courts to determine. In *Rinner-Kühn* v *FWW Spezial-Gebäudereinigung GmbH* Case 171/88 [1989] ECR 2743 the Court stated that to objectively justify indirect discrimination the employer had to show that the measures were part of a necessary aim of social policy and were suitable and requisite to achieve that purpose. In the case the claim that the measure was justified because part-time workers were not as dependent on their employers was concluded to be a gross generalisation and was not acceptable objective justification: see also *Nimz* v *Freie und Hansestadt Hamburg* Case 184/89 [1991] ECR 297.

'Equal pay' is defined in art 141 EC as 'the ordinary basic or minimum wage or salary and any other consideration, whether in cash or kind, which the worker receives, directly or indirectly, in respect of his [or her] employment from his [or her] employer'.

The European Court has defined 'pay' in broad terms. Article 141 EC defines pay as the 'ordinary basic or minimum wage or salary or any other consideration, whether in cash or in kind, which the worker receives directly or indirectly, in respect of his employment from his employer'. This forms the basis of the liberal interpretation offered by the European Court, although it should be noted that social security is not pay: *Defrenne* v *Sabena (No 2)* Case 43/75 [1976] ECR 455. In *Garland* v *British Rail Engineering* Case 12/81 [1982] ECR 359 the Court concluded that special travel facilities were pay. Sick pay has been concluded also to be pay: *Rinner-Kühn* (above). In *Commission* v *Belgium* Case C–173/91 [1993] ECR I–673 the Belgian government attempted to argue that redundancy supplements were social security and outside of the ambit of art 141 EC – the European Court disagreed. Supplementary payments (for example, to top-up gross salary for contribution to a compulsory occupational pension scheme) and maternity pay are also pay within art 141 EC: *Worringham and Humphreys* v *Lloyds Bank* Case 69/80 [1981] ECR 767 and *Gillespie* v *Northern Ireland Health and Social Services Board* Case C–342/93 [1996] ECR I–475.

In the landmark judgment of *Barber* v *Guardian Royal Exchange Assurance Group* Case C–262/88 [1990] ECR I–1889 the European Court also came to the conclusion that a contracted-out occupational pension scheme was not social security but pay for the purposes of art 141 EC. This was an important decision, since until this case the Community institutions and Member States were operating under the principle that such pensions were forms of social security and outside the ambit of the Treaty principle. Instead, the institutions were preparing a directive (Council Directive 86/378) to deal with equality issues. The Directive contains numerous exceptions, but since the decision in *Barber* an employee can rely on the Treaty, which contains no express exceptions and attracts both vertical and horizontal direct effect. However, due to the claim by the Member States that such a decision could have serious financial implications, the Court limited the retrospective effect of the decision. This was clarified by the addition of a protocol attached to the EC Treaty by the Treaty on European Union. Thus, only pay attributable to periods of service after 17 May 1990 will constitute pay within art 141 EC, except for those that had already instigated proceedings.

A number of Community directives have also been adopted by the Community to add substance to the general obligation of non-discrimination in the workplace: see Council Directive 76/207, Council Directive 79/7 and Council Directive 86/613.

Article 226(4) EC was added by the Treaty of Amsterdam to allow positive discrimination programmes in favour of underrepresented genders in specific areas of employment. This new provision is intended to overrule the European Court's decision in *Kalanke* v *Freie Hansestadt Bremen* Case C–450/93 [1995] ECR I–3051 which ruled against such schemes.

The protection of human rights in Community law

The European Court has acknowledged that 'the fundamental rights generally recognised by the Member States form an integral part of [the] Community system': *Nold* v *Commission* Case 4/73 [1974] ECR 491. In the past, the European Court has considered issues of human rights relating to the following matters:

a) the right to privacy: *National Panasonic* v *Commission* Case 136/79 [1980] ECR 2033;

b) freedom to practise a religion: *Prais* v *Council* Case 130/75 [1976] ECR 1589;

c) the right to possess property: *Hauer* v *Land Rheinland-Pfalz* Case 44/79 [1979] ECR 3727;

d) the right of lawyer/client confidentiality: *AM and S Europe Ltd* v *Commission* Case 155/79 [1982] ECR 1575;

e) issues of substantive and procedural due process of law: *Musique Diffusion Française SA* v *Commission* Cases 100–103/80 [1985] ECR 1825;

f) the right to refrain from self-incrimination: *UNECTEF* v *Heylens and Others* Case 222/86 [1987] ECR 4097.

In *Internationale Handelsgesellschaft GmbH* v *EVGF* Case 11/70 [1970] ECR 1125 the

Court expressly stated that respect for fundamental human rights formed an integral part of those general principles it was to protect. However, the Court has rejected the proposition that the Community can accede as a whole to the European Convention on Human Rights. In its Opinion in *Re the Accession of the European Community to the ECHR* Opinion 2/94 [1996] ECR I–1759, the Court firmly ruled that joining the European Convention on Human Rights (ECHR) would undermine the principle of the supremacy of Community law by allowing a non-EC institution to judge whether a rule of Community law was compatible with a set of external legal principles. If such review was to be possible, the EC Treaty itself would require amendment.

The importance of the protection of human rights can now be seen in the treaties. Article 6(1) EC, as amended by the Treaty of Amsterdam, states:

> 'The Union is founded on the principles of liberty, democracy, respect for human rights and fundamental freedoms, and the rule of law, principles which are common to the Member States.'

In addition, the Council now also has the power to suspend the voting rights of any Member State found to have breached these principles: art 7(2) TEU. Instead of acceding to the ECHR, the ECJ may apply the principles of the Convention insofar as they relate to matters that are within the competence of the Community under art 6(2) TEU.

A more recent development is the creation of an EU Charter of Fundamental Rights, which was published in draft form in July 2000. The Charter identifies six fundamental values, namely: dignity; freedom; equality; solidarity; citizenship and justice. The rights protected under the Charter are generally available to all, although there are some that are targeted to offering protection for distinct categories of persons, such as children and workers. European Union citizens are specifically targeted and are given a range of rights, such as: to settle; to access social security benefits and welfare assistance; and diplomatic and consular protection. EU citizens and non-EU nationals residing in the EU are also granted rights, such as: to access institution documents; to refer cases to the Ombudsman and to petition the European Parliament. Limitations to these rights may only be introduced under law, must be proportionate, and must be necessary to meet the general interests of the Union or to protect the rights and freedoms of others: art 52(1) of the Charter.

The Charter takes the unusual step of incorporating social, economic, civil and political rights in one place, and codifies rights previously contained in a wide range of national and international sources. It remains to be seen whether the Charter will remain merely declaratory, or whether it will be incorporated into the treaties, as suggested by the European Commission.

Other general principles of Community law

As well as those principles such as equality and the protection of human rights referred to above, the European Court has established other general principles of Community law (sometimes also referred to as tertiary sources of EC law). These general principles of EC law include the following.

a) Proportionality: this principle ensures that administrative measures are proportionate to their aims. In *Internationale Handelsgesellschaft GmbH v EVGF* Case 11/70 [1970] ECR 1125 the Court referred to the need for an individual not to have their freedom of action limited to an extent that was beyond the public interest. The principle has been used in economic cases: see, for example, *R v Intervention Board, ex parte Man (Sugar) Ltd* Case 181/84 [1985] ECR 2889. The principle can also be witnessed in non-economic matters, especially in cases involving the use by Member States of any rules allowing derogation from the basic rules of the Treaty, such as *Watson (Lynne) and Belmann (Alessandro)* Case 118/75 [1976] ECR 1185 and *R v Pieck* Case 157/79 [1980] ECR 2171.

b) Legal certainty: this principle was invoked by the Court in *Defrenne v Sabena (No 2)* Case 43/75 [1976] ECR 455 as an important ground for refusing to permit art 141 EC to have retrospective effect. In *Officier van Justitie v Kolpinghuis Nijmegen BV* Case 80/86 [1987] ECR 3969 the ECJ stated that national courts must interpret national law to comply with EC law in a manner that respected the principles of legal certainty and non-retroactivity.

c) Protection of legitimate expectations: this principle was accepted as part of Community law in *Deuka* Case 5/75 [1975] ECR 759 and *Mulder v Minister of Agriculture and Fisheries* Case 120/86 [1988] ECR 2321. This principle, though, cannot be used in a manner that constrains the Community's freedom of action.

d) Natural justice: often referred to by the Court as simply 'fairness', this principle equates to the rules in English law that a person is entitled to an unbiased hearing and the right to be heard: see, for example, *UNECTEF v Heylens and Others* Case 222/86 [1987] ECR 4097.

e) Legal professional privilege: written communications between an independent lawyer and client are privileged under Community law according to *AM and S Europe Ltd v Commission* Case 155/79 [1982] ECR 1575.

7.3 Key cases and materials

- *Accession of the Community to the ECHR, Re the* Opinion 2/94 [1996] ECR I–1759
  The Community is not capable of acceding in its own right to the ECHR

- *Barber v Guardian Royal Exchange Assurance Group* Case C–262/88 [1990] ECR I–1889
  A contracted-out occupational pension scheme was not social security but pay for the purposes of art 141 EC

- *Bilka-Kaufhaus GmbH v Karin Weber von Hartz* Case 170/84 [1986] ECR 1607
  Established a test that an employer is required to meet in order to objectively justify indirect discrimination

- *Defrenne* v *Sabena (No 2)* Case 43/75 [1976] ECR 455
  Article 141 EC has direct effect, although this case concluded that this would only be the case where the discrimination was direct/overt

- *Garland* v *British Rail Engineering* Case 12/81 [1982] ECR 359
  Example of the wide interpretation of pay for the purposes of art 141 EC – the Court concluded that special travel facilities were pay

- *Internationale Handelsgesellschaft GmbH* v *EVGF* Case 11/70 [1970] ECR 1125
  Respect for fundamental human rights form an integral part of those general principles that the European Court must protect

- *Jenkins* v *Kingsgate (Clothing Productions) Ltd* Case 96/80 [1981] ECR 911
  Discrimination in relation to pay that is disguised or indirect may also come within the ambit of art 141 EC

- *Rinner-Kühn* v *FWW Spezial-Gebäudereinigung GmbH* Case 171/88 [1989] ECR 2743
  To objectively justify indirect discrimination the employer has to show that the measures are part of a necessary aim of social policy and are suitable and requisite

- EC Treaty

  - art 6 – the Union is founded on the principles of liberty, democracy, respect for human rights and fundamental freedoms, and the rule of law

  - art 12 – prohibits any discrimination on the basis of nationality

  - art 13 – gives the Council of Ministers power to adopt legislation to expand the prohibition against discrimination on grounds other than nationality, such as that on the basis of sex, race, ethnicity, religion or belief, disability, age and sexual orientation

  - art 141 – men and women are entitled to receive equal pay for equal work or work of equal value

- Council Directive 75/117 – assessing work of equal value

- Council Directive 76/207 – equal treatment in the workplace

- Council Directive 97/80 – burden of proof rests on the employee to establish the facts from which indirect discrimination may be presumed to exist

- Council Directive 79/7 – equality in matters of social security

- Council Directive 86/378 – equal treatment in occupational pension schemes

- Council Directive 86/613 – equal treatment for the self-employed

7.4 Questions and suggested solutions

QUESTION ONE

The elimination of sex discrimination has become a major objective of the European Community. Discuss its development from the Treaty of Rome and through the case law of the European Court of Justice.

University of London LLB Examination
(for External Students) European Community Law June 1996 Q4

General Comment

A straightforward essay question requiring an account of the development of sex discrimination law within the Community.

Skeleton Solution

Article 141 EC: principle of equal pay for equal work for men and women – *Defrenne* v *Sabena* – meaning of pay – meaning of equal pay for equal work – direct and indirect discrimination; Council Directives 75/117, 76/207 (equal treatment Directive), 79/7, 86/378, 86/613.

Suggested Solution

The basic Community law against sex discrimination is contained in art 141 EC. Article 141 EC provides that each Member State shall maintain the principle of equal pay for equal work for men and women. This Article was considered by the ECJ in *Defrenne* v *Sabena (No 2)* Case 43/75 [1976] ECR 455 in which it was stated that art 141 EC had a dual aim. First, the principle was to ensure a level playing field so that the Member States who had implemented this principle, with all the attendant costs, should not be competitively disadvantaged in relation to those Member States that had not. Second, the Article formed part of the broader social policy of the Community, the aims of which are 'social progress' and 'the improvement of the living and working conditions of their peoples'. The provisions of art 141 EC therefore apply within Member States without any necessity for there to be trans-border activity. Its application is restricted to the field of employment.

It was further decided in *Defrenne* v *Sabena (No 2)* Case 43/75 [1976] ECR 455 that art 141 EC was directly effective – both horizontally and vertically. The *Defrenne* case is a rare example of the ECJ limiting the retrospective effect of its judgement. It held that art 141 EC could be relied upon solely in respect of claims made after its judgement or claims that had already been initiated prior to their judgement. Predictions of the potentially disastrous economic effects for Member States of equal pay claims dating back a number of years persuaded the ECJ to take this stance. Nevertheless, the fact that art 141 EC can be invoked against the State and private parties means that access to and enforcement of the principle of equal pay is now widespread.

Article 141 EC defines pay as 'ordinary basic or minimum wage or salary and any other consideration, whether in cash or in kind, which the worker receives, directly or indirectly'. The ECJ has played an important part in the development of Community anti-discrimination law by giving the notion of 'pay' an extended meaning. 'Pay' covers those benefits which are received as a result of employment (*Garland* v *British Rail Engineering* Case 12/81 [1982] ECR 359), and these include bonus payments or sick pay (*Rinner-Kühn* v *FWW Spezial-Gebäudereinigung GmbH* Case 171/88 [1989] ECR 2743), post-retirement travel concessions (*Garland*, above) and private pension schemes (*Bilka-Kaufhaus GmbH* v *Karin Weber von Hartz* Case 170/84 [1986] ECR 1607).

The applicability of the equal pay principle to pensions has been the most vexed question in this area. Originally, in *Defrenne* v *Belgian State (No 1)* Case 80/70 [1971] ECR 445 the ECJ held that pensions set up under a social security scheme were not 'pay' within art 141 EC. Subsequently, in *Barber* v *Guardian Royal Exchange Assurance Group* Case C–262/88 [1990] ECR I–1889 a pension payable under a 'contracted out' scheme, which was a substitute for a state pension, was found to be pay and therefore subject to the equal pay principle.

It appears, therefore, that only statutory social security pension schemes payable from public funds are now excluded from the equal pay principle. Again, it is noteworthy that the ECJ limited the retrospective effect of the *Barber* decision. Claims were restricted to those relating to benefits payable for periods of employment after the judgement save where proceedings had already been commenced prior to the judgement.

The meaning of 'equal pay for equal work' in the then EEC Treaty was clarified by Council Directive 75/117 to mean equal pay for the same work or for work to which equal value is attributed. Work does not have to be identical to fall within the concept of the 'same' work, provided it is very similar: *Macarthys* v *Smith* [1980] ECR 1275.

In *Commission* v *United Kingdom (Re Equal Treatment for Men and Women)* Case 165/82 [1983] ECR 3431 the UK was found to have breached its Treaty obligations in failing to set up a system whereby an assessment of claims of work of equal value might be made. The assessment of whether one job is of equal value to another can be done by a variety of means, for example, a job evaluation scheme. No specific method of assessment is set out in art 141 EC or Council Directive 75/117. Community law does require, however, that some mechanism is established to assess a claim of work being of equal value.

The principle of equal pay under art 141 EC covers both direct discrimination (different treatment on the basis of sex alone) or indirect discrimination (different treatment on the basis of factors other than sex is disadvantaged by the difference in treatment). Although it was first considered by the ECJ to apply only to direct and overt discrimination (*Defrenne* v *Sabena (No 2)* Case 43/75 [1976] ECR 455), it was later stated to apply to all forms of discrimination. Whilst direct discrimination can never be justifiable, it may be possible to justify indirect discrimination.

In *Jenkins* v *Kingsgate (Clothing Productions) Ltd* Case 96/80 [1981] ECR 911 the part-time employees, who were mainly women, were paid a lower hourly rate than the full-time employees. The ECJ held that the differential treatment was permissible if it could be objectively justified by reasons unrelated to gender. Similar reasoning was adopted in *Bilka-Kaufhaus GmbH* v *Karin Weber von Hartz* Case 170/84 [1986] ECR 1607. A difference in treatment will be objectively justified if three conditions are fulfilled.

a) It must fulfill a real need on the part of the employer.

b) It must be appropriate to attain the objective of the employer.

c) It must be necessary to attain the objective.

Arguments put forward to justify a difference in treatment between categories of workers have been mainly economic in nature. In *Bilka-Kaufhaus GmbH* a difference in pay between full-time and part-time staff which affected women disproportionately (since they formed a higher percentage of part-time workers) was justified on the grounds that part-timers were less economic. It was said that they were generally not willing to work unsociable hours and a higher rate of pay was necessary to attract full-time employees.

In *Handels-og Kontorfunktionaerernes Forbund i Danmark* v *Dansk Arbejdsgiverforening* Case 109/88 [1989] ECR 3199 higher rates of pay to reward flexibility in working hours and sites were, in principle, objectively justifiable. Ultimately, the question of objective justification must be decided by national courts according to the criteria laid down by the ECJ.

This area of sex discrimination law has also developed as a result of secondary legislation, in particular, as a result of Council Directive 76/207, the equal treatment Directive.

Council Directive 75/117 was passed to implement the terms of art 141 EC. It does not in the view of the ECJ alter the scope of art 141 EC (*Jenkins* v *Kingsgate (Clothing Productions) Ltd*), but sets out the obligations of Member States to take measures to ensure the application of the principle of equal pay. Article 2 of Council Directive 75/117 provides that Member States should ensure that there are effective judicial remedies for those denied the principle of equal pay.

Council Directive 76/207 takes the principle of equality beyond the area of pay and has been the source of some of the most far-reaching decisions in relation to sex discrimination. It provides for equal treatment for both sexes with regard to access to employment, promotion, working conditions, including dismissal, and all types and levels of vocational training. Equal treatment is defined in Article 2 of the Directive as 'no discrimination on the grounds of sex ... marital or family status'.

Council Directive 76/207 has been used in the UK to challenge the existence of different retirement ages for men and women. It was thought that different retirement ages were not subject to the equal treatment principle since under Council Directive 79/7 the 'determination of pensionable age for the purposes of granting old-age and retirement pension' was excluded from the equality principle in 76/207. In *Marshall* v *Southampton and South-West Hampshire Area Health Authority (Teaching) (No 1)* Case 152/84 [1986] ECR 723, it was held that different retirement ages did fall within the scope of the equal treatment Directive and were contrary to the rule against equal treatment. The exclusion in Council Directive 79/7 applied only to the determination of age for the receipt of a pension, not for the purposes of retirement.

The equal treatment principle has also been applied to pregnant women. A refusal to employ a woman because of her pregnancy is direct discrimination: *Dekker* v *Stichting Vormingscentrum voor Jong Volwassenen* Case C–177/88 [1990] ECR I–3941. Dismissal on the grounds of a woman's pregnancy also breaches the equal treatment rule: *Webb* v *EMO Air Cargo* Case C–32/93 [1994] ECR I–3567. These decisions have led to a number of claims being made in the UK, most notably by former members of the armed services, dismissed because of pregnancy.

Article 6 of Directive 76/207 requires Member States to introduce into their legal systems the means by which individuals not accorded equal treatment may pursue such claims. The duty under art 6 is to provide 'real and effective remedies': *Von Colson and Kamann* v *Land Nordrhein-Westfalen* Case 14/83 [1984] ECR 1891.

In *Marshall* v *Southampton and South-West Hampshire Area Health Authority (No 2)* Case C–271/91 [1993] ECR I–4367 it was held that art 6 of Council Directive 76/207 required that where compensation was payable, that compensation should enable all loss and damage sustained to be recovered. No ceiling could be imposed on the amount of damages recoverable. This ruling has resulted in a change (in the United Kingdom) to the statutory maximum award of damages imposed in industrial tribunals when dealing with sex discrimination claims.

Other relevant directives include Council Directive 79/7 which relates to equal treatment in relation to social security benefits, Council Directive 86/378 which provides for equal treatment in occupational social security schemes and Council Directive 86/613 which covers equal treatment for the self-employed. All three directives are vertically directly effective.

It is self-evident that there is now a considerable body of Community sex discrimination law in existence which has had a considerable effect on the national laws of Member States, not least on the UK. That law is restricted to the field of employment but it has a powerful effect on the rights, in particular, of women in the Community. Much of the credit for the steps taken to eliminate sex discrimination must be given to the ECJ, which has through its judgments established an effective body of rights enforceable in national courts.

QUESTION TWO

Describe the way in which the Court of Justice has developed unwritten general principles of law in the interests of the Community.

University of London LLB Examination
(for External Students) European Union Law June 1999 Q5

General Comment

This question was designed to require discussion of the unwritten, general principles of Community law. The treaties failed to include many of these principles, such as the protection of human rights, and their historical development by the ECJ should have been the heart of this essay. General principles such as freedom from discrimination, proportionality, legal certainty, etc, are all examples of some of the general principles that could have been discussed in this answer. The answer should not have referred to direct effect, supremacy or subsidiarity (the latter being a Treaty based concept). The former are doctrines of Community law and are covered by other questions.

Skeleton Solution

The sources of Community law – primary, secondary and tertiary sources – general principles of Community law – protection of fundamental human rights – proportionality – legal certainty – protection of legitimate expectations – equality – natural justice.

Suggested Solution

The Community treaties do not define the sources of Community law, although they do instruct the European Court of Justice (ECJ) to ensure that in the interpretation and application of the treaties the 'law is observed': art 220 EC. The sources of Community law, however, may be classified into three main categories, namely, primary, secondary and tertiary. The two primary sources of Community law are the treaties creating the European Union and treaties entered into by the European Community with third States. The secondary sources stem from art 249 EC, which provides the Community institutions with the power to produce secondary legislation in the form of regulations, directives, and decisions, which are legally binding, and recommendations and opinions, which are non-legally binding. In addition, there are tertiary sources, the legal authority of which rests generally not in the treaties but in the jurisprudence of the ECJ. These principles often fill a legal vacuum in the treaties. This essay will discuss one of the most significant tertiary sources, that of general principles of Community law.

It is generally accepted in Community law that the general principles of the legal systems of the Member States will be incorporated into the 'common law' of the Community. Over time a number of such principles have been recognised by the ECJ.

Protection of fundamental human rights

The original Treaty of Rome included no explicit reference to the protection of human rights, although there is reference to some limited protection, such as that prohibiting discrimination on the basis of nationality under art 12 EC (see below). The reason for this may simply have been due to the pervading culture at the time the Treaty was drafted, or perhaps the fact that the Treaty was designed to promote economic objectives rather than social ones. Over time the ECJ recognised the need to extend Community law to protect fundamental human rights, although it took some time to achieve this.

In *Stauder v City of Ulm* Case 29/69 [1969] ECR 419 the ECJ recognised in an implicit way that Community law should not infringe human rights, since such rights had to be protected under Community law and protected by the Court itself. The European Court expanded this principle in the case of *Internationale Handelsgesellschaft GmbH v EVGF* Case 11/70 [1970] ECR 1125.

In *Internationale Handesgesellschaft* the ECJ was asked under the preliminary reference procedure to consider whether a deposit system under Council Regulation 120/67 was contrary to national constitutional law. The Court concluded that recourse to national laws was capable of breaching the uniformity of Community law, but that respect for fundamental human rights did form an integral part of the general principles of law protected by the Court. However, at the same time those rights had to be protected within the existing structure and objectives of the Community. This assertion was repeated in the case of *Nold v Commission* Case 4/73 [1974] ECR 491 in which the Court referred not only to the human rights protection offered in the constitutional traditions of the Member States, but to international treaties too. One such treaty is the European Convention for the Protection of Human Rights and Fundamental Freedoms 1950 (ECHR) to which all Member States are party.

The treaties themselves now directly refer to the protection of human rights and formally recognise the jurisprudence of the Court outlined above. Article 6(1) Treaty on European Union (TEU), as amended by the Treaty of Amsterdam (ToA), states that the Union is founded on principles of liberty, democracy, respect for human rights and fundamental freedoms and the rule of law. The ToA inserted a new art 7 TEU providing that Member States may find their rights, such as voting rights, suspended if they breach these principles. Under art 6(2) TEU the Community is to respect those rights protected under the ECHR as being general principles of Community law. However, the Community has also recognised that it lacks the necessary competence to actually accede to the Convention in its own right: *Accession of the Community to the ECHR, Re the* Opinion 2/94 [1996] ECR I–1759.

The European Court has referred to the following rights of the ECHR. Article 1 of the First Protocol ECHR protects the right to property and the freedom to choose a trade or profession. In *Wachauf v Germany* Case 5/88 [1989] ECR 2609 the Court upheld these principles, although it should be noted that the Court does not consider them to be absolute, which may be limited in order to meet Community general objectives. Article 8 ECHR offers protection to family life, home and family correspondence. In the case of *National Panasonic* v *Commission* Case 136/79 [1980] ECR 2033, the ECJ held that these principles were applicable to the carrying out of investigations by the Commission into anti-competitive practices. Freedom of expression is protected under art 10 ECHR and the Court has concluded that the interpretation of Treaty rights on the free movement of services/establishment under arts 46 and 55 EC must be done in light of this protection: *Elliniki Radiophonia Tileorassi* v *Dimotiki Etaria Pliroforissis* Case C–260/89 [1991] ECR I–2925.

Proportionality

This principle is based on the notion that administrative measures must be proportionate to the aim or objective to be achieved. The concept of proportionality was first mooted in the case of *Internationale Handelsgesellschaft GmbH* v *EVGF* Case 11/70 [1970] ECR 1125 and was later expanded on in another economic based case: *R* v *Intervention Board, ex parte Man (Sugar) Ltd* Case 181/84 [1985] ECR 2889. In this case Man had been late in applying for an export licence from the Board. The short delay of only four hours resulted in their losing all their bank securities, in accordance with Community law. Under the preliminary reference procedure the Court concluded that the penalty imposed by Community law was disproportionate and too drastic.

The application of proportionality can also be witnessed in non-economic matters, such as in the use of the derogations to free movement: art 39 EC. In the case of *Watson (Lynne) and Belmann (Alessandro)* Case 118/75 [1976] ECR 1185, Watson was to be deported from Italy for failure to comply with administrative requirements. It was concluded that this was disproportionate.

The need for proportionality will apply to both Community legislation (stemming from art 249 EC) and to actions of the Community institutions. As regards the need for legislation to be proportionate, the Court has declared that it should be examined to assess whether the means employed are suitable to achieve the desired objectives or whether they are more than is necessary: *United Kingdom* v *Council (Re Working Hours Directive)* Case C–84/94 [1996] ECR I–5755. In relation to the need for the Community institutions to operate in a manner that is proportionate, the Court will exercise the power of judicial review. However, in the above case the Court did state that they would permit the Council a wide measure of discretion particularly since it was legislating for an area (social policy) that required difficult and complex assessments. In such cases judicial review will only examine the measure in terms of whether the discretion used by the institution was affected by a manifest error, misuse of powers or was a manifest excess of the limits of discretion.

Legal certainty

This principle was first recognised early in the Court's jurisprudence in the case of *Da Costa en Schaake NV* v *Nederlandse Belastingadministratie* Cases 28–30/62 [1963] ECR 31. In the context of the case it was argued by the Advocate-General that altering the law was something that should be done prudently, since it had the potential to destroy legal certainty. Recognition of the need to protect legal certainty was also used as justification for the non-retrospective effect of the decision in *Defrenne* v *Sabena (No 2)* Case 43/75 [1976] ECR 455 on art 141 EC. This was confirmed in *Officier van Justitie* v *Kolpinghuis Nijmegen BV* [1987] ECR 3969 where the Court concluded that national courts had to interpret their national law to comply with EC law in a manner that respected the general principles of Community law, in particular legal certainty and non-retroactivity. Again, though, this is not an absolute rule, since if the Court believes that the grant of retrospective effect is essential in order for a piece of Community law to meet its objective, then it will be prepared to do so: *Amylum (GR) NV* v *Council* Case 108/81 [1982] ECR 3107.

Protection of legitimate expectations

This principle, common to a number of national legal systems, has also been recognised by the ECJ: *Mulder* v *Minister of Agriculture and Fisheries* Case 120/86 [1988] ECR 2321. In this case it can be seen that the Court equated the protection of legitimate expectation with the provision of a fair process. Again, however, there is a limitation to the scope of this principle in that it may not be relied upon of the result is to fetter the Community's freedom to act. If this should occur, the Court will need to undertake a balancing of interests, in which the Community's freedom of action may prevail: *O'Dwyer and Others* v *Council* Cases T–466, 469, 473, 474 and 477/93 [1995] ECR II–2071.

Equality

This principle was considered by the Court in *Ferrario* Case 152/81 [1983] ECR 2357 to be one of the basic and fundamental principles of the Community legal order. This is one area where the principle has been formally recognised in the EC Treaty. It prohibits three specific types of discrimination: discrimination on the grounds on nationality (art 12 EC); discrimination between producers and consumers under the Common Agricultural Policy (art 34(2) EC); and discrimination in relation to pay for work of equal value between men and women (art 141 EC). In addition, the Treaty of Amsterdam amended art 2 EC so that it now includes the general principle of securing equality between men and women, rather than confining the principle to the workplace only.

These Treaty Articles have been used as the basis for securing equality in the broadest means possible by the ECJ exercising teleological interpretation. For example, workers and their families are provided with specific provisions of Community law (ie Council Regulation 1612/68) under which they may enforce their right to equality. No such legislation exists to protect the self-employed. However, the ECJ has used art 12 EC to come to their aid. In, for example, *Commission* v *Italy (Re Housing Aid)* Case 63/86 [1988] ECR 29 the Court concluded that any restriction on housing facilities granted to nationals to alleviate financial burdens must also be granted to non-nationals, such as those attempting to exercise their right to freedom of establishment.

Natural justice

The concept of natural justice may be found in English administrative law and is closely linked to that of equity. In brief it comprises of two main rules: the right to a fair hearing and the right to be heard. In Community law the Court is more likely to refer to the need for fairness.

The principle can be found in judgements of the Court in cases such as *UNECTEF* v *Heylens and Others* Case 222/86 [1987] ECR 4097, where the Court spoke of the need for individuals to be provided with the best possible conditions in which to make their defence. In this case, it was the need for reasons to be given if a decision unfavourable to the applicant was made.

The principle is also formally enshrined in the legislation of the Community. For example, Council Directive 64/221: arts 5–7 require that these principles are adhered to when individuals are to be deprived of rights to free movement on the grounds of public policy, security or health under art 39(3) EC. In particular, those exercising their rights to free movement have the right to be officially informed of decisions within a specified timeframe. They must also be provided with clear and comprehensive reasons for any decision not in their favour; to have access to all legal remedies available to nationals; and to have the right to appeal to a court of law or a competent authority.

QUESTION THREE

'Discrimination has been elevated to a general principle of Community law by the European Court of Justice.'

Discuss, and elaborate particularly on the development of art 141 (ex 119) EC.

University of London LLB Examination
(for External Students) European Union Law June 1999 Q8

General Comment

This question, an essay one, requires a discussion of the development of the principle of non-discrimination. Discussion should have included reference to art 12 EC, which prohibits discrimination on the basis of nationality, but would have centred on art 141 EC as required by the terms of the question itself. This provision relates to the principle of equal pay for men and women, although the area has been considerably expanded by legislation and the interpretative role of the European Court of Justice.

Skeleton Solution

The principle of non-discrimination – art 12 EC: discrimination on the basis of nationality prohibited – new enabling clause in art 13 EC – art 141 EC: equal pay – elaboration on the general principle by the production of secondary legislation – expansion of the principle by the European Court of Justice; for example, direct and indirect discrimination and the definition of pay, with particular reference to the issue of pensions.

Suggested Solution

The European Court of Justice has recognised that freedom from discrimination, or equality, is a fundamental principle of Community law: *Ferrario* Case 152/81 [1983] ECR 2357. The application of this principle can be witnessed most clearly in cases involving discrimination on grounds of nationality, under art 12 EC, and gender, under art 141 EC.

Article 12 EC prohibits discrimination imposed on the basis of nationality. It applies to any matter covered by the EC Treaty and is perhaps invoked most often in relation to aspects that may affect an individual's ability to enter or reside in another Member State. This can be witnessed clearly in relation to rights available to those seeking free movement of establishment and provision or receipt of services.

Council Regulation 1612/68 provides for equal access to employment and other benefits for workers and their families. There is no corresponding secondary legislation providing for such rights for the self-employed, in relation to establishment or providing/ receiving services. The Court, though, has come to the aid of those Community nationals by relying on art 12 EC. For example, Council Regulation 1612/68 has been applied to secure rights for workers (and their families) in relation to housing and the criminal process. The Court has made use of art 12 EC to secure similar rights for the self-employed.

In *Commission* v *Italy (Re Housing Aid)* Case 63/86 [1988] ECR 29 the Court stated that any restriction on housing facilities granted to nationals to alleviate financial burdens must also be granted to non-nationals, since to do otherwise would be a breach of art 12 EC. The same conclusion was reached in relation to the access of leisure facilities in *Commission* v *France* Case C–334/94 [1996] ECR I–1307. In *Hayes* v *Kronenberger GmbH* Case C–323/95 [1997] ECR I–1711 the Court concluded that a requirement that non-nationals pay a court security deposit was a breach of art 12 EC, since nationals were not required to make such a payment. The case of *Cowan* v *Trésor Public* Case 186/87 [1989] ECR 195 centred on a British citizen who was assaulted outside a Paris metro station but denied access to compensation from the French equivalent of the Criminal Compensation Board. The principle of freedom of discrimination on the basis of nationality was concluded by the Court to be applicable to those seeking services, and consequently any law or regulation that prevented a Community national from receiving a service because of their non-national status was discriminatory and a breach of the EC Treaty.

The equality principle was further enhanced by the Treaty of Amsterdam (ToA) when it amended old art 6a of the EC Treaty (now art 13 EC) to provide for a new non-discrimination provision, which confers legislative competence on the Community to combat discrimination based on sex, racial or ethnic origin, religion or belief, disability, age or sexual orientation. It should be noted that this provision does not per se prohibit such discrimination, but does provide a means of producing legislation to combat it. Hence, the Council of Ministers, acting unanimously, can under art 13 EC adopt such measures that are appropriate to secure such objectives upon a Commission proposal, after having consulted the Parliament.

One of the areas in which the ECJ has been most proactive in securing equality as a general principle of Community law is that of equality for men and women under art 141 EC. Whilst the equal pay for equal work provision was perhaps included in response to economic arguments, the Court has held that equal treatment is a fundamental general principle of Community law. It is a personal human right that Community law and national courts must protect: *Defrenne* v *Sabena (No 3)* Case 149/77 [1978] ECR 1365 and *P* v *S and Cornwall County Council* Case C–13/94 [1996] ECR I–2143. Indeed, in *Defrenne* v *Sabena (No 2)* Case 43/75 [1976] ECR 455 the Court concluded that art 141 EC pursued a double aim, both economic and social.

The proactive approach of the Court in its interpretation of this important Treaty provision has done much to secure some measure of equality between the treatment of men and women. Two important areas in which this can perhaps be best seen include the types of discrimination prohibited, and extension of the definition of pay to which there is entitlement to equality.

In *Defrenne (No 2)* (above) the Court held that direct and overt discrimination was identifiable under the conditions in art 141 EC and would not be justifiable, but that indirect or disguised discrimination was not identifiable under its terms. Consequently, an individual suffering indirect discrimination – discrimination not based on sex but which has the practical effect of disadvantaging one particular sex – would not be able to bring their claim under the Treaty. This was resolved to some extent by the introduction of Council Directive 75/117, which extended equality in pay to those doing work of equal value, and which was concluded to merely be an extension of art 141 EC so that claims could be brought directly under the Treaty. Indeed, art 141 EC was amended by the Treaty of Amsterdam to extend to work of equal value. However, before this Treaty development the Court itself recognised that claims for indirect discrimination could be brought under art 141 EC in the case of *Jenkins* v *Kingsgate (Clothing Productions) Ltd* Case 96/80 [1981] ECR 911.

In *Jenkins* the ECJ concluded that indirect discrimination, in this case paying full and part-time workers differing hourly rates although the latter were predominately women, was a form of indirect discrimination. This would breach the Treaty, unless there were reasons, other than those based on sex, for the inequality in treatment. Hence, indirect discrimination is now within the ambit of art 141 EC, although the burden of proof to establish that a distinct class of persons are affected rests with the employee (*Enderby* v *Frenchay Health Authority and the Secretary of State for Health* Case C–127/92 [1993] ECR I–5535) and the employer has the opportunity to objectively justify the difference. In order to justify the difference the employer must, according to the Court in *Bilka-Kaufhaus GmbH* v *Karin Weber von Hartz* Case 170/84 [1986] ECR 1607, prove: that the offending measure corresponds to a real need on the part of the undertaking; that it is proportionate to achieve that need; and that it is necessary. They may not, however, rely on economic or general considerations: *Rinner-Kühn* v *FWW Spezial-Gebäudereinigung GmbH* Case 171/88 [1989] ECR 2743.

The ECJ has also been influential in extending the definition of 'pay' under art 141 EC. This has been held to include 'perks', such as travel facilities in *Garland* v *British Rail Engineering* Case 12/81 [1982] ECR 359, and sick-pay in *Rinner-Kühn* v *FWW Spezial-Gebäudereinigung GmbH* Case 171/88 [1989] ECR 2743. In *Barber* v *Guardian Royal Exchange Assurance Group* Case C–262/88 [1990] ECR I–1889 the definition of pay was held to include redundancy payments, regardless of whether they are made on a contractual or voluntary basis or under national legislative obligations. Maternity pay has also been concluded to be within art 141 EC – in *Gillespie* v *Northern Ireland Health and Social Services Board* Case C–342/93 [1996] ECR I–475 the Court held that the amount of maternity pay must be calculated so as to reflect any increases awarded during the actual maternity period itself. The area in which the ECJ has been most influential, and one in which it has been arguably more proactive than the Community institutions, is that of pensions.

In *Defrenne* v *Belgian State (No 1)* Case 80/70 [1971] ECR 445 the Court declared that retirement pensions governed by legislation were a form of social security and were not within the ambit of pay for the purposes of art 141 EC. Equal treatment in social security is provided for under Council Directive 79/7, but this includes a number of express exceptions to equality. In relation to occupational pensions schemes the Community institutions were devising another directive (Council Directive 86/378), which was to declare such pensions to be a form of social security and consequently also outside the scope of art 141 EC. The ECJ, however, was faced in the case of *Bilka-Kaufhaus GmbH* v *Karin Weber von Hartz* Case 170/84 [1986] ECR 1607 with having to consider whether an employer's occupational pension scheme was 'pay'.

In *Bilka* the Court came to the conclusion that employer's contributions to an occupational pension scheme under contractual obligation was pay. This was due to the fact that the employer's contributions were paid to supplement existing statutory security schemes, so they were consideration paid by the employer to the employee; occupational pension schemes were devised and regulated as an integral part of employment contracts. It was thought that this decision would not apply to those occupational schemes that were in direct substitution for statutory schemes and therefore Council Directive 86/378 was still adopted. Its importance was subsequently made effectively redundant by the landmark decision of the Court in *Barber* (above).

In this case the pension scheme was a contracted-out scheme; a private, non-statutory scheme approved by UK law as a direct substitute for the earning-related part of the State pension scheme. After examining its characteristics, the Court concluded that the scheme was one that fell within the definition of pay, and that art 141 EC could be relied upon to secure equality. This was because the scheme was agreed and entirely financed by the employer: it was not compulsory and was regulated by its own rules.

The importance of this decision rests in the fact that it extends the definition of pay to an area that the Member States and Community institutions believed was outside the scope of the Treaty Article. They had produced a Directive to secure equality, but this of course contained a number of express exceptions and had limited direct effect of a vertical nature only. The Court's insistence that occupational pensions are within the definition of pay means that claims may be brought directly under the Treaty Article, with its vertical and horizontal direct effect and no exceptions. This was an important development in securing equality, but was limited by the Court in one respect.

In response to claims by the Member States that they would face a heavy financial burden because of the decision, the Court decided to limit the retrospective effect of the case and make it prospective only, except for those that had already instigated proceedings. Hence art 141 EC may not be relied on to secure equality for periods before the date of *Barber* v *Guardian Royal Exchange Assurance Group* Case C–262/88 [1990] ECR I–1889 (17 May 1990) as confirmed in the Protocol attached to the EC Treaty by the Treaty on European Union. This limitation, though, only applies to the benefits from such a scheme and not the right to join in the first place.

This right had been denied to many women on the basis that they were not full-time workers or were married. The Court has held that such discrimination breached art 141 EC, since occupational pensions were pay and women should have had the right to join these schemes from the date of *Defrenne* v *Sabena (No 2)* Case 43/75 [1976] ECR 455: *Fisscher* v *Voorhuis Hengelo BV and Stichting Bedrijfspensioenfonds voor de Detailhandel* Case C–128/93 [1994] ECR I–4583. The practical impact of this decision, though, is tempered by the fact that whilst women may assert that they had the right to join such schemes, they must still pay the back-payments into the scheme – something the majority of women are unable to afford.

In conclusion, the elimination of discrimination and the promotion of equality has become an important principle of Community law. The Community institutions have been responsible for developing the concept through both Treaty amendments and the introduction of secondary legislation, such as Council Directive 76/207 providing for equal treatment in employment; Council Directive 75/117 extending equal pay to work of equal value; and Council Directive 86/613 providing equal treatment for the self-employed. Simultaneously, and sometimes in direct conflict with the intensions of the Member States and Community institutions, the ECJ has expanded and developed the concept so that provisions perhaps intended to have economic objectives have become used to secure social goals and non-discrimination has become a central concept of Community law.

Chapter 8

The Free Movement of Persons

8.1   Introduction

8.2   Key points

8.3   Key cases and materials

8.4   Questions and suggested solutions

8.1 Introduction

The free movement of labour is recognised by the EC Treaty as essential to achieve the goal of a common market. The essence of this freedom is the abolition of discrimination between nationals and workers from other Community Member States as regards employment, remuneration and other conditions of work. In the realisation of this object, a distinction is made between 'workers' and 'self-employed persons'. 'Workers' enjoy the freedom of movement, while 'self-employed persons' enjoy the freedom of establishment. Both freedoms serve the same purpose – the liberalisation of the supply of labour.

8.2 Key points

Part 1

Freedom of movement of workers

Article 39 EC regulates the free movement of workers. It creates four rights which are inherent in the exercise of this freedom:

a) the right to accept offers of employment actually made;

b) the right to move freely within the territory of Member States for this purpose;

c) the right to reside in a Member State for the purpose of employment in accordance with the provisions governing the employment of nationals of that State as laid down by law, regulations or administrative action;

d) the right to remain in the territory of a Member State after having been employed in that State, subject to conditions laid down by the European Commission.

Article 40 EC authorises the Council of Ministers to issue regulations and directives to implement art 39 EC. However, this has not prevented the European Court from declaring that art 39 EC has direct effect: *Commission* v *France (Re French Merchant Seamen)* Case 167/73 [1974] ECR 359 and *Van Duyn* v *Home Office* Case 41/74 [1974] ECR 1337.

Article 40 EC provides for art 39 EC to be supplemented by secondary legislation. The secondary legislation relevant to the free movement of workers includes:

a) Council Regulation 1612/68 providing rights for workers and their families;

b) Council Regulation 1251/70 on remaining after employment;

c) Council Directive 68/360 on entry and residence permits; and

d) Council Directive 64/221 on justifying exclusions.

In addition, art 12 EC prohibits discrimination on the basis of nationality (see Chapter 7).

Definition of 'worker' under Community law

The right to the freedom of movement is expressly restricted to 'workers' under art 39 EC. Whether a person qualifies as a worker depends on whether or not he or she satisfies the relevant criteria laid down in Community law: *Lawrie-Blum* v *Land Baden-Württenburg* Case 66/85 [1986] ECR 2121.

In order to qualify as a worker under art 39 EC, a person must be employed. The essential feature of an employment relationship is that, for a certain period of time, a person performs services for and under the direction of another person in return for which he or she receives remuneration: *Lawrie-Blum* v *Land Baden-Württenburg* Case 66/85 [1986] ECR 2121. The term 'worker' therefore includes all persons engaged in a contract of employment, including executives, salaried employees and manual workers.

The definition of 'worker' is not restricted to full-time employees. A person who is employed on a part-time basis may acquire the right of freedom of movement provided that he or she pursues an activity as an employed person which is 'effective and genuine': *Levin* v *Staatssecretaris van Justitie* Case 53/81 [1982] ECR 1035. Even a worker who is engaged in part-time employment, and who receives public assistance to supplement his or her income, may exercise this right: *Kempf* v *Staatssecretaris van Justitie* Case 139/85 [1986] ECR 1741.

The Court has teleologically interpreted art 39 EC so that it extends beyond those that have an offer of employment. In *R* v *Immigration Appeal Tribunal, ex parte Antonissen* Case C–292/89 [1991] ECR I–745 the Court declared that a Community national could enter a Member State to search for work as a migrant worker. The migrant worker has to prove that they are genuinely searching and have a genuine chance of securing employment. Only if the migrant worker is unable to do this are the authorities permitted to deport them. The migrant worker also has to be given a reasonable time within which to secure employment; in this case six months was considered reasonable.

However, the Court has left the exact time period open-ended, only stating that three months should be the minimum entitlement: *Procureur du Roi* v *Royer* Case 48/75 [1976] ECR 497.

Although not strictly workers in the true sense of that term, students enjoy special rights due to the vocational nature of their studies. A special regime has been introduced to regulate their right to exercise this freedom. In particular, Council Directive 93/96 confers on students the right of residence when pursuing their studies in Member States other than their own.

The scope of art 39 EC

Article 39 has direct effect: *Kenny* v *Insurance Officer* Case 1/78 [1978] ECR 1489. This extends to the actions of both public authorities and those adopted by private persons: *Walrave and Koch* v *Association Union Cycliste Internationale* Case 36/74 [1974] ECR 1405. In other words, art 39 EC has both vertical and horizontal direct effect.

The ECJ has given an extremely expansive definition to the prohibition on discrimination contained in art 39 EC, specifically in its judgment in *Union des Associations Européenes de Football* v *Jean-Marc Bosman* Case C–415/93 [1995] ECR I–4921. This case concerned, inter alia, the imposition of transfer fees which allowed national football clubs to impose a transfer fee when a player moved from one club to another. In the absence of such a fee, which was set by the transferring club, a player could not move from one club to another. These requirements were written into individual players' contracts. If a club refused to accept the fee offered by another club, it could prevent the player moving, in which case the player in question would be unable to break his contractual link with his club.

The Court held that the transfer fee system contravened the prohibition on discrimination contained in art 39 EC because it interfered with the right of free movement for football players. The Court accepted that the same rules applied inside Member States but held that the nature of these rules was excessive and constituted a barrier to the cross-border movement of players inside the Community. The fact that the contracts were incompatible with this prohibition rendered them unenforceable.

However, although Community countries have created the principle of the free movement of persons, Community law has not excluded the power of Member States to adopt measures enabling the national authorities to have an exact knowledge of population movements affecting their territory: *Watson (Lynne) and Belmann (Alessandro)* Case 118/75 [1976] ECR 1185.

Rights of workers exercising the freedom of movement

a) Council Directive 68/360 abolishes restrictions on the movement and residence of workers within the Community. Under this Directive, workers may exercise the freedom of movement on production of a valid identity card or passport: art 3 of the Directive.

Also, workers taking up employment in another Member State are entitled to a residence permit as proof of the right of residence: art 4(2) of the Directive. This permit must be renewed unless justified reasons may be given for not doing so.

A valid residence permit may not be withdrawn from a worker solely on the ground that he is no longer in employment due to illness or involuntary unemployment.

b) Council Regulation 1612/68 provides a number of substantive rights. Article 1 of the Regulation provides that workers are entitled to take up employment with the same priority as nationals. Articles 3 and 4 prohibit direct and indirect discrimination in relation to reserving posts for nationals, advertising and applications, and setting special recruitment or registration processes. Article 5 requires employment offices to give the same assistance to non-nationals as they do nationals. Under art 6, discriminatory vocational or medical criteria for recruitment or appointment are prohibited.

The most fertile source of rights though is probably art 7 of the Regulation. Article 7(1) prohibits all forms of discrimination, be they direct or indirect: *Sotgiu* v *Deutsche Bundespost* Case 152/73 [1974] ECR 153. Article 7(2) requires that workers are provided with all social and tax advantages granted to nationals. These rights extend to family members (defined below): *Fiorini (née Christini)* v *SNCF* Case 32/75 [1975] ECR 1085. The rights available under this provision are extremely extensive, ranging from the right to access old age pensions and childbirth allowances to speaking ones own language in judicial proceedings. However, migrant workers are not entitled to access such rights until they are employed: *Centre Public de l'Aide Sociale de Courcelles* v *Lebon* Case 316/85 [1987] ECR 2811. Article 7(3) provides the worker with the right to receive vocational education; art 8 provides the right to belong to a trade union; and art 9 requires that non-nationals be provided with the same rights to housing as nationals.

c) Council Regulation 1251/70 provides the right to remain after having been employed. To benefit from these rights the worker must have reached pensionable age having been employed for the previous 12 months and resided in the State continuously for more than three years. Alternatively, the worker may stay if they become permanently incapable of work after two years continuous residence. These rights are extended to the worker's family (defined below) in certain circumstances.

The right to remain also extends to employees and self-employed persons who have decided to retire. Council Directive 90/365 requires Member States to grant the right of residence to non-nationals who have been employed or self-employed and are recipients of an invalidity or early retirement pension, an old-age pension or a pension for industrial accident or disease. To be entitled to these rights, the non-national has to prove that they receive a sufficient enough income to not be a burden on the social security system of the State they wish to remain in.

In addition to the above rights, Council Regulation 1612/68 permits workers to 'install' their family with them, subject to the worker having adequate housing.

Family is defined in art 10(1) of the Regulation as the spouse, descendants under 21 or who are dependent, and dependent relatives in the ascendant line of both the worker and the spouse. Dependency is a question of fact, not law: *Centre Public de l'Aide Sociale de Courcelles* v *Lebon* Case 316/85 [1987] ECR 2811. The nationality of family members is not relevant, although any non-EC nationals require a visa.

The definition of spouse is that of someone legally married to the worker and this status remains until the full, legal dissolution of the marriage: *Diatta* v *Land Berlin* Case 267/83 [1985] ECR 567. A cohabitee is not considered to be a spouse. However, the ECJ in *Netherlands* v *Reed* Case 59/85 [1986] ECR 1283 concluded that the worker could rely on alternative provisions of EC law to secure the right to install a cohabitee, namely art 7(2) of Regulation 1612/68 (see above) and art 12 EC which prohibits discrimination of the basis of nationality. In other words, if nationals are entitled to cohabit, depriving workers of such rights would constitute discrimination and would breach their entitlement to the same social and tax advantages granted to nationals.

Under art 11 of the Regulation, family members are entitled to take up employment: see, for example, *Gül (Emir)* v *Regierungspräsident Düsseldorf* Case 131/85 [1986] ECR 1573.

Employment in the public service

Article 39(4) EC exempts employment in the public sector from the scope of the free movement of workers. The Member States of the Community all vary from each other in their characterisation of public service. For the purposes of the application of this exemption, whether or not a position constitutes employment in the public service depends on whether or not:

> '... the posts in question are typical of the specific activities of the public service in so far as the exercise of powers conferred by public law and responsibilities for safeguarding the general interests of the State are vested in it.' (*Commission* v *Belgium (Re State Employees)* Case 149/79 [1980] ECR 3881.)

Therefore, in order for this exemption to apply, it must be shown that the persons employed are charged with the exercise of powers conferred by public law or, alternatively, have been given responsibility for protecting the special interests of the state: *Commission* v *Italy (Re Public Service Employment)* Case 225/85 [1987] ECR 2625.

This may be described as a functional rather than institutional test, in other words it is the work that is being undertaken that is the relevant factor, not the nature of the employer.

Derogations

Article 39(3) EC limits the exercise of the free movement of workers on the grounds of public policy, public security and public health. Council Directive 64/221 creates rules to regulate the exercise of discretion conferred on Member States.

Public policy and security

These grounds may be exercised to prevent a person from entering a Member State, from residing there or may be used to justify their deportation, although it should be noted that they are restrictively interpreted by the Court: *Van Duyn* v *Home Office* Case 41/74 [1974] ECR 1337. To exercise these grounds the Member State must prove that the person is a genuine and serious threat: *Rutili* v *Minister for the Interior* Case 36/75 [1975] ECR 1219. To ascertain whether the threat is genuine one should consider the treatment nationals receive when committing the same action. In *Adoui and Cornvaille* v *Belgian State* Cases 115 and 116/81 [1982] ECR 1665, the Court emphasised the need for there to be some repressive measures of an equivalent nature imposed on nationals. In addition, according to art 32 of Council Directive 64/221, these grounds may only be exercised on the basis of the personal conduct of the individual, and criminal convictions per se are insufficient justification for their exercise.

Personal conduct may include the membership of an organisation: *Van Duyn* (above). However, the organisation must not receive the full protection of the law and the membership must be present with active participation or support of its aims.

Criminal convictions cannot be used to justify the use of these grounds as a general preventative measure or as a means of deterring others: *Bonsignore* v *Oberstadtdirektor of the City of Cologne* Case 67/74 [1975] ECR 297. Previous convictions may be used as evidence of personal conduct that the person constitutes a present threat in the context that they have a propensity to act again in the same manner in the future: *R* v *Bouchereau* Case 30/77 [1977] ECR 1999. However, the Court accepted in *R* v *Secretary of State for the Home Department, ex parte Santillo* Case 131/79 [1980] ECR 1585 that the person's conduct must be considered at the time of deportation to ensure that there have been no changes since the offending activity and the issuing of the order: *Proll* v *Entry Clearance Officer, Düsseldorf (No 2)* [1988] 2 CMLR 387.

Public health

Restrictions on the movement of persons based on the ground of public health have been codified in Council Directive 64/221. This lists the only diseases and disabilities which justify refusing entry into a territory or a refusal to issue a residence permit. Diseases or disabilities occurring after a residence permit has been issued do not justify a refusal to renew the permit.

Diseases which are considered to constitute a danger to the pubic health include tuberculosis of the respiratory system, syphilis, and other infectious diseases or contagious parasitic diseases. Disabilities which constitute a threat to public health include drug addiction and profound mental disturbance.

Procedural safeguards

Council Directive 64/221 provides a number of Articles relating to procedural safeguards designed to secure minimum protection for those subject to derogation from the free movement for workers. These safeguards include the following:

a) art 5 – the right to wait no longer than six months for a decision on the issuing of the first residence permit;

b) art 6 – clear and comprehensive reasons for any decision must be provided (unless this prejudices national security);

c) art 7 – a minimum period of leave must be provided: this is 15 days if the person does not have a residence permit and one month is they do;

d) art 8 – non-nationals must be entitled to all legal remedies available to nationals; and

e) art 9 – that if there is no appeal available to a court of law there must be one available to a competent authority.

Part 2

Freedom of establishment and services

The EC Treaty provisions providing for free movement of establishment and services are provided by arts 43 and 49 EC respectively. These provisions ensure that restrictions on the self-employed that are providing professional or commercial services from either a permanent establishment or on a temporary basis are to be abolished. This obligation rests on the Member States, any competent bodies and legally recognised professional bodies too: see, for example, *Steinhauser* v *City of Biarritz* Case 197/84 [1985] ECR 1819.

The exception to these rights of free movement can be found in arts 45 and 55 EC, which provide that they do not extend to activities connected, even occasionally, with the exercise of official authority. This exception has been narrowly construed by the Court so, for example, it does not include lawyers: *Reyners (Jean)* v *Belgium* Case 2/74 [1974] ECR 631.

Any form of direct discrimination in breach of arts 43 or 49 EC may only be justified under the grounds in arts 46 (establishment) and 55 EC (services) of public policy, security or health (as with the free movement of workers – see above).

Freedom of establishment

Direct effect

Article 44 EC required the creation of a General Programme to ensure the abolition of restrictions on the freedom of establishment and art 47 EC required the development of directives for the mutual recognition of qualifications. Consequently, further legislative action on the part of the Community institutions was required and for this reason it was thought that art 43 EC would not have direct effect – it was dependent and thus failed the *Van Gend en Loos* v *Netherlands* Case 26/62 [1963] ECR 1 test.

However, in *Reyners* (above) the Court concluded that since the transitional period for the above action had expired, and the obligation was sufficiently clear and precise, art 43 EC could generate direct effect. Thus, art 43 EC could be relied upon to secure the removal of restrictions in relation to discrimination imposed on the basis of nationality and residence.

Qualifications – art 43 EC

In *Reyners* the Court also stated that whilst art 43 EC could be relied upon to remove discrimination on the basis of nationality, or measures that prevented a person entering a profession or impeded their performance of a certain activity, it did not believe that the Article could be relied on in the case of recognising qualifications. In this respect, the Court stated that the issuing of directives was still important. Hence, it was thought that art 43 EC could be used to secure the removal of discrimination on the basis of nationality, but not when it was based on the possession of different qualifications compared to those of nationals.

This position changed with subsequent decisions. In *Thieffry* v *Conseil de l'Ordre des Avocats à la Cour de Paris* Case 71/76 [1977] ECR 765 the Court ruled that Thieffry could rely directly on art 43 EC to secure recognition of his qualification, regardless of the lack of any harmonising directive. In *UNECTEF* v *Heylens and Others* Case 222/86 [1987] ECR 4097 the Court concluded that the Member State and any professional bodies are obligated to consider the equivalence of a non-national's qualifications, with reference to the nature and duration of their studies and any practical training they had undertaken. In addition, reasons for any decision had to be provided, as did a right of appeal. The ECJ has also concluded that reference should be made to any experience the applicant has: *Vlassopoulou* v *Ministerium für Justiz, Bundes-und Europaangelegenheiten Baden-Württenburg* Case C–340/89 [1991] ECR I–2357.

Qualifications – secondary legislation

The Court made significant improvements in its decisions to extend art 43 EC direct effect (see above). However, the Community institutions were also obligated to produce directives to secure the recognition of equivalent qualifications. The approach originally adopted by the Council was that of harmonisation. This involved identifying a profession and securing agreement on its minimum standards. A directive would then be issued listing all the qualifications considered as equivalent. If a Community national's qualifications are listed in the directive they have an absolute right to have them recognised in any other Member State. For example, architects can find Community qualifications harmonised in Council Directive 85/384 and veterinary surgeons have rights to freedom of establishment by virtue of Council Directives 78/1026 and 78/1027. However, reaching consensus for the production of these directives was extremely slow and the Council responded by changing its approach to one described as 'mutual recognition'.

Council Directive 89/48 adopts an approach of 'mutual trust' – if an individual is adequately qualified in one Member State they are assumed to be adequately qualified in all Member States. This drops the profession-by-profession approach described above, in favour of one, broad directive, although if the profession is covered by a harmonising (or sectoral) directive the individual should rely on that, since it gives them automatic rights to recognition of their qualifications.

Council Directive 89/48 only applies if the individual has at least three years education at university level, has completed any necessary practical training or has undertaken the profession for at least two years in a State that does not regulate the profession: art 3 of the Directive. However, it does not provide any absolute right to have qualifications recognised, but to have them assessed for equivalence.

If the education and training are at least one year less than that required in the State where the person desires recognition, the State must consider professional experience of no more than four years. If there are any major differences in the education, training or structure of the profession compared to the national requirement, or the applicant's State did not regulate the profession, an applicant may be required to undertake an adaptation period (of no more than three years) or an aptitude test: art 4(b). The choice is the applicants unless the profession requires precise knowledge of the law (although Council Directive 98/5 now provides that lawyers with at least three years experience of their home-State's legal system, the State in which to establish themselves or Community law are now exempt). Article 8 states that a right of appeal must be available.

Council Directive 92/51 extends this system of recognising qualifications to diplomas and certificates of at least one years duration, or professional practice periods or vocational training, if the diploma or certificate entitles them to pursue a regulated profession.

Non-discriminatory rules

The ECJ originally concluded that non-discriminatory rules, such as those in relation to professional standards and ethics, were outside of the scope of art 43 EC: see, for example, *Commission* v *Belgium* Case 221/85 [1987] ECR 719. However, the Court has adopted a more proactive approach by assessing whether the non-discriminatory rules are in fact a form of indirect discrimination. Hence in *Ordre des Avocats* v *Klopp* Case 107/83 [1984] ECR 2971, the Court declared that the requirement to have only one office in the region of practice in France, whilst applied in an apparently non-discriminatory manner, was in reality a form of indirect discrimination that prevented the very essence of the rights in art 43 EC from being attained. The Court appreciated that the Paris Bar was attempting to ensure that professional standards were being maintained, but concluded that the measure adopted was not proportionate.

In *Gebhard* v *Consiglio dell'Ordine degli Avvocati e Procuratori di Milano* Case C–55/44 [1995] ECR I–4165 the ECJ offered a test that may objectively justify such measures. The test provides that the measure must:

a) be applied in a non-discriminatory way;

b) be justified as being in the general good;

c) be suitable to achieve that purpose; and

d) be proportionate.

The free movement of services

Direct effect

Under art 49 EC services may also freely move, although in order to benefit from this right the individual must first be established in one of the Member States. Services are defined in art 50 EC as those that are normally provided for remuneration and the State must impose the same conditions on the provision of these services as those imposed on nationals.

Similar to establishment, art 52 EC required the adoption of directives and for this reason it was thought that art 49 EC did not have direct effect. However, in *Van Binsbergen* v *Bestuur van de Bedrijfsvereniging voor de Metaalnijverheid* Case 33/74 [1974] ECR 1299 the Court stated that art 49 EC was capable of direct effect, so that the imposing of a residence requirement before the provision of services could be permitted was capable of being challenged.

Article 49 EC only applies where there is an inter-state element and there must be some element for remuneration: *Belgium* v *Humbel* Case 263/86 [1988] ECR 5365.

Freedom to receive services

Whilst the Treaty provides only for the free movement to provide services, in *Luisi and Carbone* v *Ministero del Tesoro* Cases 286/82 and 26/83 [1984] ECR 377, the Court declared that a right of free movement to receive services also exists. This extends to education, training, vocational programmes, business, medical services and tourism.

Illegal or immoral services

In *Society for the Protection of Unborn Children (Ireland)* v *Grogan* Case C–159/90 [1991] ECR I–4685 the ECJ stated that it would not impose its judgement on whether a Member State should consider a particular service illegal and/or immoral. Hence, each State is free to regulate such services, although they must do so in a manner that is proportionate and non-discriminatory: *Customs and Excise* v *Schindler* Case C–275/92 [1994] ECR I–1039.

Non-discriminatory rules

As with establishment, the Court has extended the scope of art 49 EC to include non-discriminatory rules, although such rules may be objectively justified according to

Van Binsbergen v *Bestuur van de Bedrijfsvereniging voor de Metaalnijverheid* Case 33/74 [1974] ECR 1299. In order to objectively justify such a measure the State must prove the following.

a) That the measure is designed to achieve a factor of legitimate public interest (such as those in relation to organisation, qualifications, professional ethics, supervision, liability and the sound administration of justice).

b) The measure must be non-discriminatory.

c) The measure must be proportionate and necessary: *Commission* v *Germany (Re Insurance Services)* Case 205/84 [1986] ECR 3755. If such a measure is already imposed by the State in which the applicant is established there will be no need to impose it again in the State in which they wish to provide a service: *Criminal Proceedings against Webb* Case 279/80 [1981] ECR 3305.

Some professions have been covered by the issuing of directives, which harmonise the professional rules that may be applied. If a measure comes within such a directive it has to comply with its terms. If a measure does not then it will have to meet the objective justification test outlined above if it is applied in a non-discriminatory manner.

Social benefits

There is no equivalent secondary legislation to Council Regulation 1612/68 for those wishing to exercise their rights to freely move in order to establish themselves or provide/receive services. However, the Court has declared that such rights should be made available where they are connected to the ability to exercise the rights of establishment or to provide or receive services. For example, in relation to establishment, in *Commission* v *Italy (Re Housing Aid)* Case 63/86 [1988] ECR 29, the Court concluded that facilities designed to alleviate financial burdens on nationals must also be provided to non-nationals on the basis that to do otherwise would constitute a barrier to the ability to exercise the right of establishment.

In addition, the Court has also referred to art 12 EC, and declared that where non-nationals have been denied access to social benefits there has been discrimination on the basis of nationality: *Hayes* v *Kronenberger GmbH* Case C–323/95 [1997] ECR I–1711.

Rights of entry, residence and to remain

Council Directive 73/148 provides for conditions on entry and residence and applies to those wishing to establish, provide/receive services and their families (defined in the same manner as that in Council Regulation 1612/68 – see above). There must be no visa requirements unless the person is a non-Community national. Article 4 of the Directive provides that those establishing themselves are provided with a permanent right of residence, whilst those providing/receiving services have temporary rights. This is known as a right of abode if their stay exceeds three months.

Council Directive 75/34 provides that persons exercising their rights of establishment as self-employed persons in another State (as well as their family) have the right to stay there.

8.3 Key cases and materials

- *Adoui and Cornvaille* v *Belgian State* Cases 115 and 116/81 [1982] ECR 1665
  To assess whether the threat is genuine the Court emphasised the need for there to be some repressive measures of an equivalent nature imposed on nationals

- *Bonsignore* v *Oberstadtdirektor of the City of Cologne* Case 67/74 [1975] ECR 297
  Criminal convictions cannot be used to justify the use of one of the grounds for derogation as a general preventative measure or as a means of deterring others

- *Centre Public de l'Aide Sociale de Courcelles* v *Lebon* Case 316/85 [1987] ECR 2811
  Migrant workers are not entitled to access social and tax rights under art 7(2), Regulation 1612/68 until they are employed

- *Customs and Excise* v *Schindler* Case C–275/92 [1994] ECR I–1039
  Each State is free to regulate the provision of illegal/immoral services, although they must do so in a manner that is proportionate and non-discriminatory

- *Fiorini (née Christini)* v *SNCF* Case 32/75 [1975] ECR 1085
  Article 7(2), Regulation 1612/68 requires that workers are provided with all social and tax advantages granted to nationals but this case extends these rights to family members too

- *Gebhard* v *Consiglio dell'Ordine degli Avvocati e Procuratori di Milano* Case C–55/44 [1995] ECR I–4165
  Provides a test that may objectively justify non-discriminatory measures on the freedom of establishment

- *Kempf* v *Staatssecretaris van Justitie* Case 139/85 [1986] ECR 1741
  A person who pursues part-time employment, and who receives supplementary benefits to his income, is still a worker for the purposes of the freedom of movement of workers

- *Luisi and Carbone* v *Ministero del Tesoro* Cases 286/82 and 26/83 [1984] ECR 377
  A right of free movement to receive, as well as provide, services exists

- *R* v *Bouchereau* Case 30/77 [1977] ECR 1999
  Previous convictions may be used as evidence of personal conduct that the person constitutes a present threat in the context that they have a propensity to act again in the same manner in the future

- *R* v *Immigration Appeal Tribunal, ex parte Antonissen* Case C–292/89 [1991] ECR I–745
  A Community national can enter a Member State to search for work as a migrant worker via a teleological interpretation of art 39 EC

- *Reyners (Jean)* v *Belgium* Case 2/74 [1974] ECR 631
  Article 43 EC is capable of direct effect

- *Rutili* v *Minister for the Interior* Case 36/75 [1975] ECR 1219
  Definition of the concept of 'public policy' as contained in the exception to art 39(3) EC

- *Thieffry* v *Conseil de l'Ordre des Avocats à la Cour de Paris* Case 71/76 [1977] ECR 765
  Individuals may rely on art 43 EC to secure recognition of their qualifications, regardless of the lack of any harmonising directive

- *UNECTEF* v *Heylens and Others* Case 222/86 [1987] ECR 4097
  The Member State and any professional bodies are obligated to consider the equivalence of a non-national's qualifications, with reference to the nature and duration of their studies and any practical training: in addition, reasons for any decision must be provided, as should a right of appeal

- *Van Binsbergen* v *Bestuur van de Bedrijfsvereniging voor de Metaalnijverheid* Case 33/74 [1974] ECR 1299
  Article 49 EC is capable of direct effect: non-discriminatory measures on the provision of services may breach the EC Treaty unless they are objectively justified

- *Van Duyn* v *Home Office* Case 41/74 [1974] ECR 1337
  The grounds of public policy, security and health under art 39(3) EC are restrictively interpreted: personal conduct may be evidenced by membership of an organisation as long as that organisation does not receive the full protection of the law and the membership is present and active or supportive

- *Vlassopoulou* v *Ministerium für Justiz, Bundes-und Europaangelegenheiten Baden-Württenburg* Case C–340/89 [1991] ECR I–2357
  Reference should be made to any experience the applicant has in assessing whether their qualifications are equivalent

- EC Treaty

  - art 39 – provides for the free movement of workers

  - art 43 – provides for the freedom of establishment

  - art 49 – provides for the freedom to provide services (extended via jurisprudence to receiving services too)

- Council Regulation 1612/68 – provides rights for workers and their families

- Council Regulation 1251/70 – provides rights to remain after employment

- Council Directive 68/360 – on entry and residence permits

- Council Directive 64/221 – justifying exclusions to free movement and procedural safeguards

- Council Directive 89/48 – on the mutual recognition of qualifications

- Council Directive 92/51 – on the mutual recognition of diplomas and certificates of one year's duration, professional practice periods and vocational training

8.4 Questions and suggested solutions

QUESTION ONE

Gerhardt is of German nationality. He speaks fluent English and is practically bilingual in English and German. He wishes to take a secretarial course in the United Kingdom in order to become a bilingual secretary. He is accepted by the Stenoland Secretarial College which charges him a 'supplementary fee' as he is not a native English speaker. The College maintains that this charge is justified because students whose first language is not English require more intensive tuition than native English speakers.

Gerhardt lives in the United Kingdom with a family as an 'au pair'. He receives accommodation and £30 a week in return for baby-sitting and helping with domestic chores.

As he cannot afford Stenoland's fees, Gerhardt turns to his local University, the University of East Wessex, which offers a one-year diploma for bilingual secretaries. He applies for and is accepted for a place on this course. As the University is too far away for him to continue to live with the family where he is an 'au pair', he applies to his local Education Authority for a grant to fund his studies in respect of maintenance and tuition, but his application is rejected.

Gerhardt finds an evening job as a shelf-stacker in a supermarket. The pay is not enough for him to live on and he applies for income support. Whilst processing his application, the local authority discovers he does not have a residence permit. His application is rejected and at the same time a deportation order is made against him.

Advise on each of the following.

a) Is the 'supplementary fee' charged by Stenoland legal under Community law?

b) Does Gerhardt have a right to a grant in respect of tuition and maintenance which is paid to local United Kingdom students, in order to pursue his bilingual secretarial course at the University of East Wessex?

c) Does Gerhardt have a right of residence in the United Kingdom on the strength of his job?

d) May Gerhardt be expelled from the United Kingdom because he does not possess a residence permit?

University of London LLB Examination
(for External Students) European Community Law June 1995 Q6

General Comment

This is a problem type question based on a series of hypothetical facts. Since four specific points are raised, the answer must be confined to addressing these issues even though the question raises a number of other aspects of Community law. The law in this area is relatively well-settled and a high score is possible for the prepared student.

Skeleton Solution

a) Supplementary fee – principle of non-discrimination on the grounds of nationality – right to receive services – obligations of public bodies – no duty on private bodies.

b) Right to a grant – judgment of the ECJ in *Brown* – changes made by the TEU.

c) Right of residence – judgments of the ECJ in *Levin* and *Kempf* – principle of effective and genuine economic activity.

d) Power to expel – provisions of art 39(3) EC – Council Directive 64/221 – no power to deport.

Suggested Solution

a) *The supplementary fee charged by Stenoland*

Article 12 EC prohibits discrimination on the grounds of nationality in relation to the scope of the application of the Treaty itself. Although this provision has been given direct effect by the European Court (or ECJ), this has only been in conjunction with other Articles of the Treaty.

In these circumstances, Gerhardt would have to establish that the supplementary fee which Stenoland charges violates the right of a Community citizen to go to another Member State for the purposes of receiving services. This right, although not expressly stated in the EC Treaty, has been created by the European Court from the freedom to supply services in art 49 EC. The Court implied the existence of this right as the converse of the freedom to supply services: *Luisi and Carbone* v *Ministero del Tesoro* Cases 286/82 and 26/83 [1984] ECR 377.

When exercising this freedom, a person is entitled to the protection offered by art 12 EC. Once an individual has travelled to another Member State, he or she is entitled to obtain these services free from discrimination on the grounds of nationality. For example, in *Gravier* v *City of Liège* Case 293/83 [1985] ECR 593, a registration fee charged by a Belgian university only to non-Belgian Community students was held to be contrary to the principle of non-discrimination on the grounds of nationality.

It is not clear, however, if the Stenoland College is a public or private institution. If it is a public institution, then it is under an obligation to refrain from this form of discrimination. The EC Treaty imposes duties on Member States and rarely on private individuals. States are required to refrain from introducing discriminatory measures in the forms of laws, administrative rules, etc. Equally, as State emanations, public bodies, including universities and colleges, are subject to the same duties. Hence, if Stenoland College is a public body, it is prohibited from discriminating on the grounds of nationality and will be unable to charge the supplementary charge if Gerhardt can prove that the charge is discriminatory.

Conversely, if the Stenoland College is a private body or even a private company, it is not subject to the same obligation to refrain from this form of discrimination. Private bodies which are detached from the operations of the government cannot be compelled to refrain from such discrimination. In these circumstances, the supplementary charge would not contravene Community law since the College would owe no duty to Gerhardt.

If the College is a public body, Gerhardt would then have to prove that discrimination on the grounds of nationality has occurred. From the facts presented, there appears to be a prima facie argument that the charge amounts to de facto discrimination. First, it only applies to non-native English speakers despite their relative competencies. Second, no test is offered to assess competence to speak English. Third, the practical effect of such a charge is to discriminate between United Kingdom nationals and other Community nationals. Finally, if the quality of the tuition given to non-English speakers is not, in fact, more intensive or specialised, the charge cannot be justified.

b) *The right to a grant from government sources*

The local Education Authority is clearly part of the government apparatus and therefore subject to the obligation of non-discrimination on the grounds of nationality. However, Gerhardt must establish that he is exercising rights under a provision of the EC Treaty before this obligation comes into effect.

A worker may gain educational rights under art 7(3) of Council Regulation 1612/68, which refers to accessing vocational schools and retraining centres. This would have applied to his secretarial course at the College, but unfortunately it will not apply to any course undertaken at a university, according to the case of *Brown* v *Secretary of State for Scotland* Case 197/86 [1988] ECR 3205.

Some relief to this decision may extend from the Court's conclusions in *Lair* v *University of Hanover* Case 39/86 [1989] ECR 3161. In this case the Court suggested that an alternative route to gain access to such courses and facilities associated with them, such as grants, would be to use art 7(2), Regulation 1612/68. However, in order to do this the worker must prove that there is some link between their previous forms of employment and the education they wish to receive, and that they are 'genuine' workers prior to applying for a place. Hence in *Brown* (above) the applicant had accepted a place at Cambridge before moving to Scotland and was not therefore a worker for the purposes of claiming educational rights under art 7(2). Lair was more successful, since he had worked periodically for five years before applying for an educational place. Gerhardt worked in the UK (as an au pair) before applying for the university course, but it is not clear whether the course in some way relates to any previous employment experience he has.

It is not clear whether the European Court would be prepared to extend its position on this point bearing in mind the new areas of competence brought by the amendments to the EC Treaty by the Treaty on European Union. Broader powers have been expressly conferred on the Community. In particular, art 3(g) EC, which was inserted by the Treaty on European Union, brings 'education and training' within the competence of the Community. If Gerhardt can argue that the provision of grants is no longer an exclusive matter of national competence, but one in which the Community has an interest, he may be successful in challenging the decision of the Education Authority.

c) *The right of residence*

To be entitled to a residence permit, Gerhardt must show that he is exercising his freedom of movement as established under art 39 EC and as supplemented by Community secondary legislation. Article 39 EC confers on 'workers' the right to travel to a Member State other than his own and to take up employment there on the same terms as workers from that country.

Gerhardt has been both an au pair and a shelf-stacker in the UK – the question is whether this gives him worker status under art 39 EC. It should be noted that Gerhardt had the right to enter the UK to search for work for a period of three to six months according to the case of *R v Immigration Appeal Tribunal, ex parte Antonissen* Case C–292/89 [1991] ECR I–745. According to *Levin v Staatssecretaris van Justitie* Case 53/81 [1982] ECR 1035 a worker is someone pursuing a genuine and effective economic activity. This may be the case even if the person is employed on a part-time basis and receives below subsistence remuneration so that they need to rely on social benefits: *Kempf v Staatssecretaris van Justitie* Case 139/85 [1986] ECR 1741. To be a worker, Gerhardt needs to establish that he is providing a service, under the direction of another, for which he receives remuneration, as explained by the Court in the case of *Lawrie-Blum v Land Baden-Württenburg* Case 66/85 [1986] ECR 2121.

Applying these criteria, it is likely that Gerhardt has activated his right of free movement and therefore is entitled to the protections of art 39 EC, one of which is the grant of a residence permit on the production of a valid passport or identity document: Council Directive 68/360. The refusal by the United Kingdom authorities to issue Gerhardt with a residence permit is itself a violation of Community law and the fact that Gerhardt does not presently have such a document does not change this situation since a worker can be employed prior to the completion of the formalities for obtaining a permit.

d) *The right to expulsion granted to the United Kingdom*

Article 39(3) EC specifies the grounds on which the exercise of the right of free movement of workers may be withdrawn and deportation permitted. A Member

State may deviate from applying this right on grounds of public policy, public security and public health. Council Directive 64/221 also elaborates on some more of the detailed provisions allowing Member States to act to limit the rights of workers. At the same time, this legislation provides a number of safeguards against arbitrary expulsion by a Member State.

None of these grounds gives the United Kingdom the right to expel Gerhardt. The fact that he has no residence permit is not a criminal offence since Gerhardt has the right to obtain such a document. No justification for the deportation can be manifested on the grounds of public security or public health since his continued residence constitutes no threat to these interests. Indeed, the European Court has pointed out that to justify expulsion, the threat to public safety must be genuine and serious: *Rutili* v *Minister for the Interior* Case 36/75 [1975] ECR 1219.

Further, national authorities cannot use an individual case to make an example to others. Thus, in *Bonsignore* v *Oberstadtdirektor of the City of Cologne* Case 67/74 [1975] ECR 297, the European Court considered the case of an Italian worker in Germany who had been convicted and fined for the unlawful possession of a pistol. The plaintiff was convicted and the German court ordered his deportation. The European Court held that exceptions to the principle of free movement should be construed strictly. Deportation should be consequent on the behaviour of the individual in question and should not be for the purposes of deterring others from unlawful behaviour.

In the event that the authorities refuse to accept these arguments, Gerhardt has the right to appeal this decision since he has the same legal remedies as are available to British nationals under art 8 of Council Directive 64/221. The European Court has also held that a person challenging a deportation order in such circumstances is entitled to obtain a stay of execution of the order pending the appeal: *Procureur du Roi* v *Royer* Case 48/75 [1976] ECR 497. In addition, Gerhardt has, under art 7 of Council Directive 64/221, the right to claim a minimum of 15 days before the execution of the deportation order without a residence permit.

QUESTION TWO

'The right of free movement of persons started out as an economic right, but developments in European law have moved it well away from this.'

Discuss.

University of London LLB Examination
(for External Students) European Community Law June 1996 Q8

General Comment

An essay question which requires an account of the extent to which the free movement of persons provisions of the Treaty relate to the economically active migrant alone.

Consideration of the development, if any, of the right of free movement from an economic right to a fundamental right available to citizens of the Union should be made.

Skeleton Solution

Original aims and tasks of the Community as they relate to free movement of persons – arts 2 and 3 EEC Treaty and preamble to Treaty of Rome – free movement of persons provisions – secondary legislation – extension of rights to non-economically active groups – Council Directive 90/364 – Council Directive 90/365 – Council Directive 93/96 – The Schengen Agreement – European Union citizenship.

Suggested Solution

In 1957, the Community's task was the establishment of a common market: art 2 EEC Treaty. A common market is a customs union which also permits the free movement of the factors of production, that is, goods, services, persons and capital. In art 3(c) EC, the abolition of obstacles to the free movement of goods, persons, services and capital was said to be one of the Community's activities. Thus, the ability of persons to move freely within the Community was an integral part of the establishment of the common market.

Even at this early stage, however, there were references in the preamble to the Treaty of Rome that suggest that the peoples of Europe were not seen solely as units of production. The preamble refers to the signatories' determination to 'lay the foundations of an ever-closer union among the peoples of Europe' and to improve 'the living and working conditions of their peoples'. In *F (Mr and Mrs) v Belgium* Case 7/75 [1975] ECR 679, Advocate-General Trabuchi stated that the migrant worker was not regarded solely as a source of labour but also as a human being. Therefore, Community law should remove obstacles to free movement and assist in their and their family's integration into the host State.

The main provisions of the EC Treaty concerning free movement of persons are contained in arts 39–42 EC (free movement for workers), arts 43–48 EC (free movement for the self-employed) and arts 49–55 EC (free movement of services). All of these freedoms relate to persons who exercise an economic activity. The approach of the Community, as evidenced by decisions of the European Court of Justice and secondary legislation passed, has been to recognise that measures which assist in the integration of persons into the host State will encourage the exercise of free movement rights.

Whilst the provisions relating to free movement of workers are the most developed, the ECJ has held that all three freedoms are based on similar principles in relation to entry into and residence in Member States and that they are all covered by the prohibition against discrimination on the grounds of nationality: *Procureur du Roi v Royer* Case 48/75 [1976] ECR 497.

Workers have a range of rights under primary and secondary legislation. A worker has the right of residence (art 39(3) EC), the right to equality of treatment in the field of employment (art 39(2) EC) and the right to stay in a Member State after employment has been terminated.

Secondary legislation has augmented and clarified these rights. Under Council Regulation 1612/68, a worker has the right to non-discriminatory access to social and tax advantages: art 7(2) of the Regulation. Social and tax benefits have been interpreted widely to mean all social advantages which accrue from the fact of residence in a Member State irrespective of whether they derive from the contract of employment: *Ministère Public* v *Even and ONPTS* Case 207/78 [1979] ECR 2019. Such advantages have included travel concessions for large families (*Fiorini (née Christini)* v *SNCF* Case 32/75 [1975] ECR 1085), and a minimum income allowance (*Hoeckx* v *Openbaar Centrum voor Maatschappelijk Welzijn, Kalmthout* Case 249/83 [1985] ECR 973).

Workers also have equal access to housing as nationals (art 9) and the right to bring their spouse, dependent children and dependant ascending relatives to live with them, regardless of their nationality (art 10(1)). The worker's spouse and dependent children are able to take up employment (art 11) and have access to educational, apprenticeship and vocational training courses (art 12). The right to educational facilities includes access to measures, such as grants and loans, which enable the exercise of the right: *Casagrande* v *Landeshauptstadt München* Case 9/74 [1974] ECR 773.

Moreover, under Council Regulation 1251/70, workers and their families have the right to remain in a Member State after the worker's employment has ended in the following circumstances.

a) Where the worker has reached retirement age, having been employed for at least the previous 12 months and having resided in the State for a continuous period of three years.

b) Where the worker has resided for more than two years in the Member State and is permanently incapacitated and unable to work.

c) Where a worker who was employed in a State for three years, then works in another State whilst retaining a home in the first State.

Similar rights attach to the self-employed and the service provider although access to social benefits for such persons does not arise because of secondary legislation but as a result of the rule against discrimination on the grounds of nationality: art 6 EC Providers of services will generally not benefit from a full range of social benefits because of their temporary status within a Member State: *Commission* v *Italy (Re Housing Aid)* Case 63/86 [1988] ECR 29.

All of these rights are available to a wide range of persons because of the extended meaning given to the term 'worker' by the ECJ.

According to the case of *Levin* v *Staatssecretaris van Justitie* Case 53/81 [1982] ECR 1035 a worker is someone who performs a genuine and effective economic activity. This extends to part-time workers, even if their income is so low they qualify for state benefits: *Kempf* v *Staatssecretaris van Justitie* Case 139/85 [1986] ECR 1741. Indeed, the Court extended art 39 EC via teleological interpretation in *R* v *Immigration Appeal Tribunal, ex parte Antonissen* Case C–292/89 [1991] ECR I–745 to even include those that are actively searching for work.

The extent of these rights and the wide range of their recipients might suggest that free movement for persons has moved beyond the economic sphere. However, although it is certainly true that the ECJ, in particular, has interpreted Treaty provisions generously in order to provide workers and others with protection over and above that given in the Treaty, the above provisions remain inextricably linked with the objective of the establishment of the common market. All of the above decisions and measures can be justified on the basis that they serve to further the aim of the integration of the common market.

There are signs, however, that in recent years free movement is moving away from the economically active person to the European citizen.

Directives have been passed giving the right of residence in Member States to categories of persons who are not economically active: students (Council Directive 93/96), persons of independent means (Council Directive 90/364) and the retired (Council Directive 90/365). All such persons must be medically insured and must have sufficient means to avoid reliance on the state.

Lastly, the establishment by the Treaty on European Union 1992 of citizenship of the European Union provides an opportunity for further development in this area. Article 18 EC provides that all Member State nationals shall be citizens of the Union and goes on to provide that EU citizens have the right to move and reside freely within Member States' territory. That right is subject at present to the limitations and conditions laid down in the Treaty but there is provision for Council measures to be taken to facilitate this right. In this regard, the Treaty also provides for inter-governmental co-operation on justice and home affairs which will include common policies on immigration and the control of crime and international fraud. Such common policies will facilitate an extension of free movement for all European citizens.

It appears therefore that whilst free movement of persons remains fundamentally an economic right, it has moved beyond the economic sphere and is likely to continue to do so in the future.

QUESTION THREE

A British engineering company with its headquarters in Guildford has decided to establish a branch in Greece. They are sending out an exploration team of engineers who intend to spend three months exploring suitable sites and looking at the available skilled labour.

If all goes well, the company will then open the branch and bring the managerial staff over from England.

Before embarking on this venture, they come to you for advice. They want to know:

a) whether the 'exploration team' will encounter any difficulties with regard to residence and work permits;

b) once the branch is open, whether they can send any of their staff members out to work there, and, in particular:

   i) Mary, deputy head of the accountancy department. She is British, but has been co-habiting with Jason, an Australian who is an engineer with the firm, for five years and the company intends to send them out together;

   ii) Malcolm, a computer specialist, whose wife Deirdre has a criminal conviction for possession of cannabis which she received three years ago.

Advise them.

University of London LLB Examination
(for External Students) European Community Law June 1994 Q7

General Comment

This question combines two separate principles of Community law, namely the right of establishment and the freedom of movement of workers. The general principle behind both is the same – the elimination of discrimination based on nationality. There are no particularly difficult points raised and, in fact, the part concerning criminal convictions is a common theme for examination.

Skeleton Solution

Right of establishment: art 43 EC – Council Directive 73/148 – art 39 EC and the concepts of 'worker', family rights and right to reside – non-application of the principle to non-Community nationals who are not married to Community nationals – right to reside and the question of previous criminal convictions.

Suggested Solution

It is the intention of the British company to carry out two separate activities in Greece. First, it intends to investigate the feasibility of establishing a branch in Greece and, for that purpose, wishes to dispatch the exploration team to that country. Second, in the event that this project is successful, it will establish a permanent branch office. This distinction is important because two separate principles of Community law apply to these two particular activities.

Sending the team to investigate the possibilities of the market is covered by the right of freedom of establishment in Community law. Article 43 EC prohibits restrictions on the freedom of establishment of Community nationals. This applies to the setting up of agencies, branches and subsidiaries by nationals of one Member State in the territory of another Member State.

The impact of these Articles is to prohibit restrictions on the exercise of this freedom if based on discrimination on the grounds of nationality. In other words, companies exercising this freedom must be treated in the same way as nationals of that Member State.

In the event that the Greek authorities deny residence permits or work permits to the exploration team then prima facie they would be guilty of a violation of art 43 EC if, in identical circumstances, they would not have done so had the application been made by Greek nationals. Any refusal must be based on objective criteria unrelated to nationality.

Article 43 EC has been held to have direct effect: *Reyners (Jean)* v *Belgium* Case 2/74 [1974] ECR 631; and *Costa* v *ENEL* Case 6/64 [1964] ECR 585. The British company can therefore rely on these provisions to create directly enforceable private rights.

Council Directive 73/148 provides for conditions on entry and residence and applies to those wishing to establish, provide/receive services and their families. There must be no visa requirements unless the person is a non-Community national. Article 4 of the Regulation provides that those establishing themselves are provided with a permanent right of residence whilst those providing/receiving services have temporary rights. This is known as a right of abode if their stay exceeds three months.

If the company proceeds to open a branch office and wishes to send personnel from the United Kingdom to operate the office, another set of principles will be involved. Article 39 EC creates the right of free movement of workers and requires Member States to abolish any discrimination based on nationality between workers as regards employment, remuneration and other conditions of work and employment. Once again, the European Court has given direct effect to this provision of the EC Treaty: *Van Duyn* v *Home Office* Case 41/74 [1974] ECR 1337.

This freedom includes the rights to accept offers of employment, to move freely within the territory of the Member State for this purpose and to reside in a Member State for the purposes of employment in accordance with the laws of that Member State governing the employment of nationals.

The key to the operation of this provision is the term 'worker'. If a person qualifies as a worker, he or she is entitled to exercise this freedom and his or her family is also entitled to the protections granted to them as members of the family of a worker. As long as an individual is pursuing an effective and genuine activity which is not marginal or ancillary, he will be deemed a worker: *Levin* v *Staatssecretaris van Justitie* Case 53/81 [1982] ECR 1035. Even part-time work qualifies a person as a worker for the purposes of applying this right: *Kempf* v *Staatssecretaris van Justitie* Case 139/85 [1986] ECR 1741.

Workers are entitled not only to the rights contained in art 39(2) EC but also the rights conferred by the secondary legislation in this field, namely Council Regulation 1612/68 and Council Directive 64/221. According to the terms of the first measure, a worker has the right to take employment with the same priority as nationals of the United Kingdom and to exercise this right free from discrimination on the grounds of nationality.

Applying these provisions to the four individuals specified in the question, quite clearly Mary is entitled to exercise the right of free movement. She is a British (and hence Community) national travelling to another Member State for the purposes of taking up an employment position.

Jason, her partner, is not a Community national and therefore is not entitled to exercise this right. Had he been married to Mary, he would have been able to rely on the rights conferred on spouses of workers to remain with spouses exercising the freedom of movement: art 10(1) of Regulation 1612/68. This right applies regardless of whether the unemployed spouse is a Community national or not: *R v Immigration Appeal Tribunal and Surinder Singh, ex parte Secretary of State for the Home Department* Case C–370/90 [1992] ECR I–4265. However, Mary and Jason are not married and Regulation 1612/68 is quite explicit in restricting the right to residence to 'spouses' of workers.

The other couple is Malcolm and Deirdre. Like Mary, Malcolm is a British national and therefore entitled, without doubt, to exercise the right of free movement. His wife Deirdre, therefore, would prima facie be entitled to reside as the spouse of a Community worker. Unfortunately she has a previous conviction for possession of cannabis which she received three years ago. The question is whether this conviction would prevent her exercising the right to remain with Malcolm.

Council Directive 64/221 does confer on Member States certain rights to restrict the free movement of persons within their territories. This Directive applies to all measures concerning the entry and expulsion of nationals from other Community countries. In certain circumstances, denial of entry and deportation may be justified on the grounds of public policy, public security or public health: art 39(3) EC.

However, it is unlikely that the Greek authorities could rely on these grounds to justify a refusal to admit Deirdre. At the outset, it can hardly be justifiably maintained that a conviction for possession of a drug constitutes a genuine threat to public policy, public security or public health: *Rutili v Minister for the Interior* Case 36/75 [1975] ECR 1219. Further, in assessing whether a decision to expel a Community national from a Member State, the Directive requires the government to take into account a number of factors. First, a decision to deny entry must be based exclusively on the personal conduct of the individual concerned. In addition, denial of entry for the purposes of deterring foreign nationals from acting in a similar manner is not permissible: *Bonsignore v Oberstadtdirektor of the City of Cologne* Case 67/74 [1975] ECR 297.

Also, previous criminal convictions are not in themselves sufficient for taking such measures unless these indicate a propensity to act in a similar manner in the future: *R* v *Bouchereau* Case 30/77 [1977] ECR 1999. A single conviction for possession of cannabis would probably not provide such an indication. If Deirdre had only received a small fine and not imprisonment, it would also indicate that the offence was a minor one which did not justify the claim that her presence would be a danger to the general public welfare: *Adoui and Cornvaille* v *Belgian State* Cases 115 and 116/81 [1982] ECR 1665.

QUESTION FOUR

'Article 18 of the EC Treaty creates the status of European citizenship for all European Union citizens, but this provision adds nothing to the free movement of persons provisions already contained in the Treaty of Rome.'

Discuss.

University of London LLB Examination
(for External Students) European Union Law June 1997 Q8

General Comment

This question requires an assessment of European citizenship – regarded by many as a token gesture – and its impact, if any, on the free movement of persons provisions of the EC Treaty.

Skeleton Solution

Articles 17–22 EC: European citizenship and consequential rights – arts 49–55 EC: free movement of persons provisions – secondary legislation – workers – self-employed – service providers and recipients – extension of rights to non-economically active groups – assessment of benefits and limitations of citizen's rights.

Suggested Solution

Article 17 EC was amended by the Treaty on European Union to create the concept of European Union citizenship. By art 17 EC, Union citizenship is to be held by all European Community Member State nationals. Union citizens have the right of free movement within the European Union.

In addition, arts 18–21 EC set out further rights for Union citizens. They include: the right to vote and stand in local and European parliamentary elections in the citizen's state of residence (but not national parliamentary elections); the right to diplomatic protection by other Member States in third countries where a citizen's own State of nationality is not represented; and the right to petition the European Parliament as well as to apply to the Ombudsman appointed by the European Parliament.

Together with the re-christening of the European Economic Community to the European Community and the creation of the two inter-governmental pillars (co-operation in the field of Foreign and Security Policy and co-operation in Justice and Home Affairs), the notion of European Union citizenship appeared to represent a move away from an economic community into a more explicitly political and social union. The concept of Union citizenship has been criticised, however, as a token gesture of symbolic rather than actual significance. Criticisms tend to centre on two areas: the fact that existing social rights have not been extended by the creation of citizenship; and the failure to address the issue of third country nationals lawfully resident within the European Community.

Although the rights bestowed on the EU citizen include a number of political rights, as outlined above, the principal right bestowed is that of free movement. However, this right is said to be subject to the limitations and conditions laid down in the Treaty. This suggests that rights of free movement are not extended beyond those already in existence in 1992.

Originally, free movement was a right primarily reserved for the economically active. Such rights are contained in arts 39–42 EC (free movement for workers), arts 43–48 EC (free movement for the self-employed) and arts 49–55 EC (free movement for the provider of services). It has always been recognised that European nationals would be unlikely to exercise the rights of mobility unless additional social rights were granted and such rights were extended to the families of the economic migrant. Extension of the basic right of mobility has taken place at legislative and judicial level.

Thus Council Regulation 1612/68 was passed to give rights of residence to a worker's spouse, their children aged under 21 or who are dependent and dependent ascending relatives. Moreover, the worker's family are also allowed to take up employment, irrespective of their nationality. Regulation 1612/68 also provides for equal access to social benefits for both the worker and his/her family. Both workers and their families may remain in a Member State after their employment has ceased in certain circumstances (Council Regulation 1251/70).

Similar provisions apply for the benefit of the families of the self-employed and providers of services under Council Regulation 148/73 and Council Directive 75/34.

The European Court of Justice (ECJ) has also been instrumental in expanding the right of free movement for European citizens. In *R v Immigration Appeal Tribunal, ex parte Antonissen* Case C–292/89 [1991] ECR I–745 it was held that the art 39 EC right of entry and residence applied not only to the employed person but also to the person seeking employment. Similarly, the art 49 EC right of entry and residence for the service provider was held also to cover the recipient of services: *Luisi and Carbone v Ministero del Tesoro* Cases 286/82 and 26/83 [1984] ECR 377. The rights of residence for members of the worker's family have been held to continue for a non-EC spouse of a worker, separated and living apart from the worker (*Diatta v Land Berlin* Case 267/83 [1985] ECR 567) and for the children of an EC worker for the duration of an educational course, even though the worker had returned to their country of origin: *Echternach and Moritz v Netherlands Minister for Education* Cases 389 and 390/87 [1989] ECR 723.

However, the provisions of Community law have been held not to apply where there is no economic activity followed by the individuals concerned (*Walrave and Koch* v *Association Union Cycliste Internationale* Case 36/74 [1974] ECR 1405) or where there is no Community law element (*Morson and Jhanjan* v *Netherlands* Cases 35 and 36/82 [1982] ECR 3723). It seems, therefore, that the citizen's rights can only be invoked within the context of the economic aim of the EC Treaty, that of establishing a common market in, inter alia, labour.

In 1990, EC nationals' rights of freedom of movement were extended beyond the boundaries of participation in the economic aims of the Community when three directives were passed. Council Directive 90/364 gave rights of entry to, and residence, in all Member States to financially independent persons and their families. Similar rights were conferred on retired persons and families by Council Directive 90/365. Council Directive 90/366 (subsequently replaced by Council Directive 93/96) applied the same rights to students and their families.

The common theme of the three Directives is that the rights are dependent upon individuals establishing access to sufficient means which prevent them becoming a burden on a State's social security systems and health insurance.

Thus, it would seem that an EU citizen's right of free movement remains subject to the limitations already in existence under the EC Treaty and that arts 17–18 EC have done nothing to alter the position that mobility is dependent upon economic activity, a connection to an economically active person or financial independence.

It is also noteworthy that EU citizenship has been seen as a concept which is a means of forging a common European identity and, consequently, the removal of 'nationality and state affiliation ... as the principal referent for transnational human intercourse' (Weiler 'The Transformation of Europe' (1991) 100 Yale LJ 2403). Such an objective would accord with the basic aims of the Community as set out in the preamble to the EC Treaty, namely a determination 'to lay the foundations of an ever closer union among the peoples of Europe' and the preservation of 'peace and liberty'.

Nationality remains, however, a matter for Member States to determine and EU citizenship does not replace, but adds to, national citizenship rights. Excluded from this Community, however, is the extensive group of third country nationals who are lawfully resident and employed within the Union. Third country nationals in such a position are given the rights under arts 194 and 195 EC to petition the European Parliament and the Ombudsman appointed by the Parliament, but have no rights in relation to free movement. Extension of such rights is unlikely to take place unless or until EU citizenship is disassociated from national citizenship. Existing EC law does little to assist the third country national. Article 22 EC does allow for the adoption of further measures to strengthen the citizenship provisions; the nature of such measures remains to be seen.

QUESTION FIVE

François, a French national, is a promising rugby player and has just been given a contract by the Poitiers Pierrots, one of the top national clubs in France who are pleased to have signed him up as the International Rugby Federation have just adopted a rule restricting the number of foreign players in any one match for all clubs. Having been taken on for a trial period of a year he plays for them for about six months. He is then approached by Epsom Clowns, a major English club, to come and play for them. Poitiers decide they need the money even more than they need François, and consent to let him go, subject to a one million Francs (about £100,000) transfer fee. Epsom Clowns consider this excessive, as François is a foreign player and, however good he is, they will not be able to use him in all their matches. They therefore reluctantly withdraw their offer.

François is, of course, very disappointed. He has heard something about European law being able to help him and asks you for advice.

University of London LLB Examination
(for External Students) European Union Law June 1999 Q7

General Comment

This problem question relates to the free movement of workers, but deals primarily with the application of art 39 EC and the prohibition on discrimination based on nationality. The question requires detailed knowledge of *Union des Associations Européennes de Football* v *Jean-Marc Bosman* Case C–415/93 [1995] ECR I–4921 and the ability to apply its principles to this situation. This question should not have been attempted by those that had only a working knowledge of the free movement of workers provisions or/and had not read or studied the *Bosman* ruling in some detail.

Skeleton Solution

Article 12 EC prohibition on discrimination based on nationality – art 39 EC free movement of workers – the definition of a worker – the direct effect of art 39 EC and the application of art 39 EC in a horizontal manner and to non-discriminatory measures with reference to the decision in *Bosman*.

Suggested Solution

Under art 12 EC one of the Community's fundamental principles is enshrined, namely the prohibition on discrimination based on nationality. This important provision of Community law is an essential one in terms of securing equality throughout the Union. In addition, the EC Treaty states that one of the activities of the Community will be the creation of an internal market, characterised by the abolition of obstacles to the free movement of goods, persons, services and capital. This was expanded upon by the inclusion of specific provisions providing free movement for workers (arts 39–42

EC), for establishment (arts 43–48 EC) and services (arts 49–55 EC). These areas have subsequently been expanded by the introduction of secondary legislation.

These rights are collectively considered one of the cornerstones – or four fundamental freedoms – of the European Community. Developments have ensured that the law has moved from its original economic basis (ensuring that labour and skill shortages in one Member States could be resolved via surpluses from another) to one that is perhaps better described as social or humanitarian. With Treaty amendments, the introduction of secondary legislation and teleological interpretation by the ECJ, this area has become a fertile source of rights for Community nationals, such as François, particularly since the majority of these rights have direct effect.

Article 39 EC provides for the free movement of workers. It also provides that discrimination between workers of the Member State and those who originate from other Member States regarding employment, remuneration and other conditions of work and employment shall be prohibited.

Article 39(3) EC provides that workers shall be entitled, subject to limitations justified on grounds of public policy, security and health, to: accept offers of employment actually made; move freely within the territory of Member States for this purpose; stay in a Member State for the purpose of employment; and remain in the territory of a Member State after having been employed there. The freedom does not apply to those working in the public service under art 39(4) EC, although this has been restrictively interpreted by the ECJ's application of a functional rather than institutional test: see, for example, *Commission* v *Belgium (Re State Employees)* Case 149/79 [1980] ECR 3881.

Article 40 EC provides that art 39 EC will be supplemented by secondary legislation. The main secondary legislation in this area includes the following: Council Regulation 1612/68 providing for worker's rights; Council Regulation 1251/70 on the right to stay; Council Directive 68/360 on rights of entry and residence; and Council Directive 64/221 on justifying exclusions to free movement.

In order to benefit from the right of free movement provided under art 39 EC, three basic conditions must be met. First, the right only extends to Community nationals, such as French nationals in this scenario. Second, it should be noted that art 39 EC may only be relied upon where there is some element of movement from one Member State to another, and therefore cannot be used for purely internal situations: *R* v *Saunders* Case 175/78 [1979] ECR 1129. In other words, François would not be able to rely on the provisions in art 39 EC if he wished to move from Poitiers Pierrots to another French club, but may attempt to rely on its provisions to secure free movement to an English club. Finally, in order to benefit from free movement the person must be considered to be a 'worker'.

A worker is not defined in either the Treaty or the secondary legislation. The ECJ has stated that the term must have a Community definition so that the objective of free movement is not undermined: *Hoekstra* v *Bestuur der Bedrijfsvereniging voor Detailhandel en Ambachten* Case 75/63 [1964] ECR 177. In *Levin* v *Staatssecretaris van Justitie* Case 53/81 [1982] ECR 1035 the Court declared that a worker would be a person pursuing a genuine and effective economic activity that was not marginal or ancillary. It was further stated in *Kempf* v *Staatssecretaris van Justitie* Case 139/85 [1986] ECR 1741 that part-time work was capable of coming within this definition, even if the wages drawn were so low as to require the individual to apply for social assistence. The Court established a test in *Lawrie-Blum* v *Land Baden-Württenburg* Case 66/85 [1986] ECR 2121 that requires a worker to be: providing services for another for a period of time; under the direction of another; and receiving pay or remuneration. François should come within this definition as a rugby player. However, he may alternatively wish, if his contract expires, to enter the UK to search for work. Since the influential decision in the case of *R* v *Immigration Appeal Tribunal, ex parte Antonissen* Case C–292/89 [1991] ECR I–745, it is now possible under a teleological interpretation of art 39 EC to enter a Member State to search for work. Should François wish to avail himself of this right, he will find that he has a limited time period within which to find employment, around three to six months, and the burden of proof will rest on him that he is genuinely searching and has a genuine chance of securing employment. The minimum time period within which he would have to search for work was confirmed in *Commission* v *Belgium* Case C–344/95 [1997] ECR I–1035 as three months.

The question here though is whether François may rely on art 39 EC as against private bodies, in other words whether art 39 EC has horizontal direct effect. In addition, there is the issue of whether the Article may be relied on as against what appears to be a non-discriminatory measure. The answers to these questions were provided in the case of *Union des Associations Européennes de Football* v *Jean-Marc Bosman* Case C–415/93 [1995] ECR I–4921. The body UEFA is responsible for regulating the national football associations of around 50 countries, including those of the Member States, similar to the International Rugby Federation in this scenario. In *Bosman* the ECJ was asked to consider the compatibility of two of the regulations imposed by UEFA.

The first regulation permitted the application of transfer fees that allowed national football clubs to impose a transfer fee when a player moved from one club to another. In the absence of the transfer fee, imposed by the transferring club (such as Poitiers Pierrots in this case), a player could not move from one club to another. These requirements were written into the individual player's contract and applied even if the contract had expired. If the club refused to accept the fee offered, the player would be unable to move. In Bosman's case the situation was somewhat different, since his contract had actually expired, unlike that of François. Bosman, a Belgian footballer, was therefore prevented from securing employment with a French football club since his Belgian one refused to accept the transfer fee offered and his career was effectively halted. The transfer system applied equally to all players moving from one club to another, both within a Member State and from one State to another, regardless of the player's nationality. This measure was, therefore, applied in a non-discriminatory manner by a private body, as in this scenario, but did it still breach art 39 EC?

The second regulation in *Bosman*, similar to that imposed by the International Rugby Federation, was one that concerned restrictions placed on the number of non-national players that could be fielded by any club. The number of non-nationals that could be fielded in any one match was three. UEFA claimed that this was a justifiable measure in that it assisted in the preservation of a national element within football clubs.

The ECJ held that the imposition of the transfer fee contravened art 39 EC. The transfer system may have been imposed in a non-discriminatory manner but was nevertheless a form of indirect discrimination. This was because it was capable of constituting an obstacle to free movement in that it could impede access to the employment market in other Member States, as Bosman had discovered. The Court recognised, though, that this indirect discrimination could be objectively justified as pursuing a legitimate aim compatible with the Treaty. However, to be successful in justifying this measure the body would have to prove that there were important reasons in the public interest for imposing the measure and that it was proportionate. (The Court made reference to the application of this test in relation to the free movement of services and cited the case of *Gebhard* v *Consiglio dell'Ordine degli Avvocati e Procuratori di Milano* Case C–55/44 [1995] ECR I–4165.)

In relation to the nationality requirement, the Court held that the measure contravened both the free movement of workers protected under arts 39 and 12 EC prohibiting discrimination on the basis of nationality. This measure was not justifiable because it was excessive and therefore breached two of the fundamental provisions of the EC Treaty.

The conclusion is that art 39 EC may be relied upon by François as against both public and private bodies, such as the International Rugby Federation, although it should be noted that in this case François is still under contract, since it has not yet expired. François should meet his contractual requirement for the remaining six months of his contract, at which point the imposition of any transfer fee will breach art 39 EC in that it will prevent him from entering the rugby employment market in England, or indeed potentially any other Member State.

The Article may also be relied upon to challenge non-discriminatory or indirectly discriminatory measures, such as those applied in François' case – the limitation on the number of non-nationals fielded in any one rugby game and the transfer fee system. These indirectly discriminatory measures may be objectively justified as in the public interest and compatible with the aims of the EC Treaty, but the burden of proof to establish this will be on the International Rugby Federation, and will be assessed by the national court. The body imposing the measure will, in addition, have to prove that the measure is imposed in a proportionate manner. The International Rugby Federation would be wise to note that the Court insists that such measures are very closely examined. Any justification offered will also be carefully scrutinised in terms of its validity and may be rejected, deemed inappropriate or declared non-proportionate.

QUESTION SIX

Christophe, a Frenchman, travels to the University of Graz, in Austria, to take up a job as a teacher of French law. He soon settles in and meets Katrina, a lawyer from Slovenia, with whom he moves in as her partner. They are popular and have an open house for students. One evening, the police arrive and find one of the students in possession of a prohibited drug. They also have obtained confidential records on Christophe from his French university where he was known as a leftist sympathiser who organised regular student protest meetings.

They arrest Christophe and start a prosecution for having prohibited drugs on his premises. They offer to drop the charges if he leaves the country immediately. Katrina is served with a deportation order.

Advise Christophe and Katrina as to their possible rights under Community law.

University of London LLB Examination
(for External Students) European Union Law June 2000 Q6

General Comment

This problem question is on the free movement of workers. The answer needed to discuss the definition and rights available to workers under art 39 EC, the secondary legislation and the case law, with better answers applying that law to the facts of the problem. A distinction should have been made between the two situations in the question; the possession of drugs by a visiting student and the possibility of Christophe being a possible political agitator. Katrina has no independent rights as a Slovenian, hence any discussion of the freedom of establishment was irrelevant. Instead, emphasis should have been made of whether she gains rights as the cohabitee of a worker.

Skeleton Solution

Article 39 EC – definition of a worker, relevant cases eg *Levin, Lawrie-Blum, Kempf* – does not include the public service: art 39(4) EC – definition of family: Council Regulation 1612/68 – cohabitees: *Netherlands* v *Reed* – grounds for derogation: art 39(3) EC – justifying measures and safeguards under Council Directive 64/221 – relevant cases, eg *Van Duyn, Bouchereau, Adoui* etc.

Suggested Solution

Article 6 EC prohibits any discrimination on the basis of nationality. In addition, art 39 EC provides for the free movement of workers, one of the fundamental freedoms of the Treaty: *F (Mr and Mrs)* v *Belgium* Case 7/75 [1975] ECR 679. The Article states that discrimination on the basis of nationality in relation to employment, remuneration and other conditions of work and employment is prohibited. These rights do not apply to non-Community nationals, such as Katrina, although she may gain rights indirectly. There must be some inter-State movement, which exists in this case, since these rights do not apply to internal situations: *Iorio (Paulo)* v *Azienda Autonomo delle Ferrovie dello Stato* Case 298/84 [1986] ECR 247.

Article 39 EC has direct effect according to the case of *Kenny* v *Insurance Officer* Case 1/78 [1978] ECR 1489 so individuals may rely on it. *Walrave and Koch* v *Association Union Cycliste Internationale* Case 36/74 [1974] ECR 1405 concluded that art 39 EC may be relied upon in both a vertical and horizontal manner, and it prohibits both direct and indirect discrimination according to *Union des Associations Européennes de Football* v *Jean-Marc Bosman* Case C–415/93 [1995] ECR I–4921.

In order for Christophe and Katrina to have any means of securing rights, Christophe must be a 'worker'. No definition is offered in the EC Treaty or in any of the secondary legislation. The definition, as provided by the European Court of Justice via teleological interpretation, is a wide one that the Court insists in *Hoekstra* v *Bestuur der Bedrijfsvereniging voor Detailhandel en Ambachten* Case 75/63 [1964] ECR 177 must be supranational. The Austrian courts will assess whether Christophe is a 'worker' and should refer to the following jurisprudence of the ECJ.

In *Levin* v *Staatssecretaris van Justitie* Case 53/81 [1982] ECR 1035 a person employed on a part-time basis was a worker for the purposes of art 39 EC; a worker was someone pursuing an effective and genuine economic activity that was not marginal or ancillary. This was followed in *Kempf* v *Staatssecretaris van Justitie* Case 139/85 [1986] ECR 1741 where a German national working as a music teacher received such low pay that he was entitled to claim social security benefits. The Court concluded that Kempf fulfilled the test in *Levin* v *Staatssecretaris van Justitie* Case 53/81 [1982] ECR 1035 and that hours worked and pay levels were merely factors to be taken into account when assessing whether the work was genuine and effective.

This broad interpretation of a worker was maintained in *Lawrie-Blum* v *Land Baden-Württenburg* Case 66/85 [1986] ECR 2121, which involved a British trainee teacher in Germany. She was paid less than her fully qualified counterparts but was still considered to be performing a genuine and effective economic activity. The Court suggested that a worker would be someone: providing services for another over a period of time; that they would be under the direction of that other; and that they would receive remuneration. Such remuneration may be low or below the national minimum wage, as in *Kempf* v *Staatssecretaris van Justitie* Case 139/85 [1986] ECR 1741 and *Lawrie-Blum*, it may also consist of 'payment in kind' such as the meeting of material needs in *Steymann* v *Staatssecretaris van Justitie* Case 196/87 [1988] ECR 6159.

Article 39(4) EC excludes free movement from those workers in the public service. This is identified by using a functional test: *Commission* v *Belgium (Re State Employees)* Case 149/79 [1980] ECR 3881. Christophe will probably not be within this exception, since his teaching job will not involve the exercise of powers conferred by public law or duties designed to safeguard the interests of the State.

A worker is entitled to 'install' their family with them. According to Council Regulation 1612/68, art 10(1), a worker's family includes their spouse. The nationality of the spouse is irrelevant, although if they are not a Community national they will require a visa. The definition of spouse is that of someone legally married to the worker, and this remains the case according to *Diatta* v *Land Berlin* Case 267/83 [1985] ECR 567 until the formal dissolution of the marriage. Katrina, a non-Community national, is not a spouse but a cohabitee. The question of whether such individuals may come within the definition of spouse was considered in the case of *Netherlands* v *Reed* Case 59/85 [1986] ECR 1283.

Reed, a British national who was unmarried, sought work in The Netherlands. She did not find employment, but then moved in with Mr W, another British national working in The Netherlands. Reed applied for a residence permit (Council Directive 68/360) but was refused on the basis that Dutch law only permitted non-nationals to extend their rights of residence to cohabitees if the relationship had begun prior to entry into The Netherlands. This rule did not apply to Dutch nationals. On a preliminary reference the ECJ concluded that a cohabitee was not a spouse for the purposes of Regulation 1612/68. Instead, the Court relied on art 12 EC and art 7(2) of Regulation 1612/68. The former provides that discrimination on the basis of nationality is prohibited. The latter states that non-nationals are entitled to the same 'social and tax' advantages as nationals. The Court concluded that since Dutch nationals were permitted to live with a cohabitee even if that relationship had begun in The Netherlands, non-nationals must be entitled to the same social advantage. Consequently, as long as Austria permits its nationals to cohabit with non-nationals, Katrina gains the right to remain with Christophe on the basis that to deprive him of the right to live with the person of his choice will be a violation of the right to the social advantages granted to Austrian nationals, and will violate the principle of the prohibition of discrimination on the basis of nationality.

Article 39(3) EC provides that the right to free movement is subject to derogation on the grounds of public policy, security and health. These grounds are exhaustive and have been narrowly interpreted by the European Court; hence any deportation of Christophe must be based on these grounds alone. The grounds must be exercised with respect for fundamental human rights, including those protected under the European Convention on Human Rights: *Elliniki Radiophonia Tileorassi* v *Dimotiki Etaria Pliroforissis* Case C–260/89 [1991] ECR I–2925. Council Directive 64/221, which has direct effect, provides additional conditions under which Member States must exercise these derogations. This Directive, though, does not apply to non-Community nationals unless they are members of the worker's family; hence it will not apply to Katrina's deportation.

Austria will have to rely on the grounds of public policy and/or security to deport Christophe. Article 2 of Council Directive 64/221 provides that the derogations may not be exercised for economic purposes. Article 3 of the Directive states that decisions on these grounds must be based exclusively on the personal conduct of the individual. At this point we should identify that there may be two grounds under which Christophe may find the derogations of public policy and/or security being applied. First, on the basis of a student having prohibited drugs on his premises and, second, that he is a possible political agitator. In both cases, the Austrian authorities will have to prove that he poses a genuine and sufficiently serious threat affecting one of the fundamental interests of society: *Rutili* v *Minister for the Interior* Case 36/75 [1975] ECR 1219.

In the case of the drugs charge, the Austrian authorities may have some difficulty in establishing that this is based on Christophe's personal conduct, since it was a student that was actually found in possession of the prohibited drugs. Even if Christophe is convicted, art 3 of Council Directive 64/221 provides that criminal convictions per se are insufficient grounds for exercising one of the derogations. In *Bonsignore* v *Oberstadtdirektor of the City of Cologne* Case 67/74 [1975] ECR 297 the Court held that a criminal conviction could not justify derogation as a general preventative measure to deter others from committing the same or similar offences. The criminal conviction would have to prove that Christophe is a present threat to public policy or security in that it shows a propensity to act in the same way in the future: *R* v *Bouchereau* Case 30/77 [1977] ECR 1999. In *Criminal Proceedings against Calfa* Case C–348/96 [1999] ECR I–11 Greek law required immediate deportation of those convicted of possession of drugs. The Court required the Greek authorities to assess the personal conduct of the individual, as well as the commission of the offence. If we apply this to Christophe's situation, it is unlikely that the Austrian authorities will be able to rely on the drugs charge/conviction.

The Austrian authorities may wish to deport Christophe on the basis of his political agitator status. In the case of *Rutili* (above) the French authorities attempted to confine an Italian national to certain parts of France because he had been involved in political and trade union activity similar to Christophe. The Court held that the concept of public policy had to be restrictively interpreted, so the threat has to be one that is genuine and sufficiently serious. However, the ECJ also emphasised that art 8 of Council Regulation 1612/68 provides the right for non-national workers to belong to trade unions, and consequently derogation cannot be invoked as a result of exercising those rights. The Court also referred to the European Convention on Human Rights, which provides that limitations in the interests of national security or public safety cannot be invoked unless they are necessary to protect democratic society.

Again the decision must be based on Chistophe's personal conduct; if he is the present member of an organisation prescribed or controlled by Austrian law, this may be used, according to *Van Duyn* v *Home Office* Case 41/74 [1974] ECR 1337, as evidence of personal conduct. However, the wide discretion offered Member States under the *Van Duyn* decision to define prohibited conduct was narrowed by the important decision in *Adoui and Cornvaille* v *Belgian State* Cases 115 and 116/81 [1982] ECR 1665. To assess whether the deportation is based on a genuine threat, Christophe's treatment must be compared with that of Austrian nationals. Hence, non-nationals should receive no arbitrary distinction in terms of their treatment, and there must be comparative measures placed on those nationals in similar situations.

Finally, Christophe is entitled to procedural safeguards under Council Directive

64/221. These include the right under art 6 to be given the grounds for the reason to deport him, and the reasons should be clear, precise and comprehensive. The only exception is where such disclosure would harm national security. Article 7 states that Christophe will have to be officially notified. He also is entitled to a minimum 15 days before deportation if he does not hold a residence permit, and one month if he does. He is entitled to access all legal remedies available to nationals under art 8 and the right to appeal to a court of law or competent authority under art 9.

Chapter 9

The Free Movement of Goods

9.1　Introduction

9.2　Key points

9.3　Key cases and materials

9.4　Questions and suggested solutions

9.1　Introduction

The creation of a more efficient market through the reduction of obstacles to transnational commerce has always been a fundamental aim of the European Community. The need to achieve the free movement of goods, persons, services and capital throughout the Community was recognised as an express goal of the EEC Treaty (now the EC Treaty) and was reaffirmed by the Single European Act 1986. Of these freedoms, the free movement of goods has traditionally been acknowledged as being of paramount significance. The free movement of goods implies that goods can move from one Community country to another without having to pay customs duties or charges having an equivalent effect to customs duties and also that goods will not be subject to quantitative restrictions or measures of equivalent effect when moving from one Community country to another.

9.2　Key points

Elimination of customs duties between Member States

The six original Member States of the Community agreed to a series of progressive reductions in the customs duties which existed between them prior to the EC Treaty, culminating in the elimination of all customs duties on both import and export transactions. Customs duties were officially eliminated between the original six on 1 July 1968.

States acceding to the Community are obliged, as a condition of membership, to eliminate all customs duties between them and the other Member States over negotiated transitional periods. The United Kingdom, Ireland, Denmark, and Greece have all eliminated customs duties for intra-Community trade in goods, while Spain and Portugal removed such restrictions on 1 January 1993. Subject to limited derogations for certain products, particularly agricultural goods, Austria, Sweden and

Finland were required to remove all customs duties for trade in goods between the countries of the European Community and themselves by 1 January 1995, as a requirement of the 1994 Treaty of Accession.

Article 25 EC expressly prohibits the re-introduction of any custom duties on imports and export for goods passing between Community States.

Elimination of charges having an equivalent effect to customs duties

Member States are also obliged to eliminate all 'charges having an equivalent effect to customs duties' on imports and exports and to refrain from re-introducing such charges on intra-Community transactions. No definition of 'charges having an equivalent effect' is elaborated in the EC Treaty and interpretation of this term has been left to the European Court. The Court has elaborated on the nature of this concept in a number of cases, and it has stated that:

> '[A]ny pecuniary charge, whatever its designation and mode of application, which is imposed unilaterally on goods by reason of the fact that they cross a frontier, and is not a customs duty in the strict sense, constitutes a charge having equivalent effect to a customs duty.' (*Commission* v *Germany (Re Animals Inspection Fees)* Case 18/87 [1988] ECR 5427.)

Hence, there is no requirement to consider the name of the charge (see, for example, *Commission* v *Luxembourg (Re Import Duties on Gingerbread)* Cases 2 and 3/62 [1963] CMLR 199), the reason for its introduction, or whether it is applied in a discriminatory manner. The Court will instead examine the effect of the measure.

A charge may take a number of forms but is often called a 'tax'. If the measure is indeed a genuine tax it will not fall within art 25 EC but will be governed by art 90 EC. A genuine tax is defined as one that relates to 'a general system of internal dues applied systematically to categories of products in accordance with objective criteria irrespective of the origin of the products': *Commission* v *France (Re Levy on Reprographic Machines)* Case 90/79 [1981] ECR 283. A genuine tax will be examined under art 90 EC to identify whether it is discriminatory (see p210).

Not all charges imposed on goods crossing a frontier between Member States will be deemed to have an equivalent effect to a customs duty. In particular, an expense will not be prohibited as a charge having an equivalent effect in three separate circumstances.

a) If the charge relates to a general system of internal dues applied systematically within a Member State without discrimination between domestic and imported products: *Denkavit* v *France* Case 132/78 [1979] ECR 1923.

b) If the charges constitute payment for a service in fact rendered and the charge is proportionate to the costs of receiving that service: *Commission* v *Denmark* Case 158/82 [1983] ECR 3573.

c) If the charges are levied in accordance with the terms of a Community measure. In this case, a number of conditions must be satisfied: *Bauhuis* v *Netherlands* Case 46/76 [1977] ECR 5.

Charges levied under the authority of Community legislation for services actually rendered (category (c) above) do not constitute charges of equivalent effect if four conditions are satisfied:

a) the charges do not exceed the actual costs of the services rendered in connection with the charge;

b) the inspections are obligatory and uniform for all products throughout the Community;

c) the charges are prescribed by Community law in the general interest of the Community; and

d) the service promotes the free movement of goods by neutralising obstacles which arise from unilateral measures of inspection.

There is no means of justifying the imposition of a customs duty or equivalent effect: *Commission* v *Italy (Re Export Tax on Art Treasures)* Case 7/68 [1968] ECR 423. Any payment of a sum breaching art 25 EC is recoverable under by the national law of the State that imposed the charge according to *Amministrazione delle Finanze dello Stato* v *San Giorgio* Case 199/82 [1983] ECR 3595. The one exception to this is if the charge has been passed on to the consumer. In such situations the trader may have made up their loss and consequently have suffered no damage.

Elimination of quantitative restrictions between Member States

A quantitative restriction is a national measure that restrains the volume or amount of imports or exports, not by artificially raising the costs of importing or exporting (as would be the case with a tariff or export tax), but by placing direct or indirect limits on the physical quantity of the imports or exports that may enter or leave the market: *Riseria Luigi Geddo* v *Ente Nazionale Risi* Case 2/73 [1973] ECR 865. The most common examples of quantitative restrictions are bans or quotas.

Quantitative restrictions between the original six Member States were gradually phased out and acceding Members must observe a similar obligation: arts 28–30 EC. Article 28 EC prohibits the re-introduction of quantitative restrictions and measures of equivalent effect on imports while art 29 EC imposes the same obligation for exports.

The explicit prohibition on the introduction of quotas is periodically violated. For example, in 1978, the United Kingdom restricted imports of Dutch potatoes while France imposed an embargo on sheepmeat from the United Kingdom. Similarly, in 1982, the United Kingdom limited imports of French UHT milk by establishing a quota. Each of these actions resulted in litigation before the European Court: *Commission* v *United Kingdom (Re Imports of Dutch Potatoes)* Case 231/78 [1979] ECR 1447; *Commission* v *France (Re Sheepmeat from the United Kingdom)* Case 232/78 [1979] ECR 2729; and *Commission* v *United Kingdom (Re UHT Milk)* Case 124/81 [1983] ECR 203.

Measures having an equivalent effect to quantitative restrictions (MEQRs)

Article 28 EC also prohibits all measures having an equivalent effect to quantitative restrictions. The concept of 'measures having an equivalent effect to quantitative restrictions' should be distinguished from that of 'charges having an equivalent effect to customs duties'. Charges having an equivalent effect to customs duties impose direct costs on imported products while measures having an equivalent effect to quantitative restrictions are national measures – either legislative or administrative – which affect the amount (quantity or volume) of products imported.

Again the EC Treaty contains no definition of the concept of measures having an equivalent effect. In order to fill this vacuum, the European Court has adopted the following definition:

> 'All trading rules enacted by Member States which are capable of hindering directly or indirectly, actually or potentially, intra-Community trade are to be considered as measures having an effect equivalent to quantitative restrictions.' (*Procureur du Roi* v *Dassonville* Case 8/74 [1974] ECR 837.)

The term 'measures having an equivalent effect' includes all laws and practices attributable to public authorities as well as government funding of activities which have the effect of restricting imports. For example, in 1982, the Irish government was held responsible for infringement of art 28 EC because it financed a 'Buy Irish' campaign which encouraged consumers to purchase goods produced in Ireland in preference over competitive goods from Community countries: *Commission* v *Ireland (Re Buy Irish Campaign)* Case 249/81 [1982] ECR 4005.

Article 28 EC and the relevant legislative measures also apply to the activities of local and regional government agencies which are required to respect the terms of such measures. The European Court will not permit any distinction to be drawn between measures enacted at local, regional or national level as long as the enacting authority exercises the necessary legislative competence. A Member State cannot therefore argue that it bears no liability for infringements of art 28 EC caused by the actions of such agencies.

There are two types of MEQR that may be imposed, namely, discriminatory MEQRs (also described as distinctly applied MEQRs) and non-discriminatory MEQRs (or indistinctly applied MEQRs). This is recognised under Commission Directive 70/50, although it should be noted that the Directive has no legally binding effect.

Discriminatory MEQRs are imposed either only on the imported product, or promote the domestic product placing the imported one at a disadvantage. Such discriminatory practices include:

a) measures designed to specify less favourable prices for imports than for domestic prices;

b) practices which establish minimum or maximum prices below or above which imports are prohibited or reduced;

c) standards which subject imports to conditions relating to shape, size, weight or composition and which cause imported products to suffer in competition with domestic products: see, for example, *Verein Gegen Unwese in Handel und Gewerbe Köln* v *Mars GmbH* Case C–470/93 [1995] ECR I–1923; this may also include the imposing of a test or inspection on the imported product: *Rewe-Zentralfinanz GmbH* v *Landwirtschaftskammer* Case 4/75 [1975] ECR 843;

d) laws which restrict the marketing of imported products in the absence of an agent or representative in the territory of the importing Member State;

e) laws that promote the domestic product to the detriment of the imported product may also constitute a discriminatory MEQR. In *Commission* v *Ireland (Re Buy Irish Campaign)* Case 249/81 [1982] ECR 4005 the Irish government created the Irish Goods Council with the objective of switching 3 per cent of consumers from buying imported to domestic products. The campaign that followed included the creation of exhibition facilities for Irish goods and use of the Buy Irish symbol. Whilst the campaign failed, it was concluded by the Court to still fall within the *Procureur du Roi* v *Dassonville* Case 8/74 [1974] ECR 837 formula, in other words, it was capable of potentially affecting the free movement of goods because it was an integrated programme for promoting domestic products: *Commission* v *Ireland (Re Dundalk Water Supply)* Case 45/87R [1987] 2 CMLR 197.

Exceptions to restrictions on discriminatory quantitative restrictions and discriminatory measures having an equivalent effect

Specific exceptions to art 28 EC are made by art 30 EC. Quantitative restrictions and discriminatory measures having equivalent effect on either imports or exports may be permitted in four circumstances.

The protection of public morality, public policy and public security

Restrictions justified on the basis of public morality have frequently been upheld by the European Court. In fact, the Court allows a considerable degree of discretion (or 'margin of discretion') on the part of Member States to make such determinations.

However, in order to be justifiable as a genuine measure designed to protect public morality there must be some form of equivalent repressive measure on the domestic product: *Conegate Limited* v *HM Customs and Excise* Case 121/85 [1986] ECR 1007.

The concept of public policy is capable of a greater application than public morality, although surprisingly few measures have been justified on this ground. In *R* v *Thompson and Others* Case 7/78 [1978] ECR 2247 the European Court upheld convictions for fraudulently importing gold coins into the United Kingdom on the basis that such practices circumvented the right of a State to mint coinage for circulation, a prerogative traditionally recognised as involving the fundamental interests of the State.

However, in *Cullet* v *Centre Leclerc* Case 231/83 [1985] ECR 305 the ECJ refused to extend public policy to include the prevention of civil disturbance. In this case the French government claimed that fixed prices for fuel were required to prevent blockades and civil violence. The Court concluded that the French government had not proved that such disturbances would occur if the fixed prices were removed, or that they lacked the resources to deal with such problems, and consequently the measures were not proportionate. The Advocate-General stated that such an interpretation of public policy would permit private interest groups to dictate the actions of governments and the Community.

Public security was the ground argued in the case of *Campus Oil Ltd* v *Minister for Industry and Energy* Case 72/83 [1984] ECR 2727. The Irish government required that importers of petrol had to purchase 35 per cent of their requirements at fixed prices from Irish oil refineries. This promotion of the domestic product constituted a discriminatory MEQR that the Irish government claimed was justifiable in the interest of public security. The ECJ accepted the justification on the basis that petrol was of exceptional importance as an energy source, so the aim of ensuring a minimum supply of the product was justifiable in the interests of public policy. However, the Court emphasised that the fixed price had to be proportionate to meet the objective.

The protection of the health and life of humans, animals or plants

This is the most often used of the grounds available under art 30 EC. However, the Court will closely examine a claim under this ground. To be successful the claim will have to be based on a real and genuine risk, based on evidence, and be proportionate and non-arbitrary: see, for example, *Commission* v *United Kingdom (Re Imports of Poultry Meat)* Case 40/82 [1982] ECR 2793, *Commission* v *United Kingdom (Re UHT Milk)* Case 124/81 [1983] ECR 203 and *Commission* v *Germany (Re German Beer Purity Law)* Case 178/84 [1987] ECR 1227.

However, if there is some scientific/medical evidence, but no consensus, according to *Officier van Justitie* v *Sandoz BV* Case 174/82 [1983] ECR 2445 the State retains discretion in how to react to the perceived threat. The measures adopted, though, must be proportionate and must be set aside if any Community harmonising measure is later produced on the subject.

The protection of national heritage

Member States can maintain restrictions necessary to protect national treasures which have artistic, historic, or archaeological value. This exception, however, only applies to treasures which remain in the public domain. As a general rule, only works of art which have not been placed on the market may benefit from this exception. Thus, in *Commission* v *Italy (Re Export Tax on Art Treasures)* Case 7/68 [1968] ECR 423, the European Court held that an export tax introduced by the Italian government could not be justified as a measure intended to protect national heritage because the items in question had entered the commercial market and had become sources of revenue for the national authorities.

Protection of industrial and commercial property

National legislation may be maintained to protect the intellectual property rights of patent holders, licensees and copyright holders. The European Court has held that measures to protect patent holders may only be maintained if the products have been manufactured without the permission of the holder of the intellectual property right. Such protection cannot be afforded where the imported product has been lawfully placed in circulation by the property right holder, or with his consent, in the Member State from which it has been imported.

Non-discriminatory MEQRs and their justification

MEQRs may also be imposed in a non-discriminatory manner, ie they are imposed on both imported/exported and domestic products equally. Such measures may also breach the Treaty, but the Court has created alternative means of justifying them.

In addition to the express exceptions enumerated in art 30 EC, the European Court has acknowledged that, in the marketing of products, Member States may regulate marketing activities as long as the objectives of the regulatory measures are legitimate. Most notably, in *Rewe-Zentrale AG* v *Bundesmonopolverwaltung für Branntwein (Cassis De Dijon)* Case 120/78 [1979] ECR 649 (commonly referred to as *Cassis De Dijon)*, the Court expressly observed that national laws imposing 'mandatory requirements' are permissible in certain circumstances.

This is known as the *Cassis* rule of reason test. In order to be justifiable as necessary to protect a mandatory requirement the measure must be proportionate, in other words no more than is necessary to meet the objective. According to *Cassis*, the measure must also respect the principle of mutual recognition. This raises a presumption that if the product is lawfully produced and/or marketed in one Member State, it is presumed lawful in all Member States. This presumption may be rebutted on the production of evidence that the additional measure is necessary.

The examples of mandatory requirements given in *Cassis* are a non-exhaustive list and the Court has been prepared to add others. One example of an acceptable mandatory requirement is consumer protection. However, to be successful, the measure introduced must be proportionate. In many cases the Court has declared the adopted action to be non-proportionate and has often suggested that a labelling requirement would be a more proportionate means of protecting consumers: for example, see *Verband Sozialer Wettbewerb eV* v *Clinique Laboratories SNC* Case C–315/92 [1994] ECR I–317, *Walter Rau Lebensmittelwerke* v *De Smedt PVBA* Case 261/81 [1982] 2 CMLR 496 and *Cassis* (above). Other mandatory requirements include: public health (*Commission* v *Germany (Re German Beer Purity Law)* Case 178/84 [1987] ECR 1227); the fairness of commercial transactions (*Oosthoek's Uitgeversmaatschappij BV* Case 286/81 [1982] ECR

4575); protecting the environment (*Commission v Denmark (Re Returnable Containers)* Case 302/86 [1988] ECR 4607); and protecting art (*Cinéthèque SA v Fédération Nationale des Cinémas Français* Cases 60 and 61/84 [1985] ECR 2605.

The European Court has developed the law in this area in a rare example of it changing its approach. This change was introduced as a reaction to criticism based on the distinction between equal burden and dual burden rules. The latter relate to the characteristics of a product, even though those products have already complied with similar standards set in the State in which they were produced or manufactured. Equal burden rules are those that apply equally to all products in the way in which they are sold. Such rules affect the volume of trade, regardless of the origin of products, and are not designed to be protectionist.

In *Criminal Proceedings against Keck and Mithouard* Cases C–267 and 268/91 [1993] ECR I–6097 the Court stated that equal burden rules in the form of selling arrangements were outside the scope of art 28 EC and therefore required no justification. In order to benefit from this distinction the measure must apply to all traders operating within the national territory, and apply to the marketing of domestic and imported goods in the same manner in both law and in fact.

Hence, measures that relate to the characteristics of a product, such as size, weight, packaging, contents, etc, are considered to be dual burden rules and will breach art 28 EC unless they can be justified under the *Cassis De Dijon* rule of reason test. Measures relating to the circumstances in which products are sold are considered to be equal burden rules, outside of the prohibition in art 28 EC.

The *Keck* principle has been extended to both static and non-static selling arrangements, such as advertising and sales promotions: see, for example, *Hünermund v Landesapothekerkammer Baden-Württenburg* Case C–292/92 [1993] ECR I–6787 and *Konsumentombudsman v De Agostini* Case C–34–36/95 [1998] 1 CMLR 32.

Discriminatory domestic taxation

Article 90 EC expressly prohibits Member States from imposing – directly or indirectly – internal taxes of any kind on Community products if such taxes exceed those imposed on identical or similar domestic products. This provision only applies to the levying of internal taxes where imported goods compete with domestic products. If there are no similar products, or no products capable of being protected, the prohibition in art 90 EC is inapplicable. The products must therefore be in actual or potential competition.

The degree of competition required was illustrated in *Commission v United Kingdom (Re Wine and Beer Tax)* Case 170/78 [1983] ECR 2265, which concerned British internal taxation policy on wines and beer. The United Kingdom imposed greater taxes on wine products, which were almost exclusively imported, than on beer products, which were mainly domestically produced. The Commission argued that, since wine and beer were conceivably interchangeable products, this tax differential created an artificial separation of the market which had the effect of de facto discrimination. The European

Court agreed with this submission and held that beer and wine were competing products and therefore the United Kingdom was guilty of discrimination by levying different levels of tax.

Harmonisation of barriers to trade

Measures having an equivalent effect to quantitative restrictions form the greatest obstacles to the free movement of goods within the Community. These measures fall into three categories:

a) physical barriers to trade – for example, the systematic stopping and checking of goods and people at national frontiers;

b) technical barriers to trade – for example, national legislation regulating product standards, conditions of marketing, or the protection of public health or safety;

c) fiscal barriers to trade – for example, the divergence in types and rates or indirect taxes levied on goods within the Community.

The EC Treaty specifically identifies the harmonisation (or approximation) of the laws of the Member States in order to remove these obstacles as an objective of the Community: art 3(h) EC. Articles 94, 95 and 308 EC confer authority on the Community to enact legislation to harmonise such measures and standards throughout the Community. A number of Community measures have been adopted to eliminate such barriers through harmonisation. Products which satisfy such standards are entitled to unimpeded entry into the markets of all Member States.

Where Community legislation has been enacted to harmonise the legislation of the Member States, as regards a particular restriction based on art 30 EC, any additional requirements imposed under national law which extend or exceed those contained in the Community measure are not permitted: *Dansk Denkavit* v *Ministry of Agriculture* Case 29/87 [1988] ECR 2965.

However, it is only when Community legislation provides for complete harmonisation that recourse to art 30 EC itself is no longer justified: *Oberkreisdirektor* v *Moorman* Case 190/87 [1988] ECR 4689.

The single internal market programme

The Single European Act 1986 also introduced the single market programme, also known as the 1992 programme. The internal market is defined as:

> '… an area without internal frontiers in which the free movement of goods, persons, services and capital is ensured in accordance with the provisions of the [EC Treaty].' (Article 14 EC.)

The programme itself was a package of measures designed to eradicate barriers to trade and measures having an equivalent effect to quantitative restrictions. The deadline for the achievement of this goal was set for 31 December 1992. A total of 282 measures were introduced to tackle barriers to trade in the areas of customs, tax, public procurement, capital movements, company law, employment, transport and safety standards.

As noted above, the target set for the enactment of all proposals was 31 December 1992. While the Council was unable to adopt all the measures proposed by the Commission under the programme, around 95 per cent of this total was in fact enacted.

Council Regulation 2679/98 was adopted to further remove obstacles to free movement within the internal market, particularly in respect of goods. Under the system established by this Regulation, when an obstacle occurs or a threat thereof emerges, any Member State which has relevant information can transmit this to the Commission. The Commission will then immediately transmit to the Member States that information and any information from any other source which it may consider relevant. If the Commission considers that the obstacle exists, it will notify the Member State concerned and request it to take all necessary and proportionate measures. The Member States shall, within five working days of receipt of the text, either inform the Commission of the steps which it has taken or intends to take, or communicate a reasoned submission as to why there is no obstacle constituting a breach of arts 28–30 EC.

The Council also adopted a Resolution concerning the free movement of goods. Member States undertook to do all within their power to maintain the free movement of goods and to deal rapidly with actions which seriously disrupt the free movement of goods. They also agreed to ensure that effective review procedures are available for any person who has been harmed as a result of a breach of the principle of free movement of goods.

Trade in goods from non-Community states

Goods entering the Community from non-Community countries are subject to the Common Customs Tariff (CCT) which is a comprehensive Community-wide regime for assessing customs duties on non-EC goods. The CCT supersedes the individual tariff schedules and customs laws of the Member States, although the Community relies on national customs officials to enforce its provisions. The present CCT is based on Council Regulation 2913/92 (1992) as supplemented by Commission Regulation 2454/93 (1993).

Article 24(1) EC provides that products from third countries shall be considered to be in 'free circulation' within the Community if:

a) the relevant import formalities have been completed;

b) any customs duties or charges having an equivalent effect have been levied; and

c) the goods have not benefited from a total or partial drawback of such duties or charges.

According to art 23(2) EC, once foreign goods are in free circulation, they may not be subject to customs duties, quantitative restrictions or measures having an equivalent effect during intra-Community trade: *Grandes Distilleries Paureux* v *Directeur des Services Fiscaux* Case 86/78 [1979] ECR 975.

9.3 Key cases and materials

- *Commission* v *France (Re Levy on Reprographic Machines)* Case 90/79 [1981] ECR 283
  Defines a genuine tax (art 90 EC) as one that relates to 'a general system of internal dues applied systematically to categories of products in accordance with objective criteria irrespective of the origin of the products'

- *Commission* v *Germany (Re Animals Inspection Fees)* Case 18/87 [1988] ECR 5427
  Definition of the concept of 'charges having an equivalent effect to customs duties'

- *Commission* v *Ireland (Re Buy Irish Campaign)* Case 249/81 [1982] ECR 4005
  Offers an example of the wide definition given to the State for the purposes of applying arts 28–29 EC: the campaign itself was concluded to be a discriminatory MEQR since it promoted domestic products to the detriment of imports

- *Commission* v *United Kingdom (Re Imports of Poultry Meat)* Case 40/82 [1982] ECR 2793; *Commission* v *United Kingdom (Re UHT Milk)* Case 124/81 [1983] ECR 203
  To justify a measure under the grounds in art 30 EC of protecting the life and health of humans, animals and plants the claim must be based on a real and genuine risk, supported by evidence, and be proportionate and non-arbitrary

- *Conegate Limited* v *HM Customs and Excise* Case 121/85 [1986] ECR 1007
  In order to be justifiable as a genuine measure designed to protect public morality under art 30 EC there must be some form of equivalent repressive measures on the domestic product

- *Criminal Proceedings against Keck and Mithouard* Cases C–267 and 268/91 [1993] ECR I–6097
  Selling arrangements fall outside the scope of art 28 EC: the measure must apply to all traders operating within the national territory and apply to the marketing of domestic and imported goods in the same manner in both law and in fact

- *Cullet* v *Centre Leclerc* Case 231/83 [1985] ECR 305
  The ECJ refused to extend public policy to include the prevention of civil disturbance

- *Officier van Justitie* v *Sandoz BV* Case 174/82 [1983] ECR 2445
  The State retains discretion in how to react to a perceived threat that is supported by some medical/scientific evidence, although there is no consensus: any measures adopted must be proportionate and set aside if any Community harmonising measure is later produced on the subject

- *Procureur du Roi* v *Dassonville* Case 8/74 [1974] ECR 837
  Defines MEQRs as measures that are capable of hindering, directly or indirectly, actually or potentially, intra-Community trade

- *Rewe-Zentrale AG* v *Bundesmonopolverwaltung für Branntwein (Cassis De Dijon)* Case 120/78 [1979] ECR 649
  Provides that non-discriminatory MEQRs may come within the ambit of art 28 EC but may be justified as necessary to protect a mandatory requirement – known as the *Cassis* rule of reason

- *Riseria Luigi Geddo* v *Ente Nazionale Risi* Case 2/73 [1973] ECR 865
  Defines a quantitative restriction for the purposes of arts 28 and 29 EC as a total or partial restraint on the free movement of goods

- EC Treaty

  - art 14 – defines the internal market

  - art 23 – non-EC goods in free circulation may not be subject to customs duties, quantitative restrictions or measures having equivalent effect

  - art 25 – prohibits the re-introduction of any customs duties and charges having equivalent effect on imports and exports between Member States

  - art 28 – prohibits Member States from imposing quantitative restrictions and measures equivalent to quantitative restrictions on imports

  - art 29 – places the same obligation as above on Member States in relation to exports

  - art 30 – offers an exhaustive set of grounds permitted to justify the use of quantitative restrictions or measures of equivalent effect

  - art 90 – prohibits Member States imposing direct or indirect internal taxes on Community products if they exceed those imposed on identical or similar domestic products

- Commission Directive 70/50 – distinguishes between discriminatory and non-discriminatory measures equivalent to quantitative restrictions and provides examples

- Council Regulation 2679/98 – designed to promote the removal of obstacles to free movement within the internal market

9.4 Questions and suggested solutions

QUESTION ONE

Martin NV exports TV aerials from the Netherlands to the United Kingdom. It enters into a contract with Nairn Ltd to supply 1,000 aerials a month. The first shipment from Martin to Nairn is stopped by United Kingdom customs authorities. The authorities state that:

a) United Kingdom law requires that such products be inspected at the port, the inspection has been carried out and a fee is now due;

b) the aerials are made partly of an aluminium alloy which United Kingdom legislation prohibits from being used in the United Kingdom for reasons of consumer protection;

c) the strength of the aerials is below that required by standards adopted by the United Kingdom pursuant to the procedure permitted by art 95(4).

Advise Martin NV as to any rights and remedies which it may have under European Community law.

University of London LLB Examination
(for External Students) European Community Law June 1992 Q6

General Comment

A problem type question requiring the student to analyse the facts presented in light of arts 28–30 EC. There appear to be no real difficulties presented by the facts of the question and so a familiarity with the basic elements of this part of the syllabus should secure a reasonable score.

Skeleton Solution

General principles relating to the free movement of goods – restrictions on customs duties and charges having similar effect: art 25 EC – restrictions on the use of quantitative restrictions and measures having equivalent effect: arts 28–30 EC – exemptions for Member States from the rigours of harmonising legislation under art 95(4) EC.

Suggested Solution

There are three separate measures preventing Martin NV from importing the aerials from the Netherlands into the United Kingdom: inspection charges; consumer protection legislation; and product technical standards. While each of these measures constitutes a barrier to trade in terms of the free movement of goods, each is subject to different Community rules. It is therefore necessary to consider each measure separately.

a) Article 25 EC expressly prohibits the introduction of any customs duties, or charges having an equivalent effect to customs duties, on imports and exports from different Member States of the Community. This provision has been given direct effect by the European Court and may therefore be relied upon by private individuals in national courts without reference to the European Court.

Charges having equivalent effect to customs duties have been defined by the European Court as 'any pecuniary charge, whatever its designation and mode of application, which is imposed unilaterally on goods by reason of the fact that they cross a frontier, and is not a customs duty in the strict sense': *Commission* v *Germany (Re Animals Inspection Fees)* Case 18/87 [1988] ECR 5427. A charge imposed on importation which has the effect of discriminating between domestic goods and similar goods of Community origin, and which cannot be justified by provisions in the EC Treaty or Community legislation, will therefore amount to a charge having equivalent effect.

Charges having an equivalent effect can only be justified in three circumstances: (i) if the charges relate to a general system of internal levies applied systematically within a Member State and without discrimination; (ii) if the charges constitute payment for a service in fact rendered and are in proportion to the costs of receiving that service; and (iii) if the charges are levied under the authority of a Community measure harmonising customs procedures.

According to the facts of this case as presented in the question, UK law requires inspection of these products at the port of entry and a charge is due for such an inspection. It is unlikely that such inspections are made of domestically-produced aerials and there is therefore a presumption that such charges are unlawful under Community law. Further, although the charge imposed was for a service rendered, in the event that this charge is disproportionate to the costs of rendering the service, again the charge may be illegitimate: *Commission* v *Denmark* Case 158/82 [1983] ECR 3573.

Further, no direct benefit accrued to either Martin NV or Nairn Ltd by virtue of the inspection. Community law requires that the importer receives some benefit from the service, which has not happened in this case. Obviously a direct benefit will not accrue to an importer if the charges are made in the interests of the inspecting State: *Commission* v *Italy ((Re Statistical Levy)* Case 24/68 [1969] ECR 193.

In these circumstances, it is unlikely that Martin NV or Nairn Ltd will be liable for the charges and the appropriate action can be raised on these grounds to reject such a claim.

b) The second barrier to import is the fact that the aerials are made of an aluminium alloy prohibited under United Kingdom consumer protection legislation.

Article 28 EC prohibits quantitative restrictions on imports along with all measures having an equivalent effect to quantitative restrictions. Measures having an equivalent effect to quantitative restrictions have been defined as 'all trading rules enacted by Member States which are capable of hindering directly or indirectly, actually or potentially, intra-Community trade': *Procureur du Roi* v *Dassonville* Case 8/74 [1974] ECR 837. All rules enacted by a Member State to regulate trade, and which have the effect of hindering commerce, may contravene art 28 EC unless they can benefit from an exception to this rule.

The seizure of the aerials because they contain an aluminium alloy is a measure equivalent to a quantitative restriction pertaining to the characteristics of a product.

However, it is a measure applied in a non-discriminatory manner. As such, the UK may attempt to justify its action under the *Cassis de Dijon* rule of reason.

In the *Cassis de Dijon* case (*Rewe-Zentrale AG* v *Bundesmonopolverwaltung für Branntwein* Case 120/78 [1979] ECR 649), the European Court considered the question of national restrictions affecting the free movement of goods. It concluded that, in the absence of Community-wide measures of harmonisation, Member States retain authority to enact laws and regulations in relation to products but only so far as such provisions are necessary to satisfy 'mandatory requirements'.

Consumer protection has been accepted by the European Court as a valid mandatory requirement: see, for example, *Walter Rau Lebensmittelwerke* v *De Smedt PVBA* Case 261/81 [1982] 2 CMLR 496. However, to be successful the UK will have to prove that the measure is proportionate, in that it is the least restrictive way of protecting consumers: *Cassis* (above).

At the same time, there is a presumption that if goods satisfy the safety standards established in one Member State, they will satisfy the counterpart standards in other Member States.

This presumption may be rebutted by the UK if it can prove that the alloy is indeed a threat to consumers: *Commission* v *Germany (Re German Beer Purity Law)* Case 178/84 [1987] ECR 1227.

In the event that the prohibition does not satisfy these conditions, the British authorities may rely on art 30 EC which allows measures designed to ensure the protection of the health and lives of humans. Naturally, however, in order to rely on this provision, the United Kingdom would have to establish that the material presents a genuine threat to the health of the general population: *Commission* v *United Kingdom (Re Imports of Poultry Meat)* Case 40/82 [1982] ECR 2793 and *Commission* v *United Kingdom (Re UHT Milk)* Case 124/81 [1983] ECR 203. However, it should be noted that art 30 EC is strictly interpreted by the European Court, and in general terms if the measure fails under the less rigorous test of *Cassis*, it is unlikely to be justified under art 30 EC.

c) The final measure preventing importation is the technical standards relating to the strength of the aerials.

From the facts presented, it appears that Community-wide measures have been adopted to harmonise these standards otherwise the United Kingdom could not have made use of the art 95 EC exception.

Article 95 EC provides that a Member State may derogate from the application of a harmonisation measure enacted to secure the internal market so long as the justification for the derogation can be based on either the terms of art 36 EC or on the ground that it relates to the protection of the environment or working conditions. If the United Kingdom has secured such a derogation, the exception will be legitimately based on one of these grounds.

However, derogations must be notified to the Commission and if this has not been properly done the exception cannot be relied upon by the British government. It must therefore be verified that the appropriate procedures have been complied with by the United Kingdom.

The second ground which may be founded upon by Martin stems from the fact that often such derogations are of a temporary nature. In other words, Member States are allowed to rely on the derogation only for a particular period. If the period of authorisation has expired, the derogation will no longer be valid and the measures cannot be justified.

QUESTION TWO

Discuss the legal principles which form the basis of the European internal market envisaged by Article [14] EC and evaluate the legislative mechanisms available for the implementation of these principles. In your answer you should also consider what other legal means, if any, might be necessary to achieve European economic integration.

University of London LLB Examination
(for External Students) European Community Law June 1992 Q8

General Comment

An essay type question requiring a narrative answer on the subject of the internal market programme. The question has three distinct parts and the answer must address each of these aspects of the question individually.

Skeleton Solution

Legal basis for the internal market programme: art 14 EC – fundamental principles of the programme – legislative procedures for the enactment of appropriate legislation – suggested improvements to the existing process.

Suggested Solution

The Single European Act (SEA) 1986 introduced a number of new policy objectives for the European Community by amending the EC Treaty. Of these, one of the most significant and successful was the initiation of a programme designed to create a single internal market. Article 14 EC, as amended, defines the internal market as 'an area without internal frontiers in which the free movement of goods, persons, services and capital is ensured in accordance with the provisions of the [EC Treaty]'. The deadline for the achievement of this goal was set as 31 December 1992.

The internal market programme is designed to eliminate or reduce all major physical, technical and fiscal barriers to trade thereby attaining free movement of goods, persons, services and capital. The programme entails an extensive legislative agenda harmonising national legal provisions relating to customs procedures, taxation, public procurement, capital movements, company law, intellectual property, employment and investment. These measures are required because the existing disparities between each of the Member States in these areas impede the creation of a harmonious and consistent environment for the production and sale of goods and the conduct of commerce.

Within the Community, physical barriers to the free flow of goods presently exist for many reasons such as to enforce national quotas for certain products, to collect VAT and excise duties, to carry out health inspections and checks, to operate the Community system of compensation under the Common Agricultural Policy, to ensure compliance with transportation regulations and to collect statistical information.

To reduce the effect of these barriers and to facilitate the free movement of goods, simplified customs procedures have been adopted. The adoption of the Single Administrative Document (SAD) is intended to reduce delays caused by the multiple processing of customs forms. The introduction of common border posts (banalisation) where all formalities are confined to a single stopping point between each Member State has been introduced to pave the way for the eventual removal of all systematic controls at frontiers.

It is the existence of technical barriers to the construction of the internal market that causes the greatest problems. These barriers result in standards and conditions which retard the practical exercise of the four freedoms. Technical barriers to trade in goods include the diversity of national regulations and standards for testing products or for the protection and safety of the consumer, the duplication of product testing and certification requirements (such as exist in the pharmaceutical industry) and the reluctance of public authorities to open their procurement contracts to the nationals of other Member States.

There are two fundamental legal principles behind the elimination of the technical barrier to the proper functioning of the free movement of goods. These are the principle of equivalence and the principle of harmonisation.

The principle of equivalence or mutual recognition requires that, once a product has been manufactured in one Member State, it is capable of being sold without restrictions throughout the Community. In other words, if a product meets the technical or safety standards of one Member State, there is a presumption that it will meet the counterpart requirements in other Members. The use of this principle was sanctioned in the *Cassis de Dijon* case (*Rewe-Zentrale AG* v *Bundesmonopolverwaltung für Branntwein* Case 120/78 [1979] ECR 649) and was also reiterated in *Commission* v *Germany (Re German Beer Purity Law)* Case 178/84 [1987] ECR 1227.

The second principle is that of harmonisation. This requires that measures standardising technical and safety requirements within the Community are adopted at the Community level. Generally, this requires the passing of Community legislation. The SEA 1986 ensures that legislation for this purpose will receive expedited passage by lowering the voting requirements in the Council of Ministers to enacting such measures to majority voting.

Where harmonising legislation is not absolutely required, the Commission has expressed its intention to rely on the principle of equivalence as applied by the European Court to attack remaining barriers. A substantial amount of Community legislation pertaining to the harmonisation of technical standards, mostly in the form of directives, has been passed to approximate technical standards on products.

Failure to achieve the four freedoms before the Single European Act 1986 was widely attributed to the legislative process which existed within the Community prior to 1986. In order to realise the achievement of these four goals, it was necessary to liberate the legislative process from the stranglehold of the requirement for unanimity among all Member States. Article 95 EC, as amended, introduced qualified majority voting for all proposed legislation enacted to secure the internal market. Measures enacted under art 95 EC are designed to approximate or harmonise national measures relating to technical barriers to trade.

Measures designed to tackle the problem of fiscal barriers and proposals relating to the free movement of persons or the rights and interests of employed persons are specifically excluded from the scope of art 95 EC. Adoption of measures relating to these subjects will continue to require unanimity under art 94 EC. Further, art 95 EC allows a Member State to derogate from measures enacted on a majority vote if the measure is alleged to adversely affect the security or welfare of that Member State.

At the same time, measures enacted under art 95 EC are subject to the co-operation procedure which requires that the Commission fully consult the European Parliament as regards proposed legislation. The co-operation procedure adds a second reading stage for certain types of proposed legislation. Under the co-operation procedure, responsibility for the initiation of proposals continues to reside in the European Commission which formulates proposals taking into account the views of the European Parliament, before submitting the proposals to the Council of Ministers for approval.

There is little doubt that the amended legislation procedure has contributed significantly to the passage of legislation to create a single internal market. Member States can no longer veto such measures because the requirement of unanimity has been removed. Similarly, the European Parliament has made a significant contribution to the content of proposed legislation.

Yet, at the same time, the creation of the art 95 EC process has opened the door to potential abuse of the legislative process. Thus, frequently Member States and the Commission clash on the legitimate basis for a particular measure. Naturally, if a measure is based on a provision of the Treaty that requires unanimity, it is easy for the Commission to assert that the proper legal basis for the measures is art 95 EC and thereby substitute majority voting for unanimity.

For example, the European Commission suggested that the controversial Fifth

Company Directive on the Statute for European Companies could be enacted by means of art 95 EC and not art 94 EC as originally proposed. The difference was that unanimity was required under art 94 EC but qualified voting applied to measures processed through art 95 EC. The United Kingdom government threatened to take this matter to the European Court if the European Commission tried to follow this route. Eventually, the European Commission withdrew its proposals on this matter.

Legislation is a potent means of achieving European economic integration. Community regulations and directives can effectively harmonise whole areas of national laws. However, their are limits to the effectiveness of legislation. For example, Community legislation must rest on some form of political consensus within the Community that the measure is necessary and appropriate. Often there is a feeling that the European Commission is too far ahead of this political consensus in its proposals. The result is conflict among the Member States and the Community institutions.

At the same time, the creation of a single market will not, by itself, significantly advance the cause of European economic integration. This is clear because the concept of the internal market is considerably more refined than that of a common market which in turn is significantly looser than a European union of states. The internal market programme concentrates on achieving the basic goals of the free movement of goods, labour, services and capital. This reflects a desire on the part of the Member States to achieve at least a bare minimum level of economic integration to sustain the momentum towards true economic, political and monetary union among the Member States.

Action is required in other fields such as social policy, cultural relations, and social interaction. This implies that a number of important political decisions must be made. Political and monetary union can only occur when there is a sufficient degree of economic and social integration among the peoples of Europe.

QUESTION THREE

Consider the following from the point of view of Community law:

a) legislation by a Member State imposing a financial levy on all books published in a foreign language published within or imported into the country;

b) legislation by a Member State requiring all novels sold in the country to state on the title page the nationality of the author;

AND

c) legislation by a Member State banning the sale of all alcoholic drinks but permitting freely their manufacture in private households.

University of London LLB Examination
(for External Students) European Community Law June 1993 Q6

General Comment

This is a three-part question concerning the application of arts 28–30 EC with the exception of part (a) which requires consideration of the concept of charges having an equivalent effect to customs duties. The issues raised are relatively novel and require a moment of reflection prior to answering the question properly.

Skeleton Solution

a) Article 25 EC and the principle of charges having an equivalent effect – art 90 EC prohibition on discriminatory taxation.

b) The *Cassis de Dijon* case and the principle of mandatory requirements – the requirements of non-discrimination and proportionality.

c) The principles behind the ECJ decision in *Stoke-on-Trent* v *B & Q plc* – concept of socio-economic function and the requirements on non-discrimination and proportionality.

Suggested Solution

a) It is likely that the financial levy imposed on the importation of foreign language books infringes art 25 EC. This provision prohibits all charges having an equivalent effect to customs duties. These are defined as 'any pecuniary charge, whatever its designation and mode of application, which is imposed unilaterally on goods by reason of the fact that they cross a frontier': *Commission* v *Germany* (*Re Animals Inspection Fees*) Case 18/87 [1988] ECR 5427.

If the legislation imposes a charge on the importation of the foreign language books when they cross the frontiers into the Member State, this will involve a violation of art 25 EC unless the charge relates to a general system of internal dues applied systematically within a Member State without discrimination between domestic and imported products: *Denkavit* v *France* Case 132/78 [1979] ECR 1923.

In this case the pecuniary charge may be considered discriminatory even though it applies to both national publishers and foreign publishers, because it causes de facto discrimination.

This is because in effect it will cause discrimination by burdening foreign producers with higher costs than those incurred by national producers publishing in their own language. This is an example of de facto discrimination.

The imposing of the financial levy may alternatively be concluded to be a tax: art 90 EC. The obligation on Member States under art 90 EC is not that they adopt a uniform system of internal taxation, but that the system adopted is non-discriminatory: *Hansen* v *Hauptzollamt Flensburg* Case 148/77 [1978] ECR 1787. This prohibition also extends to indirectly discriminatory taxation, which the levy may amount to. Such a tax will be one that, whilst applied to both domestic and imported products, has the effect in practice of being discriminatory on imports. In *Humblot* v *Directeur des Services Fiscaux* Case 112/84 [1985] ECR 1367 indirectly discriminatory taxation was defined as a system that 'manifestly exhibits discriminatory or protective features'.

The Member State may be able to objectively justify an indirectly discriminatory tax: *Chemical Farmaceutic* v *DAF SpA* Case 140/79 [1989] ECR 1. This will require the State to prove that the tax is based on objective criteria, that it is non-discriminatory and that it is not protectionist.

b) The legislation of the Member State requiring all novels sold in the country to state on the title page the nationality of the author requires scrutiny under art 28 EC to verify whether or not it amounts to a measure having an equivalent effect to a quantitative restriction.

The measure may amount to a MEQR, defined in *Procureur du Roi* v *Dassonville* Case 8/74 [1974] ECR 837 as any measure capable of hindering, directly or indirectly, actually or potentially, intra-Community trade. The measure imposed here is done so in a non-discriminatory manner and hence may be justifiable under the *Cassis De Dijon* (*Rewe-Zentrale AG* v *Bundesmonopolverwaltung für Branntwein* Case 120/78 [1979] ECR 649) rule of reason.

The rule of reason states that measures may be justified if they are necessary to satisfy or protect a mandatory requirement. The most suitable mandatory requirements in this case would perhaps be the fairness of commercial transactions or to protect consumers from unfair trade practices, but it would be unlikely that this would be acceptable since the measure fails to really be in the general interest. In addition, the rule of reason requires the presumption to be rebutted that since the goods are lawfully marketed in other Member States, they should be lawful in the State that wishes to impose this additional requirement: *Commission* v *Germany (Re German Beer Purity Law)* Case 178/84 [1987] ECR 1227.

One final point to note is the case of *Commission* v *United Kingdom (Re Origin Marking Requirements)* Case 207/83 [1985] ECR 1202. In this case the UK imposed a requirement that clothes indicated their country of origin. The Court concluded that whilst seemingly non-discriminatory in application, the measure was in effect a discriminatory measure since it allowed consumers to assert their national prejudices. Being a discriminatory MEQR the measure could only be justified under art 30 EC, which does not include the ground of consumer protection.

c) A ban on all alcoholic drinks will amount to a quantitative restriction: *Riseria Luigi Geddo* v *Ente Nazionale Risi* Case 2/73 [1973] ECR 865. Since it is applied in an apparently non-discriminatory manner is may be justifiable under the *Cassis* rule of reason. In *Cassis* (above) the Court concluded that, in the absence of Community rules relating to the production and marketing of alcohol products, it was for the Member States themselves to regulate such matters. The Court also stated that such measures could be legitimate since they protected the health of the consumer.

However, any measures adopted by the Member State have to be proportionate. In *Cassis* the conclusion was that a minimum alcohol content was disproportionate, since a labelling requirement would have been a less restrictive means of achieving the objective of consumer protection. This may be the conclusion here, especially since the State permits nationals to produce alcohol in their own homes.

In addition, the State will have to respect the principle of mutual recognition. This will require the State to rebut the presumption that since alcohol is legally marketed and produced in other Member States, it should be lawful in their national territory. This will require the State to produce evidence that the additional measures they have adopted are necessary: *Verband Sozialer Wettbewerb eV* v *Clinique Laboratories SNC* Case C–315/92 [1994] ECR I–317.

In some cases the Court has not been prepared to apply *Cassis*, even though the measure appears non-discriminatory on face value, and has instead applied art 30 EC: for example, see *Commission* v *United Kingdom (Re UHT Milk)* Case 124/81 [1983] ECR 203. If this were the case, the Member State would have to prove that there was a real risk, based on evidence, to the health and life of their nationals. In addition, the measure would have to be proportionate and non-arbitrary. In *Officier van Justitie* v *Sandoz BV* Case 174/82 [1983] ECR 2445 a ban was imposed on certain products containing added vitamins. The measure was concluded to be justifiable under art 30 EC to protect the life and health of humans. This was the case because there was medical evidence indicating health risks due to excessive vitamin consumption, even though there was no consensus on what exactly constituted 'excessive'. The Court concluded that in such circumstances the State retains discretion in how to react. However, any measures adopted must be proportionate and later set aside if any Community harmonising measure is produced on the subject.

Finally, it could perhaps be argued that the measure is a selling arrangement within the ambit of the decision in *Criminal Proceedings against Keck and Mithouard* Joined Cases C–267 and 268/91 [1993] ECR I–6097. Under *Keck*, a selling arrangement relating to the circumstances in which a product is sold will not fall within the ambit of the prohibition in art 28 EC. In order to be successful under this principle the measure adopted must affect the volume of trade in a non-discriminatory manner and treat imports and domestic products in the same way in both law and in fact. In this scenario, the continued production of domestic alcohol may indicate that in fact there is discrimination, in which case the measure will still require justification.

QUESTION FOUR

Manuel owns a small car mechanic's business in Barcelona. He has developed an environmentally friendly type of exhaust, which works particularly well on cars which take leaded petrol. Although most cars in Spain still use this type of petrol, he is not very successful in marketing this exhaust in Spain, as it is about 20 per cent more expensive than regular exhausts routinely sold there. Manuel therefore decides to try and export the exhaust to countries which are particularly concerned about environmental pollution and sends a trial lot of 100 such exhausts to Denmark. In Denmark, leaded petrol is not sold at many garages, but it is not outlawed. Besides, there is a flourishing club of vintage car owners, which is expanding its membership. All the members have cars which can only take leaded petrol.

Knud, Manuel's colleague in Copenhagen, has ordered the entire lot of 100 exhausts and has advertised heavily in the vintage car press. He is offering them at a particularly advantageous 'introductory' price, which is the same as that of the normal exhausts sold in Denmark.

The exhausts arrive directly at Knud's premises in Copenhagen. As soon as they do, inspectors raid Knud's premises and confiscate the exhausts. They inform him that:

a) environmental policy in Denmark is aimed at phasing out leaded petrol and they must first ascertain whether these exhausts can be legally imported;

b) if they are legal, Knud will nevertheless be required to pay an inspection fee to ascertain that the exhausts are environmentally clean;

c) Knud will not be able to sell them at the price indicated, as this is below their cost price and selling at that price is unlawful in Denmark.

Advise Knud as to his position under European Community law in respect of all three requirements.

University of London LLB Examination
(for External Students) European Community Law June 1999 Q3

General Comment

This question on the free movement of goods and custom duties is in the form of a complex problem question requiring application, and not merely description, of the relevant law. The question has three distinct parts and any answer must ensure that it has addressed all three aspects individually.

Skeleton Solution

Free movement of goods (arts 28–30 EC) – the elimination of customs duties and charges of equivalent effect (art 25 EC) – the prohibiting of direct or indirect discriminatory taxation (art 90 EC).

a) Article 28 – define quantitative restrictions and measures of equivalent effect – apply the *Dassonville* formula – apply the possible exhaustive art 30 EC exceptions – identify that if the measure is an indistinctly applicable measure it may be justified under the non-exhaustive rule of reason of the *Cassis De Dijon* case – is the measure (confiscation) proportionate?

b) When are inspection fees legal – arts 25 and 90 EC – apply relevant case law – Articles are mutually exclusive.

c) Application of *Keck and Mithouard* – define selling arrangement outside the scope of art 28 EC – or could it be considered a selling condition or condition of access to the market?

Suggested Solution

Under arts 28–30 EC Member States are prohibited from imposing quantitative restrictions (QRs) and measures equivalent to QRs (MEQRs) on imports and exports. Member States are prohibited under art 25 EC from re-introducing customs duties and are obligated to eliminate all 'charges having an equivalent effect to customs duties'. In addition, according to art 90 EC, Member States are prohibited from imposing direct or indirect discriminatory taxation or imposing internal taxation in such a way as to afford indirect protection to other products.

a) The confiscation of the exhausts by the Danish authorities may amount to a breach of art 28 EC in that it constitutes a barrier to free trade between Member States. Member States are obliged to refrain from applying QRs and MEQRs on imports. A QR was defined in the case of *Riseria Luigi Geddo* v *Ente Nazionale Risi* Case 2/73 [1973] ECR 865 as a measure that amounts to a total or partial restraint of imports, exports or goods in transit. If, after their investigations, the Danish authorities conclude that these particular exhausts are illegal, they will be effectively banned – a measure that will amount to a QR in breach of art 28 EC.

A MEQR has proved more difficult to define, but in the case of *Procureur du Roi* v *Dassonville* Case 8/74 [1974] ECR 837 the ECJ defined one as a measure capable of hindering, directly or indirectly, actually or potentially, the free movement of goods. Confiscation of the exhausts in order to ascertain whether they are legal, even if they are later returned to Knud, will amount to a measure capable of hindering the free movement of goods. There is no requirement for an actual effect on inter-State trade since a potential one will suffice: *Criminal Proceedings against Prantl* Case 16/83 [1984] ECR 1299. The intent behind the imposition of the measure, such as checking the legality of the product, is also irrelevant since only the effects of the measure are considered.

If the confiscation of such exhausts only extends to those that have been imported, the measure will be one that is imposed in a discriminatory manner, referred to as a discriminatory or distinctly applied MEQR. Alternatively, if the measure applies regardless of origin and includes domestically produced exhausts of the same type, the measure will be a non-discriminatory or indistinctly applied MEQR.

The Danish authorities may wish to justify their action. This is permitted in the case of QRs and discriminatory MEQRs under an exhaustive range of grounds in art 30 EC, which have been strictly construed by the ECJ. To justify use of one of these grounds the measure must not 'constitute a means of arbitrary discrimination or a disguised restriction on trade between Member States'. The burden of proof will be on the Danish authorities to establish that their action is within one of the express derogations and is proportionate.

The most pertinent ground would be protection of the life and health of humans, plants and animals. The Member State must prove that there is a real risk and that their action is non-arbitrary and proportionate: see, for example, *Commission* v *United Kingdom (Re UHT Milk)* Case 124/81 [1983] ECR 203 and *Commission* v *United Kingdom (Re Imports of Poultry Meat)* Case 40/82 [1982] ECR 2793. Protection of the environment, as may presumably be claimed by the Danish authorities, will not succeed here, since any genuine claim for protection of the environment would immediately require the measure to be non-discriminatory. In other words, applying either a QR or discriminatory MEQR on the imports of certain exhausts will not be perceived as a genuine, non-arbitrary measure designed to protect the environment, since by implication it can be assumed that domestic production of such exhausts is permitted.

If it is established that the Danish authorities have imposed an indistinctly applied MEQR, there will have been a breach of art 28 EC, but they may have recourse to an alternative means of justifying the measure. The landmark decision of the Court in *Rewe-Zentrale AG* v *Bundesmonopolverwaltung für Branntwein (Cassis De Dijon)* Case 120/78 [1979] ECR 649 states that non-discriminatory obstacles to free movement may be acceptable insofar as they are necessary in order to satisfy mandatory requirements. Hence certain measures, if imposed in a manner that does not discriminate between imported or domestically produced goods, may be justified under a rule of reason test: *Commission* v *Ireland (Re Irish Souvenirs)* Case 113/80 [1981] ECR 1625.

The mandatory requirements listed in *Cassis* are non-exhaustive and in *Commission* v *Denmark (Re Returnable Containers)* Case 302/86 [1988] ECR 4607 protection of the environment was accepted as one. However, the ECJ insisted in *Cassis* that such measures be proportionate to the aim being pursued, and comply with the principle of mutual recognition. This latter point establishes that if a product is lawfully produced and marketed in one Member State, it is presumed to be lawful in all other Member States, unless proved otherwise. Hence the Danish authorities will have to establish that the confiscation is proportionate and provide evidence to rebut the presumption that since such exhausts are lawful in, for example, Spain, they are lawful in Denmark.

b) Under art 25 EC Member States are obliged to eliminate all charges having an equivalent effect to customs duties on imports and exports. In *Commission* v *Italy (Re Statistical Levy)* Case 24/68 [1969] ECR 193 the Court defined the term as any pecuniary charge, however small and whatever its designation, imposed on an imported product by virtue of the fact that it has crossed a frontier. The reason for the imposition of such a charge and whether it is imposed in a discriminatory manner are irrelevant factors.

The Court appears to have concluded that a charge levied on an importer for a service is a type of measure that may not breach art 25 EC: *Commission v Italy* (above). In order to benefit from this apparent exception, the Danish charge must be for a service that provides something of tangible benefit to the importer. The charge applied must also not be based on the value of the products or goods being imported, in this case the exhausts, and must be no more than, or proportionate to, the actual value of the service provided: *Rewe-Zentralfinanze GmbH v Direktor der Landswirtschaftskammer Westfalen-Lippe* Case 39/73 [1973] ECR 1039. A national Danish court will determine whether this is the case.

However, in this scenario Knud has been informed that the inspection fee being imposed is to ascertain whether the exhausts are environmentally friendly. This may amount to an inspection test in the 'general interest' or an administrative formality, and charges for such services, according to *Dubois et Fils SA and General Cargo Services SA v Garoner Exploitation SA* Case C–16/94 [1995] ECR I–2421, are not justifiable. If the inspection test is permissible under Community law, then a charge still cannot be imposed since, according to *Commission v Belgium* Case 314/82 [1984] ECR 1543, this will not be considered as a service for the benefit of the importer.

Alternatively, the inspection test may be a mandatory service under Community law. If the charge is imposed in this context then under *Commission v Germany (Re Animals Inspection Fees)* Case 18/87 [1988] ECR 5427 it must meet the following conditions. First, it must be proportionate to the actual cost of providing the service. Second, the inspection must be obligatory and uniform for all products. Third, the inspection must be prescribed by Community law and be in the Community's general interest and, finally, it must promote the free movement of goods, in particular by neutralising obstacles that could arise from unilateral inspections.

The charge may alternatively be considered to be an internal tax – an additional charge incurred once the product is within the territory of the Member State. A genuine tax will not breach art 25 EC but will be examined under the terms of art 90 EC to assess whether it breaches the prohibition on discriminatory taxation. Article 90 EC does not require that Member States adopt a uniform system of internal taxation, but that any system adopted is non-discriminatory in its treatment of domestic and imported products: *Hansen v Hauptzollamt Flensburg* Case 148/77 [1978] ECR 1787. If the tax is indirectly discriminatory it may be objectively justified by reference to both economic and/or social objectives, such as protection of the environment, as concluded in *Commission v Greece* Case C–132/88 [1990] ECR I–1567. However, the Danish authorities will have to establish that the tax complies with the following cumulative criteria: first that it is based on objective criteria; second, that it is non-discriminatory; and, third, that it is not protectionist.

c) Finally, Knud has been informed that he will be unable to sell the exhausts at below cost price under Danish law. The Danish authorities may argue that this is a selling arrangement within the terms of the *Criminal Proceedings against Keck and Mithouard*

Joined Cases C–267 and 268/91 [1993] ECR I–6097 case and consequently falls outside the prohibition in art 28 EC. The *Keck* case was similar to this Danish law in that it involved the legality of a French law that prohibited the resale of goods in an unaltered state at a price lower than the actual purchase price in order, the French claimed, to prevent predatory pricing. The Court concluded that such a measure (also known as an equal burden trade law) was a 'selling arrangement' and that contrary to what had been previously decided it was not capable of falling within the *Procureur du Roi* v *Dassonville* Case 8/74 [1974] ECR 837 formula. As a direct result the measure was not in breach of art 28 EC.

In order to benefit from this exception to the prohibition in art 28 EC, the Danish measure must apply equally to all traders operating within Denmark and apply to the marketing of domestic goods and imported goods in the same manner in both law and fact. If the measure fails to treat both in the same way in law and in fact, it will require justification under the *Cassis* rule of reason.

The law has been developed by later cases, for example *Hünermund* v *Landesapothekerkammer Baden-Württemburg* Case C–292/92 [1993] ECR I–6787, so that it now also extends to non-static forms of selling arrangement or conditions of access to the market, such as limited bans on advertising. Indeed, in this scenario, by not permitting the introductory price, access to the market may be hindered since the price that will have to be charged will be higher than normal exhausts sold in Denmark. However, if the Danish measure results in affecting the actual content of the product itself, as occurred in *Vereinigte Familiapress Zeitungsverlags-und Vertreibs GmbH* v *Heinrich Bauer Verlag* Case C–368/95 [1997] ECR I–3689, it will fall outside of Keck and consequently require justification.

QUESTION FIVE

Jens, a Danish dairy farmer has developed an unusual (for Denmark) type of soft cheese, which he markets under the name of Storost. Wanting to expand, Jens decides to test out foreign markets. He decides to try England where soft (mainly foreign) and hard (mainly domestic) cheeses are equally favoured. The cheese arrives at the border and the authorities block its entry.

The cheese is packaged in boxes exactly resembling those in which French Camembert comes. Camembert is very popular in England and the authorities think this will lead to confusion.

They say they will allow the cheese to be imported only if:

a) it is re-packaged in recognisably different packaging;

b) an inspection of a sample of cheese shows it is free of listeria, a bacteria harmful to humans, which tends to be prevalent in soft cheese. Charges for the inspection are to be borne by Jens.

Jens complies and the re-packaged consignment is offered for sale in a specialised cheese shop in London. Its price is about half that of the French Camembert sold there. The local council inspectors descend on the shop and confiscate the cheese. They say the law forbids the sale at such a low price as it is anti-competitive.

Advise Jens as to European Law. Should he get the cheese back? Should he be allowed to sell it? Does he have any claims for reimbursement of the charges for re-packaging and/or inspection?

University of London LLB Examination
(for External Students) European Union Law June 1997 Q4

General Comment

This is a problem question concerning the free movement of goods provisions of the EC Treaty and the remedies available when those provisions are breached. The question touches on charges imposed when goods cross a frontier (art 25 EC), but focuses on non-fiscal obstacles to trade prohibited under art 28 EC. The student is required to be familiar with the distinction between distinctly and non-distinctly applicable measures and the different treatment accorded to such measures. In addition, art 30 EC should be discussed as well as the recent line of authority established by the *Criminal Proceedings against Keck and Mithouard* Joined Cases C–267 and 268/91 [1993] ECR I–6097 decision.

Skeleton Solution

Article 25 EC: prohibition on customs duties and charges having equivalent effect (CEEs) – exceptions to art 25 EC: charge for a service; charge for a mandatory inspection – art 28 EC: prohibition on quantitative restrictions (QRs) and measures having equivalent effect (MEQRs) – definition of MEQR: *Dassonville* formula – *Cassis De Dijon*: existence of mandatory requirements for indistinctly applicable measures – *Keck and Mithouard*: non-discriminatory selling arrangements: art 30 EC: derogations – arts 25 and 28 EC: direct effect – remedies.

Suggested Solution

Article 2 EC provides that the task of the Community is the establishment of the common market. In order to achieve this aim, the activities of the Community are set out at art 3 EC and include, inter alia:

a) the elimination, as between Member States, of customs duties and quantitative restrictions on the import and export of goods and of all other measures having equivalent effect; and

b) an internal market characterised by the abolition as between Member States, of obstacles to the free movement of goods, persons, services and capital.

These provisions are amplified by Articles, such as arts 25 and 28 EC, which abolish both fiscal and non-fiscal barriers to trade. Jens may, therefore, be able to rely upon such Articles in order to challenge the measures adopted by the United Kingdom government which have hindered, and ultimately prevented, the sale of his products within the United Kingdom.

Article 25 EC provides that no new customs duties or charges having equivalent effect to customs duties (CEE) shall be introduced by Member States on imports or exports. A CEE was defined in *Commission* v *Italy (Re Statistical Levy)* Case 24/68 [1969] ECR 193 as 'any pecuniary charge, however small and whatever its designation and mode of application, which is imposed unilaterally on domestic or foreign goods by reason of the fact that they cross a frontier'. In deciding if a charge amounts to a CEE, it is irrelevant that the charge is imposed neither to raise revenue for the State nor to protect a home industry, or even that the charge is raised for a worthy cause: *Sociaal Fonds voor de Diamantarbeiders* v *Brachfeld and Chougol Diamond Co* Cases 2 and 3/69 [1969] ECR 211.

The prohibition on any charges being imposed on goods entering a Member State is therefore strict, and it would appear that the charge imposed for inspection of Jens' goods will amount to an unlawful CEE. Support for this conclusion may be found in the case of *Commission* v *Belgium* Case 314/82 [1984] ECR 1543 in which it was held that a charge for a health inspection, permitted although not compulsory under EC law, would amount to a CEE.

However, there are two situations in which the European Court of Justice (ECJ) has established that a charge imposed by a Member State will not fall within the art 25 EC prohibition. The first is when the charge is imposed as a result of a service being rendered by a Member State to a trader. Such a charge will only be allowable if the service provides a specific benefit to an individual trader. In addition, the charge must be proportionate to the value of the service provided: *Commission* v *Denmark* Case 158/82 [1983] ECR 3573. Public health inspections carried out in the general public interest do not fall within this exception: *Bresciani* v *Amministrazione Italiana delle Finanze* Case 87/75 [1976] ECR 129. The second is when the charge is imposed for the cost of an inspection which is mandatory under either EC law (*Commission* v *Germany (Re Animals Inspection Fees)* Case 18/87 [1988] ECR 5427) or international law (*Netherlands* v *P Bakker Hillegom BV* Case C–111/89 [1990] ECR I–1735). This 'exception' is subject to stringent criteria, as follows:

a) the charge must not exceed the actual cost of the inspection;

b) the inspections must be obligatory and uniform for all products concerned;

c) the inspections must be prescribed by EC law in the general interest of the Community; and

d) the inspections must promote free movement of goods, by neutralising obstacles to trade which would otherwise arise: *Commission* v *Germany (Re Animals Inspection Fees)* Case 18/87 [1988] ECR 5427.

There is no indication in the question that the United Kingdom is undertaking this inspection as a result of an EC or international obligation. It would, therefore, seem unlikely that the United Kingdom authorities are able to rely upon this 'exception'. In any event, compliance with all of the above criteria would also have to be established. Advice to Jens concerning future action will be set out below under 'Remedies'.

In contrast to art 25 EC, art 28 EC focuses on non-fiscal barriers to trade in the form of physical, technical and intangible obstacles to the free flow of goods across frontiers. Article 28 EC prohibits the imposition of quantitative restrictions (QRs) or measures equivalent to quantitative restrictions (MEQRs) on imports between Member States. Such measures may be permitted if necessary to protect one of the interests set out in art 30 EC, one of which is the protection of the health and life of humans, animals or plants.

A MEQR has been widely defined in the case of *Procureur du Roi* v *Dassonville* Case 8/74 [1974] ECR 837 to mean 'all trading rules enacted by Member States which are capable of hindering, directly or indirectly, actually or potentially intra-Community trade'. This definition makes no distinction between trading rules which are distinctly applicable (rules applied only to imports) or those which are indistinctly applicable (rules applied to domestic goods and imports), but concentrates on the rules' detrimental effect on intra-Community trade.

A distinction between distinctly and indistinctly applicable measures was made in the *Cassis de Dijon* case (*Rewe-Zentrale AG* v *Bundesmonopolverwaltung für Branntwein* Case 120/78 [1979] ECR 649) in which the ECJ established two principles. The first, the rule of equivalence, provides that goods lawfully manufactured and marketed in one Member State should have access to the markets of all other Member States. The second, the rule of reason, recognises that national marketing rules may amount to an obstacle to free movement of goods, but such rules may still be justifiable on the grounds of mandatory requirements. Mandatory requirements identified in *Cassis de Dijon* included 'the protection of public health and the defence of the consumer'.The categories of mandatory requirements have been expanded to include, inter alia, protection of the environment: *Commission* v *Denmark (Re Returnable Containers)* Case 302/86 [1988] ECR 4607.

Mandatory requirements are subject to the proportionality principle, that is, measures adopted by a Member State to protect a mandatory requirement must be no more stringent than necessary to achieve the desired aim: *Walter Rau Lebensmittelwerke* v *De Smedt PVBA* Case 261/81 [1982] 2 CMLR 496. Mandatory requirements can only be used to justify indistinctly applicable trading rules; distinctly applicable measures are only justifiable under art 30 EC derogations: *Commission* v *Ireland (Re Irish Souvenirs)* Case 113/80 [1981] ECR 1625. Article 30 EC justifications, as with all derogations from fundamental principles of the EC Treaty, are interpreted strictly and cannot be expanded. Article 30 EC permits Member States to adopt measures which hinder intra-Community trade if justified, inter alia, on the grounds of 'health and life of humans, animals or plants'. Measures adopted under art 30 EC, however, must not arbitrarily discriminate nor amount to a disguised restriction on trade. Accordingly, in order to rely upon art 30 EC a Member State must establish that its action is objectively justifiable (*Commission* v *United Kingdom (Re UHT Milk)* Case 124/81 [1983] ECR 203) and proportionate.

The ECJ has recognised a further category of measures which fall outside art 28 EC in *Criminal Proceedings against Keck and Mithouard* Joined Cases C–267 and 268/91 [1993] ECR I–6097. In the wake of what were regarded by many as unmeritorious Euro-defences raised by traders, the ECJ reconsidered the application of art 28 EC to non-discriminatory trading rules which restricted the manner in which goods could be sold, such as the former Sunday trading rules in the United Kingdom. *Keck* concerned the application of art 28 EC to a rule which prohibited the sale of goods at a price lower than their purchase price. The Court held that national rules restricting selling arrangements would not fall within the *Procureur du Roi* v *Dassonville* Case 8/74 [1974] ECR 837 formula, provided those rules applied to all affected traders in the Member State concerned, and that they affected in the same way as a matter of law and fact the marketing of domestic products and imports.

The United Kingdom rules applied to Jens, that is, the re-packaging requirements, the inspection and the prohibition on the sale of products at a low price, are all capable of hindering and ultimately preventing the sale of Jens' products in the United Kingdom and, therefore, intra-Community trade.

Re-packaging

A re-packaging requirement will fall within the *Dassonville* (above) test for MEQRs. In other words, it is a measure capable of hindering, directly or indirectly, actually or potentially, intra-Community trade.

It is unclear whether the re-packaging requirement imposed is a distinctly or indistinctly applicable measure. If United Kingdom producers of soft cheese are not faced with this requirement, then the measure will be discriminatory and capable of justification under art 30 EC only. If that is the case, it is unlikely that the requirement will be unlawful since there appears to be no appropriate derogation under art 30 EC especially since consumer protection is not included. Alternatively, if the measure is indistinctly applicable, it may be justifiable under the mandatory requirements of defence of the consumer or fairness of commercial transactions (*Cassis*, above).

The United Kingdom authorities may have difficulty in establishing that this measure is necessary to protect the consumer, in that the aim of avoiding confusion between Camembert and Jens' cheese may be achievable by the simple expedient of labelling: *Walter Rau Lebensmittelwerke* v *De Smedt PVBA* Case 261/81 [1982] 2 CMLR 496. In other words, the re-packaging requirement is not proportionate.

Inspection

A test or inspection will also fall within the definition of MEQRs given in the *Dassonville* case (above). For example, in *Rewe-Zentralfinanz GmbH* v *Landswirtschaftskammer* Case 4/75 [1975] ECR 843 the Court concluded that a test/inspection on imported plants was a MEQR. Commission Directive 70/50 also offers tests and/or inspections as examples of MEQRs. From the facts given, it appears that the inspection is distinctly applied in that it is only placed on imported cheese. If this is the case, the *Cassis* rule of reason will not be available as a means of justifying the measure: *Commission* v *Ireland (Re Irish Souvenirs)* Case 113/80 [1981] ECR 1625.

In principle, the inspection is justifiable under art 30 EC in order to protect public health. The inspection must have an objective basis, which would be established by the production of scientific evidence. Even if the scientific evidence concerning the presence and threat of listeria is conflicting, the United Kingdom authorities are entitled to take appropriate measures to protect their population. Such measures will be subject to the principle of proportionality: *Officier van Justitie* v *Sandoz BV* Case 174/82 [1983] ECR 2445.

Prohibition on sale at a low price

Such a prohibition will be subject to the decision in *Criminal Proceedings against Keck and Mithouard* Joined Cases C–267 and 268/91 [1993] ECR I–6097, provided that it can be established that a prohibition on the sale of goods at a low price amounts to a selling arrangement and is not a rule concerning the characteristics of a product. Since the decision in *Keck* concerned a rule which prevented the resale of goods at a loss, it is submitted that the United Kingdom rule will constitute a selling arrangement. If so, the United Kingdom rule will fall outside art 28 EC provided it is legally and factually non-discriminatory. However, if this rule applies only to soft cheeses (mainly foreign, as stated in the question), it may well be discriminatory in effect (ie in fact) and fall within art 28 EC. If this is the case it will require justification under the *Cassis* rule of reason test.

Remedies

Both arts 25 and 28 EC are directly effective (*Van Gend en Loos* v *Netherlands* Case 26/62 [1963] ECR 1 and *R* v *Henn and Darby* Case 34/79 [1979] ECR 3795) and may, therefore, be relied upon by Jens in the United Kingdom courts. Jens will, therefore, be able to recover an unlawfully levied charge and challenge the legality of the inspections, re-packaging and price requirements. In the event that art 28 EC has been breached by the re-packaging requirements, Jens may be able to establish a claim for damages against the United Kingdom government in respect of the re-packaging costs: *Francovich and Bonifaci* v *Italian Republic* Cases C–6 and 9/90 [1991] ECR I–5357. Jens may also be able to make a claim for loss of profits if access to the United Kingdom market is unlawfully denied to him: *Brasserie du Pêcheur SA* v *Federal Republic of Germany; R* v *Secretary of State for Transport, ex parte Factortame Ltd* Joined Cases C–46 and 48/93 [1996] ECR I–1029.

Chapter 10

European Competition Law
– Article 81 EC

10.1   Introduction

10.2   Key points

10.3   Key cases and materials

10.4   Questions and suggested solutions

10.1 Introduction

Articles 81 and 82 EC are the pillars of the Community competition policy. Each of these Articles addresses different forms of anti-competitive behaviour. Article 81 EC (the subject of this chapter) prohibits agreements and concerted practices among private commercial bodies if they affect trade between Member States and distort, prevent or restrict competition. Article 82 EC (the subject of the next chapter) prohibits commercial practices by one or more enterprises where such practices amount to an abuse of a dominant position with the Community. These two provisions therefore seek to achieve separate objectives. Article 81 EC attempts to eradicate unfair commercial practices which result from collaboration between enterprises while art 82 EC strikes at companies taking advantage of dominant or monopoly positions in the market place.

10.2 Key points

The subjects of European Community law

Both arts 81 and 82 EC apply to 'undertakings' although this term is not expressly defined. The European Court has, however, defined an undertaking as:

> '... a single organisation of personal, tangible and intangible elements, attached to an autonomous legal entity and pursuing a long-term economic aim.' (*Mannesmann* v *High Authority* Case 8/61 [1962] ECR 357.)

This definition embraces all natural and legal persons engaged in commercial activities, whether profit-making or otherwise. The fact that an entity is a non profit-making organisation is irrelevant for the purpose of identifying an undertaking: *Heintz van Landewyck Sarl* v *Commission* Case 108/78 [1980] ECR 3125. The critical characteristic is whether or not the entity is engaged in economic or commercial activities.

The application of European competition law is not restricted to undertakings located within the Community, but extends to undertakings whose registered offices are situated outside the Community. This is because European competition law is not concerned with the behaviour of entities but rather the effects of such behaviour on the competitive environment within the Community: *Ahlström and Others* v *Commission (Re Wood Pulp Cartel)* Cases 89, 104, 114, 116, 117 and 125–129/85 [1994] ECR I–99.

Commercial practices prohibited by art 81 EC

Article 81(1) EC addresses different forms of concerted behaviour between two or more undertakings and specifically provides:

'The following shall be prohibited as incompatible with the common market: all agreements between undertakings, decisions by associations of undertakings, and concerted practices which may affect trade between Member States and which have as their object or effect the prevention, restriction or distortion of competition within the common market, and in particular those which:
a) directly or indirectly fix purchase or selling prices or any other trading conditions;
b) limit or control production, markets, technical development, or investment;
c) share markets or sources of supply;
d) apply dissimilar conditions to equivalent transactions with other trading parties, thereby placing them at a competitive disadvantage;
e) make the conclusion of contracts subject to acceptance by the other parties of supplementary obligations which, by their nature or according to commercial usage, have no connection with the subject of such contracts.'

All agreements, decisions and practices prohibited under art 81(1) EC are automatically void under art 81(2) EC unless exempt from the scope of this subsection by virtue of art 81(3) EC.

The Article itself specifically enumerates a number of examples of anti-competitive behaviour in order to illustrate the types of conduct which the provision is intended to limit.

Price fixing

Practices which have the effect of directly or indirectly fixing buying or selling prices for products are incompatible with competition policy. This includes arrangements whereby undertakings agree on the particular trading conditions which are applicable to their business dealings, such as discounts or credit terms. Another example of prohibited practices is agreements to fix prices and to apportion markets: *Società Italiana Vetro* v *Commission (Re Italian Flat Glass Suppliers)* Cases T–68, 77 and 78/89 [1992] 5 CMLR 302.

Limitation or control of production

Quotas on production and supply cartels are contrary to competition policy, as are arrangements to control marketing, technical development or investment. An illustration of this type of practice is the setting of volume targets for production: *PVC Cartel* [1990] 4 CMLR 45.

Allocation of markets

Practices which allow potential competitors to apportion a market in a particular product amongst each other on a mutually exclusive basis are prohibited. This practice is condemned when the apportionment is made on the basis of either geography or product ranges: *Siemans-Fanne* [1988] 4 CMLR 945; *ACF Chemiefarma NV* v *Commission* Cases 41, 44 and 45/69 [1970] ECR 661.

Application of dissimilar conditions

By applying dissimilar sales conditions to identical transactions one undertaking may place another at a competitive disadvantage. For example, an agreement to provide one purchaser with more advantageous purchasing conditions than another purchaser would result in unfair discrimination.

Imposition of supplementary obligations

Agreements requiring the fulfilment of supplementary obligations which, by their nature or commercial usage, have no connection with the original subject matter of a contract, are prohibited. For example, agreements which require a buyer of one product or service to purchase another product or service unconnected with the first transaction would amount to the imposition of a supplementary obligation.

This list of anti-competitive behaviour is intended to illustrate the most common forms of conduct which will infringe art 81(1) EC and is not intended to be exhaustive.

Agreements, decisions by associations of undertakings and concerted practices

Article 81 EC identifies three separate arrangements which may contravene competition law: agreements, decisions, and concerted practices. Each of these concepts refers to a different form of commercial practice among undertakings.

Agreements

The term 'agreements' includes all contracts in the sense of binding contractual obligations, whether written, verbal, or partly written and partly verbal. Further, an arrangement between two or more parties may constitute an agreement for the purposes of art 81(1) EC even although the arrangement in question has no binding legal effect: *Atka A/S* v *BP Kemi A/S* [1979] CMLR 684.

Unrecorded understandings, the mutual adoption of common rules, and so-called 'gentlemen's agreements' are also agreements for the purposes of competition law: *Boehringer* v *Commission* Case 45/69 [1970] ECR 769.

Agreements which prevent, distort or restrict competition are classified either as horizontal agreements or vertical agreements. Horizontal agreements are arrangements made between competitors, or potential competitors, while vertical agreements are arrangements between undertakings at the differing stages of process through which a product or service passes from the manufacturer to the final consumer.

Illustrations of horizontal agreements include agreements dividing markets among competitors, price fixing, export and import bans, cartels, and boycotts. Examples of vertical agreements include exclusive distribution agreements, exclusive patent licensing agreements, exclusive purchasing agreements and tying.

Decisions of associations of undertakings

The concept of decisions of associations of undertakings refers to the creation of rules establishing trade associations, as well as any other formal or informal decisions or recommendations made under such rules.

Prohibited decisions of trade associations would include recommending prices, fixing discounts, collective boycotts and the negotiation of restrictive contract clauses. A recommendation by a trade association may constitute a decision, even although such acts are not binding under the constitution of the association in question: *Cementhandelaren* v *Commission* Case 8/72 [1972] ECR 977.

Concerted practices

The term 'concerted practice' refers to commercial co-operation in the absence of a formal agreement. The European Court has defined a concerted practice as:

'… a form of coordination between enterprises that has not yet reached the point where it is a contract in the true sense of the word but which, in practice, consciously substitutes practical co-operation for the risks of competition.' (*Imperial Chemical Industries Ltd* v *Commission (Dyestuffs)* Case 48/69 [1972] ECR 619.)

Manufacturers and producers are, of course, entitled to take into consideration prices set for similar goods by competitors. It is only when potential competitors deliberately and intentionally agree to coordinate pricing policy that a concerted practice arises.

Commercial co-operation will likely amount to a concerted practice if it enables the entities under investigation to consolidate their market positions to the detriment of the principle of free movement of goods within the Community and the freedom of consumers to select products: *Suiker Unie* v *Commission* Cases 40–48, 50, 54–56, 111, 113 and 114/73 [1975] ECR 1663.

It is contrary to the rules on competition contained in art 81 EC for a producer to cooperate with its competitors in order to determine a coordinated course of action relating to pricing policy, particularly if this co-operation ensures the elimination of all uncertainty among competitors as regards matters such as price increases, the subject matter of increases, and the date and place of increases.

In determining whether a concerted practice exists there may be heavy reliance placed on an economic analysis of the market to assess the parties' behaviour, especially since in many cases any substantive evidence is difficult, if not impossible, to acquire. However, in *Ahlström and Others* v *Commission (Re Wood Pulp Cartel)* Cases 89, 104, 114, 116, 117 and 125–129/85 [1994] ECR I–99 the Court refined how such evidence of a concerted practice may be used. The Commission had concluded that a concerted practice existed after an economic analysis revealed the charging of similar prices with uniform and simultaneous increases. The Court annulled much of the Commission's Decision, concluding that such parallel activity in the market would only be evidence of a concerted practice if there were no other plausible explanation. Therefore, the burden of proof shifts to the undertakings alleged to have entered into the concerted practice to justify the parallel behaviour. If there is no objective justification, then the Commission and/or Court will probably conclude that there has been a concerted practice.

Effect on trade between Member States

No agreement, decision or concerted practice may be held contrary to Community competition law unless it affects patterns of trade between Member States. As the European Court has observed:

> 'It is only to the extent to which agreements may affect trade between Member States that the deterioration in competition falls under the prohibition of Community law contained in art 81; otherwise it escapes the prohibition.' (*Consten and Grundig* v *Commission* Cases 56 and 58/64 [1966] ECR 299.)

This requirement is intended to enable a distinction to be drawn between unfair commercial practices which have only national ramifications and those practices which have Community implications.

The effect of an agreement on trade between Member States is ascertained by reference to the principle of free movement of goods and, in particular, the realisation of the objective of creating a single market among all the Member States of the Community. An agreement, decision or practice will affect trade between Member States if it is capable of constituting a threat, either direct or indirect, actual or potential, to the freedom of trade between Member States in a manner which might harm the attainment of the objective of a single market between States: *Société Technique Minière* v *Maschinenbau Ulm GmbH* Case 56/65 [1966] ECR 235.

Actual harm need not be established. It is sufficient that the agreement is likely to prevent, restrict or distort competition to a sufficient degree.

It should also be noted that there is no need for there to be any overt cross-border element in the transaction for an arrangement to affect trade between Member States. Thus, arrangements between producers to set target prices for the sale of products, even although they applied in only one Member State, have been considered by the Commission to infringe art 81(1) EC: *Cementhandelaren* v *Commission* Case 8/72 [1972] ECR 977.

There is no violation of art 81 EC if an agreement or practice has only a negligible effect on trade between Member States. Early in the jurisprudence of competition law, the European Court held that:

'[A]n agreement falls outside the prohibition in art 81 when it has only an insignificant effect on the markets, taking into account the weak position which the persons concerned have on the market of the product in question.' (*Völk v Etablissements Vervaecke Sprl* Case 5/69 [1969] ECR 295.)

Insignificant agreements escape the prohibition of art 81 EC because their relative effect on trade between Member States is negligible. This is discussed in further detail below.

The object or effect of preventing, restricting or distorting competition within the Community

Agreements, decisions and practice are only prohibited under art 81 EC if, in addition to satisfying all other relevant criteria, they have as their object or effect the prevention, restriction or distortion of competition within the Community. Such arrangements may have either the object or the effect of distorting competition. These options are clearly intended to be alternative, not cumulative, tests.

An agreement will have the object of distorting competition if, prior to its implementation, it can be determined that the agreement would prevent or restrict competition which might take place between the parties to the agreement: *Consten and Grundig v Commission* Cases 56 and 58/64 [1966] ECR 299. If an agreement does not have the object of restricting competition, whether or not an agreement has the effect of distorting competition may be determined by market analysis.

Activities outside the scope of art 81(1) EC

An agreement, decision or practice may be excluded from the scope of art 81(1) EC on four principal grounds: where an agreement has been given negative clearance by the Commission; where an agreement is of minor importance; where an agreement regulates relations between undertakings to which the competition rules are inapplicable; and where agreements and practices benefit from the exemptions under art 81(3) EC.

Negative clearance

An undertaking proposing to enter into an agreement or engage in a practice which might be considered to restrict, prevent or distort competition may apply to the Commission for negative clearance in respect of the arrangement. Negative clearance is a determination made by the Commission that, on the basis of the facts in its possession, it believes that there are no grounds under art 81(1) EC for action to be taken against the submitted agreement, decision or practice.

In order to obtain negative clearance, the undertakings submitting the application must prove that the agreement, decision or practice is excluded from the scope of the applicable competition provision. Negative clearance is therefore not strictly a separate ground for exclusion from the competition provisions of the EC Treaty, but rather certification that an agreement or practice, in the opinion of the Commission, falls outside Community competition law.

Frequently, instead of making a formal decision on a matter, the Commission may notify the undertaking by correspondence that no action is required to conform to the terms of art 81(1) EC. Such correspondence is known as a 'comfort letter'. It offers no absolute protection from investigation by the Commission, particularly where the facts submitted by the undertaking vary from the true facts of the case. But, if an investigation is subsequently initiated, the statement may be pleaded in mitigation should an infringement be established.

Agreements of minor importance

Agreements which would otherwise be caught by art 81(1) EC may nevertheless be exempt from its scope if they are incapable of affecting trade between Member States or restricting competition to any appreciable extent. This principle is known as the de minimus rule and was originally conceived by the European Court in *Völk* v *Etablissements Vervaecke Sprl* Case 5/69 [1969] ECR 295. Agreements fall outside the prohibition of art 81(1) EC if they have an 'insignificant effect' on the market in such products.

The Commission published a Notice in 1986 (updated in 1997) intended to establish guidelines for the application of the de minimus rule, the basis of which is the jurisprudence of the European Court in this subject. The Commission has indicated that, in normal circumstances, agreements would fall outside art 81(1) EC by virtue of the de minimus rule, if:

a) in the case of vertical agreements (ie agreements operating between different levels in the market), the agreements apply between undertakings with less than a 10 per cent market share for the relevant product;

b) in the case of horizontal agreements (ie agreements between companies at the same level in the market), the agreements apply to undertakings with less than a combined 5 per cent market share.

However, the Notice introduces a blacklist of restrictive clauses which will not be tolerated even where the agreement is within the threshold limits. These include contractual provisions in horizontal agreements which are intended to fix prices, limit production or sales or divide up supply sources, as well as clauses in vertical agreements which fix resale prices or give territorial protection for contracting companies or third parties. The intention of the Notice is to allow small and medium sized undertakings to benefit from the rule exempting minor agreements from the rigours of art 81(1) EC.

Commercial relations to which competition rules do not apply

The competition rules established under art 81 EC do not apply to two particular commercial relationships: between principals and agents; and between parents and subsidiaries.

From the beginning of Community competition policy administration contracts entered into between principals and commercial agents have been traditionally excluded from the scope of art 81(1) EC so long as the agent is concerned with the simple negotiation of transactions on behalf of the principal: Commission Notice Relating to Exclusive Dealing Contracts with Commercial Agents 1962. While the non-application of art 81(1) EC to such relationships legally has the form of a group negative clearance, the application of competition rules to such relations is clearly contrary to the policy of promoting competition throughout the Community.

A subsidiary which is under the control of a parent company is not considered to be capable of anti-competitive behaviour in relation to its parent since it has no autonomous decision-making capacity. Restrictive agreements and anti-competitive concerned practices between parents and non-autonomous subsidiaries are therefore not subject to the rules of Community competition law. As the European Court has explicitly ruled:

> 'Article 81 is not concerned with agreements or concerted practices between undertakings belonging to the same concern and having the status of parent company and subsidiary, if the undertakings form an economic unit within which the subsidiary has no real freedom to determine its course of action on the market, and if the agreements or practices are concerned merely with the internal allocation of tasks as between the undertakings.' (*Hydrotherm Gerätebau* v *Audreoli* Case 170/83 [1984] ECR 2999.)

Two conditions are therefore required in order to avoid the application of art 81(1) EC on this basis.

a) The subsidiary cannot have any real freedom to dictate its own course of action in the market place. Control over the conduct of a subsidiary is determined by reference to the size of the shareholding held by the parent.

b) The restrictive agreement itself must relate only to the allocation of responsibilities and tasks between the parent and the subsidiary. For example, see *Racal Group Services* [1990] 4 CMLR 627.

Exempt agreements and practices

Article 81(3) EC specifically creates criteria for exempting agreements, decisions and concerted practices from the effects of art 81(1) EC. Agreements and practices which satisfy the exemption criteria established by art 81(3) EC are not void under art 81(2) EC nor subject to the imposition of fines. Two positive and two negative tests must be satisfied for an agreement to be exempt and the onus is on the applicant to establish these conditions are present:

a) the agreement, decision or practice must contribute to improving the production or distribution of goods or promoting technical or economic progress;

b) a fair share of the resulting benefit must accrue to the consumer;

c) the agreement or practice must not impose any restrictions which go beyond the positive aims of the agreement or practice; and

d) these restrictions must not create a possibility of eliminating competition in respect of a substantial part of the products in question.

An example of the Commission's application of this four-part test can be witnessed in *Prym-Werke* [1973] CMLR C250.

Two types of exemption are granted on the basis of the authority of this provision: individual exemptions which are issued on the basis of an individual application; and block exemptions which are applicable to categories of agreements. Subject to review by the Court of First Instance and thereafter the European Court itself, the European Commission has exclusive authority to create exemptions on the basis of art 81(3) EC.

The procedure for obtaining an individual exemption is specified in Council Regulation 17/62. Individual exemptions are granted in the form of Commission decisions. These decisions are issued for a limited period and may be conditional on the fulfilment of certain obligations. A decision may be renewed if the relevant conditions continue to be satisfied. The Commission may revoke or amend a decision granting an individual exemption in the event of a change of circumstances. Naturally an individual exemption will only be granted if the four conditions on art 81(3) EC are satisfied.

To reduce the bureaucratic burdens imposed by applications for individual exemption, the Commission is empowered to establish group exemption categories: Council Regulation 19/65 and Council Regulation 2821/71. The Commission has enacted a number of Regulations in order to grant group exclusive distribution agreements, exclusive purchasing agreements, specialisation agreements, research and development agreements, franchising agreements and technology transfer agreements.

If an agreement falls within the scope of a group exemption under a Commission regulation, the parties to the agreement are not required to notify the Commission of the agreement and the parties cannot be fined by the Commission for violating competition law on that basis.

The Commission initiated a review of the application of competition rules to vertical agreements because of the changing structure of the Community market. One factor of specific significance is the near-completion of the single internal market which required that the Commission give greater emphasis on the economic impact of vertical restraints on the structure of individual product markets.

The result of the review was the adoption of Commission Regulation 2790/99 in December 1999. The Regulation came into force on 1 June 2000 and will run for a period of ten years.

Article 2(1) of the Regulation defines a vertical agreement as:

'... agreements or concerted practices entered into between two or more undertakings, each of which operates, for the purpose of the agreement, at a different level of the production or distribution chain, and relating to the conditions under which the parties may purchase, sell or resell certain goods or services.'

Article 3(1) provides that block exemption is available for suppliers that hold a maximum of 30 per cent of the relevant market in which they sell goods or services. Article 3(2) states that block exemption is available to vertical agreements containing exclusive supply obligations if the market share held by the buyer does not exceed 30 per cent of the market in which it purchases the goods or services. If the market share is more than 30 per cent, the undertakings will have to apply for individual exemption (see above).

Article 2(4) states that block exemption will not apply to vertical agreements entered into between competing undertakings, as opposed to those on 'different levels'. However, it will extend to such agreements if they are non-reciprocal and meet the following criteria:

a) the buyer's total annual turnover does not exceed Euro 1,000 million; or

b) the supplier is both a manufacturer and distributor of goods, while the buyer is a distributor not manufacturing goods competing with the contract goods; or

c) the supplier is a provider of services at several levels of trade whilst the buyer does not provide competing services at the level of trade where it purchases the contract services.

Article 4 of the Regulation identifies vertical agreements that are outside of the scope of block exemption – the black list. Known as forbidden 'hardcore' restraints, these include the following:

a) resale price maintenance (except for maximum prices or recommended sale prices);

b) restriction on resales (with some exceptions);

c) restrictions on sales to users in selective distribution agreements (except if operating out of an unauthorised place of distribution);

d) restrictions on cross-supplies between distributors in a selective distribution system; and

e) restrictions on the sale of spare parts.

Article 5 provides for restraints that are prohibited, but which can be severed from the agreement permitting the rest to remain valid. These include: non-competition obligations for a maximum of five years; post-termination non-compete clauses unless they protect know-how for a maximum of one year; and obligations relating to specified competitor brands imposed on selective distribution. A non-compete obligation is defined in art 1(b) as any direct or indirect obligation causing the buyer not to manufacture, purchase, sell or resell goods or services that compete with the contracted goods or services.

Article 6 states that block exemption can be withdrawn by the Commission if it finds that the agreement violates the principles of art 81(3) EC, particularly if market access is denied or significantly restricted. The authorities of the Member State have similar powers under art 7 of the Regulation.

In addition, Council Regulation 1216/99 provides for new rules on the notification of vertical agreements/restraints. Undertakings do not have to notify the Commission at the start of the agreement and any late application for exemption will be post-dated.

Remedies through the national courts

Articles 81 and 82 EC have direct effect and may be relied on by private individuals against other private parties in the national courts. Three remedies in particular should be noted.

a) These provisions may form the basis for an action of damages against the party indulging in anti-competitive practices for injury caused to the business activities of the plaintiff: *Garden Cottage Foods Ltd* v *Milk Marketing Board* [1984] AC 130.

b) Article 81(2) EC declares that any agreement contrary to art 81(1) EC is void. The European Court has however applied the doctrine of severability to this provision and only those terms of an agreement which are contrary to the Article are void and the rest remain in force: *Delimitis* v *Henninger Braü AG* Case C–234/89 [1992] 5 CMLR 210.

c) An infringement of art 81(1) EC may also form the basis of an action of injunction to prevent the party allegedly infringing competition law from continuing to do so.

In order to develop co-ordination between the Commission and the national courts in this area, the Commission has published a Notice to National Courts on the Application of Articles 81 and 82 1993. This Notice sets out in detail the procedure which national courts should follow if an allegation of an infringement of Community competition law arises before them.

In fact, the Commission has adopted a deliberate policy of encouraging private parties to use domestic court procedures rather than complaining direct to the Commission by declining to investigate complaints unless there are important 'Community considerations' to be taken into account. This policy has been supported by the European Court: *Automec* v *Commission (No 2)* Case T–24/90 [1992] ECR II–2223.

10.3 Key cases and materials

- *Ahlström and Others* v *Commission (Re Wood Pulp Cartel)* Cases 89, 104, 114, 116, 117
  and 125–129/85 [1994] ECR I–99
  Example of the extraterritorial effect of art 81 EC and the way in which evidence of
  a concerted practice from an economic analysis may be used

- *Consten and Grundig* v *Commission* Cases 56 and 58/64 [1966] ECR 299
  Provides a definition of the effect on inter-State trade required for a breach of art
  81 EC

- *Imperial Chemical Industries Ltd* v *Commission (Dyestuffs)* Case 48/69 [1972] ECR 619
  Definition of the concept of concerted practice, together with the identification of the
  requisite criteria

- *Metro-SB-Grossmärkte GmbH* v *Commission (No 2)* [1986] ECR 3021
  Identification of the scope of the requirement that an agreement must have the
  effect of distorting competition before contravening Community competition law

- *Società Italiana Vetro* v *Commission (Re Italian Flat Glass Suppliers)* Cases T–68, 77 and
  78/89 [1992] 5 CMLR 302
  The Commission is permitted to apply arts 81 and 82 EC to the same parties and
  the application of these Articles is not mutually exclusive

- *Société Technique Minière* v *Maschinenbau Ulm GmbH* Case 56/65 [1966] ECR 235
  Extends art 81 EC to those agreements, etc, that may have an effect on inter-State
  trade, ie those agreements that may, directly or indirectly, actually or potentially,
  have an effect on trade between Member States

- EC Treaty

  - art 81 – prohibits agreements, decisions and concerted practices among private
    commercial bodies if they affect inter-state trade and distort, prevent or restrict
    competition

- Commission Notice 1997 – provides thresholds for the application of the de
  minimus doctrine

- Council Regulation 17/62 – establishes the Commission's powers in relation to
  enforcing competition law, including the granting of individual exemptions

- Commission Regulation 2790/99 – block exemption for vertical agreements

10.4 Questions and suggested solutions

QUESTION ONE

British Breweries plc is an important producer of beer in the United Kingdom. Statistics
show that British Breweries account for some 12 per cent of all beer sold in the United

Kingdom but that its British Brewlite is especially successful and accounts for 40 per cent of all non-alcoholic beer consumed in the UK.

British Breweries want to establish a German subsidary but have been advised that most retailers in Germany have agreed to purchase non-alcoholic beer only from the German Brewers' Association. The Association checks the quality of its members' products. However, there is a two-year trading requirement in Germany before a new brewery can be admitted to the Association.

Advise British Breweries as to the significance, if any, of EC law for each of the above aspects of its business.

Adapted from University of London LLB Examination
(for External Students) European Community Law June 1990 Q7

General Comment

A problem type question involving the application of art 81 EC to hypothetical circumstances.

Skeleton Solution

Is there a prohibited practice – does this practice affect trade between Member States and distort competition – application of individual or group exemption – alternative methods of challenge.

Suggested Solution

In order to ascertain whether or not a practice infringes Community competition policy, three separate determinations must be made: the activity in question must constitute an agreement, decision or concerted practice as prescribed by art 81(1) EC; the practice must affect trade between Member States; and the practice must prevent, restrict or distort competition.

Both the German beer retailers and the German Brewers Association (GBA) are undertakings for the purpose of art 81(1) EC. All natural and legal persons engaged in economic activities constitute undertakings, regardless of whether or not they are profit-making or otherwise: *Heintz van Landewyck Sarl* v *Commission* Case 108/78 [1980] ECR 3125. The fact that the GBA is a non-profit making organisation would be irrelevant for the purpose of identifying it as an undertaking.

Article 81(1) EC addresses decisions of associations of undertakings, whether formal or informal. Therefore any decision made by the GBA – as an association of undertakings – is subject to review under Community competition law. Further, its decisions need not be legally binding: *Cementhandelaren* v *Commission* Case 8/72 [1972] ECR 977.

In these circumstances, the relevant agreement is between the GBA and the retailers in Germany. This agreement is therefore a vertical one, since the parties are at different levels in the chain of manufacturing, distribution and sale. The relevant product market consists of the market for the product under investigation together with the market for products that are identical or substantially equivalent to the product. Identical and substantially equivalent products must be interchangeable with the original product. Whether or not this requirement is satisfied is normally judged from the perspective of the consumer, taking into account the characteristics, price and intended use of the products. The relevant product market in this case will probably be non-alcoholic beer, since alcoholic beer is not a substantially equivalent product, nor, it is suggested, are soft drinks in general.

The relevant geographical market is the area in the Community in which the agreement or concerted practice produces its effects: *Delimitis* v *Henninger Braü AG* Case C–234/89 [1992] 5 CMLR 210. In the circumstances of the present case the relevant market is Germany, since that is the area where the agreement produces its effects.

Naturally, the decisions of the GBA may affect trade between Member States. A decision will affect trade between Member States if it is capable of constituting a threat, either direct or indirect, actual or potential, to the freedom to trade between Member States in a manner which might harm the attainment of the objectives of a single market: *Société Technique Minière* v *Maschinenbau Ulm GmbH* Case 56/65 [1966] ECR 235. The fact that the GBA effectively prevents foreign sellers from entering the German non-alcoholic beer market is more than sufficient to establish that its decisions affect trade between Member States.

Article 81(1) EC refers to decisions which 'have as their object or effect the prevention, restriction or distortion of competition' within the common market, to an appreciable degree. It is sufficient that a decision of an association of undertakings has as its object the restriction of competition without this necessarily representing the common intention of the parties: *Consten and Grundig* v *Commission* Cases 56 and 58/64 [1966] ECR 299.

Competition is clearly severely restricted if not prevented by the two-year trading requirement imposed in Germany by the GBA. Since most retailers purchase non-alcoholic beer only from members of the GBA, any brewery attempting to enter the market would have to trade for two years, selling to a very limited number of retailers – a venture which would not be commercially viable. The two year trading requirement acts as a disincentive to new competitors entering the market and effectively closes the market to new entrants to the market.

The GBA may attempt to argue that the two-year trading requirement may be justified. First, it could be argued that the de minimus rule should apply. In such cases the effect on competition is considered to not be significant enough to breach art 81 EC: *Völk* v *Etablissements Vervaecke Sprl* Case 5/69 [1969] ECR 295. The arrangement here is one of a vertical nature; it operates between different levels in the market. In the 1997 De Minimus Notice published by the Commission, vertical agreements concerning less than a 10 per cent market share will not breach art 81 EC. Since 'most retailers in

Germany' have entered into the agreement, the de minimus rule is unlikely to be applicable.

Second, the GBA could seek individual exemption under art 81(3) EC. To be successful the Association will have to prove that the agreement contributes to improving the production or distribution of goods, or promotes technical or economic progress, and that a fair share of the resulting benefits accrue to consumers. In addition, it will have to be established that the agreement does not impose any restriction that is beyond the positive aims of the agreement, nor create the possibility of eliminating competition in respect of a substantial part of the market.

The GBA could argue that the two-year trading requirement ensures that any new brewer is a reliable, quality producer of non-alcoholic beers. This supervision process, it could be argued, contributes to improved production that inevitably benefits consumers and retailers. However, these arguments are likely to fail. The benefit of the two-year trading requirement is not strictly economic. The requirement also goes beyond what is absolutely necessary to achieve the objectives regarded as beneficial. Finally, the measure probably results in the elimination of a substantial degree of competition in the market.

British Breweries should therefore be advised to make a complaint to the Commission under Council Regulation 17/62, arts 3(1) and 3(2). British Breweries is a party with a sufficient legitimate interest. If the Commission decides not to initiate proceedings and notifies British Breweries accordingly, British Breweries will have sufficient locus standi to bring an action for annulment under art 230 EC. Further, if the Commission takes no action British Breweries can bring art 232 EC proceedings.

British Breweries could also challenge the decision of the GBA on the ground that it breaches the right of an undertaking to establish itself anywhere in the Community under art 43 EC.

QUESTION TWO

It has been suggested that Article [81] EC is intended only to support the rules for the movement of goods. Comment on this suggestion in the light of the case law of the European Court of Justice, particularly the judgment in *Consten and Grundig* v *Commission.*

University of London LLB Examination
(for External Students) European Community Law June 1992 Q3

General Comment

A question dealing with two separate areas of Community law but both concerning trade in goods. To answer the question, it is necessary to compare and contrast the policy reasons behind Community competition law with the principle of the free movement of goods.

Skeleton Solution

Purposes of European competition law and policy – relationship between art 81 EC and the provisions relating to the free movement of goods – decision of the ECJ in *Consten and Grundig* – limitations applying to the relationship.

Suggested Solution

Article 81 EC prohibits all agreements, decisions and concerted practices between commercial enterprises if they affect trade between Member States and have, as their object or effect, the prevention, restriction or distortion of competition within the Community. Together with art 82 EC, this provision forms the basis of the competition policy of the Community.

The purpose of art 81 EC is relatively straightforward; it is intended to prevent commercial parties erecting barriers to trade between Member States by means of private agreements or contracts. For example, if a British company and a German company are both engaged in the production or supply of the same goods and agree not to sell their products in the national market of the other party, goods would not flow from Germany to the United Kingdom and vice versa. In the absence of competition both companies could set their prices in their respective markets without reference to the prices charged by the other. This would undoubtedly have the effect of depriving consumers of lower prices which generally result from competition between producers and supplies.

Agreements fixing prices, controlling or limiting production, or permitting price discrimination are potentially anti-competitive because they prevent or restrict distortion. Each of these arrangements impedes the normal free flow of goods by erecting artificial barriers to trade.

There is little doubt that, at least theoretically, competition policy and the principle of the free movement of goods are related because both seek to reduce barriers to trade within the Community.

It will be recalled that art 14 EC introduced the concept of an internal market, defined as an area 'without internal frontiers in which the free movement of goods ... is ensured'. Article 25 EC prohibits customs duties and any charges having equivalent effect on the flow of goods between Member States while arts 28 and 29 EC prevent the imposition of quantitative restrictions and measures having an equivalent effect on imports between Member States.

These are measures taken by the relevant national authorities of each Member State for particular purposes. These rules, and the objective which they seek to achieve, namely the free movement of goods, would be circumvented if private parties were allowed to substitute private barriers to prevent effective competition and the free movement of goods. The decision of the European Court in *Consten and Grundig* v *Commission* Cases 56 and 58/64 [1966] ECR 299 supports this view.

In this case, Grundig, a German manufacturer of electrical equipment, entered into a distribution agreement with Consten, a French distributor. This agreement appointed Consten as Grundig's exclusive agent in certain regions of France. However, a French competitor imported Grundig's products, in free circulation in Germany, into France where they were sold at prices beneath those being offered by Consten.

Consten brought an action in the French courts to prevent its rival from importing in this manner, but the European Commission objected to this procedure and commenced an investigation into the commercial activities of Consten. The Commission found that the distribution agreement was contrary to art 81(1) EC because the agreement had the effect of distorting competition in the Community because it restricted trade. Both parties brought an action against the Commission in the European Court to have this decision annulled.

The Court held that an agreement could only be contrary to art 81(1) EC if it affected trade between Member States. It is only to the extent that an agreement affects trade between Member States that the deterioration in competition caused by the agreement falls within art 81 EC; otherwise it would escape the prohibitions contained in art 81(1) EC.

To assess whether an agreement affects trade between Member States, it is necessary to assess whether an agreement is capable of constituting a threat, either direct or indirect, actual or potential, to the free movement of goods between Member States in a manner which might harm the attainment of the objectives of a single market among the Member States: *Société Technique Minière* v *Maschinenbau Ulm GmbH* Case 56/65 [1966] ECR 235. In other words, the degree to which an agreement affects trade between Member States is determined by reference to the amount of distortion, even potentially, that it causes to the achievement of the free movement of goods.

If commercial agreements do not impede the free flow of goods from Member States, they do not fall within the scope of art 81(1) EC. But, for this condition to be satisfied, it is not necessary that there is actual trade between parties situated in different countries. In the past, the Commission and the Court have held that agreements between two or more parties in the same Member State may be anti-competitive even though there is no element of transnational trade. For example, in *Cementhandeleren* v *Commission* Case 8/72 [1972] ECR 977, the Court held that a price fixing cartel between cement manufacturers in the Netherlands was contrary to art 81 EC even though no participant was from outside the Netherlands, simply because the effect of the cartel inside the Netherlands prevented or impeded imports from other Member States.

Similarly, in *Delimitis* v *Henninger Braü* Case C–234/89 [1992] 5 CMLR 210, the Court held that an exclusive supply agreement between a bar owner and a brewery was contrary to art 81(1) EC even though both parties conducted business in Germany because of the cumulative effect of similar agreements between the brewery and various third parties.

The degree to which competition law and the principle of the free movement of goods complement each other is also evidenced by the fact that the operation of both is primarily in the interest of the consumer. Naturally, it is in the interests of the consumer that no customs duties, quantitative restrictions or measures having an equivalent effect are imposed on goods since these would merely increase the final price or limit the choice of goods available to consumers. Competition between producers and suppliers also has the overall effect of lowering average prices.

However, while the relationship between art 81 EC and the principle of the free movement of goods is certainly tangible, it may be going too far to suggest that art 81 EC is intended only to support the rules for the free movement of goods. The purpose of art 81 EC is wider than mere support for the principle of the free movement of goods. It provides a comprehensive framework for the operation of an effective Community policy on competition.

The purpose of competition policy in a market economy is more than merely protecting consumer interests. It is intended to promote efficiency by allowing businesses to compete with each other, generally on fair terms and without one or the other having an unfair competitive advantage. It would be grossly unfair, for example, for a number of businesses to group together and pool their resources merely for the purposes of eliminating a competitor from the market.

The Commission itself has observed that arts 81 and 82 EC are intended to provide a commercial environment where competition is not distorted: *EC Competition Policy in the Single Market* (3rd ed, 1997). In other words, competition policy provides a level playing field throughout the Community where companies can compete in the knowledge that their competitors are subject to similar commercial and trading conditions.

Further, art 81 EC applies not only to goods, but also to the supply of services. It is therefore equally applicable to the freedom to provide services as it is to the free movement of goods. In the past, for example, banking services have been the subject of investigation by the Commission: *Zuchner v Bayerische Vereinsbank* Case A2/80 [1981] ECR 2021. Similarly, in *Ahmed Saeed Flugreisen and Silver Line Reisbüro GmbH v Zentrale zur Bekämpfung Unlauteren Wettbewerbs eV* Case 66/86 [1989] ECR 803, the economic activity under review was the supply of airline services. So, there is no logical restriction of art 81 EC to its relationship with the principle of the free movement of goods.

QUESTION THREE

Plato, a small but exclusive firm of concert piano manufacturers in Sparta, Greece wish to expand their market. They investigate the situation in the rest of the European Union and find that the market is divided as follows: the major German manufacturers, Klavier, have about 30 per cent of the entire piano market in the EU. They aim their production at the mass market and concert pianos are only a small part of their production. The rest of the market is divided among five or six other firms, some in Germany, some in other parts of the Union.

Plato select two German firms which make pianos very similar to their own. They approach them and invite them for talks in Sparta. During the talks, they find that by pooling their expertise with these firms they will be able to produce even better quality sound without increasing their cost. They have also preliminary and exploratory talks about joint enterprises in marketing their pianos.

Klavier hear about this meeting and alert the European Commission authorities. Have Plato offended against EC competition law?

University of London LLB Examination
(for External Students) European Community Law June 1999 Q4

General Comment

This problem question required application of Community competition law, although the question did not require any discussion of the Merger Regulation. Candidates should have identified that this question involved potential application of both arts 81 (restrictive trading practices) and 82 EC (abuse of a dominant position), although it should be noted that art 82 EC is discussed in detail in the following chapter. Candidates must be aware that any answer omitting case law is unwise, but in this area it is almost impossible, since many of the relevant principles (for example, a concerted practice) have been defined by the Commission, European Court of Justice and/or the Court of First Instance.

Skeleton Solution

Introduction – define purpose of competition provisions, namely arts 81 and 82 EC; the power of the Commission to investigate under Council Regulation 17/62; the possibility of applying both provisions to this behaviour (ie possible oligopolistic market) – art 81 EC: define and explain – relevant case law – define concerted practice – apply to meeting between firms – possibility of exemption/comfort letter – art 82 EC: define and explain – relevant case law – assess relevant product and geographical market – define dominant position/market share, etc – identify the 'abuse' types – no possibility of exemption – Commission's powers of sanction: Regulation 17/62.

Suggested Solution

In the context of private undertakings the substantive rules of competition law are to be found in arts 81 and 82 EC. Article 81 EC prohibits agreements, decisions and concerted practices between undertakings that have the object or effect of preventing, restricting or distorting competition within the Community. Article 82 EC prohibits any abuse of power by one or more parties of a dominant position within a particular market that affects trade between Member States. Competition law is enforced by the Commission under Council Regulation 17/62. Once the Commission has received a complaint, it may investigate the situation by obtaining information (art 11, Regulation 17/62); conducting inspections (art 14); and convening hearings (art 19). Klavier should be aware that they are not automatically entitled to damages even if an infringement is established, nor are they able to compel the Commission to investigate: *Star Fruit Co SA v Commission* Case 247/87 [1989] ECR 291.

Article 81 EC applies where there is an agreement, decision or concerted practice between a number of undertakings. Although art 82 EC is traditionally applied to the activities of an individual undertaking, it does refer to the abuse of a dominant position by 'one or more undertakings'. Therefore oligopolistic market behaviour may breach arts 81 and 82 EC: *Società Italiana Vetro* v *Commission (Re Italian Flat Glass Suppliers)* Cases T–68, 77 and 78/89 [1992] 5 CMLR 302 and *Municipality of Almelo* v *NV Energiebedriff Ijsselmij* Case C–393/92 [1994] ECR I–1477. Hence we must consider the potential application of both Treaty Articles to the behaviour of Plato and the two German firms.

The three firms in question will have to be 'undertakings'. This term has been given a wide interpretation by the Commission and the ECJ to include all natural and legal persons engaged in commercial activities, whether or not they are profit-making: *Heintz van Landewyck Sarl* v *Commission* Case 108/78 [1980] ECR 3125.

Article 81 EC prohibits agreements, decisions and concerted practices between undertakings that affect trade between Member States and that have the object or effect or preventing, restricting or distorting competition within the Community. According to art 81(2) EC, such agreements, etc, will be automatically void, although there exists the possibility of exemption under art 81(3) EC should the agreement, etc, have compensating beneficial facets.

In this scenario, the three firms may have entered into an agreement or potential concerted practice. An agreement has been defined widely so as to include unrecorded understandings and gentlemen's agreements: *Boehringer* v *Commission* Case 45/69 [1970] ECR 769 and *ACF Chemiefarma NV* v *Commission* Cases 41, 44 and 45/69 [1970] ECR 661. In this case the agreement is horizontal in that it is made between competitors or potential competitors. A concerted practice may alternatively be concluded to be in operation here, in that there are informal talks of an exploratory and preliminary nature.

A concerted practice was defined in the case of *Imperial Chemical Industries Ltd* v *Commission (Dyestuffs)* Case 48/69 [1972] ECR 619 as a situation where undertakings aim to remove any uncertainty as to their future conduct through either direct or indirect contact, regardless of whether any coherent plan is agreed. However, if the Commission need to carry out a market analysis to identify the existence of the concerted practice the evidence produced will not per se be indicative of a concerted practice. This will only be the case if there is no other plausible explanation, as concluded in *Ahlström and Others* v *Commission (Re Wood Pulp Cartel)* Cases 89, 104, 114, 116, 117 and 125–129/85 [1994] ECR I–99.

There will be no breach of art 81 EC unless there is an effect on inter-State trade: *Consten and Grundig* v *Commission* Cases 56 and 58/64 [1966] ECR 299. To determine whether there has been such an effect, the Commission will first assess the relevant product market, in this case concert pianos, and the relevant geographical market, probably consisting here of at least the German and Greek markets. However, art 81 EC also applies to those agreements, decisions or concerted practices that may have an effect. In *Société Technique Minière* v *Maschinenbau Ulm GmbH* Case 56/65 [1966] ECR 235 the ECJ held that this is the case where the agreement, etc, is capable of directly or indirectly, actually or potentially, affecting the pattern of trade between Member States. However, the effect will have to be one that is not purely minimal. This may be determined by application of the Commission's guidance in the De Minimus Notice of 1997. In the case of a horizontal agreement such as this one, the parties will have to affect at least 5 per cent of the relevant market. Although unlikely given these particular facts, should this be the case, the Commission will usually not open the investigation and if the agreement, etc, is later found to be a breach of art 81 EC the parties will not be fined if they acted in good faith. However, horizontal agreements are blacklisted by the Notice if they are intended to fix prices, limit production/sales, or divide up supply sources.

Article 81(1) EC contains a list of types of agreements, etc, that are prohibited. This list is non-exhaustive, and the practices outlawed will potentially extend to research and development agreements and joint ventures on development, as being considered by the three firms. Article 81(2) EC declares that those agreements, etc, falling within art 81(1) EC are automatically void, although it should be noted that severance may be available.

The parties could be eligible for exemption. Under art 81(3) EC the parties may be awarded individual exemption (although it should be noted that in practice it is important that they notify the Commission). To acquire exemption the parties will have to prove that their agreement, etc, is capable of contributing to the production or distribution of concert pianos or of promoting technical or economic progress, and that a fair share of the resulting benefit (such as improved sound quality without increased cost) accrues to the consumer. In addition, the parties will also have to prove that they have not imposed any restriction beyond the positive aims of the agreement or practice and that there is no possibility of eliminating competition in respect of a substantial part of the market.

Alternatively, the parties may be eligible for block exemption under the terms of various Commission Regulations. Should their agreement or practice come within the terms of one of these regulations (such as Commission Regulation 418/85 on research and development agreements) there will be no breach of art 81 EC; there will be no requirement to notify the Commission; and there will be no possibility of incurring a fine.

Finally, if the parties notify the Commission they may receive a comfort letter. This will state that in the opinion of the Commission the agreement or practice does not come within the ambit of art 81 EC or that it would be eligible for individual exemption. If the parties receive such a letter they may assume that the file has been closed, although they should note that such comfort letters are non-legally binding: *SA Lancôme v Etos BV* Case 99/79 [1980] ECR 2511 and *Procureur de la République v Giry and Guerlain* Case 253/78 [1980] ECR 2237 (the *Perfumes* case).

Alternatively, the parties' behaviour may constitute a breach of art 82 EC as abuse of a dominant position. Article 82 EC shares a number of common features with art 81 EC such as the need for undertakings to have committed the action and the need for an effect on inter-State trade. It is possible to apply both Articles to the same behaviour, but if the Commission did so it would not be entitled to simply reiterate the same facts: *Societá Italiana Vetro v Commission (Re Italian Flat Glass Suppliers)* Cases T–68, 77 and 78/89 [1992] 5 CMLR 302.

The first step is to identify the relevant product market (RPM). According to guidelines in the Commission Notice 1997, this is comprised of all products regarded as interchangeable or substitutable by the consumer by reason of the products' characteristics, price and intended use. In assessing the RPM the Commission will consider the following factors: the evidence of past substitution; views of customers and competitors; consumer preferences; barriers and costs to changing demand; and the different categories of customers and price discrimination. Commission and Court practice in cases such as *Michelin v Commission* Case 322/81 [1983] ECR 3461 indicates that a narrow RPM will traditionally be identified, either based on interchangeability or on cross-elasticity of demand and supply: *United Brands & United Brands Continental BV v Commission* Case 27/76 [1978] ECR 207 where it was concluded that bananas, rather than fresh fruit, was the RPM because of the lack of such interchangeability. In this case the RPM will probably be comprised of concert pianos for the same reasons.

The second step is to ascertain the relevant geographical market (RGM), which must be the common market or a substantial part of it. In this case the products are regularly bought and sold in all Member States and therefore the RGM will be the whole of the Community. Alternatively, the RGM may merely constitute Greece and Germany, which should still be sufficient since a single Member State may constitute a significant part of the common market: *BP v Commission* Case 77/77 [1978] ECR 1513.

It can then be assessed whether there is a dominant position, defined by the ECJ as a position of economic strength so that the undertakings may operate independently of competitors, customers and consumers. The Commission will begin by considering the market share held by the parties. According to *Hoffman-La Roche v Commission* Case 85/76 [1979] ECR 461 a large market share will be evidence of a dominant position. However, there may be a dominant position with less than 50 per cent market share if the rest of the market is highly fragmented, as was the case in *United Brands* (above). Other factors that the Commission may take into account will, according to *Hoffman-La Roche*, include: the market share of competitors; financial and technological resources held by the parties; their control of production and distribution; any absence of potential competition; and their conduct and performance.

However, even if a dominant position is found to exist, there will be no breach of art 82 EC unless there has been an abuse. Examples are found in art 82 EC but this is a non-exhaustive list. Generally, types of abuse may be categorised as exploitative or anti-competitive. The former may be defined as acts that occur when the dominant undertaking takes advantage of its position, often by imposing unfair conditions. The latter occurs when there is a reduction or attempt to eliminate competition by undermining or eliminating existing competitors, or preventing new competitors from entering the market. There is no possibility of exemption for breaches of art 82 EC.

If competition law is breached the Commission may impose a fine under Council Regulation 17/62, art 15, the maximum level of which will be Euro 1 million or 10 per cent of the annual global turnover of the undertaking, whichever is the greatest. To assess the level of the fine, the Commission traditionally considers: the size of the undertakings; the steps if any taken by the parties to mitigate their infringement; and the nature of the infringement itself. The Commission Notice 1998 on the method of setting fines refers to a range of minor to very serious infringements, the latter including horizontal agreements. The Notice also refers to the need to assess the duration of the offending action, which in this case will be minor since at this stage only exploratory talks have taken place. If the parties are found to have infringed competition law and are fined they may appeal to the CFI (and then the ECJ but only in terms of reducing or cancelling the fine) but they should be aware of the fact that they are liable for any interest in the interim period. Klavier could seek interim relief, which may be granted by the Commission if: the practice they have complained of is likely to be a per se breach of competition law; there is urgency; and there is a need to avoid serious and irreparable damage: *La Cinq* v *Commission* Case T–44/90 [1992] ECR II–1.

Chapter 11

European Competition Law and Merger Control – Article 82 EC

11.1   Introduction

11.2   Key points

11.3   Key cases and materials

11.4   Questions and suggested solutions

11.1 Introduction

This chapter will deal mainly with the restraints imposed on commercial practices by art 82 EC and also the regulation of mergers within the Community by competition law. In addition, a number of other matters of general competition law will be considered in order to provide a comprehensive description of the Community competition policy scheme. This includes the proper procedure for the initiation of a complaint, the determination of infringements, the powers of the Commission to investigate complaints, and the imposition of fines. These matters are equally relevant to the application of art 81 EC as well as art 82 EC, but are included in this chapter to avoid duplication and repetition.

11.2 Key points

Commercial practices prohibited by art 82 EC

Article 82 EC prohibits practices which constitute an abuse of a dominant position within the Community market. Article 82 EC expressly provides:

'Any abuse by one or more undertakings of a dominant position within the common market or in a substantial part of it shall be prohibited as incompatible with the common market in so far as it may affect trade between Member States. Such abuse may, in particular, consist in:

a) directly or indirectly imposing unfair purchase or selling prices or other unfair trading conditions;

b) limiting production, markets or technical developments to the prejudice of consumers;

c) applying dissimilar conditions to equivalent transactions with other parties, thereby placing them at a competitive disadvantage;

d) making the conclusion of contracts subject to acceptance by the other parties of supplementary obligations which, by their nature and according to commercial usage, have no connection with the subject of such contracts.'

Articles 81(1) and 82 EC are not mutually exclusive. The Commission has discretion in selecting the appropriate instrument to enforce competition policy. Consequently, the possibility that both arts 81 and 82 EC may be applicable to a particular case cannot be ruled out: *Ahmed Saeed Flugreisen and Silver Line Reisbüro GmbH* v *Zentrale zur Bekämpfung Unlauteren Wettbewerbs eV* Case 66/86 [1989] ECR 803.

The existence of a dominant position per se is not prohibited under art 82 EC, only any abuse of the market power which accompanies such a position. Article 82 EC is not intended to penalise or punish efficient forms of economic behaviour. On the contrary, art 82 EC seeks to discourage the acquisition or maintenance of a dominant position through anti-competitive practices which create artificial competitive conditions.

The existence of a dominant position

The concept of dominant position is not defined in the EC Treaty but, in effect, is analogous to the existence of a monopoly in a particular sector of the economy. The European Court has defined dominant position in the following terms:

'Undertakings are in a dominant position when they have the power to behave independently, which puts them in a position to act without taking into account their competitors, purchasers or suppliers. That is a position when, because of their share of the market, or of their share of the market combined with the availability of technical knowledge, raw materials or capital, they have power to determine prices or to control production or distribution for a significant part of the products in question.' (*Europemballage Corporation and Continental Can Co* v *Commission* Case 6/72 [1973] ECR 215.)

Article 82 EC does not, however, only apply to the activities of single companies. For example, in *Societá Italiana Vetro* v *Commission (Re Italian Flat Glass Suppliers)* Cases T–68, 77 and 78/89 [1992] 5 CMLR 302, the European Court held that the provision could be applied to three Italian glass producers. The number of parties is not the critical factor although in investigations under art 82 EC this number does tend to be small. The important element is the position of the parties in the relevant market and their behaviour.

The two key concepts in establishing the existence of a dominant position are: the definition of the relevant product market (RPM) and the relevant geographic market (RGM); and the calculation of the market share.

Definition of the relevant market

The Commission Notice on Relevant Markets 1997 explains the application of the concept of relevant product and geographic markets for the purposes of EC competition law. It is first necessary to identify what the relevant market is in order to decide whether there is or might be a restriction of competition or the abuse of a dominant position. The Notice sets out basic principles for market definition, recognising that firms are subject to three main elements: demand substitutability; supply substitutability; and potential competition.

In defining the relevant product market, the Commission first analyses the product's characteristics and its intended use. As for whether two products are demand substitutes, the Commission looks at: evidence of substitution in the recent past; the views of customers and competitors; consumer preferences; barriers and costs associated with switching demand to potential substitutes; and the different categories of customers and price discrimination.

For examples of identification of the RPM on the basis of the interchangeability or substitutability, see the cases of *Michelin* v *Commission* Case 322/81 [1983] ECR 3461; *Hilti AG* v *Commission* Case T–30/89 [1991] ECR II–1439; *Hugin Kassaregister AB and Hugin Cash Registers Ltd* v *Commission* Case 22/78 [1979] ECR 1869 and *AKZO Chemie BV* v *Commission* Case C–62/86 [1991] ECR I–3359. For examples of the identification of the RPM on the basis of the cross-elasticity of demand and supply, see *United Brands & United Brands Continental BV* v *Commission* Case 27/76 [1978] ECR 207 and *Tetra Pak Rausing SA* v *Commission (No 1)* Case T–51/89 [1991] 4 CMLR 334.

To define geographic markets, the Commission looks at the distribution of the parties' and their competitors' market shares and will usually conduct a preliminary analysis of pricing and price differences at national and Community level. It also checks supply factors to ensure that companies located in distinct areas are not prevented from developing their sales in competitive terms throughout the whole geographic market. Finally, the Commission takes into account the continuing process of market integration, particularly in areas of concentrations and structural joint ventures.

In general, the relevant geographical market will be assumed to be the whole of the Community. The relevant geographical market will be smaller than the Community in three main instances:

a) if the nature and characteristics of the product restrict distribution: *Napier Brown-British Sugar* [1988] 4 CMLR 347;

b) where the movement of the product within the Community is hindered by barriers to entry into another national market caused by state intervention; and

c) where the marketing and sales efforts by the company under investigation are intentionally restricted to a particular part of the Community.

A single Member State has been concluded to be the relevant geographical market in that it was a substantial part of the common market: for example, see *Michelin* (above) where Belgium was concluded to be the relevant geographical market.

Finally, it should be noted that the relevant geographical market may shift over time, since consumer preferences may change, there may be technical developments, and/or the product may exist in a temporal market, ie one that is only available on a seasonal basis.

Calculation of market share

No particular share of a market is required to prove the existence of a dominant position. In *United Brands & United Brands Continental BV v Commission* Case 27/76 [1978] ECR 207 the European Court stated that the fact that an undertaking possessed around 40 per cent of the relevant market was not itself sufficient to establish market dominance. Other factors contributed to the determination that United Brands maintained a dominant position, including the facts that the company controlled its own shipping fleet, could regulate the volume of the product entering the Community regardless of weather conditions and subjected distributors to rigorous restrictive covenants.

On the other hand, in *Europemballage Corporation and Continental Can Co v Commission* Case 6/72 [1973] ECR 215, the Commission decided that a company with a share of approximately 50 per cent of the relevant market occupied a dominant position.

In *Hoffman-La Roche v Commission* Case 85/76 [1979] ECR 461 the Court identified other factors relevant in determining whether there is a dominant position held by the undertaking. The Court referred to the following:

a) the market share of competitors;

b) financial and technological resources held by the undertaking;

c) the undertaking's control of distribution and production;

d) the absence of any potential competition; and

e) the conduct and performance of the undertaking.

Investigation period for determination of market share

The period selected for the calculation of market share and the determination of a dominant position must be sufficient to facilitate the proper appraisal of market conditions, dominant position and the alleged abusive practice. Failure to properly assess these conditions may lead to the partial or complete annulment of any Commission measures designed to penalise findings of abuse: *BPB Industries v Commission* Case T–65/89 [1993] ECR II–389.

Abuse of a dominant position

Abuse is an objective concept which relates to the behaviour of the undertaking alleged to be in a dominant position. It is behaviour which modifies the structure of a market in such a way as to reduce the levels of competition or retard the growth of competition in a particular economic area.

Article 82 EC lists a number of practices which are specifically identified as perpetrating such abuse, including the following.

a) Directly or indirectly imposing unfair purchase or selling prices or other unfair trading conditions: see, for example, *Bodson v Pompes Funèbres des Règions Libérées SA* Case 30/87 [1988] ECR 2479.

b) Limiting production, markets or technical development to the prejudice of consumers.

c) Applying dissimilar conditions to equivalent transactions with other trading parties, thereby placing them at a competitive disadvantage.

d) Making the negotiation of contracts subject to acceptance by the other parties of supplementary obligations which, by their nature or according to commercial usage, have no connection with the subject of such contracts.

e) Refusal to give access to essential facilities. Such practices are abusive, in the view of the European Court in *Oscar Bronner GmbH & Co KG v Mediaprint Zeitungs-und Eitschriftenverag GmbH & Co KG* Case C–7/97 [1998] ECR I–7701, if: the refusal of the service is likely to eliminate all competition in the market; such refusal is incapable of being objectively justified; and the service in itself is indispensable to carrying on the activities of the undertaking making the challenge.

This catalogue is intended to be illustrative and, in common with the list elaborated in relation to art 81(1) EC, is not exhaustive.

In *Michelin v Commission* Case 322/81 [1983] ECR 3461 abuse was defined as behaviour that has the effect of hindering the maintenance of the degree of competition still existing in the market or the growth of that competition. In general, the abuses that are prohibited under art 82 EC fall into two main categories:

a) exploitative abuses, where the undertaking takes advantage of its dominant position, which will usually detrimentally affect consumers; and

b) anti-competitive abuses, where the undertaking in the dominant position commits action that is not necessarily unfair to consumers, but which will reduce or eliminate competition within the relevant market.

Examples of exploitative abuses include unfair prices (*United Brands & United Brands Continental BV v Commission* Case 27/76 [1978] ECR 207); unfair trading conditions (*United Brands*); discriminatory treatment (*Tetra Pak Rausing SA v Commission (No 2)* Case T–83/91 [1994] ECR II–755) and refusal and supply (*United Brands* and *BP v Commission* Case 77/77 [1978] ECR 1513).

Examples of anti-competitive abuses include predatory pricing (*Tetra Pak Rausing SA*, above); exclusive reservation of activities (*CBEM v CLT & IPB (Re Telemarketing)* Case 311/84 [1985] ECR 3261); import and export bans (*Suiker Unie v Commission* Cases 40–48, 50, 54–56, 111, 113 and 114/73 [1975] ECR 1663); loyalty rebates (*Hoffman-La*

Roche v *Commission* Case 85/76 [1979] ECR 461); and refusal to supply (*ICI SpA & Commercial Solvents Corporation* v *Commission* Cases 6 and 7/73 [1974] ECR 223); tying-in (*Hilti AG* v *Commission* Case T–30/89 [1991] ECR II–1439); and threatening behaviour (*Irish Sugar plc* v *Commission* Case T–228/97 [1999] ECR II–2969).

Merger control in the European Community – the original provisions

The Community competition provisions make no express reference to the control of mergers among undertakings in the Community. Notwithstanding this omission, the Commission has been prepared to apply both arts 81(1) and 82 EC to mergers and takeovers.

a) A dominant position in the manufacturing or distribution of a product or service may also lead to abuse where one producer or supplier is able to absorb competitors by way of an acquisition or merger: *Tetra Pak Rausing SA* v *Commission (No 1)* Case T–51/89 [1990] ECR II–309.

b) Article 81(1) EC may be applied to acquisitions of shareholdings where a company acquires a minority stake in a competitor as leverage for the coordination of marketing strategy between the two undertakings: *British American Tobacco (BAT) & RJ Reynolds Industries Inc* v *Commission* Cases 142 and 156/84 [1987] ECR 4487.

c) Article 81(1) EC may also be infringed if a company enters into a joint venture or acquires an interest in a third company where the other principal shareholder is in a related field of business.

d) Consortium bids may also violate art 81 EC if the consortium involves competitors seeking to acquire a competitor or attempting to influence its behaviour.

Notwithstanding the application of these provisions to individual cases, until 1990, the European Commission had no specific mandate to investigate mergers or acquisitions within the Community.

Merger control in the European Community – the Merger Control Regulation 1990

After a series of controversial takeovers in the early 1980s, the Council of Ministers agreed to adopt Community legislation conferring authority on the Commission to investigate takeovers and mergers above a certain threshold. Council Regulation 4064/89 was enacted for this purpose and came into force in September 1990. This has been amended by Council Regulation 1310/97, which had effect from March 1998.

The Regulation uses the term 'concentration' to refer to mergers and takeovers. A concentration arises where either: two or more previously independent undertakings merge into one; or one or more persons already controlling at least one undertaking acquire, whether by purchase of securities or assets, direct or indirect control of the whole or part of one or more other undertakings.

Article 1 of the Regulation confers regulatory jurisdiction upon the Commission over all mergers (termed 'concentrations') involving a 'Community dimension'.

A concentration arises where either: two or more previously independent undertakings merge into one; or one or more persons already controlling at least one undertaking acquire, whether by purchase of securities or assets, direct or indirect control of the whole or part of one or more other undertakings.

Originally, a concentration had a Community dimension where:

a) the aggregate world-wide turnover of all the undertakings concerned was more than Euro 5,000 million; and

b) the aggregate Community-wide turnover of each of the undertakings concerned was more than Euro 250 million.

These thresholds were lowered by Council Regulation 1310/97. On the basis of the amending Regulation, concentrations which do not meet the above thresholds are still caught where:

a) the combined aggregate world-wide turnover of all the undertakings involved in the merger is more than Euro 2,500 million; and

b) in each of at least three Member States, the combined aggregate turnover of all the undertakings concerned is more than Euro 100 million; and

c) in each of at least these three Member States, the aggregate turnover of each of at least two of the undertakings concerned is more than Euro 25 million; and

d) the aggregate Community-wide turnover of each of at least two of the undertakings concerned is more than Euro 100 million.

However, where the undertakings concerned achieve more than two-thirds of their Community-wide turnover within the same Member State, the merger will still not have a Community dimension.

Merging companies will now have to go through two tiers of threshold in order to assess whether a merger has a Community dimension. First, they must assess whether they meet the thresholds under the original Regulation. Second, if these thresholds are not met, they must determine whether they fulfil the additional cumulative criteria in the new Regulation.

Council Regulation 1310/97 also removes the requirement that concentrative joint ventures must not involve co-ordination between the parents, or between one of them and the joint venture, in order to come within the Regulation. Joint ventures falling within the Regulation are those which perform on a lasting basis all the functions of an autonomous economic entity.

Even if a merger is approved by the Commission, Member States retain a veto over mergers in particularly sensitive sectors of their national economies. Member States may take appropriate measures to protect legitimate national interests such as public security, the plurality of the media and the maintenance of prudent rules for the conduct of commerce. However, such measures are subject to the requirement that they must be compatible with the general principles and other provisions of Community law.

Concentrations with a Community dimension must be notified to the Commission not more than one week after the conclusion of the agreement, or the announcement of a public bid, or the acquisition of the necessary controlling interest. If a merger is by consent, the notification must be made jointly by all the parties involved. In all other cases, including contested acquisitions, the notification to the Commission must be made by the acquiring undertaking.

The Commission is empowered to impose fines on persons, undertaking or associations of undertakings if they intentionally or negligently fail to notify the Commission of a concentration with a Community dimension. These fines can range from Euro 1,000 to Euro 50,000.

Once a concentration with a Community dimension is notified, two options are available to the Commission.

a) The Commission can conclude that the concentration does not fall within the scope of the Regulation and must record such a finding by means of a decision.

b) It can find that the concentration falls within the scope of the Regulation. In such a case, it may adopt one of two alternative courses of action:

   i) declare that the concentration, while within the scope of the Regulation, is not incompatible with the common market and will not therefore be opposed; or

   ii) find that the concentration falls within the Regulation and is incompatible with the common market in which case it is obliged to initiate proceedings.

In each of these cases, the Commission must make its decision within one month of the notification.

To appraise the compatibility of a concentration with the common market, the Commission must evaluate the implications of the concentration in the light of the need to preserve and develop effective competition within the common market, taking into account, inter alia, the structure of all the relevant markets concerned and the actual or potential competition from other undertakings both within and outside the Community. In making this assessment, the Commission must consider the market position of the undertakings concerned, their economic and financial power, the opportunities available to both suppliers and consumers, access to supplies and markets, the existence of legal or other barriers to the entry of the product into particular markets, the interests of intermediate and ultimate consumers, as well as technical and economic development and progress.

For examples of the assessment made by the Commission see, generally, *Nestlé SA*

Source/Perrier SA Case IV/M190 [1993] 4 CMLR M17 and *Aérospatiale-Alenia/de Havilland* Case IV/M53 [1992] 4 CMLR M2.

Determination of infringements of European Competition law

The Commission may investigate alleged anti-competitive behaviour either on an ex proprio motu basis, or at the instance of interested parties. Interested parties permitted to notify the Commission of anti-competitive behaviour include Member States, undertakings and individuals who are affected by the alleged infringement of the competition rules.

Although the Commission has discretion whether or not to pursue an investigation after allegations have been made by interested parties (*GEMA* v *Commission* Case 125/75 [1979] ECR 3173), it is obliged to notify a petitioner if no action is to be taken. If the Commission reaches the conclusion that no action is warranted, it must at least have conducted a proper preliminary investigation and cannot dismiss a complaint without exhausting the proper standard of appraisal in such an investigation: *Asia Motor France SA* v *Commission* Case T–387/94 [1996] ECR II–961.

Generally, the Commission concentrates its investigations to matters that are of sufficient Community interest: see, for example, *BENIM* v *Commission* Case T–114/92 [1995] ECR II–147. If such an interest is not present and the Commission refuses take action, the parties can seek relief through national courts. The Commission advocated this in its 1993 Notice on Co-operation between Community Institutions and National Courts. This is possible because arts 81 and 82 EC have horizontal direct effect: *Belgische Radio en Télévisie (BRT)* v *SABAM* Case 127/73 [1974] ECR 313.

In conducting its investigations, the Commission has a right to obtain all necessary information from the competent authorities of Member States as well as from undertakings and associations subject to investigation. The owners of undertakings or, in the case of companies, the persons authorised by the articles of association to represent incorporated bodies, are obliged to supply such information.

Commission's powers to enforce competition rules – Council Regulation 17/62

The Commission has the authority to deal with the notification of agreements that may potentially breach art 81 EC. If an agreement, decision or concerted practice is to fall within the scope of art 81 EC it should be notified to the Commission unless:

a) notification is not necessary due to the existence of a dispensation; or

b) the agreement or contract falls within a block exemption.

The latter is discussed in detail in Chapter 10. Dispensation includes application of the de minimus principle (see Chapter 10); the commercial agents rule; and the parent/ subsidiary rule. The Community's competition rules do not apply to agreements between agents and principles and transactions between parents and subsidiaries, on the basis that such agreements relate only to the exercise of the authority of one party.

The response to notification may include the following.

a) Negative clearance – this occurs where the Commission concludes that the agreement does not breach art 81 EC. The approval is called negative clearance and can take the form of a formal 'decision' or the issuing or a non-legally binding comfort letter.

b) Individual exemption – the undertakings must officially apply for this when it is clear that their notification includes a breach of art 81 EC. This is discussed in further detail in Chapter 10. It should be noted that the Commission rarely exempts price-fixing or market-sharing agreements. However, those agreements that increase efficiency or expand consumer choice, such as licensing, distribution and joint venture agreements, and those agreements that protect small to medium-sized undertakings are often granted exemption.

The Commission's powers to investigate are contained in Council Regulation 17/62 and can be broadly classified as follows.

Power to obtain information

Under art 11(1) of the Regulation, in carrying out its duties, the Commission may obtain 'all information necessary' for the purposes of the investigation from interested private parties and the governments and competent authorities of the Member States.

The scope of information 'necessary' for the purposes of conducting the investigation falls broadly within the discretion of the Commission to decide: *Samenwerkende Elektriciteits Produktiebedrijven (SEP) NV* v *Commission* Case T–39/90 [1991] ECR II–1497.

Article 20(1) of the Regulation provides that the information may only be used for the purpose of the relevant request, so the Commission cannot use the information except for in the context of the reasons stated.

Private parties subject to a request for information may decline to provide information protected on the basis of client/lawyer confidentiality: *AM and S Europe Ltd* v *Commission* Case 155/79 [1982] ECR 1575. In addition, further protection is offered by virtue of the fact that private parties are entitled to legal representation (*Hoechst AG* v *Commission* Cases 46/87 and 227/88 [1989] ECR 2859) and cannot be forced to respond to leading questions if their answers would amount to an admission of unlawful conduct: *Orkem* v *Commission* Case 374/87 [1989] ECR 3283.

Power to conduct inspections

Again the Commission's powers to conduct on-the-spot investigations are extensive. Article 14(1) of the Regulation allows Commission officials to:

a) examine the books and business records of the company;

b) to take copies of books and business records;

c) to ask for oral explanations on the spot; and

d) to enter any premises, land or means of transport of parties under investigation.

The Commission exercises these powers in two stages. First, Commission officials visit premises with a simple mandate from the Commission authorising inspection. If these officials are refused access to premises or records, the Commission may adopt a decision under art 14(3) of the Regulation requiring companies to submit to investigations authorised by the decision.

The Commission may proceed with a search after obtaining the necessary permission from the national authorities and can impose fines on companies for failing to comply with the Commission's requests. The European Court has held that such searches must be subject to procedural safeguards. In particular:

'... if the Commission intends, with the assistance of the national authorities, to carry out an investigation other than with the co-operation of the undertakings concerned, it is required to respect the relevant procedural guarantees laid down by national law.' (*Hoechst AG* v *Commission* Cases 46/87 and 227/88 [1989] ECR 2859.)

Power to convene hearings

The Commission is required to allow interested parties an opportunity to present their arguments and views directly to its officials. The procedures for the convening of hearings to discharge this obligation are regulated by Council Regulation 2842/98.

The main purpose of holding such meetings is to allow parties to make representations in their favour at various stages in the proceedings.

Power to grant interim relief

No such power is expressly conferred in Council Regulation 17/62, but the Commission has been deemed to possess an inherent power to issue decisions providing interim relief to complaining parties to prevent injury caused by the anti-competitive practices of business competitors: *Camera Care Ltd* v *Commission* Case 792/79R [1980] ECR 119.

The Court of First Instance has recently confirmed that the Commission can adopt interim measures of protection if the following three conditions were satisfied:

a) the practices against which a complaint was lodged were prima facie likely to infringe Community law;

b) proven urgency existed; and

c) there is a need to avoid serious and irreparable damage to the party seeking relief: *La Cinq* v *Commission* Case T–44/90 [1992] ECR II–1.

Power to fine

According to art 15 of Council Regulation 17/62, as amended, the Commission may impose fines ranging from Euro 1,000 to Euro 1,000,000, or a sum in excess of this limit but not exceeding 10 per cent of the turnover, against any undertakings found in violation of arts 81(1) and 82 EC. In addition, fines can be imposed for the supply of false or misleading information, for the submission of incomplete books or other documents or for refusal to submit to an investigation.

The policy of the Commission towards fining is a matter which is influenced by many factors. However, the following factors are considered most relevant to such a determination.

a) The size of the companies engaged in the anti-competitive behaviour: *Belasco* v *Commission* Case T–124/89 [1989] ECR 2117.

b) The steps taken by the party to mitigate the infringement prior to the decision imposing fines has been rendered: *National Panasonic* v *Commission* Case 136/79 [1980] ECR 2033.

c) The nature of the infringement. For example, the Commission considers certain practices, such as predatory pricing, to be particularly repugnant to Community competition policy: *Tetra Pak Rausing SA* v *Commission (No 1)* Case T–51/89 [1991] 4 CMLR 334.

The application of these principles can been seen by reference to two recent cases. In 1998 the European Commission adopted a decision imposing fines on the parties to the Trans-Atlantic Conference Agreement (TACA). The members of TACA had a joint market share in excess of 60 per cent and included 15 of the world's largest shipping lines which dominated container trade across the North Atlantic. Three practices were found to infringe EC competition law, including unjustified price-fixing. The Commission found that the TACA members had collectively abused their dominant position. The total fines imposed amounted to Euro 273 million.

In the same year, the Commission also fined the German car maker, Volkswagen, Euro 102 million for persistent infringement of EC competition rules. The fine was the largest ever imposed on an individual company: *Volkswagen* (1999) OJ L124/60 (Decision 98/273). The Commission's investigation revealed that the company sought to partition the single market, contrary to EC competition rules. The company prevented its Italian dealerships supplying its cars for export to German and Austrian final customers. Finally, the company penalised dealers who sold models outside their territory, for example by threatening termination of the dealer's contracts, actual termination of such contracts and the reduction of profit margins and bonuses for such dealers.

On appeal, however, the fine was reduced to Euro 90 million because the Commission was unable to prove that the infringement's duration exceeded three years: *Volkswagen* v *Commission* Case T–62/98 [2000] 5 CMLR 948.

To clarify the position on the setting of the level of fines, the Commission published a Notice in 1998, providing guidelines. The Notice adopts the method of determining the basic fine amount on the basis of the gravity and duration of the infringement. The gravity of infringements can range from:

a) minor, usually trade, restrictions of a vertical nature that affect only a limited part of the Community: the fine will usually be from Euro 1,000 to Euro 1 million;

b) serious, which have a wider market impact or occur where there has been an abuse of a dominant position: the fine will usually be from Euro 1 million to Euro 20 million; to

c) very serious, usually horizontal in nature, and includes clear-cut abuse of a dominant position, price fixing and market sharing: the fine will usually be above Euro 20 million.

The duration of infringements can range from:

a) short duration, usually less than one year, when there will be no increase in the fine;

b) medium duration, between one to five years, where the fine will be increased by up to 50 per cent; and

c) long duration, exceeding five years, where the fine will be increased by up to 10 per cent for every year the infringement occurred.

The Commission adopted a Notice in 1996 on reduced fines for cartel informers designed to encourage participants in cartels to offer evidence of such activities to the Commission. The Notice is not a codification of the Commission's previous practice, but a statement of the future policy which will be pursued in the future by the Commission against cartels.

The Notice gives much greater discretion to the Commission as to how it will treat cartel informers. The two main guidelines set down are as follows.

a) Total immunity from fines for companies reporting cartels is subject to the broad discretion of the Commission. However, as a general rule, such companies will benefit from a minimum reduction of 75 per cent of the fine which would have been imposed had the company not come forward.

b) Companies first reporting cartelistic behaviour immediately after an investigation has been opened by the Commission may obtain a reduction of between 50 per cent and 75 per cent of the final fine, again subject to the discretion of the Commission.

In both cases, reporting companies must satisfy a number of pre-conditions before being granted immunity. First, the informing company must not have been a ringleader in setting up the cartel. Second, the company must be the first to come forward to the Commission with substantial evidence of the cartel. Third, the company must pull out of the cartel no later than the time disclosure is made to the Commission. Fourth, it must provide the Commission with all information it possesses in relation to the activities of the cartel and must maintain continuous and complete co-operation with the Commission throughout the investigation. Failure to meet these requirements may mean the withdrawal of exemption.

The Commission also has authority to require undertakings to adopt particular courses of action including:

a) discontinuing infringements of arts 81(1) and 82 EC;

b) discontinuing action prohibited under art 8(3) of Council Regulation 17/62;

c) supplying completely and truthfully any information requested under art 11(5) of Council Regulation 17/62; and

d) submitting to any investigation ordered under the investigative powers of the Commission.

The Commission also has power under art 16 of Council Regulation 17/62 to impose periodic penalty payments of up to Euro 1,000 per day for each day that an undertaking refuses to rectify its breach of competition rules. Penalty payments can also be imposed on undertakings that refuse to supply information, or submit, to an investigation if such requests are formal.

While the Commission has authority to fix the level of fines, the national authorities concerned enforce the decision by virtue of art 256 EC in accordance with their rules of civil procedure.

Co-operation with national competition authorities

The enforcement of Community competition law is also partly the responsibility of national competition authorities. In 1998 the Commission published a Notice setting out the ways in which the European Commission and the national competition authorities of the Member States can co-operate in handling cases which fall within arts 81 and 82 EC. This Notice is the counterpart to the 1993 Co-operation Notice on Relations between National Courts and the Commission on Competition Matters.

Under the framework of Community competition law, both the national authorities and the Commission are jointly responsible for applying arts 81 and 82 EC, although it is only the Commission who can grant an individual exemption under art 81(3) EC. The Notice sets down rules which, generally, allow national authorities to deal with cases having a mainly local impact and which, prima facie, are unlikely to be exempted under art 81(3) EC. However, the Commission reserves the right to handle cases involving a 'particular Community interest' even if they could be dealt with by a national authority. These include cases which: raise a new point of law; or involve alleged anti-competitive behaviour by a public undertaking or an undertaking with an interest in the operation of services of general economic interest.

Judicial review of the Commission's decisions in competition law

This can be reviewed by the Court of First Instance (CFI) under art 230 EC. Four grounds for review are provided:

a) lack of competence;

b) infringement of an essential procedural requirement;

c) infringement of the Treaty or any rule relating to its application; and

d) misuse of powers.

Further discussion of the interpretation and application of art 230 EC can be found in Chapter 3.

The ECJ can hear an appeal against a decision of the CFI, but only on a point of law, and the ECJ can only set aside a CFI judgement if it has erred in law: art 225 EC. The CFI can cancel or vary the level of fine imposed by the Commission under art 229 EC and art 17 of Council Regulation 17/62. If this is then appealed to the ECJ the European Court cannot substitute its own determination, but may consider whether the CFI responded sufficiently to any arguments.

11.3 Key cases and materials

- *Belgische Radio en Télévisie (BRT)* v *SABAM* Case 127/73 [1974] ECR 313
  Individuals may access their national courts to seek redress for breaches of competition rules because arts 81 and 82 EC have horizontal direct effect

- *BENIM* v *Commission* Case T–114/92 [1995] ECR II–147
  The Commission concentrates its investigations to matters that are of sufficient Community interest

- *Europemballage Corporation and Continental Can Co* v *Commission* Case 6/72 [1973] ECR 215
  Provides a definition of a dominant position

- *Hilti AG* v *Commission* Case T–30/89 [1992] 4 CMLR 16
  Identification of the relevant product markets for the purposes of ascertaining the dominant position of an undertaking

- *Hoffmann-La Roche & Co AG* v *Commission* Case 85/76 [1979] ECR 461
  Examines the criteria to be used to determine whether a dominant position exists

- *La Cinq* v *Commission* Case T–44/90 [1992] ECR II–1
  Principles behind the grant of interim measures of relief by the Commission

- *Michelin* v *Commission* Case 322/81 [1983] ECR 3461
  Provides an example of determining the relevant product market and offers a definition of 'abuse' for the purposes of art 82 EC

- *Samenwerkende Elektriciteits Produktiebedrijven (SEP) NV v Commission* Case T–39/90 [1991] ECR II–1497
  The Commission has the discretion to decide what information is necessary for the purposes of conducting its investigation

- *United Brands & United Brands Continental BV v Commission* Case 27/76 [1978] ECR 207
  Identification of the criteria applied in order to determine the relevant product market

- EC Treaty

  - art 82 – prohibits practices that constitute an abuse of a dominant position

  - art 230 – judicial review (of Commission decisions in relation to competition law)

- Commission Notice on Relevant Markets 1997 – explains the concept and application of the relevant product and geographic markets

- Commission Notice on the Method of Setting Fines 1998 – provides guidelines on the setting of fines for breaches of EC competition law

- Council Regulation 17/62 – powers of the Commission to investigate and enforce EC competition law

- Council Regulation 4064/89 as amended by Council Regulation 1310/97 – confer authority on the Commission to investigate takeovers and mergers above certain threshold limits

- Commission Leniency Notice 1996 – encourages cartel participants to notify the Commission in return for reduced fine levels

11.4 Questions and suggested solutions

QUESTION ONE

British Breweries plc is an important producer of beer in the United Kingdom. Statistics shown that British Breweries account for some 12 per cent of all beer sold in the United Kingdom but that its British Brewlite is especially successful and accounts for 40 per cent of all non-alcoholic beer consumed in the UK.

a) British Breweries has been negotiating with County Beers Ltd with a view to merger. County Beers is the principal other producer of non-alcoholic beers and after merger the new company, British County Breweries, will control 65 per cent of the market in non-alcoholic beer.

b) British Breweries includes in its standard supply contract a requirement that pubs and other purchasers must display prominently its non-alcoholic beer and advertising materials. The advertising materials offer consumers 'healthy drinking discounts' whereby the more non-alcoholic beer they buy, the lower the price they have to pay. Since the healthy drinking discounts were introduced two years ago, British Breweries' sales have doubled and several small-scale producers of non-alcoholic beers have gone out of business.

Advise British Breweries as to the significance, if any, of EC law for each of the above aspects of its business.

Adapted from University of London LLB Examination
(for External Students) European Community Law June 1990 Q7

General Comment

A problem question requiring the application of art 82 EC to hypothetical facts.

Skeleton Solution

British Breweries as an undertaking – do the practices affect trade between Member States? – application of art 82 EC – dominant position and abuse.

Suggested Solution

a) British Breweries is clearly an undertaking for the purposes of art 82 EC, as is County Beers Ltd. Further, art 82 EC covers all sectors of the economy and the sale of drink is not covered by any derogation to the Treaty. Therefore, whether the proposed merger amount would to an abuse of a dominant position depends on whether the criteria established under art 82 EC are satisfied.

The acquisition of a competitor by a company which maintains a dominant position in the market may infringe art 82 EC if the merger results in an abuse of a dominant position, and this abuse affects trade between Member States.

British Breweries could feasibly argue that, since its activities only take place in the United Kingdom, trade between Member States is not affected. In this case, British law would apply and not Community competition law. However, in *Hugin Kassaregister AB and Hugin Cash Registers Ltd* v *Commission* Case 22/78 [1979] ECR 1869, the European Court stated that the test for effect on trade is whether the practice constitutes a threat to the freedom of trade between Member States in a way that might harm the attainment of a single market. In other words, it is only necessary that it is possible to foresee with a sufficient degree of probability that the practice in question would influence, directly or indirectly, actually or potentially, the pattern of trade between Member States.

The broad wording of this test means that it is not difficult for the Commission to establish that an effect on trade exists. Activities by an undertaking which create artificial divisions of the national market have been found to have an indirect effect on trade, for example, by making it harder for imports to penetrate the market: *Cementhandelaren* v *Commission* Case 8/72 [1972] ECR 977. Specifically, under art 82 EC, the European Court has held that where a dominant company refused to sell chemicals to the smaller company which sold almost all of its production outside the common market, that the requirement of an effect on trade was satisfied by the impairment of the competitive structure in the Community. Thus, it would seem likely that Community law would apply to the activities of British Breweries.

Next, it is necessary to ascertain whether British Breweries holds a dominant position, a term not defined in the EC Treaty, but which has been interpreted to mean an overall independence of behaviour on the market 'which puts [undertakings] in a position to act without taking into account their competitors, purchasers or suppliers': *Europemballage Corporation and Continental Can v Commission* Case 6/72 [1973] ECR 215. Absolute domination is not necessary.

There are two tests to establish a dominant position: the identification of the relevant market; and the assessment of the strength of the undertaking in question on the market.

To assess the relevant market, reference needs to be made to both the relevant product market (RPM) and the relevant geographic market (RGM). The RPM should be determined with reference to the Commission Notice 1997. In defining the RPM the Commission will analyse the product's characteristics and its intended use. As to whether two products are interchangeable, the Commission will consider evidence of past substitution, the views of customers and competitors, consumer preferences, barriers and costs associated with switching demand to potential substitutes, and different categories of customers and price discrimination.

It would be in British Breweries' interest to define the relevant market as broadly as possible, such as the market for all drinks, alcoholic and non-alcoholic, or at least the market for non-alcoholic drinks. In *United Brands & United Brands Continental BV* v *Commission* Case 27/76 [1978] ECR 207, the Court had to decide whether bananas should be regarded as an independent market in themselves or, alternatively, part of the general market for fresh fruit. In this case, the Court adopted the test of limited interchangeability and decided that the banana could be 'singled out by such special features distinguishing it from other fruits that it is only to a limited extent interchangeable with them and it is only exposed to their competition in a way that is hardly perceptible'.

The same argument may be used to distinguish alcoholic beer from non-alcoholic beer, the latter being developed expressly for its non-alcoholic content. Following the Court's reasoning in *Michelin* v *Commission* Case 322/81 [1983] ECR 3461 which distinguished the market in retreaded tyres from the market in replacement tyres, it could be argued that although other soft drinks are to some extent interchangeable with non-alcoholic beer, and hence in competition with such beer, sales of soft drinks do not sufficiently undermine the sales of non-alcoholic beer, which has been specifically developed for its similarity to beer and not just as another soft drink.

The RGM needs to be the common market or a substantial part of it for the purposes of art 82 EC. Since non-alcoholic beer is regularly bought and sold in all Member States, the RGM is presumed to be the entire Community.

In assessing the strength of an undertaking in a market, the most important factor is the size of the undertaking's share of the relevant market. Market shares have normally been relatively high. In the *Continental Can* case, the undertaking accounted for 50–60 per cent of the market in Germany for meat tins, 80–90 per cent of fish tins and 50–55 per cent for metal closures for glass jars. In *Hoffman-La Roche* v *Commission* Case 85/76 [1979] ECR 461, the undertaking held an 80 per cent share of the vitamin market. However, in *United Brands & United Brands Continental BV* v *Commission* Case 27/76 [1978] ECR 207 the Court was content to hold a figure of 40–45 per cent of the relevant market as constituting a dominant position. The Commission has said that a dominant position will usually be found once a market share of the order of 40–45 per cent is reached, but cannot be ruled out even as regards shares of between 20 and 40 per cent.

Furthermore, the rest of the market is likely to be fragmented – County Beers holds a 25 per cent share and the remaining 35 per cent is likely to belong to smaller producers. This factor underlines British Breweries' dominance.

Although nothing is known about British Breweries' financial resources or its performance, these factors suggest that the Commission would have a strong case for establishing the existence of a dominant position after merger.

However, to violate art 82 EC, British Breweries must be abusing their dominant position. It is not clear whether acquisitions can still be considered abusive under art 82 EC now that the Merger Control Regulation (MCR) 4064/89, as amended, has been put in place. The MCR imposes market share criteria above which certain acquisitions and mergers may be considered to constitute the creation of a dominant position. Market shares which give rise to concern vary according to whether the concentration increases the position of the merger entity in terms of horizontal or vertical integration in the relevant market.

However, in order to breach the MCR, the acquisition needs to involve a merger with a 'Community dimension'. This is defined as occurring where the aggregate annual turnover of all participating undertakings exceeds Euro 5,000 million, and the aggregate annual Community-wide turnover of each of the undertakings exceeds Euro 250 million. However, even if the proposed acquisition does not meet these criteria it may still have a Community dimension if it has the qualities introduced under amendments brought about by Council Regulation 1310/97. Hence, a Community dimension will also exist where:

i) the combined aggregate world wide turnover of all the undertakings is more than Euro 2,500 million;

ii) in each of at least three Member States the combined aggregate turnover of all the undertakings is more than Euro 100 million;

iii) in each of at least these three Member States the aggregate turnover of each of at least two of the undertakings is more than Euro 100 million; and

iv) the undertakings do not generate two-thirds of their turnover in a single Member State.

Given the facts it is unlikely that the proposed acquisition will fall either within the criteria of the MCR or those introduced by the amending Regulation. In particular, the acquisition may fall within the exception provided for those undertakings that generate more than two-thirds of their Community-wide turnover in one Member State, ie the United Kingdom.

b) Tying arrangements may also constitute an abuse of a dominant position. As illustrated by art 82(d) EC, where a person is required to accept, as a condition of entering into a contract, 'supplementary obligations which, by their nature or according to commercial usage, have no connection with the subject of such contracts', a prima facie infringement of competition law arises. An example of 'tying' can be seen in the case of *Hoffman-La Roche* v *Commission* Case 85/76 [1979] ECR 461, where the Court concluded that the action breached art 82 EC even though consumers liked the practice and had requested it.

The conditions that public houses and other purchasers must display British Breweries products and also advertisements in a prominent position appears to fall inside art 82(d) EC.

Such conditions may, however, be objectively justified, but they must be proportionate. The onus would therefore be on British Breweries to establish that such conditions are objectively justified as commercial practice that is proportionate. However, such conditions must not strengthen the dominant position, which appears to be the case here.

In this particular case the advertising goes beyond describing the attributes of the non-alcoholic beer by offering financial incentives towards its purchase, thus locking the consumer into the purchase of a single brand name, to the exclusion of other products. The main objection to tying is that it enables an undertaking with a dominant position in the market to gain a competitive advantage. Therefore, it is likely that the practices of British Breweries as regards the ancillary conditions for purchasers would fall foul of art 82 EC.

Even if British Breweries are not deemed to be abusing a dominant position, these contract terms may fall foul of art 81(1)(e) EC (*Delimitis* v *Henninger Bräu AG* Case C–234/89 [1992] 5 CMLR 210). The Brewers could, however, try to bring themselves within one of the existing exceptions to art 81(1) EC. By arguing that these contractual terms were necessary to establish non-alcoholic beer on the market, using the analogies drawn from two cases – *Société Technique Minière* v *Maschinenbau Ulm GmbH* Case 56/65 [1966] ECR 235 and *Pronuptia de Paris GmbH* v *Pronuptia de Paris Irmgard Schillgallis* Case 161/84 [1986] ECR 353 – such contractual terms might escape possible contravention of the competition provisions.

Alternatively, British Breweries could seek an exemption from liability under art 81(3) EC by arguing that the contractual terms contribute to improving the production or distribution of goods. British Breweries is likely to be on weaker ground here since the Commission insists that the gain to welfare must exceed what could have been achieved without the restriction on competition. In British Breweries' case, competition has clearly been restricted since several small-scale producers have gone out of business.

Council Regulation 17/62 provides for the Commission's powers to investigate breaches of competition rules. Under the Regulation, the Commission can request any information that it considers necessary and conduct on-the-spot inspections. If a breach of competition law is found to have taken place, in this case the abuse of a dominant position, the Commission may fine the undertaking: art 15. The Commission Notice 1998 adopts the method of determining the basic fine amount on the basis of the gravity and duration of the infringement. The gravity of infringements can range from minor to very serious, with abuses of a dominant position such as in this case often being determined to be either serious or very serious. If it is serious the fine will usually be between Euro 1–20 million. If the infringement is concluded to be very serious the fine will be over Euro 20 million. The duration of the infringement also contributes to the level of the fine. The tying-in has been taking place for two years, which the Notice determines to be of medium duration. As a result, British Breweries can expect any fine to be increased by up to 50 per cent.

QUESTION TWO

The concept of 'abuse of a dominant position' is one of the key elements in EC Competition law. How has it been used by the Commission and applied by the ECJ?

University of London LLB Examination
(for External Students) European Community Law June 1995 Q5

General Comment

This is an essay type question with quite a broad scope. While the answer must cover a number of basic points, considerable latitude is possible with regard to its content. The best way to discuss this issue is by way of examples, and there are numerous precedents from the Commission and Court in this area.

Skeleton Solution

The respective roles of the European Commission and the ECJ – the determination of a dominant position – the concept of abusive behaviour – examples to illustrate the concept of abusive behaviour.

Suggested Solution

Any abuse of a dominant position within the Community, or a substantial part of it, is prohibited under art 82 EC if such practices affect trade between Member States. The concept of an abuse of a dominant position therefore requires establishing two separate issues: whether a particular company has a dominant position in a specific market; and whether the company has been guilty of abusing that position in an anti-competitive manner. Both elements must be made out before an infringement of Community competition policy can be found to exist.

It is the European Commission which conducts investigations into allegations of abusive behaviour normally after receiving a complaint from competitors of the company accused of such practices. The Commission therefore has to apply the relevant legal principles and economic analysis to the facts gathered after an investigation to determine whether or not there has been an infringement.

Judicial review is carried out by the Court of First Instance (CFI) and the European Court (ECJ) itself. Since the CFI has only recently been given jurisdiction in this area, the majority of established principles relating to abuse of dominant positions have been developed by the ECJ. In fulfilling this role, the European Court, in conjunction with the Commission, has defined the concept in greater detail than that elaborated in art 82 EC.

The existence of a dominant position

Article 82 EC is intended to regulate the activities of generally one, or at most a selected few, companies which are engaged in anti-competitive practices. In the majority of investigations conducted by the Commission, it is a single producer which is found to have a dominant position: *Tetra Pak Rausing SA* v *Commission (No 2)* Case T–83/91 [1994] ECR II–755. In exceptional cases, two or three producers may be held to collectively hold a dominant position. For example, in *Solway* v *Commission* Case T–30/91 [1995] ECR II–1775 the CFI refused to interfere with the Commission's findings that both these producers jointly held a dominant position in the Community for the production of certain chemicals. Only on very rare occasions has the Commission found more than two companies with a collective dominant position: *Società Italiana Vetro* v *Commission (Re Italian Flat Glass Suppliers)* Cases T–68, 77 and 78/89 [1992] 5 CMLR 302.

In order to ascertain the existence of a dominant position, the Commission first identifies the relevant product market and the relevant geographical market in which dominance is believed to exist. Its approach to performing this task has been refined over the last two decades and this process has now become well-established.

To identify the relevant product market it is necessary for the Commission to isolate the product under investigation from similar products in the market place. For this purpose, the relevant product includes the actual product under investigation, together with all other products which may be substituted, in terms of both production and use, for the actual product. The test for identifying substitutable products depends on whether or not there is 'a sufficient degree of interchangeability' between all the products forming part of the same market: *Hoffman-La Roche* v *Commission* Case 85/76 [1979] ECR 461. Where a product is interchangeable with the product under investigation, then that product also forms part of the relevant product market.

Whether another product is sufficiently interchangeable with the product under investigation, and hence part of the relevant product market, is measured in terms of two factors. First, the objective physical characteristics of the product must be similar to those of the product under consideration. Second, the competitive conditions and the structure of the supply and demand for the other products must similar to those for the principal product.

The application of this test is best illustrated by the decisions of the ECJ. In *United Brands & United Brands Continental BV* v *Commission* Case 27/76 [1978] ECR 207, the Court was required to decide if bananas constituted a separate product market separate from that for fresh fruits in general. The Court ruled that the important physical qualities which required consideration were the characteristics of the product gauged in terms of appearance, taste, softness and ease of handling.

As regards competitive conditions, the Court considered four factors to be relevant: the degree to which the principal product was affected by falling or increasing prices of other fruits; the purchasing habits of consumers relative to expenditure on the principal product compared to other types of fresh fruit; the existence of special purchasing groups; and growing seasons for the product in comparison with others.

In the event that other fruits shared the same characteristics and competitive structure, consumers would select these fruits over bananas if the price of bananas was increased. Those fruits which could be identified after the application of this test formed part of the same relevant market as bananas. In the *United Brands* case itself, the Court found that there was insufficient substitutability between bananas and other fruits. Accordingly bananas formed a single relevant product market.

The relevant geographical market is considerably more easier to ascertain. It is the area within the Community 'where the conditions are sufficiently homogeneous for the effect of economic power of the undertaking to be evaluated': *United Brands*. As a general principle, the Commission will consider that the relevant geographical market will be the whole of the Community unless there are factual reasons for limiting the area to a lesser size. Factors generally pointed to in order to limit the geographical scope of the relevant market include impediments to cross-border trade such as physical, technological, legal or cultural barriers to trade, a lack of adequate transportation facilities, or an inability to extend distribution or supply networks into certain regions.

Once the relevant product and geographical markets are isolated, the Commission calculates the market share of the company alleged to have a dominant position. In normal circumstances, the turnover of the company is calculated relative to the total shares of the relevant product in the market. There is no strict market share which is used by the Commission to establish dominance. Rather, as the Court has agreed, a dominant position is defined as one which gives a company 'an ability to prevent effective competition and to behave to an appreciable extent independently of its competitors': *United Brands & United Brands Continental BV* v *Commission* Case 27/76 [1978] ECR 207.

The Commission and Court have, in the past, looked at several factors to determine the existence of dominance, but market share is undoubtedly important. As the European Court pointed out, 'very large shares are, in themselves, evidence of the existence of a dominant position': *Hoffman-La Roche* v *Commission* Case 85/76 [1979] ECR 461. However, no absolute percentage share of the relevant market has ever been considered by the Commission or the Court to definitely establish the existence of a dominant position. The Commission has, in the past, even considered that market shares of between 20–40 per cent may constitute dominance if certain circumstances are shown to exist.

Other factors contributing to a finding of dominance have included the concentrations and relative market shares of other companies in the sector, technological leads and the existence of a well-established sales and distribution network.

Abusive behaviour

The concept of abuse is not expressly defined in the EC Treaty but the European Court, in *Hoffmann-La Roche* indicated that abuse occurs when the structure of the market is weakened and competition hindered. In general, the Commission has been concerned with three main types of abusive behaviour: unfair pricing; refusal to supply; and abusive acquisitions and mergers.

Unfair pricing occurs when the prices charged by the company in the dominant position are excessive. Prices are excessive if they bear no relation to the economic value of the product supplied: *General Motors Continental NV* v *Commission* Case 26/75 [1975] ECR 1367. The Commission determines the fairness of prices in relation to the costs of production for the goods, the prices charged to consumers and the profits of the company. As a general principle, large profits margins prima facie indicate excessive pricing.

Unfair pricing also includes price discrimination where a company charges different prices to customers in order to take advantage of barriers existing in the market. Of course, a company is free to charge different prices where there are wide disparities in the volumes supplied. This is not the type of conduct that price discrimination is aimed at tackling. Instead, it is where a company charges different prices to broadly equivalent transactions with the effect of creating distortions in the market.

The Commission has aggressively pursued investigations into allegations of refusal to supply. Where a producer has a monopoly or duopoly position in the market, it often has the power to withhold goods in order to increase prices. A refusal to supply is also often damaging to those companies which use the product to manufacture a more refined product. Hence, the Commission is particularly suspicious of allegations of refusal to supply in markets for raw materials and commodities. The ECJ upheld this policy in *Istituto Chemisterapico Italiano SpA and Commercial Solvents Corporation* v *Commission* Cases 6 and 7/73 [1974] ECR 223.

However, not all refusals to supply are abusive. There may be legitimate reasons why a company cannot supply another. For example, in *BP* v *Commission* Case 77/77 [1978] ECR 1513, the ECJ held that BP's rationing of customers could be justified during periods of oil shortages.

Finally, a dominant position in the manufacturing or production of goods may also lead to abuse where one producer is able to absorb its competitors by way of acquisition or merger. For example, in *Tetra Pak Rausing SA* v *Commission (No 1)* Case T–51/89 [1990] ECR II–309, Tetra Pak was fined a record sum for engaging in predatory pricing as a means of forcing a competing company in the Italian market to allow itself to be acquired.

Acquisitions and mergers are, however, only abusive if the acquisition or merger was undertaken with an anti-competitive motive in mind. Because of this qualification, the Commission has now stepped back from many investigations into such activities, particularly since the adoption of the Merger Regulation which allows the Commission to investigate mergers notified in accordance with the Regulation.

QUESTION THREE

Diana Ltd is a British manufacturer of fashion clothes, which are mostly copies of designer originals but are much less expensive to produce and to buy and have a high turnover as a result. It contracts with Jacques SA, a French company, to distribute its clothes in France and in Italy.

Jacques SA also sells some of the designer originals which Diana Ltd copies, particularly those of the well-known fashion house of de Ribes, which has a 40 per cent share of the French fashion market. Jacques SA informs de Ribes of its contract with Diana Ltd and de Ribes writes to Jacques SA telling it that it will no longer be able to supply it with its latest lines as its prestigious reputation would be severely impaired by having its designs sold side by side with cheap copies. Jacques SA, however, decides to stand by the contract as it expects considerable benefits from it, even at the risk of losing some 'prestige business'. It asks Diana to look into the matter and to obtain advice as to how EC law might help it.

Diana's first shipment of clothes to Jacques SA is refused entry at the French port of Calais. The customs authority states that the goods are not allowed into France for two reasons:

a) French law requires the clothes to be inspected at the border for the presence of certain animal dyes, which, although permitted in Britain, are considered in France to be harmful to the human skin. An inspection fee is charged for this, which Diana refuses to pay.

b) The clothes are labelled 'Diana's designer garments'. Under French law, clothes cannot be sold under the label of 'designer garments' unless they are the product of one of ten registered designers.

Advise Diana Ltd as to the points of Community law involved and any rights and remedies it might have under European Community law.

University of London LLB Examination
(for External Students) European Community Law June 1995 Q4

General Comment

This question combines issues of Community competition law with the principles behind the free movement of goods (see Chapter 9). As long as this distinction is made at the outset, the answer is relatively straightforward.

Skeleton Solution

Article 82 EC – abuse of a dominant position – the concepts of dominance and abuse – determination of the relevant market and market share – application of the concept of abuse – refusal to supply – art 25 EC – charges equivalent to customs duties – art 28 EC – measures having equivalent effect to quantitative restrictions.

Suggested Solution

Breach of European competition law by de Ribes

The first legal problem raised by the facts presented concerns the refusal of de Ribes to supply Jacques SA with original garments from its collection. This refusal raises the question whether de Ribes has infringed art 82 EC, bearing in mind that it has a 40 per cent share of the French fashion market.

Article 82 EC prohibits all abuses of dominant positions within the Community where the commercial practice in question has an anti-competitive effect on trade between Member States. To assess whether de Ribes has a dominant position it is necessary to identify the relevant market for its products. This requires an examination of both the relevant product market and the relevant geographical market.

To identify the relevant product market it is necessary to isolate the product under investigation from similar products in the marketplace: see guidelines in Commission Notice 1997. For this purpose, the relevant product includes the actual product under consideration together with all other products which may be substituted, in terms of production and use, for the actual product. In this case, the relevant product is original designer clothes. The question is, however, whether copies of such clothes can be considered as substitutable products and therefore included within the ambit of the relevant product market.

The test for identifying substitutable products depends on whether or not there is a 'sufficient degree of interchangeability' between all the products forming part of the same market: *Hoffman-La Roche v Commission* Case 85/76 [1979] ECR 461. Where a product is interchangeable with the product under investigation, then that product too forms part of the relevant market. It is, however, unlikely that copies also form part of the relevant market. Although the objective physical characteristics of the designer garments are similar to copies, the quality of the products will be greatly dissimilar and the designer garments will more than likely bear a trademark or label which is protected under French intellectual property law. In addition, the price differential between the two types of garments will effectively exclude their substitutability. Hence, the relevant product market is likely to be confined to original designer garments.

Turning next to the relevant geographical market, this is defined as the area within the Community 'where the conditions are sufficiently homogeneous for the effects of economic power of the undertaking concerned to be evaluated': *United Brands & United Brands Continental BV v Commission* Case 27/76 [1978] ECR 207. The geographical market will be the whole Community, unless there are factual reasons for limiting the area to a lesser size while still satisfying the criterion laid down in art 82 EC of being 'a substantial part' of the Community.

Factors generally relied on to limit the geographical scope of the relevant geographical market include impediments to cross-border trade such as physical, technological, legal or cultural barriers to trade, as well as any inability to extend distribution or supply networks to certain areas. It is difficult to evaluate whether the relevant geographical market in this particular case is the whole of the Community or a smaller portion. Obviously the larger the geographical market the smaller share of the market held by de Ribes. On the other hand, if the relevant geographical market is France, de Ribes has a high enough market share – 40 per cent – to be considered dominant: *United Brands*.

If de Ribes has a dominant position, the next issue to consider is whether it has abused that position. De Ribes has refused to supply its garments to Jacques SA on the ground that it wishes to protect its reputation. As a general principle, refusal to supply is a flagrant abuse of a dominant position. Producers cannot use their positions within particular markets to impose unreasonable terms and conditions of sale on customers. Dominant companies may only refuse to supply customers where there is an objectively justifiable reason for such refusal. Where an order is made in the ordinary course of trade and can be easily satisfied, a dominant company cannot flex its economic muscle to withdraw its goods from potential customers: *Hilti AG v Commission* Case T–30/89 [1991] ECR II–1439.

If de Ribes wishes to avoid the charge of unlawfully refusing to supply, it must provide an objective and justifiable rationale for its behaviour. Only if de Ribes can establish that its reputation and economic prosperity would be threatened by continuing to supply Jacques SA would it be able to avoid the charge of abusive behaviour contrary to art 82 EC.

In the event that de Ribes is guilty of abusing its position, Jacques SA has two courses of action open to it. First, it could complaint to the European Commission alleging that de Ribes is engaging in abusive behaviour. The Commission would then investigate the matter and, if necessary, fine de Ribes for its unlawful practices. The Commission is empowered to impose fines of up to 10 per cent of the annual turnover of a company found to have violated European competition law: art 15 of Council Regulation 17/62 and Commission Notice 1998 on the setting of fine levels.

Second, Jacques SA could initiate proceedings in the French courts. Article 82 EC has direct effect and national courts are obliged to enforce the obligations contained in that provision. The abuses perpetrated by de Ribes constitute a breach of the obligations imposed in art 82 EC not to abuse a dominant position. If Jacques SA can establish that injury has been caused, it will have a claim in damages against de Ribes which can be prosecuted in the French courts.

The French legislation and the principle of the free movement of goods

The first French law requires the clothes to be inspected at the French border for the presence of allegedly harmful animal dyes and an inspection fee is payable by Diana Ltd for this service. Article 25 EC expressly prohibits the introduction of any customs duties, or charges having equivalent effect to customs duties, on imports and exports coming and going from different Member States. This provision has been given direct effect on numerous occasions by the European Court (ECJ) and may be founded upon by Diana in the French courts without reference to the ECJ.

Charges having equivalent effect to customs duties have been defined by the ECJ as any pecuniary charge, whatever its designation and mode of application, which is imposed unilaterally on goods by reason of the fact that they cross a frontier, and is not a customs duty in the strict sense: *Commission v Italy (Re Statistical Levy)* Case 24/68 [1969] ECR 193. A charge imposed on importation which has the effect of discriminating between domestic goods and similar goods of Community origin, and which cannot be justified by provisions in the EC Treaty, will therefore amount to a charge having equivalent effect.

Charges having equivalent effect can only be justified in three circumstances: if the charges relate to a general system of internal levies applied systematically within a Member State and without discrimination; if the charges constitute payment for a service in fact rendered and are in proportion to the costs of receiving that service; and if the charges are levied under the authority of a Community measure harmonising customs procedures: *Commission v Germany (Re Animals Inspection Fees)* Case 18/87 [1988] ECR 5427.

According to the facts presented, French law requires testing of the garments only on importation. It is unlikely that such tests are carried out on French-produced garments and therefore there is a presumption that such charges are unlawful under Community law. Although the charge was for a service actually rendered, in the event that the charge was disproportionate to the service provided, the charge will be illegal:

Commission v *Denmark* Case 158/82 [1983] ECR 3573. Further, no direct benefit accrued to either Diana or Jacques SA by virtue of the testing. Community law requires that the importer receives some benefit from service, which has not happened in this case: *Commission* v *Italy (Re Statistical Levy)* Case 24/68 [1969] ECR 193. Obviously, a direct benefit will not accrue to an importer if the charges are made in the interests of the inspecting State.

In the circumstances presented, it is unlikely that the French customs authorities would be allowed to impose such a charge and impede the importation of the garments. The measure is clearly discriminatory and has little basis if French garment manufacturers are not subject to a similar testing system.

The second French law concerns the labelling of particular types of garments and restrictions on the use of that labelling to products from one of ten registered designers. Article 28 EC prohibits all measures having an equivalent effect to quantitative restrictions and this concept has been defined as including 'all trading rules enacted by Member States which are capable of hindering directly or indirectly, actually or potentially, intra-Community trade': *Procureur du Roi* v *Dassonville* Case 8/74 [1974] ECR 837.

Quite clearly, the French restrictions on the use of this type of label are trading rules within the scope of art 28 EC are therefore prohibited if they are: without objective economic justification; disproportionate to the objective sought to be achieved; and discriminatory in character.

The French government would have to justify the French law as being a mandatory requirement necessary to protect the interests of consumers: *Rewe-Zentrale AG* v *Bundesmonopolverwaltung für Branntwein (Cassis De Dijon)* Case 120/78 [1979] ECR 649. In the circumstances of the facts presented, this is unlikely. Instead, it is more likely that the law facilitates the creation of a cartel among the principal French garment manufacturers. The fact that non-French producers cannot access this group is itself evidence of discrimination. Further, since the consequence of this law is the exclusion of non-French producers, the effects of the law are wholly disproportionate to the objective sought to be achieved.

Diana should be advised that both infractions of Community law can be referred to the attention of the European Commission for investigation. If the Commission fails to act on the complaint, Diana and Jacques would be entitled to initiate proceedings in the French courts against the French government for failing to comply with the obligations established under Community. If they can establish that they have been injured as a consequence of this breach, then damages may also be claimed: *Brasserie du Pêcheur SA* v *Federal Republic of Germany; R* v *Secretary of State for Transport, ex parte Factortame Ltd* Joined Cases C–46 and 48/93 [1996] ECR I–1029.

QUESTION FOUR

Rodhot, a German heating firm, has 90 per cent of the German market and 25 per cent of the market in the whole of the EU for environmentally friendly heaters. Its market share for the heater market in general is 20 per cent in Germany and 1 per cent in the EU.

Rodhot issues instructions to all its subsidiaries, which are also sole distributors of their products, not to sell their product to Blauhot in Holland and Bleuchaud in France and Belgium who are big exporters to other countries, mainly within the EU, where they offer Rodhot heaters at discounted prices, sometimes at as much as 20 per cent below Rodhot's own prices.

Do Blauhot and Bleuchaud have any redress under Community law against Rodhot?

University of London LLB Examination
(for External Students) European Community Law June 2000 Q8

General Comment

This problem question required the application of the law on competition under arts 81 and 82 EC. Some papers attempted to apply the free movement of goods and art 28 EC. This was of no relevance, particularly since art 28 EC only prohibits Member States from certain action.

Skeleton Solution

Complain to the Commission – Council Regulation 17/62 – power of investigation – art 81 EC – undertakings – agreement, decision, concerted practice – vertical agreement – effect on inter-State trade: *Consten and Grundig* – de minimus rule – exemption – art 82 EC: abuse of a dominant position – define RPM and RGM – factors indicating dominance, eg market share – abuse – powers of sanction.

Suggested Solution

Blauhot and Bleuchaud have two courses of action open to them for an alleged breach of EC competition law: lodge a complaint with the Commission (a preliminary step towards an investigation) or initiate legal proceedings in their national courts. The advantage of complaining to the Commission is that the parties will not incur legal expenses. The disadvantages are, first, that there is no guarantee that the Commission will investigate the complaint since it does so at its own discretion: *Star Fruit Co SA v Commission* Case 247/87 [1989] ECR 291. Second, even if an infringement is found, there is no automatic right to be awarded damages. Alternatively, they may proceed by way of their national courts, since arts 81 and 82 EC have direct effect. Whilst this procedure is perhaps more likely to secure the companies damages to compensate for any injury suffered, such proceedings can be very costly and protracted.

If the companies complain to the Commission, it must at least consider the issues in a careful and diligent way or it could be subject to art 232 EC proceedings: *Demo-Studio Schmidt* v *Commission* Case 210/81 [1983] ECR 3045. If it refuses to initiate an investigation it must provide reasons: *GEMA* v *Commission* Case 125/75 [1979] ECR 3173. The companies could then appeal to the Court of First Instance against the decision not to investigate.

The Commission has investigative powers under Council Regulation 17/62. It may: obtain information from the companies involved; conduct an inspection; and convene hearings. The Commission also has inherent power to grant interim relief to Blauhot and Bleuchaud if: the practices complained of are prima facie likely to infringe competition law; urgency is proven; and there is a need to avoid serious and irreparable damage to the companies: *La Cinq* v *Commission* Case T–44/90 [1992] ECR II–1.

The investigation may establish that there has been a breach of arts 81 and/or 82 EC. Article 81 EC prohibits agreements, decisions and concerted practices between undertakings that have the object or effect of preventing, restricting or distorting competition in the Community. Article 82 EC prohibits the abuse of a dominant position. In both cases the parties involved must be undertakings, broadly defined to include, according to *Mannesman* v *High Authority* Case 8/61 [1962] ECR 357, all natural and legal persons engaged in commercial or economic activities.

Articles 81 and 82 EC may be applied to the same parties for the same behaviour; however, the Commission cannot simply restate the same facts to justify simultaneous investigation: *Società Italiana Vetro* v *Commission (Re Italian Flat Glass Suppliers)* Cases T–68, 77 and 78/89 [1992] 5 CMLR 302.

Article 81 EC

This provision applies to situations involving two or more parties and may therefore be applied to Rodhot and its subsidiaries if they are legally distinct. If they are not, then the agreement will not come within art 81 EC, but there may be an abuse of a dominant position contrary to art 82 EC.

Article 81 EC extends to all agreements, decisions and concerted practices. An agreement has been broadly defined to include all binding and non-binding contracts, whether verbal or written. Unrecorded understandings, the adoption of common rules and gentlemen's agreements are also agreements within art 81 EC: *ACF Chemiefarma NV* v *Commission* Cases 41, 44 and 45/69 [1970] ECR 661. There is a potential vertical agreement in operation between Rodhot and its subsidiaries for exclusive distribution of the heaters.

To breach art 81 EC the agreement must affect trade between two or more Member States. In *Société Technique Minière* v *Maschinenbau Ulm GmbH* Case 56/65 [1966] ECR 235 the Court held that this would occur if the agreement had a direct or indirect, actual or potential, effect on trade between Member States. Hence it is not necessary for the agreement to actually affect trade in heaters, only that it may.

According to the ECJ in *Delimitis* v *Henninger Braü AG* Case C–234/89 [1992] 5 CMLR

210 there are two steps to identifying whether there is the necessary effect. The first step is to ascertain the relevant product market (RPM), which in this case may be environmentally friendly heaters if that is the only product Rodhot manufactures and to which the instructions apply; the problem is unclear on this point. Alternatively the RPM may be heaters in general, particularly if the company produces different types and the instructions apply to all their products. The second step is to identify the relevant geographical market (RGM). It can then be established whether there is the necessary effect.

This agreement is similar to that in *Consten and Grundig v Commission* Cases 56 and 58/64 [1966] ECR 299 where Consten, a French company, agreed to act as the sole distributor of the German company Grundig's products in France. Grundig agreed to not sell to any other French firm or let dealers in other States export to France. However, another French firm bought Grundig's products from a German distributor and imported them into France. The Commission, as upheld by the ECJ, concluded that the aim of the agreement was to isolate the French market with the object of preventing parallel imports. There was subsequently an effect on inter-State trade and it was irrelevant whether that was a detrimental or positive effect. The instructions issued by Rodhot will prevent parallel imports of heaters in those Member States to which Blauhot and Bleuchaud export.

The agreement will have to have an appreciable effect, since a de minimus rule applies; the effect of the agreement must be above a certain level or there will not be a breach of art 81 EC. According to the De Minimus Notice 1997 vertical agreements, such as this one, need to affect more than 10 per cent of the market. However, the Notice also contains a 'black list' of clauses that will not be tolerated. In the case of vertical agreements this includes the fixing of resale prices, which is what Rodhot is potentially attempting to do by preventing Blauhot and Bleuchaud from selling their product at 20 per cent less than they would want to.

If the agreement does fall within the prohibition in art 81(1) EC, it will be automatically void under art 81(2) EC, although a doctrine of severance may apply. Blauhot and Bleuchaud should be warned that Rodhot may be able to acquire exemption on an individual basis under the conditions set out in art 81(3) EC. Alternatively they may be eligible for block exemption particularly under Commission Regulation 1983/83 on exclusive distribution agreements (valid until 31st May 2000); or may receive a non-legally binding comfort letter.

Article 82 EC

Article 82 EC prohibits the abuse of a dominant position and may apply to this situation if Rodhot and its subsidiaries are part of the same corporate group or economic unit in a dominant position. Such a position does not constitute a per se breach of art 82 EC; the prohibition is on abusing that position.

Having established that the party is an undertaking, it is necessary to identify the relevant market in which the alleged dominant position exists. Failure to do this may render any decision of the Commission susceptible to annulment by the Court, as occurred in *Europemballage Corporation and Continental Can Co Inc* v *Commission* Case 6/72 [1973] ECR 215. This is achieved by identifying the relevant product and geographical markets.

A 1997 Notice defines the RPM as one in which the consumer regards products as reasonably interchangeable or substitutable because of their characteristics, price, and intended use. This may be a complex process, as witnessed in cases such as *Michelin* v *Commission* Case 322/81 [1983] ECR 3461 (where car/van tyres and those for heavy vehicles were distinct RPMs) and *Hilti AG* v *Commission* Case T–30/89 [1991] ECR II–1439 (where nail guns and nail cartridge strips were also concluded to be distinct RPMs). In terms of cross-elasticity, the question is whether the customer would choose a different product if the price of the product in question increased; if they would then the RPM includes those other products, and if they would not then the RPM is solely the product in question. Hence, in *United Brands & United Brands Continental BV* v *Commission* Case 27/76 [1978] ECR 207 it was concluded that bananas were the RPM, since certain consumers such as the old, sick and young would not switch to another fruit because of the special characteristics of bananas. Similarly, in *Tetra Pak Rausing SA* v *Commission (No 1)* Case T–51/89 [1990] ECR II–309 cartons for fresh milk and UHT milk were distinct RPMs because consumers would not switch between them due to their different tastes.

In practice the Commission and Court will define the RPM as narrow as possible, resulting in a greater possibility of finding a dominant position. Hence, the RPM in this case may be environmentally friendly heaters, particularly if consumers do not consider them interchangeable with other types of heater because of this particular characteristic.

The RGM is the area within the Community in which the practice produces its effects. For the purposes of art 82 EC this must be the common market or a substantial part of it. According to *Hilti AG* v *Commission* Case T–30/89 [1991] ECR II–1439, this will be the entire Community if the product is regularly bought and sold in all Member States, as appears to be the case here. Once the RPM and RGM have been identified, the Commission will assess whether the undertaking has a dominant position.

The Court in *United Brands* (above) defined a dominant position as one that permits an undertaking to enjoy a position of economic strength, preventing effective competition by behaving independently of its competitors, customers and its consumers. The first step in finding such a position is to identify the market share held by the undertaking. If the RPM is environmentally friendly heaters, the market share held by Rodhot is 25 per cent in the EU. This may constitute a dominant position if the remainder of the market is highly fragmented: *United Brands*. Alternatively, other factors may be considered to assess whether they, combined with the market share, indicate a dominant position. These factors include, according to *Hoffman-La Roche & Co AG* v *Commission* Case 85/76 [1979] ECR 461: the market share of competitors; financial and technological resources; the absence of potential competitors; the conduct and performance of Rodhot; and control of production and distribution. The facts only indicate that in terms of production and distribution Rodhot has a well developed sales network, as was the case in *Hoffman-La Roche*.

Finally, art 82 EC requires there to an abuse of the dominant position. This is not defined in the EC Treaty, but the Court in *Hoffman* concluded that it would be behaviour hindering the maintenance of competition in the market; it will influence the structure of the market and weaken or hinder competition. There are two broad categories of abuse: exploitative and anti-competitive abuses. The former occurs where the dominant undertaking takes advantage of its position often by imposing unfair conditions, such as unfair prices. An exploitative abuse will generally affect consumers in an unfair way. An anti-competitive abuse is one that is not necessarily unfair to consumers, but will reduce or eliminate competition within the relevant market. A refusal to supply, as in this case, has been held to constitute both types of abuse: *United Brands & United Brands Continental BV v Commission* Case 27/76 [1978] ECR 207 and *Istituto Chemisterapico Italiano SpA and Commercial Solvents Corporation v Commission* Cases 6 and 7/73 [1974] ECR 223. This refusal to supply may be exploitative in that it is in reaction to the sale of the product at 20 per cent less than Rodhot's prices, resulting in the consumer having to pay the higher price. It may also be anti-competitive in that it eliminates the ability of Blauhot and Bleuchaud to compete in the sale of the product.

Finally, should the Commission find that there is a breach of competition law they may, under art 15 of Council Regulation 17/62, fine the offending undertaking(s). The maximum level of the fine will be Euro 1 million or 10 per cent of the annual global turnover, whichever is the greatest. There may be an appeal against any decision and the level of any fine, but undertakings should note that they are liable for any interest in the interim period: *AEG Telefunken AG v Commission* Case 107/82 [1983] ECR 3151.

Chapter 12

The External Relations of the European Community

12.1 Introduction

12.2 Key points

12.3 Key cases and materials

12.4 Questions and suggested solutions

12.1 Introduction

The Member States of the European Community have transferred considerable external sovereignty to the Community for the purpose of conducting economic and commercial relationships with non-Community states. The European Community, on behalf of the individual Member States, negotiates trade and economic agreements with third countries and administers the various trade protection mechanisms to protect industry within the Community from unfair foreign competition. The European Commission and the Council of Ministers are the bodies responsible for the conduct of the Community's external affairs. Authority to exercise powers to regulate external affairs is vested in the Community by virtue of Common Commercial Policy (CCP) provisions of the EC Treaty.

12.2 Key points

The international legal personality of the European Community

The European Community has limited international personality and has entered a substantial number of bilateral and multilateral agreements with third states. In addition, the Community participates in a number of international organisations, including the World Trade Organisation.

Article 281 EC expressly declares that '[t]he Community shall have legal personality'; see also art 75 ECSC Treaty and art 101 EURATOM Treaty.

Types of international agreements entered into by the Community

Express capacity to enter international agreements is granted under arts 133 and 310 EC. In addition, art 300 EC specifies the procedure for the negotiation of such agreements. The Commission is empowered as the main 'negotiator', although it is the Council that will conclude any agreement on the basis of the Commission's proposals. The Parliament will also have to be consulted. The nature of the subject matter will determine the basic procedures to be applied in any particular case, such as the voting requirements and level of Parliamentary involvement. Agreements between the Community and third states may be classified according to form and content into four groups:

a) multilateral trade agreements, primarily negotiated within the context of the General Agreement on Tariffs and Trade (GATT)/World Trade Organisation (WTO);

b) bilateral free trade agreements;

c) association agreements, which are usually concluded with states about to become Members of the Community; and

d) development and assistance agreements with developing states.

These agreements vary, in both content and legal structure, according to the relationship which is to be regulated by a particular agreement.

Capacity of the European Community to enter into international obligations

The Community does not exercise unlimited capacity to enter into international agreements on behalf of its Member States. Where the subject matter of an agreement is unrelated to the objectives and purpose of the Community, the Community has no competence to act. Unfortunately, the distinction between those subjects which concern the Community under the terms of the three Community treaties and other issues of international concern is not clear cut. Often an international agreement will regulate issues of Community concern as well as unrelated issues: for example the United Nations Convention on the Law of the Sea 1982.

If the subject matter of an international agreement falls completely within the competence of the Community, the Community has exclusive capacity to negotiate the agreement and the individual Member States have no authority to negotiate. Such agreements are known as 'Community Agreements'.

Where an international agreement contains provisions relating to matters within the competence of the Community, and also issues which fall outside the scope of the Community treaties, both the Member States and the Community participate in the negotiating process and ratify the final agreement. Such agreements are known as 'mixed agreements'. For example in *Advisory Opinion on the WTO Agreement* Opinion 1/94 [1994] ECR I–5267, the European Court confirmed that the Community had exclusive competence to conclude the WTO agreements concerning trade in goods but shared competence with Member States in two other sectors. Since the Community did not have exclusive competence over all the matters contained in the agreement, a mixed agreement was required and the Member States also ratified the terms of the agreement. It should be noted that the Treaty of Amsterdam modified art 133 EC so that the Community's competence now covers some of those areas that were previously excluded.

The Member States of the Community may be parties to international treaties, in their own right, concerning matters not related to the Community. Even though all the Member States participate in such agreements, if the subject matter bears no relation to issues of Community concern, the obligations are assumed by the Member States alone. These agreements are known as 'International Agreements Assumed by the Member States'. An example of such an agreement is the European Convention on Human Rights 1950 which, despite participation by all Community Member States, is not an agreement of Community concern.

Community agreements

The Community has express capacity to enter into two forms of international agreements without the participation of the Member States in the negotiating process.

a) Article 133 EC authorises the Community to enter into commercial agreements relating to tariff and trade matters for the purpose of achieving the objectives of the Common Commercial Policy. This authority expressly extends to export aids, credit and finance, and matters relating to multilateral commodity agreements.

b) Article 310 EC authorises the Community to negotiate with third states, unions of states or international organisations, association agreements creating reciprocal rights and obligations, and facilitating common action through special procedures.

While the capacity to enter association agreements under art 310 EC is relatively defined, the exercise of power under art 133 EC has a potentially greater application since no explicit parameters have been set in relation to its application.

In order to define the scope of the Community's power under art 133 EC, the European Commission has sought a number of opinions from the European Court. In *Commission v Council (Re ERTA)* Case 22/70 [1971] ECR 263, the Court held that authority to enter international agreements not only arose from the express provisions, but also provisions of the EC Treaty which require the negotiation of international agreements for their achievement. As a result, the Court decided that:

> '... the Community enjoys the capacity to establish contractual links with third countries over the whole field of objectives defined in Part One (arts 1 to 16) of the [EC] Treaty.'

The rationale for extending the competence of the Community was the need for the Community to assume and carry out contractual obligations towards third states affecting the whole sphere of the application of the Community legal system.

This decision, along with a number of subsequent judgments of the Court (such as *Kramer* Cases 3, 4 and 6/76 [1976] ECR 1279 and *Opinion 1/76 on the Draft Agreement Establishing a Laying-up Fund for Inland Waterway Vessels* Opinion 1/76 [1977] ECR 741), established the doctrine of implied powers. These implied powers supplement the express powers of the Community to enter into international agreements. Whether an agreement with a third state in negotiated by the Community on the basis of an express power or an implied power makes no difference to its status as a 'Community Agreement'.

Mixed agreements

Since Member States have not conferred upon the Community their absolute sovereignty to negotiate treaties and in fact continue to exercise those powers not transferred to the Community, a conflict may arise where an international agreement contains provisions which fall within the competence of both the Community and the individual Member States. Implementation of such agreements requires joint action and such agreements are concluded simultaneously by the Community and the Member States.

In these mixed agreements, each party acts in its own name, undertaking to perform the obligations which fall within its competence. Mixed agreements may be concluded by the Community, acting with the participation of the Member States, under either art 133 EC or art 310 EC.

Mixed agreements have been used extensively to implement the numerous treaties between the Community and developing countries, namely Yaounde I (1964), Yaounde II (1969), Lomé I (1975), Lomé II (1979), Lomé III (1984) and Lomé IV (1989).

International obligations assumed by the Member States

The Member States of the Community were parties to a number of international agreements prior to the conclusion of the treaties forming the Community, including the European Convention on Human Rights 1950 and the WTO Agreement.

The Community is deemed to succeed to treaties concluded before the Community Treaties only if they contain matters within the competence of the Community. In one case relating to the status of the GATT in Community law, the Court declared that:

> '... in so far as under the EC Treaty the Community has assumed the powers previously exercised by the Member States in the area governed by the GATT, the provisions of that agreement have the effect of binding the Community.' (*International Fruit Company* v *Produktschap voor Groenten en Fruit* Cases 51 and 54/71 [1972] ECR 1219.)

Treaties concluded after the Community treaties by the Member States on subjects within the competence of the Community are probably void, although in practice this is an unlikely eventuality because of the propensity of the Community to participate in all agreements that might conceivably relate to its affairs.

Incorporation of treaties into European Community law

The EC Treaty itself does not specify the status and effect of international agreements within the Community legal order, nor does it identify the means through which such obligations are incorporated into Community law. Although the practice of the Council is to enact a decision or a regulation to approve an agreement, it appears that the actual instrument of approval itself is not the source of authority for an agreement in Community law. Rather, an international agreement concluded by the Community, by its mere conclusion and approval by the Council, and subsequent publication in the Community Official Journal, is incorporated into Community law: *Haegeman* v *Belgian State* Case 181/73 [1973] ECR 125.

Effect of treaties in Community law

Treaties concluded by the Community exercising its express or implied treaty-making powers are 'binding on the institutions of the Community and the Member States' by virtue of art 300 EC.

Community treaties form an integral element of Community law and have been given direct effect by the European Court. In other words, individuals may rely upon the terms of treaties negotiated by the Community. In order to have direct effect, a particular provision of a Treaty must satisfy two main criteria:

a) an individual may only rely on such a provision if it is 'capable of creating rights of which interested parties may avail themselves in a court of law': *International Fruit Company* v *Produktschap voor Groeten en Fruit* Cases 51 and 54/71 [1972] ECR 1219; and

b) in order to ascertain whether a Community agreement confers rights upon individuals, regard must be had to the 'purpose and nature of the agreement itself' to determine if the provision in question 'contains a clear and precise obligation which is not subject, in its implementation or effects, to the adoption of any subsequent measure': *Demirel* v *Stadt Schwabisch GmbH* Case 12/86 [1987] ECR 3719.

If these conditions are satisfied, then direct effect may be given to the terms of a Community agreement: *Hauptzollamt Mainz* v *Kupferberg* Case 104/81 [1982] ECR 3641.

The contents and effect of the Common Commercial Policy

The Community Common Commercial Policy (CCP) is founded on the uniform application of principles relating to tariff rates, the conclusion of tariff and trade agreements, the attainment of uniformity in measures of trade liberalisation, the formulation of a consistent export policy and the adoption of measures to protect against unfair trade practices: art 133(1) EC.

The process for the formulation of the CCP is similar to the normal decision-making procedures within the Community. The European Commission drafts proposals after consultations with interested parties, or third states in the case of negotiating agreements. These proposals are submitted to the Council of Ministers, which must adopt proposals by a qualified majority: art 205 EC. The Council has authority to enact regulations, directives and decisions in the pursuit of the Common Commercial Policy.

The creation of the CCP was a primary goal of the EC Treaty. The Treaty confers exclusive authority to formulate trade policy to the Community institutions and consequently Member States no longer retain authority to act in matters where the Community has adopted measures in pursuit of the CCP: *Donkerwolke* v *Procureur de la République* Case 41/76 [1976] ECR 1921. The practical effect of this is that Member States cannot legislate in fields covered by Community measures or enter into international obligations that could restrict the powers of the Community.

The date for the completion of the CCP's transition period has expired, but Member States have expressed a continued reluctance to transfer complete authority to the Community. Hence there is no comprehensive, coherent commercial policy, but a complex framework of international agreements and Community measures. In those areas of policy not yet covered under Community measures, the Member States may continue to act: *Bulk Oil* v *Sun International* [1986] 2 All ER 744. In addition, this failure to enact Community measures to cover all aspects of the CCP has left loopholes that may be lawfully used by Member States to restrict, prohibit and limit imports from non-EC countries: *Tezi Textiel* v *Commission* Case 59/84 [1986] ECR 887.

European Community trade protection laws

The Community has a number of powers to impose measures on imports from third countries in order to protect industry and commerce within the Community from unfair foreign trade practices. These measures may be classified into four categories: anti-dumping measures; countervailing (or anti-subsidy) measures; safeguard measures; and measures under the Trade Barrier Regulation.

Anti-dumping actions

The Community authorities are entitled to impose anti-dumping duties on foreign products which are deemed to have been 'dumped' within the Community and which have caused injury to a Community industry: Council Regulation 384/96. A foreign product has been 'dumped' inside the Community if it has been introduced into the internal market at a price less than the comparable price for the identical product in the country of manufacture.

In addition to establishing the existence of dumped products, it is also necessary under the Regulation to prove that the products have caused material injury to an industry within the Community, and that the interests of the Community require such intervention. No list of 'Community interests' is provided in the Regulation, and the concept covers a broad range of factors, such as protection of the consumer, foreign investment and employment. If the necessary elements are present, the imported product may be subject to anti-dumping duties, which are assessed on each product according to its country of origin.

Protection against dumped products is the most common form of trade protection measure employed by the European Community.

Countervailing duty (or anti-subsidy) actions

Countervailing duties are imposed by the Community on foreign products that have benefited from subsidies from foreign governments during their manufacture, distribution or export, if such products cause injury to Community industries producing similar goods. Such duties are infrequently imposed by the Community on foreign products. The authority under which the Community imposes countervailing duties is contained in Council Regulation 2026/97.

Safeguard actions

Imports into the Community from third countries may also be subject to safeguard measures under the relevant provisions of Council Regulation 3285/94. If foreign products are being imported into the Community in such increased quantities as to cause, or threaten to cause, serious injury to a Community industry, safeguard measures may be imposed to protect the Community industry, regardless of the cause or source of the increase in the volume of imports.

If the existence of increased imports can be established, and if such imports cause serious injury, the Community may impose additional duties, tariffs or quotas on the importation of such products to protect the Community industry.

The Trade Barrier Regulation (TBR)

The European Commission is empowered to investigate allegations of obstacles to trade erected by non-EC countries under the Trade Barrier Regulation (TBR) 3286/94. EC companies or industries may lodge a complaint with the Commission requesting the examination of foreign trade practices which impede EC exports. If these allegations are found to be true, and if the complainant can show injury, the Commission is required to enter into discussions with the third state with a view to removing the obstacle to trade. If a negotiated settlement proves ineffective, the matter may be brought to the attention of the WTO dispute settlement body for resolution.

12.3 Key cases and materials

*   *Commission v Council (Re ERTA)* Case 22/70 [1971] ECR 263
    Development by the Court of the doctrine of the implied powers of the Community

*   *Demirel v Stadt Schwabisch GmbH* Case 12/86 [1987] ECR 3719
    The direct effect of the EC-Turkey association agreement

*   *Hauptzollamt Mainz v Kupferberg* Case 104/81 [1982] ECR 3641
    A decision relating to the direct effect of treaties negotiated by the Community within the Community legal system

- *International Fruit Company* v *Produktschap voor Groenten en Fruit* Cases 51 and 54/71 [1972] ECR 1219
  The direct effect of treaties negotiated by the Member States prior to the adopting of the three founding Community treaties

- *Polydor* v *Harlequin Record Shops* Case 270/80 [1982] ECR 329
  The effect of free trade agreements between the Community and third states in Community law

- EC Treaty

  - arts 133 and 310 – provide the EC with the capacity to enter into various international agreements

  - art 281 – the Community is declared to have legal personality

  - art 300 – the procedure for the negotiation of international agreements, which in turn are binding on Community institutions and Member States

- Council Regulation 384/96 – provides authority to impose anti-dumping duties on foreign products deemed to have been 'dumped' within the Community and which have caused injury to a Community industry

- Council Regulation 2026/97 – authority to impose countervailing duties on foreign products in specified circumstances

- Council Regulation 3285/94 – authority to impose safeguard measures on foreign products in specified circumstances

- Trade Barrier Regulation 3286/94 – authorises Commission to investigate allegations of obstacles to trade by non-EC countries

12.4 Questions and suggested solutions

QUESTION ONE

What role has the Court of Justice played in defining the extent of the Community's powers in the external relations field?

Written by the Editor

General Comment

A general question on the function of the European Court in determining the scope of the external competence of the Community.

Skeleton Solution

Express powers of the Community to negotiate treaties – implied powers imputed by the Court – development of the doctrine through the jurisprudence of the Court.

Suggested Solution

The Community has capacity to enter international agreements between itself and third states without the participation of the Member States in the negotiating processes. Express treaty-making capacity is conferred in the EC Treaty for two particular forms of agreement.

Article 133 EC authorises the Community to conclude commercial agreements relating to tariff and trade matters for the purposes of achieving the objectives of the common commercial policy. This authority expressly extends to export aids, credit and finance, and matters relating to multilateral commodity agreements.

Article 310 EC also authorises the Community to negotiate with third states, unions of states or international organisations, association agreements creating reciprocal rights and obligations, and facilitating common action through special procedures. Association agreements perform two functions. In the case of certain European countries the purpose of this form of agreement is to act as a preliminary procedure prior to membership of the Community. Other association agreements establish free trade status between the products of the Community and the third state in each others markets.

Agreements under art 310 EC are supplemented by a special form of association agreement which provide for agreements between the Community and overseas countries and territories. These territories are listed in Annex IV to the Treaty and were originally dependencies of the Member States. The purpose of such agreements is to promote the economic and social development of these territories by establishing 'close economic relations' between the Community and the territory.

The exercise of power under art 133 EC has a potentially greater application. Two developments have significantly expanded the powers of the Community under art 133 EC to the exclusion of the participation of the Member States: the development of a broad interpretation by the Court of the concept of the Common Commercial Policy (CCP); and the creation, also by the Court, of the 'theory of parallelism'.

The intention of the European Court to interpret the concept of the CCP in broad terms was made clear in an advisory opinion on a reference by the Commission under art 300 EC. The case concerned the participation of the Community in the negotiation of an international commodity agreement to regulate the supply of rubber. The Court stressed that a coherent common commercial policy would not be feasible if the Community was unable to exercise its treaty-making powers in relation to those international agreements which, alongside traditional commercial agreements, form an important element of the international economic environment. A broad interpretation of this provision was supported by the fact that the enumeration of the individual subjects covered by the article was conceived in a non-exhaustive fashion.

However, at the same time the Court believed that an important factor in deciding whether the Community had exclusive competence in this matter was the financial burden of participating in an agreement. In the case of a commodity agreement, if the burden of financing the agreement is placed on the Community budget, the Community has exclusive jurisdiction. Alternatively, if the charges are to be borne directly by the Member States, this factor implies the participation of the Member States in the negotiation of the agreement. The effect of this decision was in fact to expand the concept of the CCP itself, and also, in turn, the powers of the Community.

While the above confirms that the Community has express authority to achieve those objectives specified for the achievement of the common commercial policy, the European Court has gone much further in developing the theory of implied powers, not only for the purposes of achieving a common commercial policy, but in fact to attain the objectives set out in Part 1 of the EC Treaty. This has been achieved by the development of the theory of parallelism by the Court which was originally elaborated *Commission* v *Council (Re ERTA)* Case 22/70 [1971] ECR 263.

In 1967 the Member States entered into negotiations with other European states to establish a European Road Transport Agreement. During these negotiations, the Council enacted a regulation which covered substantially the same subject matter, but the Member States, anxious to include third states within the scope of the agreement continued negotiations on the subject. In 1970 the Council decided that negotiations would continue on an individual Member State basis without the participation of the Commission in the process. The Commission objected to this situation and brought an action before the European Court to annul the Council resolution deciding to conduct the negotiations on a Member State basis.

The Court held that authority to enter international agreements not only arose from those provisions which granted express authority, but also from other provisions of the Treaty which require international agreement for their achievement. In particular, each time the Community adopts legislation for the purpose of implementing a common policy envisaged by the Treaty, the Member States no longer have the right, acting individually or even collectively, to undertake obligations with third countries which would affect those rules. The doctrine of parallelism therefore requires that if the Community exercises an internal power, it simultaneously acquires a parallel external power to government the subject matter.

In other words, the exercise of the internal capacity of the Community over a particular subject matter deprives the Member States of individual authority to regulate the matter by international agreement. The basis for this determination was the need for the Community to assume and carry out contractual obligations towards third states affecting the whole sphere of the application of the Community legal system. This rationale was later confirmed in *Hauptzollamt Mainz* v *Kupferberg* Case 104/81 [1982] ECR 3641.

One qualification was, in fact, made to the functioning of the theory of parallelism under the EC Treaty. The mere existence of internal legislative competence within the scheme of the Treaty was not ipso facto conclusive of the inability of the Member States to conclude international agreements bearing on such matters. Not only must legislative competence exist, but this power must be exercised by the Community: *Kramer* Cases 3, 4 and 6/76 [1976] ECR 1279. This restriction stems from the construction given by the Court to the rationale behind the theory – the desirability of avoiding conflicts between internal Community legislative and the international obligations of the Member States.

The Court has elaborated upon the doctrine of parallelism in a number of subsequent cases, one of the most significant being the *North-East Atlantic Fisheries Convention Case* [1975] ECR 1363. Seven of the nine Member States entered into a convention to conserve fishing stocks in the North-East Atlantic and the Netherlands promulgated legislation implementing the provisions of the convention which provided inter alia for criminal prosecutions. A number of Dutch fishermen were prosecuted in a Dutch court for violating this statute. In their defence, the fishermen alleged that the Member States had no authority to enter international agreements on this subject since competence to regulate fishing policy had been passed to the Community. The Dutch legislation therefore infringed Community law.

The Community had in fact passed two regulations dealing with a common fishing policy but neither concerned the issue of conservation. Therefore, no Community legislation had been passed and no express authority to enter fishing conservation agreements had been conferred by the EC Treaty. The Court held that the Community had authority to enter international commitments for the conservation of the resources of the sea, even though the Community had not passed legislation in exercise of this internal capacity. However, since the Community had not yet exercised its powers for this purpose, concurrent authority over this matter existed between the Community and the Member States and the Dutch legislation was upheld.

The Court abandoned these restrictions on the implied powers of the Community to enter international agreements in *Opinion 1/76 on the Draft Agreement Establishing a Laying-up Fund for Inland Waterway Vessels* Opinion 1/76 [1977] ECR 741. In this case, the Community had no express treaty-making power to regulate inland waterway administration, although it did have authority to pass internal legislation in pursuit of a common transport policy. This internal legislative power had not been exercised.

Nevertheless, the European Court declared that the theory of parallelism extended not only to cases in which internal legislative power had been exercised by the Community but also to those cases which the Treaty creates an internal legislative capacity and the participation of the Community in the negotiation of an agreement 'is necessary for the attainment of one of the objectives of the Community'.

However, this Opinion centred on a situation where it was necessary to adopt the international agreement (in this case with Switzerland) because it was required in order to meet an internal Community objective, and can, therefore, be distinguished on that basis.

A more recent discussion of this matter can be witnessed in the Court's deliberations in its Advisory Opinion on the *Advisory Opinion on the WTO Agreement* Opinion 1/94, [1994] ECR I–5267. In its Opinion the Court stated that in matters covered by the General Agreement on Trade in Services and the Agreement on Trade Related Intellectual Property Rights, the Community did not have exclusive competence. This was because the area did not require international action to acquire internal Community objectives. (It should be noted that art 133 EC has since been amended by the Treaty of Amsterdam to provide that the Council may now conclude agreements on services and intellectual property.)

The European Court has therefore played a significant role in the expansion of the powers of the Community in the field of external relations. This has, in turn, resulted in a restriction of the powers of the Member States to conduct international affairs. The Court has achieved this expansion primarily through the teleological interpretation of the terms of the EC Treaty.

QUESTION TWO

What criteria does the Court of Justice apply in deciding whether a provision of an international agreement has direct effects?

Written by the Editor

General Comment

A difficult question requiring detailed knowledge of the jurisprudence of the European Court.

Skeleton Solution

Legal effect of agreements within the Community – rights of individuals – criteria for establishing direct effect – examples of the application of the principle.

Suggested Solution

Treaties concluded by the Community within the powers vested by the EC Treaty are 'binding on the institutions of the Community and the Member States' by virtue of art 300(7) EC. The European Court has taken the view that treaties to which the Community is a party, either by succession or direct negotiation, are an 'integral element of community law': *Haegeman* v *Belgian State* Case 181/73 [1974] ECR 449. The Court has taken this view to ensure that international obligations assumed by the Community are consistently respected by the Member States.

In *Hauptzollamt Mainz* v *Kupferberg* Case 104/81 [1982] ECR 3641, the Court held that in order to 'ensure respect for treaty obligations concluded by the Community institutions, the Member States fulfil an obligation not only in relation to the non-Member country concerned but also and above all in relation to the Community which has assumed responsibility for the due performance of the obligation'. However, naturally a Community treaty may be binding on both the Community and the Member States without conferring rights on individuals.

While a Community treaty may form an integral element of Community law, the Court has not automatically granted directly enforceable rights to individuals to vindicate this aspect of community law in the national tribunals of the Member States. The jurisprudence of the Court establishes a number of conditions which must be satisfied before an individual may exercise rights created under a Community agreement.

First, an individual may only contest the validity of a Community regulation or a national rule of law if the treaty provision is 'capable of creating rights of which interested parties may avail themselves in a court of law': *International Fruit Company* v *Produktschap voor Groenten en Fruit* Cases 51 and 54/71 [1972] ECR 1219.

Second, in order to ascertain whether a Community agreement confers rights upon individuals, regard must be had to 'the purpose and nature of the agreement itself' to determine whether the provision in question 'contains a clear and precise obligation which is not subject, in its implementation or effects, to the adoption of any subsequent measure: *Demirel* v *Stadt Schwabisch GmbH* Case 12/86 [1987] ECR 3719. If these conditions are satisfied, then direct effect may be given to the terms of a Community agreement under Community law.

The Court has demonstrated a greater reluctance to construe treaties to which the Community has succeeded as conferring individual enforceable rights than under treaties which the Community has negotiated itself. In *Bresciani* v *Amministrazione Italiana delle Finanze* Case 87/75 [1976] ECR 129, the Court was prepared to accept that certain provisions of the Yaounde Convention of 1963 were directly enforceable after ascertaining that the purpose and nature of the provisions being relied upon was the automatic abolition of charges having an equivalent effect.

While the plaintiff in *Hauptzollamt Mainz* v *Kupferberg* Case 104/81 [1982] ECR 3641 was unsuccessful in invoking the EC-Portugal Free Trade Agreement as a defence, nevertheless the Court made a number of important points in defining the direct enforcement of Community agreements. The Court elaborated on the nature of the obligations assumed by the Community under Community agreements. On the one hand, it was the Community which was internationally responsible for the execution of the international obligations, while on the other hand, the obligation extended to the third state. A refusal by a national court to implement an obligation assumed by the Community did not invariably constitute an infringement of a reciprocal obligation since such agreements did not always require incorporation into national law. The full performance of an obligation might leave a party free to determine the legal means necessary within its legal system to pursue the objectives agreed.

Since this distinction existed, it was impossible to allow individuals to enforce rights at the national level unless the Member State in question would be failing to conform to its international obligations assumed through the Community. This was the ultimate rationale for distinguishing between the enforceable and unenforceable exercise of rights by individuals under Community treaties. In *R* v *Secretary of State for the Home Department, ex parte Narin* [1990] 2 CMLR 233, the English High Court applied this rationale in rejecting the argument that provisions of the EC-Turkey association could be given direct effect in English law.

In an earlier case relating to the direct effect of the provisions of the EC Treaty, the European Court acknowledged that 'the vigilance of individuals concerned to protect their rights amounts to an effective supervision in addition to the supervision by other states or by international organs': *Van Gend en Loos* v *Netherlands* Case 26/62 [1963] ECR 1. Where EC Treaty provisions were capable of clear, unqualified and unconditional application then they were capable of being directly effective as a source of Community law. The Court has not adopted a similar policy with regard to the enforceability of treaties in Community law.

This aims and purposes standard established for the direct enforceability of such agreements, while perhaps more rigorous than the test for the direct enforcement of EC Treaty provisions, is eminently sensible. First, the EC treaties and the related founding agreements are the constitution of the Community and should enjoy a preferred status to agreements negotiated under authority of them. Second, a dramatic expansion of enforceable rights would arise if every Community treaty was capable of conferring directly enforceable rights. Third, direct enforcement of Community treaties as an element of Community law would represent a usurpation of those legal systems which maintain a dualist legal tradition such as the United Kingdom. Fourth, considerable opposition has been manifested by a number of Member States to this limited inroad into the direct enforceability of Community treaties by the Court.

QUESTION THREE

Describe the processes which are involved in the formulation and administration of the common commercial policy within the European Community and comment on the extent to which the scope of this policy is limited by international regulations.

Written by the Editor

General Comment

A narrative question requiring a descriptive answer.

Skeleton Solution

The scope of arts 131–134 EC – procedure for the formulation of the CCP – an illustration of the tensions involved – the existence of international restraints and their effects.

Suggested Solution

The creation of a consistent trade policy among the Member States of the European

Community has been achieved by the delegation of decision-making authority over this subject matter to the centralised agencies of the Community. Both the EC Treaty and the ECSC Treaty reserve exclusive competence to the Community for the conduct of 'commercial policy': arts 131–134 EC. Individual Member States no longer retain competence to legislate or enter into international obligations relating to these matters, in the absence of specific authorisation from the Community: *Donkerwolke v Procureur de la République* Case 41/76 [1976] ECR 1921. While the exact scope of the right to formulate commercial policy has not been clearly defined, the European Commission has consistently adopted an aggressive interpretation of this authority and on the whole, this policy has been supported by the ECJ.

From an international trade policy perspective, the European Community is a customs territory which is erected on the establishment of a Common Customs Tariff and the creation of a Common Commercial Policy (CCP) towards third countries. The Common Customs Tariff has replaced individual national tariff schedules with a harmonised and comprehensive scheme to facilitate the levying of duties on goods and products entering the Community. The Community common commercial policy is founded on the uniform application of principles relating, inter alia, to tariff changes, the conclusion of tariff and trade agreements, the achievement of uniformity in measures of trade liberalisation, the formulation of a consistent export policy and the adoption of measures to protect against unfair trade practices.

The procedure for the formulation of the Common Commercial Policy is similar to the normal decision-making processes within the Community. The European Commission drafts proposals after consultations with various foreign representatives and forwards these initial draft texts to working groups composed of national representatives which negotiate a minimum acceptable proposal for submission to the Council of Ministers. The final content of the policy is the product of a continuous process of negotiation between the Commission and the Council of Ministers on the one hand, and where international agreements are involved, between the Commission and third states on the other hand. Although ultimate authority for Community legislation rests with the Council of Ministers, the powers of that organ are circumscribed by the requirement that the Council may only act on the basis of a proposal from the Commission.

This separation of powers in the adoption of trade policy is a hallmark of the institutional structure of the Community legislative process. The Commission is the initiator of policy, both within the Community itself and in relation to agreements with foreign states. The Council is compelled to act upon a formal proposal from the Commission as the basis for its final policy position. A tension has developed between the Council and the Commission, since the Member States demonstrate a propensity to attempt to preserve national control over the conduct of foreign policy.

The final content of Community trade policy is the compromise reached between the Council and the Commission, tempered by the need to accommodate international obligations assumed by the Community in the exercise of its external affairs competence.

The tension between the interests of the Member States, as manifested in the Council of Ministers, and the objectives of the Community, as advocated by the Commission, surfaced during the Tokyo Round of Multilateral Tariff Negotiations held under the auspices of the General Agreement on Tariffs and Trade (GATT), and again during the European Community – United States steel dispute in the early 1980s. After the conclusion of the Code on Technical Barriers to Trade 1979, a number of Member States of the Community argued that the subject matters of certain agreements fell within the jurisdiction of the Member States and outside that of the Community. During the steel dispute, a number of Member States pointed to the less rigorous Community provisions in the ECSC Treaty in contrast to the comparable provisions in the EC Treaty. The final resolution of this dispute required the negotiation of an extensive mandate between the Member States to allow the Commission to settle the issue with the United States government.

Despite the expiry of the transition periods for the completion of the objectives of the EC Treaty, and the renewed impetus towards the creation of an internal market by the Single European Act 1986, Member States continue to express a reluctance to transfer complete authority to the Community to formulate a comprehensive and coherent common commercial policy. This reluctance may be attributed to two separate factors. First, the institutional structure established for the creation of a commercial policy is insufficient. Second, the objectives of the Common Commercial Policy are fragmented and not comprehensively stated to a degree which would encourage transfer of competence to the Community.

Consistent commercial policy requires a centralised agency to express policy objectives. Within the Community, the Council of Ministers, which is the organ with ultimate responsibility for commercial policy, indulges in extensive internal debate and bargaining before a mandate is given to the Commission to present the policy at the global level. Since the final position within the Council is the embodiment of an internal political compromise, the final Community policy is rigid and inflexible. The internal decision-making processes, by allowing for the continued voicing of national concerns, are not suitable for consistent policy formulation.

Also the objectives of the Common Commercial Policy are organically integrated with the success of other Community policies. The ineffective control of the Community over certain areas of the Community economy, such as agriculture, has undermined even this weak policy position. While the Community has failed to adopt legislation standardising technical requirements for intra-Community trade, it is unlikely that it will succeed in doing so for foreign goods. The failure of the Community at this level, ultimately exacerbates the problems at the international level. For example, the Member States of the Community continue to negotiate voluntary export restraints with foreign nations even though this matter is an issue for Community regulation.

The ultimate consequence of the fragmented approach to policy formulation is the reluctance of Member States to transfer regulatory authority to the Community.

Community external policy depends on the Common Customs Tariff (CCT) and the Common Commercial Policy (CCP). Each of these is subject to the international regulations established under the World Trade Organisation (WTO) and assumed by the Community on behalf of the individual Member States. Non-adherence or violation of such rules would therefore ex facie give rise to a presumption of protectionism. The existence of international rules negotiated in the WTO does limit the scope of the Community to formulate the CCP, but this effect is minimised by the fact that international rules regulating economic matters are generally vague and imprecise. As a result, the normative effect of such rules is strictly circumscribed. This is particularly true as regards the international legal restraints on the use of trade protection measures such as anti-dumping duties.

The European Community appears to have tightened its legislation in the field of trade protection laws in order to take advantage of the relative laxity of the international rules. A number of trade remedy provisions do in fact seem to violate the international rules. But greater concern must be raised by the volume of actions taken under the authority of trade protection laws.

Despite recognition that the abuse of measures of contingent protection represents a serious threat to the stability of the global trading system – a fact acknowledged during the Tokyo Round of Multilateral Tariff Negotiations – the introduction of Community legislation to implement the Anti-Dumping Code 1979 has done nothing to stem the growth of anti-dumping duty actions. The conclusion must therefore be reached that the Code itself is ineffective.

At the same time, subsequent amendments to the 1979 legislation have attempted to close any loopholes in the law which may facilitate abuse. The general theme of this process has been a tightening of the regulations against the interests of foreign producers and importers. As the subject of dumping has been increasingly regulated, it has become progressively easier for a complainer to be successful in its action, or at least to harass the importer or foreign producer.

QUESTION FOUR

The Mitsubishi Corporation of Japan has been accused of dumping video cassette recorders in the European Community by the government of France. This allegation is denied by Mitsubishi who seek advice from you in relation to the nature of the investigation by the Commission into the allegation of dumping. The French government has also alleged that Mitsubishi has established a manufacturing plant in Sunderland, England, in order to circumvent the payment of earlier anti-dumping duties by importing the component parts for final assembly in Sunderland.

Advise Mitsubishi of the nature of the investigation which will be carried out by the Commission, and the legitimacy of its activities in Sunderland.

Written by the Editor

General Comment

A problem type question requiring the student to apply Community anti-dumping procedure to a hypothetical factual situation.

Skeleton Solution

Council Regulation 384/96 – the elements of a dumping action – procedure and substantive – anti-circumvention provisions.

Suggested Solution

Dumping is the practice by which goods are introduced into the Community at a price lower than the price of equivalent goods on the domestic market of the exporting country. It is deemed to be an unfair trade practice and most states, including the Community, have legislation which allows anti-dumping duties to be levied in order to prevent injury to domestic industries competing with the foreign products.

The European Commission has responsibility for investigating the facts surrounding an anti-dumping petition and determines whether or not there is sufficient evidence to justify an investigation: Council Regulation 384/96. It is also empowered under certain conditions to impose provisional anti-dumping duties for a maximum period of six months and to accept undertakings by foreign exporters. However, the Council of Ministers has sole competence to order definitive anti-dumping duties.

A dumping complaint may be lodged by any legal person (an individual or company) or by an association not having legal personality, acting on behalf of a Community industry. According to the Regulation, investigations of anti-dumping must normally be completed within a period of not less than six months immediately prior to the initiation of the complaint.

The complaint itself must contain 'sufficient evidence' of the existence of both dumping and injury to a Community industry. In general, this requires information relating to: the nature of the allegedly dumped product; the origin of the exporting country; the names of the country of origin, the producer and the exporter of the product in question; and evidence of dumping and injury resulting therefrom from the industry which considers itself injured or threatened. Upon receipt of a complaint setting forth such facts, the Commission will begin its investigation.

The Commission investigates the question of dumping until its final determination. If this is negative, the investigation terminates, but where the finding is positive, definitive anti-dumping duties may be imposed. This is done by way of a report submitted to the Council of Ministers which has the discretion to accept, modify or reject the Commission's proposal. Where duties are imposed, this is achieved by the adoption of a regulation (or a decision) sanctioning the imposition of duties.

The basic substantive elements of an anti-dumping action are the existence of dumping, injury and 'Community interests' requiring intervention.

The procedure for determining the existence of dumping in the Community is deceptively simple. It involves four basic steps: the determination of 'normal value'; the determination of 'export price'; a comparison of the normal value to export price; and the calculation of the 'margin of dumping' (the normal price minus the export price). Each of these determinations allows considerable latitude for interpretation.

Normal value is the price of the goods in the country of origin, while the export price is the price of the goods inside the Community. The margin of dumping is the difference between these two figures and is also the quantum of the anti-dumping duty which will be levied to neutralise the unfair competitive advantage enjoyed by the foreign product.

In addition to establishing the existence of actual dumped products, it is also necessary to prove that these products have caused material injury to an industry within the Community. This involves proof of actual material injury, the threat of material injury or the material retardation of an industry. In addition, the investigation must reveal that the dumped products have caused the material injury. If it cannot be shown that the dumped products are the cause of the injury, no anti-dumping duties can be imposed.

Before anti-dumping duties can be assessed, a third condition must be met; it must be decided that 'the interests of the Community call for intervention'. No list of definitive Community interests is provided in the Regulation concerning the imposition of dumping duties. However, the concept of Community interests will cover a wide range of factors, but the most important concern the interests of the consumer and processors of imported products and the need to have regard to the competitive equilibrium within the Community market.

If all these elements are established during the Commission investigation, Mitsubishi may be subject to anti-dumping duties in respect of its video cassette recorder products.

The Community has also adopted legislation to prevent foreign importers from circumventing the application of anti-dumping duties by breaking down their products into their component parts and then importing these for reassembly inside the Community. Anti-dumping duties may be imposed on the finished product even if assembled in a factory within the Community, at the rate applicable to the finished product but by reference to the value of the parts imported for assembly in this manner.

Finally, Mitsubishi, if subject to anti-dumping subsidies, may wish to challenge any regulation under art 230(4) EC. This requires Mitsubishi to prove that the act is challengeable and that they have the necessary standing. In the context of challenging regulations providing for anti-dumping duties, the European Court has been rather liberal in determining whether the measure is a decision to the applicant and whether it is of individual concern. If the applicant is the complainant or has been involved in the preliminary investigations, they will be considered as having the necessary individual concern: see, for example, *NTN Toyo v Council* Case 121/77R [1977] ECR 1721. An applicant will also have the necessary individual concern if their retail prices or business dealings are used as a basis for the Commission's decision that dumping has occurred: *Enital* v *Commission* Case C–304/86 [1990] ECR I–2939. This was extended even further by the Court's decision in *Extramet Industrie SA* v *Council* Case C–358/89 [1991] ECR I–2501. In this case an independent importer was concluded to have individual concern even though they had not been involved in the original investigation, or had had their prices/business dealings used as part of the decision that dumping had occurred. The Court held that 'other traders' could bring actions for annulment on the basis that they were individually concerned because of certain attributes peculiar to them and which differentiated them from other persons.

Unannotated Cracknell's Statutes for use in Examinations

New Editions of Cracknell's Statutes

£11.95 due 2002

Cracknell's Statutes provide a comprehensive series of essential statutory provisions for each subject. Amendments are consolidated, avoiding the need to cross-refer to amending legislation. Unannotated, they are suitable for use in examinations, and provide the precise wording of vital Acts of Parliament for the diligent student.

Commercial Law
ISBN: 1 85836 472 8

European Community Legislation
ISBN: 1 85836 470 1

Conflict of Laws
ISBN: 1 85836 473 6

Family Law
ISBN: 1 85836 471 X

Criminal Law
ISBN: 1 85836 474 4

Public International Law
ISBN: 1 85836 476 0

Employment Law
ISBN: 1 85836 475 2

For further information on contents or to place an order, please contact:

Mail Order
Old Bailey Press
at Holborn College
Woolwich Road
Charlton
London
SE7 8LN

Telephone No: 020 7381 7407
Fax No: 020 7386 0952
Website: www.oldbaileypress.co.uk

Suggested Solutions to Past Examination Questions 2000–2001

The Suggested Solutions series provides examples of full answers to the questions regularly set by examiners. Each suggested solution has been broken down into three stages: general comment, skeleton solution and suggested solution. The examination questions included within the text are taken from past examination papers set by the London University. The full opinion answers will undoubtedly assist you with your research and further your understanding and appreciation of the subject in question.

Only £6.95 Due December 2002

Constitutional Law
ISBN: 1 85836 478 7

Criminal Law
ISBN: 1 85836 479 5

English Legal System
ISBN: 1 85836 482 5

Elements of the Law of Contract
ISBN: 1 85836 480 9

Jurisprudence and Legal Theory
ISBN: 1 85836 484 1

Land Law
ISBN: 1 85836 481 7

Law of Tort
ISBN: 1 85836 483 3

For further information on contents or to place an order, please contact:

Mail Order
Old Bailey Press
at Holborn College
Woolwich Road
Charlton
London
SE7 8LN

Telephone No: 020 7381 7407
Fax No: 020 7386 0952
Website: www.oldbaileypress.co.uk

Old Bailey Press

The Old Bailey Press integrated student law library is tailor-made to help you at every stage of your studies from the preliminaries of each subject through to the final examination. The series of Textbooks, Revision WorkBooks, 150 Leading Cases and Cracknell's Statutes are interrelated to provide you with a comprehensive set of study materials.

You can buy Old Bailey Press books from your University Bookshop, your local Bookshop, direct using this form, or you can order a free catalogue of our titles from the address shown overleaf.

The following subjects each have a Textbook, 150 Leading Cases/Casebook, Revision WorkBook and Cracknell's Statutes unless otherwise stated.

Administrative Law
Commercial Law
Company Law
Conflict of Laws
Constitutional Law
Conveyancing (Textbook and 150 Leading Cases)
Criminal Law
Criminology (Textbook and Sourcebook)
Employment Law (Textbook and Cracknell's Statutes)
English and European Legal Systems
Equity and Trusts
Evidence
Family Law
Jurisprudence: The Philosophy of Law (Textbook, Sourcebook and
    Revision WorkBook)
Land: The Law of Real Property
Law of International Trade
Law of the European Union
Legal Skills and System
    (Textbook)
Obligations: Contract Law
Obligations: The Law of Tort
Public International Law
Revenue Law (Textbook,
    Revision WorkBook and
    Cracknell's Statutes)
Succession

Mail order prices:	
Textbook	£14.95
150 Leading Cases	£11.95
Revision WorkBook	£9.95
Cracknell's Statutes	£11.95
Suggested Solutions 1998–1999	£6.95
Suggested Solutions 1999–2000	£6.95
Suggested Solutions 2000–2001	£6.95
Law Update 2002	£9.95
Law Update 2003	£10.95

Please note details and prices are subject to alteration.

£4.50

To complete your order, please fill in the form below:

Module	Books required	Quantity	Price	Cost
		Postage		
		TOTAL		

For Europe, add 15% postage and packing (£20 maximum).
For the rest of the world, add 40% for airmail.

ORDERING

By telephone to Mail Order at 020 7381 7407, with your credit card to hand.

By fax to 020 7386 0952 (giving your credit card details).

Website: www.oldbaileypress.co.uk

By post to: Mail Order, Old Bailey Press at Holborn College, Woolwich Road, Charlton, London, SE7 8LN.

When ordering by post, please enclose full payment by cheque or banker's draft, or complete the credit card details below. You may also order a free catalogue of our complete range of titles from this address.

We aim to despatch your books within 3 working days of receiving your order.

Name

Address

Postcode   Telephone

Total value of order, including postage: £

I enclose a cheque/banker's draft for the above sum, or

charge my   ☐ Access/Mastercard   ☐ Visa   ☐ American Express
Card number

☐☐☐☐ ☐☐☐☐ ☐☐☐☐ ☐☐☐☐

Expiry date ☐☐☐☐

Signature: ....Date: ....